The Wild Gardener

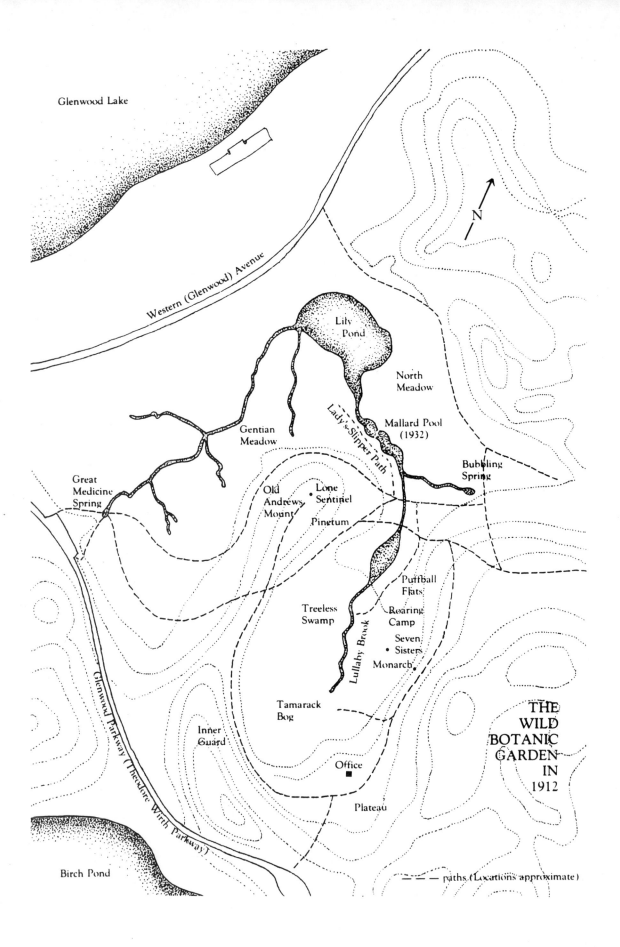

Glenwood Lake

Western (Glenwood) Avenue

Lily
Pond

North
Meadow

Gentian
Meadow

Mallard Pool
(1932)

Lady's Slipper Path

Great
Medicine
Spring

Bubbling
Spring

Old
Andrews
Mount

Lone
Sentinel

Pinetum

N

Puffball
Flats

Treeless
Swamp

Roaring
Camp

Seven
Sisters

Monarch

Lullaby Brook

Glenwood Parkway (Theodore Wirth Parkway)

Tamarack
Bog

Inner
Guard

Office

THE
WILD
BOTANIC
GARDEN
IN
1912

Plateau

Birch Pond

— — — paths (Locations approximate)

the Wild Gardener

The Life and Selected Writings
of Eloise Butler

Martha E. Hellander

North Star Press of St. Cloud, Inc.

For the Lovers of
Wild Nature
ELOISE BUTLER

Pen and ink illustrations: Jessica Allen Johnson and Corinne A. Dwyer

Calligraphy: Tim Ternes

Library of Congress Cataloging-in-Publication Data

Hellander, Martha E., 1952-
    The Wild Gardener : the life and selected writings of Eloise Butler / Martha E. Hellander.
    208 p. 26 cm.
    Includes bibliographical references and index.
        ISBN 0-87839-064-2 : $19.95
        1. Butler, Eloise, 1851-1933.   2. Botanists —United States—Biography.   3. Gardeners —Minnesota—Biography.   4. Botany— Minnesota.   5. Native plant gardening— Minnesota.   I. Butler, Eloise, 1851-1933. II. Title.
QK31.B88H45   1992
581'.092—dc20   92-3664
[B]   CIP

Published by North Star Press of St. Cloud, Inc., P.O. Box 451, St. Cloud, Minnesota 56302.

ISBN: 0-87839-064-2

Martha Hellander grew up in Nebraska and Minnesota. She is a graduate of the University of Minnesota School of Law and lives with her husband and two daughters in Edina, Minnesota. From 1985-1990, she and her family lived near the Eloise Butler Wildflower Garden and Bird Sanctuary in Minneapolis.

Acknowledgments

I AM DEEPLY GRATEFUL to the many people who contributed to the research and writing of this book. Dan Hasty and Mary Maguire Lerman of the Minneapolis Park and Recreation Board, Horticulture Department, and Ann Kessen, president of the Friends of the Wild Flower Garden, Inc., steadfastly believed in the importance of telling Eloise Butler's story, and read and commented on portions of the manuscript, for which I thank them. I benefitted from numerous conversations with Beatrice Scheer Smith, botanist and scholar on the history of women in botany, who loaned me reference books, shared my excitement at each new discovery, and offered encouragement at every step of the way. She and Elizabeth W. Reed generously shared the results of their own earlier research on Eloise Butler. Genealogical assistance was provided by Marjorie Bowers, Warren H. Hasty, Martha P. Pease, and by Theodore L. Brown; the untimely death of Theodore Brown, who invested many hours helping to research the history of the Butler family in Appleton, Maine, was a great loss to that community as well as to me personally.

Among the relatives who scoured attics and storerooms for photographs and material on the Butler family, the untiring assistance of Martha P. Pease (now deceased), and her permission to use photographs and quote from the unpublished writings of Eloise Butler and her sister, Cora E. Pease, is gratefully acknowledged. Thanks also to Nona Butler Allen, Eloise Butler (of California), Oliver Butler, Dorothy Furness Dunn, Katherine Rose Gary, Lucia Butler McKenzie, Eloise M. Riggs, Grace Butler Smith and Eva Zayha.

Thanks to those who shared their memories of Eloise Butler, especially Bessie Babcock Johnson, Jean Rohrbaugh, Elizabeth Schutt, and Lloyd and Leroy Teeuwen. Martha Crone and her daughter, Janet Prevey (both deceased since the project began), also gave me many documents, which have been donated to the Minnesota Historical Society.

Botanist Gerald B. Ownbey provided modern botanical names for the higher plants of Minnesota and patient assistance in interpreting Butler's plant records, as did botanists Alan J. Brook, Hannah Croasdale and Elizabeth Flint (on desmids), David J. McLaughlin (on mushrooms), Thomas Morley (on mosses, lichens and liverworts), and Paul C. Silva and Michael J. Wynne (on seaweeds);

Alan Brook, Barbara Delaney, Welby Smith, Paul C. Silva and Gustav A. Swanson read draft chapters and offered helpful comments.

The assistance of many archivists, librarians, and herbarium curators is acknowledged, especially David L. Anderson at the Maine State Archives, Fay Greenleaf at the Lynn Historical Society, Ellenore Doudiet at the Wilson Museum in Castine, Ruth Bauer at the Minnesota Historical Society, John A. Baule and Dorothea Guiney at the Hennepin County Historical Society, Susan M. Dreydoppel at the Moravian Historical Society, Anita F. Cholewa at the Herbarium of the University of Minnesota, Donald Pfister of the Farlow Herbarium of Cryptogamic Botany at Harvard University, Barbara M. Thiers at the Herbarium and Susan Fraser at the Library of the New York Botanical Garden, Paul C. Silva at the Herbarium of the University of California at Berkeley, Beth Carroll-Horrocks at the American Philosophical Society in Philadelphia, Penelope Krosch at the University of Minnesota Archives, Beverly Swanson at the City of Minneapolis Archives, Erin Foley at the Minneapolis Public Library, and Sally Jungers.

I also thank the following for their important contributions: Cheryl Albrecht, Kenneth Avery, Ray Bartlett, Moana Beim, Jane Blachly, John and Betty Blanchard, Betty Bridgman, Betty Bryan, Elizabeth Crosby, Marcia Cummings, Liz Curitzkis, Leon Cushing, Maynard Erickson, Timothy C. Glines, Cynthia Gonzalez, Gardiner Gregory, Cary George, Marlene Hall, Malcolm Jackson, Laleah Kennedy, Connie Lavoie, Wilmet Leak, Naja Lindberg, Roma Kay May, Patricia McKernon, Richard W. Meservey, Gary Meyer, Eric Mundell, Rita Oyaas, Bruce C. Parker, Janet Pelley, Susan Perry, Camille Richiardelli, Dan Rylance, Ruth Smith, Beverly Swanson, Larry Syverson, Wigle Tamboer, Mary Tribble, Clifford M. Wetmore, and May Wright.

I am especially grateful for the support of my husband, Lawrence Christiano, and our daughters, Carson (who gave up her "secret room" to the Eloise Butler Papers) and Haley (who slept many nights under my desk).

Grant support was provided by the Friends of the Wild Flower Garden, Inc., the Minnesota Historical Society's Grants-in-Aid Program, and the Minneapolis Woman's Club.

Contents

Forward

LADY BIRD JOHNSON, FOUNDER of the National Wildflower Research Center, observed that "almost every person, from childhood, has been touched by the untamed beauty of wildflowers." Eloise Butler's childhood memories of woods, meadows and bogs were the inspiration for her life's work, the creation of her special garden in Minneapolis. Beyond that accomplishment, if Butler were alive today she probably would have my job as program coordinator for the Midwest office of the National Wildflower Research Center. On second thought, with her energy and passion she would probably be directing a global conservation effort!

"This is a pioneering effort," wrote Lady Bird Johnson, "and sometimes I feel overwhelmed with a sense of so much to do and so little time, because of all we need to discover. Yet I can hardly wait for spring each year!" Eloise Butler felt the same way. The foresighted botany teacher who defended the beauty and utility of native plants had much in common with other pioneers like turn-of-the-century landscape architect Jens Jensen, who advocated the use of native plants in residential landscapes. Eloise wrote that she enhanced her garden with plants from land scheduled to be "made over for so-called improvements." Today, organizations exist that salvage wild plants in anticipation of development, in the name of conservation.

The art of landscape restoration with native plants is still in its infancy; we need more knowledge in propagation, establishment, and management techniques. The story of Eloise Butler's pioneering work is of great value to us today. In terms of management, she learned that a hands-off approach was impossible, and looked for control alternatives to herbicides such as planting other species to outcompete or "head off Creeping Charlie." She also used only the natural fertilizer furnished by decaying vegetation. Recognizing the importance of matching plants to the microclimates of her garden, Eloise moved soil when transplanting species such as Indian paintbrush, "suspected of root parasitism"; not until recently did research document that very phenomenon.

The records of Butler's years of work in her wild garden may further increase our knowledge of the distribution of native plants in the Twin Cities area, and give clues to local succession, or change over time, of the plant communities that existed in her garden. By studying the dynamics of such a place, restorationists will gain insight as to how to repair similar landscapes.

Modern landscape architects, such as Darrel G. Morrison, encourage landscapes that allow seasonal and successional changes not currently common in urban areas. Morrison greatly respected Jens Jensen, who wrote that the soul of our native landscape "speaks of freedom and friendliness . . . of joy and peace to the mind." That joy and peace can still be found in Eloise Butler's garden. Thank goodness, since human need for such places of solitude in the surrounding urban spaces is likely to increase over time. The garden, therefore, serves us scientifically, aesthetically, and spiritually.

The garden serves us ethically, as well. "A chance to find a pasque flower is a right as inalienable as free speech," declared Aldo Leopold. Whether a pasque flower on the upland or a marsh marigold in the bog, our children and theirs should have the right to discover wildflowers and all of nature in their lifetimes. Only if we continue the work of the Wild Gardener will our children inherit this right.

Martha Hellander has wandered far, persisted long, and labored hard with the same determination that Eloise Butler pursued in the wild garden. The soul of the Wild Gardener and the renewal offered by her garden are captured in these pages. May the peace of Eloise's wild garden be with us all!

Bonnie Harper-Lore
National Wildflower Research Center
Midwest Regional Office

Introduction

THE NEED FOR A QUIET place apart, deeply felt by many, is often disregarded in the rush and clamor of modern life. Some in Minneapolis who heed its call have long known of a secluded glen, near the old Great Medicine Spring of the Dakota Indians, where a wild garden of native plants lies deep inside the large Theodore Wirth Park on the city's western border. The unique Eloise Butler Wildflower Garden and Bird Sanctuary, originally called the Minneapolis Wild Botanic Garden, was founded in 1907 and tended until her death in 1933 by the inspired botanist and Victorian plant-hunter Eloise Butler. To walk down the winding path into the heart of Butler's garden—where sunlight filters through tall trees, dappling ferns and spring wildflowers in rippled light, and the air is fragrant with the scent of balm of gilead trees after rain—is to enter a sanctuary, a still and peaceful place that touches some elemental memory of a time when we lived closer to nature.

The ancients had a name for it: the sacred grove, a sheltered place where the spirit of a revered person was thought to linger, where water from springs flowed through untended meadows rich in wildflowers, and aged trees stood guard over the entrance to a natural garden. That such a place exists in a modern urban landscape, less than one-half mile from a busy freeway carrying traffic to and from downtown Minneapolis, is a testament both to the garden's founder, for whom the "depths of a swamp" were "an earthly paradise," and those who have followed her in caring for and ensuring the preservation of Eloise Butler's legacy.

A visit to the garden always kindles, in me, feelings of regret as well as gratitude. Knowing that this utter loveliness had existed all the while I was occupied elsewhere with the often trivial details of my life, I regret that I had not found the time to come sooner. No matter how short the time elapsed since my last visit, I am always astonished at the beauty I find there. And I am grateful that Eloise Butler, who died nearly twenty years before my birth, cared enough about those who came after her to want to share her joy with us—to make a place where we could come to experience some of the pleasure that she found among the wild plants of Minnesota, plants once common but now so rare that we might live our entire lives in the state and never encounter them, if not for her garden.

The Eloise Butler Wildflower Garden and Bird Sanctuary appears to be the oldest existing wildflower garden in the United States. Wildflower gardens and native plant preserves now exist throughout the nation; no doubt Butler's pioneering endeavor inspired the founding of others. There are many who can trace their love for nature, and interest in conservation, to childhood memories of visits to Butler's wild garden. Yet her early contribution to the native plant preservation movement has gone largely unheralded.

The research for this book began in the fall of 1987, on the day I walked into the Minneapolis Public Library in search of a biography of Eloise Butler, only to discover that none existed. I felt compelled to learn more about this woman born in 1851, who, according to a notebook of her writings kept at the rustic shelter in the garden, had written to friends at the age of sixty: "As you well know, I chiefly live and move and have my being in and for the Wild Botanic Garden." Those profound and extraordinary words, based on a passage from an ancient Greek poem quoted by Paul in the Book of Acts, convinced me that, in her life's work, Eloise Butler had experienced a rare and purposeful joy. I knew I had much to learn from Eloise about gardening with native plants, and the role of women in nineteenth-century botany; but, on another plane, I suspected that Eloise had left behind clues which might serve as signposts for my own life's journey.

The roots of this book are connected to, and take sustenance from, all that has nourished me. In 1981, after moving from Minneapolis to Chicago with my husband, Larry, I went on a camping trip with two close friends to the Boundary Waters Canoe Area of northern Minnesota. Tired, and disappointed that the last day of our otherwise-delightful trip had turned cloudy and threatened to storm before we reached our last portage, we beached our canoe at the wrong landing. Upon discovering our mistake, we resigned ourselves to putting the canoe back into the water. Just then, the sun broke through the clouds and, for a few precious moments, illuminated a small patch of the forest floor, carpeted with fallen pine needles. There, in the center of the light, was a clump of stemless lady's-slippers bearing five exquisite pink blossoms. I had never before seen wild orchids, and was awed by their beauty. My friends and I felt as though we had been purposefully drawn there. A photograph that I took of those lady's-slippers has hung above my desk for the past ten years.

Four years later, Larry and I moved back to Minnesota and bought a house near Theodore Wirth Park in Minneapolis. After signing the papers, we followed the advice of a friend and stopped for an early-morning walk in the Eloise Butler Wildflower Garden, a few blocks from our house-to-be. The woods, bathed in May sunshine, rang with birdsong; white blossoms of delicate hepatica and large-flowered trillium welcomed us. I was overjoyed at our good fortune in finding a house so close to the beautiful garden, previously unknown to me, although I had lived for years in the city.

Once settled in our new home, I walked often in Eloise Butler's garden, usually alone, sometimes with Larry and our young daughter, Carson. I began bringing my journal, books to read, special friends. In May 1987, nine months pregnant with our second child, I sat immersed in sunshine on a bench surrounded by blooming marsh marigolds, on the day before Haley was born, and wrote her a love letter. The garden had become, for me, a sacred place. When a woman whom I met in the garden confided that she had scattered the ashes of her deceased father there, I realized that others felt the same way.

During the following year, I cared for our often-ill and sleepless infant daughter and began researching Eloise Butler's life while Larry's father lay dying of brain cancer. There were dark times of despair and hopelessness mingled with flashes of light and clarity. I sought the peace of the garden at every opportunity. It never failed to renew me and heal my exhaustion and pain.

Everything I had managed to learn about Eloise confirmed my belief that hers was an uncommon life, but large parts of that life, and her work in making the garden, were still obscured from view. I knew that a woman named Martha Crone, forty-three years younger than Eloise, had befriended Eloise and, after Butler's death, had herself cared for the garden until 1959. When I learned in the spring of 1988 that Martha Crone was still living in Minneapolis at the age of ninety-four, I wrote her at once. Her daughter, Janet Prevey, responded to my card. Janet told me that her mother was in a nursing home; she was sometimes lucid, and sometimes not. I was welcome to visit her.

A few days later I drove to the Camden Care Center in north Minneapolis, where Martha Crone, seated in a wheelchair, was waiting for me by the door. With her silvery-white hair drawn tightly back into a knot, and her strong, graceful hands clasped in her lap, she had the aura and poise of a beautiful, aged dancer. I gave her a jar of wild violets from my back yard, and we talked—of the drought, of her German ancestors, of Eloise Butler. She obviously enjoyed reminiscing about "Miss Butler." She told of "botanizing" with Eloise, of being lost in a swamp together, of fighting fires that had threatened the garden. When she grew tired, she instructed me to go "mull it all over," and invited me to come again when I needed to know more.

I visited Martha Crone seven times between April and June of 1988. Her moods varied from one visit to the next; sometimes she was sunny and talkative, other times cranky and withdrawn. Once, when I complained of painful blisters on my legs from poison ivy stumbled into while searching my sister's woods for wildflowers, she scolded me: "*First* you look for the poison ivy, *then* you look for the wildflowers." Although many facts and dates were already beyond retrieval, her heart's memory was still whole. When asked if she had loved Eloise Butler, Martha Crone smiled. She nodded, and replied that she could see Eloise "almost any time" she liked. "She and I, you might say, we were one," she said.

A few days after our last meeting, Martha Crone became ill, and I never saw her again. She died the following winter. Like the lady's-slippers illuminated for a few moments by a break in the clouds, I had been granted the great privilege of witnessing the final light of this extremely old and spirited woman, who had been Eloise Butler's friend, before she passed into darkness.

One day I received a telephone call from Martha Crone's daughter. While cleaning her mother's bedroom in preparation for sale of the house, Janet had found some old papers relating to Eloise Butler and the garden. She was going to throw them out, she said, unless, perhaps, I wanted them. I spent the following day sorting through the life's accumulation of a compulsive saver. Folded in a box which

seemed to contain every Christmas card Martha Crone had ever received was a letter to Eloise Butler from Warren Upham of the Geological and Natural History Survey of Minnesota, dated 1884, asking for specimens of any rare or unusual plants she had lately found. In other boxes were letters from Eloise Butler to Martha Crone and her husband written in the 1920s and 1930s. At the bottom of an old metal cabinet lay a pair of worn and tattered black notebooks; they were the two volumes of Eloise Butler's long-lost *Garden Log*, a record of the natural history of the garden which she had kept from 1907 until her death in 1933. In a bookcase was a diary entitled *Nature's Calendar*; the handwriting I knew to be that of Eloise Butler. The entries dated from 1902. As I drove home that evening, my car heavy with the weight of the books and papers Martha Crone's daughter had given me, I began to see a way in which I might repay the gift of the garden.

Gathering and deciphering the clues to Eloise Butler's life from the places they lay hidden became my own passion. The trail led me among fragile, hundred-year-old herbarium specimens, dusty old botanical journals, scrapbooks of crumbling and yellowed newspaper clippings, and to the farmhouse in Maine, surrounded by wildflowers, where Eloise was born. My initial delight upon learning that Eloise had a beloved older sister, Cora, who accompanied her on many plant-hunting expeditions, had turned to disappointment when it appeared that their letters had not been preserved. But, as it turned out, Cora was a writer; the discovery of many of her articles, which dated from around the turn of the century and which often referred to Eloise, compensated for the lack of correspondence. In the end, the story was pieced together from many scattered sources, helped at every turn by generous individuals who came forward at just the right moment with a piece of the puzzle. The long hours in libraries and archives, my struggle to trace the Latin names of plants through several editions of *Gray's Botany* in order to interpret Eloise Butler's often cryptic records, and the many nights that I worked until nearly dawn, eventually revealed the most important gift that Eloise's life held for me. She had led me down a path into immersion in work that held greater joy than I had ever thought possible. And what a lovely path it has been! At the end, Eloise Butler, radiant once more, stepped into the light.

Since embarking upon this project, I have been sustained and inspired by Eloise Butler's writings. Her tales of adventures in plant-hunting, and her observations on the vagaries of wild gardening, gleaned from what survives of twenty-five years of contributions to the bulletins of her botanical correspondence club, are collected and reprinted here, along with a series of articles on wildflowers that she wrote for the Minneapolis *Tribune* in 1911, and a few other essays. Eloise Butler's writings often meander and sometimes stray into enchanting by-paths. Like a stroll in her garden, they are best enjoyed at a leisurely pace, and may be read in any order whatsoever; for, as Eloise wrote, "Where may one . . . wander, if not in a wild garden?"

Part I

1

Roaming the Woods in Maine

Wintergreen

IT WOULD BE DIFFICULT to imagine a more ideal setting for the childhood of a botanist than the farm in Maine, twelve miles from the sea, where Eloise Butler was born. Her parents, Oliver Butler and Margaretta Graves Butler, owned a hundred and twenty acres in the town of Appleton.[1] Their land rose gently from the St. George River through woods and pastures nearly to the crest of Appleton Ridge, an arched upfold of bedrock about five miles long, which forms the westerly border of the St. George valley. A short walk down the lane, which bisected the farm, took Eloise to the doorstep of her grandfather Levi Butler's house, the old schoolhouse to which he had retired with his second wife, Mary Walker, called "Aunt Mary" by the children. From the road, there was an expansive view of the landscape to the south, where Sennebec Pond glistened in the valley, and to the east, where the timber-covered Simmons Hill and Jones Hill lay like slumbering bears along the horizon.

Eloise enjoyed a typical rural childhood of the mid-nineteenth century, surrounded by close and distant relatives of all ages. She was born on August 3, 1851, in the farmhouse in which her father and his nine younger siblings had grown up. Eloise was the fourth child born to Oliver and Margaretta. Her older brothers were Simpson, then nearly nine, and Esbon, five and one-half; her sister, Cora, was nearly four. As she recalled in a memoir, Eloise was regarded as a "good baby," content to lie quietly in her cradle looking about, rather than demanding attention.[2] Her younger brother Arthur was born when Eloise was five, followed by Edgar's birth one year later. The Butler children had innumerable aunts, uncles and cousins who lived nearby and visited often, sometimes staying with the family for extended periods of time.

The farmhouse, covered with weathered gray shingles, was square and unadorned. It was built by Eloise's grandfather, Levi Butler, in the early Cape style common on old New England farms, of lumber cut from trees felled on the land. A long shed, or "ell," off the kitchen sheltered the fowl and eased the passage to the barn and outbuildings during bad weather. Rafters in the attic and beams in the fieldstone cellar were simply unbarked logs, and the floorboards varied in width according to the size of the tree from which they were sawed. The house still stands after more than 170 years, although the barn is long gone. The Appleton Village School, built in 1983, now occupies the pasture.

The house was comfortable and convenient, in sharp contrast to the rough log cabins built by Eloise's great-great-grandfather Oliver Robbins, who had been among the first settlers of South Thomaston, on the St. George peninsula, and her great-grandfather Phineas Butler, who had settled in Union, a few miles downstream from Appleton along the St. George River.

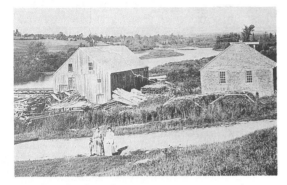

Lumber mills along the St. George River in North Appleton, c. 1900. *Richard W. Meservey.*

The Butlers claimed descent from the British Duke of Ormond, Lord Lieutenant of Ireland. The first Butlers in America settled in Boston; five or more generations later, in 1774, Phineas Butler went to the Province of Maine from Framingham, Massachusetts, with his brother, John. The two young men were indentured to a Doctor Taylor, who promised each of them one hundred acres and two suits of clothes in exchange for working on his land until they were twenty-one years old. Phineas fought in the Revolutionary War (as did his father, also named Phineas) and was with General Washington at Valley Forge; after the war he returned to Maine and married Melea Robbins.[3]

Eloise Butler's paternal grandmother, Lucy Tolman Butler, was the ninth of twenty-one children of Isiah Tolman, a wealthy farmer, mill owner and the first settler of the city of Rockland, Maine. On her mother's side, the families of her grandmother, Louisa Emery, and grandfather, Nathaniel Graves, had, since the Revolution, lived close to the sea in the small villages along the western shore of Penobscot Bay. The Emery

line descended from Anthony Emery and his son James, who came to America from England in 1635, and included Daniel Emery (great-great-grandfather of Eloise) who also fought in the Revolutionary War. The names Emery, Graves, Tolman and Butler are still common in mid-coastal Maine.

Of Eloise's female ancestors, little is known but their names; numerous Elizabeths, Margarets and Marys appear on the family tree along with the fearsome-sounding Bathsheba Graves (wife of the elder Phineas Butler) and the resonantly-named Elioenai Shepard (wife of Oliver Robbins and mother of Melea). Presumably their lives were bound up in housekeeping, childbearing, and rearing their large families of ten or more offspring, some of whom invariably died in childhood.

The lives of the early settlers of Maine were fraught with pioneer hardships, and the Butlers knew these hardships as well as the relative prosperity that came later to the family. In the town histories of Thomaston and Union, Maine, are recorded the names of newcomers without means of support who appeared likely to become a town charge. These unfortunates were "warned out" by the town officials in order that they not gain residence and thereby a claim to support. The elder Phineas Butler and his wife, Bathsheba, who followed their sons to Maine, were warned out of Thomaston in 1785 and Union in 1787.[4] The custom of warning strangers out of town was short-lived and eventually outlawed by the state of Massachusetts, according to Cyrus Eaton's *History of Thomaston* (1865):

> This ungracious salutation was bestowed by the town constable here on not less than seventeen individuals the present year [1785], including many, as it afterwards proved, of the town's most valuable and thrifty citizens. These were Phineas Butler and wife, last from Needham, and formerly of Framingham. . . .[5]

When Eloise was eight years old the family moved a short distance to another farm closer to McLains Mills, on the road which led up from the Mills to the top of Appleton Ridge. The new house had a front door ornamented with a leaded glass cornice and sidelight windows; the door, reserved for the use of company, opened onto a whimsical spiral staircase which led to the second-floor bedrooms. Oliver Butler stenciled his name and the date "1863" onto the door of the huge barn that he later built.[6]

Details of life on the Butler farm are known from a journal kept by Eloise's thirteen-year-old cousin Winnifred Furness of Indiana of a visit (1869-1870) and an article published by Eloise's sister, Cora, in 1901 entitled, "Old Time New England Industries."[7] In addition to family members, the busy household often included hired farmhands, and sometimes the local schoolteacher boarded there. Traveling peddlars frequently stopped at the farm selling tin wares, Bibles, and numerous other items of necessity or curiosity. There was a blind man who caned chairs, and a man who sold grape vines; Oliver and Margaretta usually bought something, then gave the peddlar lodgings for the night.

On their farm the Butlers grew wheat, rye, and corn, which was taken to "the Mills" (McLains Mills), to be ground into flour and meal for the bread. They kept a few sheep, pigs and cows; calfskins and cowhides were tanned at the village tannery and made into boots and shoes for the family by an old man with black shaggy hair who set up his bench and tools in Levi Butler's kitchen every autumn. Flocks of chickens, turkeys, and geese were kept in the barn and outbuildings; the geese provided feathers and down for the family's beds and pillows.

Daily life on the Butler farm meant strenuous labor for everyone, the tasks apportioned according to sex and age. The cows had to be milked, the milk had to be skimmed, and the cream had to be churned for hours at a time to make butter, chores usually done by the girls and women. Most of the family's clothes and blankets were made at home, of homespun or linsey-woolsey woven by hand of wool from the sheep, which was spun into yarn on a great spinning wheel kept in an unfinished chamber (fancy cloth, thread and trimmings could be purchased at McLains Mills). The family practiced strict economy, making over cast-off clothing to fit the younger ones; when unfit to wear any longer, the fabric was made into rugs on a huge loom. When a horse died, all other work stopped while Margaretta made soap. Sewing and quilting bees, in which all the neighboring women participated, were often held at the farm.

Gathering eggs was a job for even the littlest child, as were picking strawberries and apples, and husking corn. On days when poultry was slaughtered, everyone donned old clothes and spent the day plucking and dressing birds (one lucky child was spared from the work so as to remain presentable in case someone came to the door).

Oliver Butler and his sons did the plowing (with oxen), planting, harvesting, and butchering, and drove teams of horses loaded with the extra produce of the farm into Camden, the port town from which steamers left for markets in Portland and Boston. For additional income, Oliver cut timber on the farm and on extra woodlots which he owned up on the Ridge; the logs were hauled to the Mills (sometimes with a child riding on top). In the winter, many local farmers made barrels for the limerock industry; Oliver Butler had a share in a mill that made barrel staves and shingles. On trips to visit her mother's relatives, Eloise passed by the huge limestone quarries which scarred the land around Rockland and Thomaston in the mid-nineteenth century, and saw the lime kilns which lit up the sky, burning day and night.[8]

Her Butler forebears had been founders of the Baptist church in Appleton, and Eloise remembered her parents as "rigid Calvinist Baptists" who reared their children "in the straight and narrow way," meting out punishment and frowning upon dancing and card-playing as cardinal sins. Sundays mandated attendance at Sabbath School as well as two or more regular services, during which the children heard terrifying sermons about the "wrath to come." It was in the Baptist church in Appleton, built in 1846 and still in active use, that Eloise learned by heart "the sublimist passages of the Bible," which she drew upon in later years for words to describe her deepest feelings about nature.[9]

Although her own parents chose to anchor in safe harbor "up country," the brooding fogs which obscured the hilltops and shrouded the trees for days at a time were a reminder that Appleton was not far from the sea. The young Eloise is likely to have heard tales of foreign ports visited by the far-ranging vessels of the Maine coast during visits of a week or more to her mother's relatives in South Thomaston. On these visits, when the formal parlors and perhaps even the front doors were used, Eloise and her cousins moved among old fishermen, sea captains, and their wives like those so lovingly described in Sarah Orne Jewett's novel *The Country of the Pointed Firs* (1896), purportedly set in Tenant's Harbor, a village near South Thomaston. In her story, "The Queen's Twin," Jewett offers a clue to the roots of the grown Eloise's love of travel:

> The coast of Maine was in former years brought so near to foreign shores by its busy fleet of ships that among the older men and women one still finds a surprising proportion of travelers. . . . The sea-captains and the captains' wives of Maine knew something of the wide world, and never mistook their native parishes for the whole instead of a part thereof. They knew not only Thomaston, Castine, and Portland, but London and Bristol and Bordeaux, and the strange-mannered harbors of the China sea.[10]

There were ship captains on both sides of the family; two brothers of Eloise's mother had been lost at sea. One particularly adventurous uncle, Edward Graves, was a storekeeper and shipbuilder in South Thomaston, when not sailing to California or leading expeditions across the Dakotas by wagon on his periodic forays in search of gold.[11]

According to an article by Cora entitled, "The Eccentric Sisters-in-law" (1889), among the more interesting of the elderly neighbors were two old women, called Aunt Serena and Aunt Mandy. Aunt Serena was an herbalist and medium who held seances and rapping sessions (strictly forbidden to the Butler children) in her parlor. Serena was also a poet, and the village balladeer. Aunt Mandy dressed oddly; she trimmed her bonnets with chicken feathers and made her own ribbon dyes from the bark of trees. Highly educated for the times, she passed her days studying scripture while her pots boiled over on the stove.[12]

Eloise Butler's lifelong interest in herbal medicine was rooted in her childhood. The Butler children were reared on homemade remedies administered by the women of the family. Hyssop, flaxseed tea and a homemade concoction of white pine bark soaked in alcohol were used to treat the coughs and congestion of "lung fever"; senna was used as a laxative. The macerated leaves of common plantain made a fine poultice for scrapes and cuts. Each spring, a tea made from thorough-wort was administered to young and old alike to "purify the blood."[13]

Eloise wrote that "botany began with us through an appeal to the gustatory sense."[14] The woods in Appleton abounded in edible wild plants and berries, to which the children freely helped themselves. They "ate but little at the table when beech leaves were young and tender." Other prized delicacies were the first leaves of wintergreen (called "iv'ries" or "youngsters") and its berries, which the children called "boxberries" or "checkerberry plums." Chewing gum was easily obtained from spruce trees in the woods, slippery elm and sweet birch yielded their inner bark, and new raspberry and blackberry shoots and the tips of wild grape tendrils fell prey to the foraging children. Strenuous digging produced buds of the interrupted fern, a "delicious morsel," or the tubers of dwarf ginseng, called "ground nuts." Berries, thorn apples and bird cherries "were made to yield their pulp" and chokecherries made the girls' mouths pucker to aid in saying "papa, prunes and prisms" (in order to gain the pursed lips then fashionable for females). The boys made cigarettes from the leaves of "sweet fern." The ledgy pastures which the children used as a shortcut to school teemed with wild blueberries and strawberries, and maple trees were tapped each spring for the making of sugar and syrup.[15]

The nearest center of trade and social life for the Butlers was McLains Mills, now the village of Appleton. The white spires of its two churches, nestled in the valley, served as a local landmark; there were also a Quaker meetinghouse, a handful of houses, a hotel, a general store and other merchants clustered around the sawmills and grist mills which huddled beside the St. George river as it flowed down its rocky course towards the sea. Saturday nights were likely to bring a meeting of the Odd Fellows Lodge, and sometimes a picnic supper or entertainment (called a "levee").

Goods or services not obtainable at the Mills could be obtained in Camden, about three hours by horse and wagon. A thriving harbor town of over four-thousand inhabitants on Penobscot Bay, Camden lay at the foot of Mount Battie which, with Mount Megunticook (the highest point on the Eastern seaboard) and Bald Mountain, comprise the "three long mountains" of the opening lines in Edna St. Vincent Millay's poem, "Renascence."[16] Camden in the 1850s and 1860s was a center of shipbuilding. Thousands turned out in their

Sunday best to celebrate the launchings of her graceful four- and five-masted schooners. The road to Camden passed along the shore of Lake Megunticook. Over its opposite side loomed "Maiden Cliff," so named after thirteen-year-old Elenora French, a girl about the same age as Eloise, fell to her death while picking wildflowers (according to one account) in 1864.[17]

Born during the waning years of the cutting of Maine's virgin forests, which had provided masts for the King's ships in colonial days, the young Eloise daily witnessed the clearing of the trees she loved. While a few stands were spared for later use in furniture or as firewood, and trees too remote from the roads and mills were left untouched, much of the accessible forest was logged to become rocky, hilly pasture or fields sown with rye or corn for the farm animals. Stones stacked alongside the country roads still mark the perimeters of the fields and pastures of Eloise Butler's childhood. Second and third-growth forest, reclaiming its original domain, now stands within the old stone walls.

Despite the lumbering, plenty of woods and wetlands remained to offer the young botanist a virtual paradise in which to explore. At age sixty Eloise wrote that her "chief amusement" in childhood was "then what it still is—roaming the woods."[18] But first, Eloise and Cora were required to practice long stints, each day, of knitting and piecing patchwork with "over and over" seams that had to be taken out and redone many times during the learning process, and do their share of the day's chores. Only then were the curly-haired "Elo" and her adored older sister Cora, a "freckled tomboy," free to roam. And roam they did, cementing a lifelong shared love of "botanizing," sometimes in the company of an aunt who pressed flowers for an herbarium and taught them to know the wild plants.[19]

Without leaving the farm, Cora and Eloise could follow the rocky, fern-covered banks of several streams that wound from Appleton Ridge down toward the St. George River. Dark and silent groves of majestic white pines grew in the lower parts of the valley, and there were several cranberry bogs to explore. The woods of oak, maple, and birch harbored a myriad of spring wildflowers, including trailing arbutus, trillium, and several species of violets, while in the meadows and along the roads in midsummer Queen Anne's lace and black-eyed Susans grew in profusion. In autumn, the many species of deciduous trees produced a riot of red, orange and yellow. Years later, a similar display in her wild garden could cause Eloise to stand, transfixed, by its beauty.[20]

On longer excursions, the children could hike all the way to the top of Appleton Ridge, where outcroppings of exposed bedrock, lined with veins of quartz and granite, were partly covered with lichens or other low-growing plants. From the old stagecoach road along the top of the ridge, beyond Hart Cemetery, could be had a splendid view of the surrounding countryside in all directions. Down the other side of the ridge lay Pettengill Stream, a wild, marshy area which drained the Whitney Bog, inhabited by moose and beaver. Beyond Pettengill Stream lay the huge Cedar Swamp, with a quaking bog of sphagnum moss and tamaracks, where the fascinating pitcher plants and sundews, and the beautiful rhodora and wild orchids grew.[21]

Years later, as a botany teacher in Minneapolis, Eloise Butler would lament the lack of such wild places close by where city children could learn firsthand about growing things. Her memories of the woods, meadows and bogs she had roamed as a girl would fuel her adult passion for wildflower preservation and her drive to save one especially lovely place for all time. And the joyful immersion in nature which the mature Eloise found in her wild garden would prove equal to that of her youthful wanderings in Appleton, Maine.

Notes

1 The town of Appleton covers approximately thirty-three square miles and contained, in 1851, three settlements along the St. George River.

2 Eloise Butler to Gray Memorial Botanical Chapter, Agassiz Association, Division D (1911), copy in *Early History of Eloise Butler Plant Reserve, Theodore Wirth Park*, p. 1, at Minneapolis Public Library, Minneapolis Collection.

3 Butler genealogy from Cyrus Eaton, *History of Thomaston, Rockland, and South Thomaston, Maine*, (1865; reprint, Rockland, Maine, *Courier-Gazette, Inc.*, 1972), pp. 165-168; and John Langdon Sibley, *A History of the Town of Union, Maine*, (Boston: Benjamin B. Mussey and Co., 1851), pp. 30-33, 41, 50, 437-438. The family genealogy is summarized in letters from Simpson Butler to Cora Butler Pease dated 20 August, 1917, and 26 July 1919 (copies in Eloise Butler Papers, Minnesota Historical Society).

4 Eaton, *History of Thomaston*, p. 172; Sibley, *History of Union*, p. 271.

5 Eaton, *History of Thomaston*, p. 172. Phineas and Bathsheba Butler are buried in Butler Cemetery on Butler Road, between Thomaston and Rockland.

6 The first Butler farmhouse is owned by Larry and Mary Syverson. The second Butler farm is now owned by Mrs. Ruth Smith. The original barn has been replaced, and its door has been placed into service in the new barn.

7 Cora E. Pease, "Old Time New England Industries," *House Beautiful* 9 (March 1901), pp. 204-209.

8 Land formerly owned by Phineas and John Butler near South Thomaston is now dominated by the Dragon Cement Plant.

9 Quotes from Eloise Butler to Gray Memorial Botanical Chapter, Agassiz Association, Division D (eulogy for Cora E. Pease), April 1928, copy in Eloise Butler biographical file at Minneapolis Public Library, Minneapolis Collection.

10 Sarah Orne Jewett, "The Queen's Twin," *Best Stories of Sarah Orne Jewett (Selected and Arranged with a Preface by Willa Cather)*, Vol. I (Cambridge: Houghton Mifflin Co., 1927), pp. 242-243.

11 "Obituary of Edward Graves," unidentified newspaper clipping [c.1904], copy in Eloise Butler Papers, Minnesota Historical Society.

12 Cora E. Pease, "The Eccentric Sisters-in-law," Portland *Transcript*, 11 September 1889 (copy in Eloise Butler Papers, Minnesota Historical Society).

13 Winnifred Furness, *Journal* (1869-1875), with 14-page typescript annotation by Theodore L. Brown of Winnifred's visit to the Butler farm in Maine in 1869-1870 (entries dated 12 and 13 March and 23 February 1870) in Eloise Butler Papers at Minnesota Historical Society; Eloise Butler, Minneapolis *Tribune*, 6 August 1911 and 13 August 1911, clippings in Scrapbook I, Minneapolis Park and Recreation Board Archives.

14 See note 9.

15 Quotes from Eloise Butler to Gray Memorial Botanical Chapter, Agassiz Association, Division D (entitled "Children's Forage Plants in the Wild Garden"), January 1915, *Annals of the Wild Life Reserve*, pp. 19-21, at Minneapolis Public Library, Minneapolis Collection.

16 "All I could see from where I stood / Was three long mountains and a wood; / I turned and looked another way, / and saw three islands in a bay. . . ." Edna St. Vincent Millay, "Renascence," *Collected Poems* (New York: Harper & Row, 1956), p. 3. Millay's mother, Mary Jane Pease, was a contemporary of Eloise Butler and granddaughter of Nathan Pease, neighbor to the Butler's first farm on Appleton Ridge.

17 *Camden-Rockport Bicentennial Commemorative Book* (Camden: Camden Herald Publishing Co., 1969), pp. 5, 15-17, 26, 51, 64.

18 See note 2.

19 See note 9. The aunt who gave Eloise and Cora their first lessons in botany may have been their father's younger sister Melea, born in 1826, whose husband, Ebenezer Sibley, died in 1854 leaving Melea with four young children who were boarded with various relatives, including the Butlers; or, perhaps it was "Aunt Mary," their grandfather Levi's second wife, who prescribed flax seed for use in tea and poultices for treatment of colds.

20 Eloise Butler, *Diary*, 16 June 1916, (in Eloise Butler Papers at Minnesota Historical Society).

21 An eighty-five-acre portion of the 680-acre Cedar Swamp, which contains the northernmost stand of Atlantic white cedar, *Chamaecyparis thyoides*, is owned by the Nature Conservancy. The Cedar Swamp (as "Appleton Bog") was designated a National Natural Landmark by the U. S. Department of the Interior in 1984.

2

A Studious Girl

Wild Geranium

OLIVER AND MARGARETTA BUTLER, both teachers before their marriage, placed a high value on education for their children. Considered a "man of vision," Oliver was deeply involved with the district schools of Appleton, conducting teacher examinations, riding out to inspect the outlying schools, and serving as school superintendent. He took the helm and taught a term or two himself occasionally, urging his scholars to apply themselves with the prediction that one of them would grow up to become president.[1]

The school nearest the farm where Eloise was born was the Elmwood School, a one-room frame building set back in a clearing along the Burkettville Road beside a small creek which ran down from the ridge. In the early 1850s, during the Maine lumber boom, the population of Appleton was at its peak (about 1,700). The Elmwood school was filled to capacity; as many as forty-eight children attended at once. There Eloise began her formal lessons, perhaps as early as age three, as had Cora. It was nearly a mile west of their house by way of a shortcut through the woods and pastures of the neighboring farm. In the winter, if they were lucky, the children might get a ride to school on a horse-drawn sled, or on a wagon or sleigh if someone happened to be going that way. After the family's move in 1859, the Butler children attended the Lower Ridge school at McCorrison's Corner, a one-room, cedar-shingled building not far uphill along the road which passed by the front door of the new house.[2]

In addition to the usual school lessons, there were private classes in penmanship and other subjects offered by lecturers who stopped in Appleton for a few weeks. When a traveling grammar teacher held an evening school for adults, Margaretta Butler enrolled and took some of her children along; little Cora was the star of the class, as Eloise later recalled.[3] The children were taught grammar by parsing the long sentences of *Paradise Lost* and other classics. Bible reading was always encouraged, and the family subscribed to popular periodicals such as *Hearth and Home* and *Young Folks*. The children read *Uncle Tom's Cabin*, and wept over the injustice portrayed in the novel.[4]

The Civil War began when Eloise was ten years old. Although neither of her older brothers, Simpson (who was attending Maine State Seminary) nor Esbon, are known to have fought in the Civil War, many Appleton families sent men. The selectmen, Oliver Butler among them, were in charge of supporting the families left behind by raising money in the town. The town paid substantial bounties for enlistments, and eventually over half the men of Appleton of military age signed up.[5] The women and girls made quilts, stockings and handkerchiefs for the soldiers, and many extra hours of sewing work were required of Eloise and Cora.

After completing the eighth grade in the rural schools of Appleton, and receiving some instruction in a local private seminary about which little is known, Eloise was sent, at the age of fifteen, to stay with relatives in Lynn, Massachusetts, to attend high school. Only ten miles north of Boston, Lynn was far from Appleton. The trip there required a long steamer ride (which often caused seasickness) from Camden to Portland along the jagged coastline of Maine, followed by a four-hour train ride from Portland to Lynn. Eloise probably stayed with the family of her father's cousin Phineas W. Butler, a grocer who lived in Lynn with his wife, Caroline, and their five children. While far from her parents, Eloise was once again close to Cora, who was attending high school and living with other relatives in Charlestown, across the Charles River from Boston. Also boarding in Lynn was their eldest brother, Simpson, who, after a few years teaching district school in Maine, was learning the mercantile business.

Life in Lynn was very different from the sheltered existence Eloise had known on the farm in Appleton. The city numbered over 15,000 residents, and was a thriving center of shoe manufacturing, with many four- and five-story brick buildings in the center of town. The first organized labor strike in the United States had taken place there only a few years before Eloise arrived. Lynn was the home of Mary Baker Eddy, founder of Christian Science, who was hard at work writing *Science and Health, a Key to the Scriptures;*[6] and the town was proud of its famous female astronomer, Maria Mitchell (originally of Nantucket), who had been called in 1865 to be professor of astronomy at Vassar. The local populace was so taken by the night sky phenomena that church bells were ordered rung to awaken sleepers on the occasion of especially brilliant meteor showers. Lynn even had its own sea-serpent, said to live in the

waters off Lynn's Beach near Egg Rock.[7]

The Lynn High School was a two-story brick building on High Street across from High Rock (former home of the legendary eighteenth-century fortuneteller, Moll Flanders). The school prided itself on having on its staff a male teacher who was a graduate of Harvard. Eloise took the classical course of study, which required three full years of Latin and a year of French in addition to courses in natural philosophy, botany, English literature, rhetoric, history, algebra, geometry, and astronomy. Extra classes in Greek and geography were offered for "the preparation of boys for college"; Eloise may have received special permission to study Greek, as she is said to have later taught the subject.[8]

The Lynn High School. *Lynn Historical Society.*

In Lynn, Eloise found herself the brunt of teasing by her schoolmates about the "greenness" of "down-easters." In defense, she wrote an ironic essay entitled "The State of Maine." Maine, she wrote, was:

> . . . a "howling wilderness," inhabited by savages, bears, snakes and monstrosities. My first recollection of things in this world was of a party of Old Town Indians dancing the wardance in front of my father's cabin. . . . One of my brothers came in shortly after, very much exhausted, as he had been engaged with our neighbors all the morning in an unsuccessful attempt to pry the sun up so that we might be sure of having a good day.[9]

Eloise's studies were undoubtedly lightened by visits with her brother and his wife, Olive Warland. The couple had married in 1866, and "Ollie" was occupied for the next decade in bearing and caring for the couple's four children. Later she became an avid campaigner for women's rights and the vote and, in 1897, was among the first three women elected to the Colorado legislature.[10] A photograph of Susan B. Anthony wearing an Olive Warland Butler campaign button was cherished for many years by Simpson and Olive's descendants.[11] The adolescent Eloise may well have witnessed the first stirrings of Ollie's feminist principles.

There was much coming and going between the Butler farm in Appleton and Lynn, Massachusetts, during the late 1860s.[12] Simpson and Esbon (who had stayed in

View in Lynn. *Lynn Historical Society.*

Appleton to help on the farm) often transported produce to the markets in Lynn and Boston. Ollie and her first two children, Ralph and Grace, lived with the Butlers in Maine for months at a time. After graduating from high school in Charlestown, Cora went to stay with relatives in Indiana to teach at a country school for a year in 1868-69; on her return in September 1869, she brought back cousin Winnifred Furness, thirteen years old, to spend the coming year at the Butler farm in Appleton. They stopped to visit Eloise, eighteen and just entering her senior year of high school in Lynn, and toured the new statehouse and other attractions in Boston before catching the steamer for Portland.

Her last year of high school may have been a lonely one for Eloise, who did not go home for Christmas. Cora was back home, teaching when she could find positions in the local schools; Ollie and her babies as well as Winnie Furness were all staying with the Butlers in Appleton. Eloise would have to wait until summer to see Cora's new organ, a Christmas present from Oliver and Margaretta. An occasional letter or small gift passed between Eloise and those on the farm whenever someone made the trip between Appleton and Lynn—Winnie sent Eloise a hemmed handkerchief for Christmas, and Eloise sent tatting collars she had made for Cora and Winnie.

After graduation from the Lynn high school on May 20, 1870, Eloise went home to Appleton. She was soon installed as teacher in a one-room district school in West Appleton, about four miles down the other side of the ridge from the Butler farm. The school stood inside the low stone walls of the Weymouth cemetery, with a view of tombstones from the windows. Eloise taught the summer term, for which she earned the sum of $25.92.[13]

Of slight build and probably not more than five feet tall, Eloise considered herself homely, compared to Cora's classical good looks. Eloise was acutely conscious of her prominent nose, although photographs taken in her twenties reveal her large, serious eyes to have dominated her face, framed in curls which had darkened considerably as she matured. Back home in Appleton after being away the better part of four years, she had an opportunity to share in the usual social life of young people of her own age—meetings at the Lodge, visiting, hayrides—although the extent to which she joined in is not known.

Astride the family's horse, Pomp, riding to her school in the morning and home in mid-afternoon along the Liberty road, Eloise had plenty of time in which to ponder her future. The choices realistically open to her were few. She decided to become a teacher that summer because, as she later wrote, "at that time and place, no other career was thought of for a studious girl."[14]

In the decade after the Civil War, higher education for women was not widely available. Most of the private, financially unstable female academies and seminaries which did exist offered a watered-down curriculum; in any event, the reasons why women should obtain higher education were unclear, since no professions other than teaching were open to them. The "cult of true womanhood," so entrenched in antebellum days, still persisted. Women were taught to revere the four cardinal virtues—piety, purity, submissiveness, and domesticity. Advocates of women's education, such as Emma Hart Willard and her sister, Almira Hart Lincoln (later Phelps), author of the successful *Familiar Lectures on Botany* (1829), prudently argued that learning would benefit women in their traditional roles as wives and mothers of future citizens, and that the study of science (especially botany) would bring them closer to God.[16]

The establishment of Vassar College in New York in 1865 was an important milestone toward making educational opportunity for women equal to that available to men; and in the 1870s the state land-grant institutions were just beginning to admit women students. It was not until the 1890s and later that American universities and colleges opened their graduate schools to women.[17] When Eloise Butler graduated from high school in 1870, the most common way for women to obtain higher education was attendance at the state-supported normal schools which trained (mostly) women to be teachers, and which obtained their funding from cost-conscious legislatures at least partly on the basis that female teachers were willing to work for lower wages than males required.[18]

For Eloise Butler, fourth child of conservative Maine farmers prosperous enough to purchase an organ (and lessons) for their eldest daughter, yet not wealthy enough to pay the tuition of $400 per year at Vassar for their "studious girl," the choice for further education was obvious. A new teacher's college had recently opened in Castine, on the other

side of Penobscot Bay from Camden. Admission was granted to all who passed the entrance exam and pledged themselves to teach in the public schools of Maine. One of the Emery cousins from South Thomaston was already a pupil there. Best of all, tuition and books were free. Both Cora and Eloise, neither of whom had yet any prospects for marriage, applied for admission. On August 24, 1870, Eloise, just nineteen, and Cora, nearly twenty-two, having satisfied the examiners of their proficiency in arithmetic, spelling, reading, geography, and grammar, both enrolled at the Eastern State Normal School.[19]

Watched over by an old British fort, Fort George, and a lighthouse with a stone tower on Dyce's Head, the town of Castine lies at the tip of a peninsula which juts out into Penobscot Bay from its eastern side. Castine was then, and still is, a lovely seacoast village with a long military history, having at different times been owned by the French, the Dutch, the English, and finally the Americans. Steamers plied the waters between Camden and Castine several times a week in the summer, serving the wealthy "rusticators" who came up from Boston and New York to stay in its comfortable inns and boarding houses; students of the Normal School rode for free. In winter, the students had a choice between the mail boat (a small sailing "packet") or a long stagecoach ride to towns across the Bay.[20]

The novel *Laura, An American Girl* by Elizabeth E. Evans (1884) describes the "quiet village" of Castine, "embowered in trees," as visited by a young Boston woman in the 1870s:

> . . . The remote graveyard with its white head-stones gleaming out from a grove of pine and fir, the rounded shore and the

The road to the lighthouse in Castine, Maine. *Castine Scientific Society.*

Eastern State Normal School in Castine, Maine, 1873. *Castine Historical Society.*

broad shining bay, the varied outline of the opposite mainland, the massive cone of Blue Hill in the east, and the fainter forms of the Mount Desert range against the southern horizon, the meeting of sky and water in the wide offing, the exquisite blending of substance and shadow in the mirrored islands opposite the town—it was perfect. . . . The ladies walked past . . . cottages fronting the sea, past neglected ship-yards cumbered with weather-beaten timbers and carpeted with shiny gray chips, until they came to an open space, the commencement of a wide spreading meadow, or common, extending along the shore as far as the lighthouse. . . .[21]

The Normal School had opened its doors in the fall of 1867 in the Abbott School on the Common, and had graduated two classes from its two-year course of study by 1870. Enrollment climbed rapidly, and by the fall of 1870, one hundred and nineteen pupils were in attendance. As was true of many normal schools, far more pupils entered than ever graduated; the graduating classes averaged only fifteen or twenty per year. Many of the students, already teachers, could afford to stay only a term or two. Marriage claimed others.[22]

Having no dormitory of their own, the Normal School students boarded with families in the village who had an extra room to spare. Besides the fishermen, sea captains and widows found all along the Maine coast, Castine was home to its share of spinsters who took in boarders. Among the best-known in Castine were the Hawes sisters, Abigail and Sarah,

then in their sixties. Sarah was renowned as a scholar of Greek and mathematics, and the sisters, who studied astronomy, taught navigation to aspiring sea captains and other villagers in a red schoolhouse which stood in their yard.[23]

Neither Eloise nor Cora Butler attended the Normal School for the winter term that year; Eloise returned alone in the spring. Cora cut short her studies to teach in country schools and later accepted a position as principal of a grammar school in Rockland. Eloise, granted advanced placement because of the fine education she had received at Lynn High School, continued intermittently with the course; her young brother Arthur attended with her for the spring term in 1873. Eloise graduated with high grades in a class of ten from the Eastern State Normal School on May 22, 1873; the commencement program indicates that she gave a speech entitled "Public Opinion."[24]

On September 9, 1872, Cora Butler had married Curtis S. Pease, whom she had met while attending high school in Charlestown, Massachusetts. Years later, Eloise would write with unusual frankness: "My sister's marriage was my first great grief."[25] The lives of the two inevitably diverged with Cora's entry into marriage and, a few years later, motherhood, while Eloise was to turn her nurturant instincts and creative energy toward her friends and students, her botanical interests, and, eventually, the cause of wildflower preservation. Despite Cora's marriage and their

Cora Butler, c. 1870. She was married in 1872. *Martha P. Pease.*

later geographical separation, the sisters managed to remain emotionally close throughout their entire lives, renewing their ties with shared interludes focused on the study of botany.

In the three decades after the Civil War, when Eloise Butler came of age and the movement for woman's suffrage was gaining momentum, there was a significant rise in American spinsterhood. Although its causes are not clear, it coincided with the rise of the women's rights movement.[26] Eloise Butler was one of many unmarried women who made substantial contributions to society as teachers and social reformers. She also became part of a large network of women, married and single, who were interested in studying science, who, increasingly excluded from the male societies and academic circles where "professional" science took place, nevertheless pursued their researches on their own and in correspondence with one another and with sympathetic men, sharing contacts and encouragement with the younger generation. The first such woman Eloise Butler encountered was Helen Coffin, botany teacher at the Eastern State Normal School.

Helen Coffin, eleven years older than Eloise, had already taught six years in the Normal School at Farmington, Maine, and had transferred to the Normal School in Castine the year before Eloise enrolled.[27] Besides botany, she taught physiology, history, geology, and drawing. An energetic and inspired teacher, she was not averse to dissecting the heart and lungs of an ox before her students. Regarded as a gifted speaker, Helen Coffin must have made an impression on Eloise, recently bereft of Cora's attention. Isolated in the small village of Castine, teachers and pupils had plenty of opportunity—indeed, need—to get to know each other well, and it is likely the young teacher and her promising student became friends.

In the summer of 1873, immediately following Eloise's graduation, Helen Coffin attended a summer school for teachers on Penikese Island off the coast of Massachusetts taught by Louis Agassiz, marine biologist of the Harvard Museum of Comparative Zoology and the most influential scientist of the time in the United States. The teachers at the school, called the Anderson School of Natural History, conducted experiments based on their observations of marine life and absorbed

Agassiz's methods of laboratory instruction. Agassiz was an early advocate of scientific education for women, and the thirty women teachers who attended his short-lived summer school in 1873 and 1874 went on to inspire the next generation of American women who wished to study science.[28] Although no letters between Coffin and Butler have survived, Helen Coffin may well have served as a role model or mentor (by correspondence) and contributed to igniting Eloise Butler's interest in algae, soon to become her foremost passion.[29]

Eloise Butler's graduation from Normal School coincided with her parents' sudden decision to sell their farm in Appleton and move west. Maine land was rocky, the soil poor, and farming was difficult; open lands to the west, with rich soil waiting to be homesteaded, enticed many families to leave Maine in the 1870s. There may, however, have been a more tragic reason for their departure. According to a family story, Oliver Butler was forced to sell the farm after the town treasurer of Appleton embezzled the town funds—then a handsome sum. The town had just taxed its citizens to contribute to the cost of the new Knox County courthouse, and the town treasurer fled to Canada with this money, leaving Oliver Butler, as surety, to make up the missing cash.[30] The Butlers sent their seventeen-year-old son, Arthur, an adventurous boy, to Kansas to scout ahead and see what land could be had there, while they settled their affairs in Appleton and prepared to go west.

Esbon, who had married his sweetheart Maria Stoddard of Appleton in 1871, would stay in the East.[31] So would Simpson, who, with Ollie and their four young children, were established in Lynn, and Cora, whose husband was employed by the Boston Ice Company. The three youngest—Eloise, Arthur and Edgar—would go west with their parents. Ultimately, they decided to head for Porter County, Indiana, to settle near Margaretta's younger sister, Louisa, whom she hadn't seen in twenty years, and Sophia, who had joined Louisa in Indiana and married a poet and Civil War veteran there in 1865. Following Arthur, the Butler party, consisting of Oliver, Margaretta, and Edgar, along with Aunt Melea, arrived by train in Furnessville, Indiana, in November of 1873.[32] Eloise, who may have stayed behind to finish a term of schoolteaching, joined them later.

Furnessville, Indiana, was a small settlement about two miles south of the dunes along the southern shore of Lake Michigan. The town was named for its founder, Edwin Leigh Furness, husband of Louisa. Originally from Maine, and after having gone to sea as a boy, Furness had migrated to Indiana in 1856 and became a prosperous lumberman and farmer. By 1873, he owned more than two thousand acres of land in Pine and Winchester townships (including what is now Beverly Shores). He was the station agent of the railroad, the postmaster, a Republican, and a candidate for state senator on the temperance platform in 1874.[33]

Edwin Leigh Furness obligingly sold his in-laws a farm of two hundred and forty acres a short distance down the road from his own place. The newcomers were made to feel at home with invitations to Christmas dinner and frequent visits to the Furness homestead.[34] Social life for the young people was much like that in Maine; there were weekly meetings of the Grange (National Grange of the Patrons of Husbandry), then more of a social than political group, and spelling bees, debates and exciting lectures by touring temperance workers and women's rights speakers. The latter were warmly received in Furnessville, where Louisa Furness believed in teaching girls to harness horses and boys to clean house and cook. In warm weather there were picnics and swimming parties at the nearby dunes, which were reached by walking through a seemingly-endless marsh with tall grasses that reached high overhead; the sand hills were covered with blue lupine and chokecherries.

Eloise taught two terms in one-room schools in Porter County, Indiana, in 1874. On a cold day in January, her brother Arthur and Winnie Furness took her seven miles in a wagon over rough roads to a school near Baileytown in Westchester Township, where Eloise taught a term in the District Four school, for which she received about thirty-eight dollars per month. She boarded with families of her pupils, and went home on weekends and holidays. That spring and summer she taught another term in the Pine Township First District school, a large, crowded one-room schoolhouse in which she was in charge of more than seventy students and earned thirty-five dollars per month.[35] When Eloise's school closed on July 3, 1874,

Winnie and five other young people went to fetch her home in a lumber wagon.

Fleeting glimpses of Eloise Butler's life in those days appear in the journal kept by her cousin Winnifred Furness in 1874. On a Saturday in March, Winnie wrote:

> Had a rag bee—all of our folks, Aunt and Ello, etc. happened in so we gave [them] a needle—we all sewed steady for an hour, only once we went out to get weighed.

On the Fourth of July, there was a gathering at the shore of Lake Michigan:

> . . . we all went to the Lake to the grand fourth of July Picnic. There was a large crowd there when we arrived. Strolled around watching them dance, etc. etc. We [ate] our dinner up on the hills, then we went down to our tent and went in bathing. I think there is no better fun on a warm day.

On Saturday, August 1, a group of thirteen, including Winnie and Arthur (and probably Eloise), went to nearby Chesterton in a railroad handcar to attend the Peach Festival. And Winnie wrote on Wednesday, August 26: "Ello taught me to embroider a handkerchief."

Eloise made an effort to fit into rural life in Indiana, but she was not happy there. She was twenty-two, no longer a child, yet not safely married (marriage and motherhood then being regarded as the only natural state for women). With her normal school education and experience of big-city life gained during her high school years near Boston, she felt stifled and ill at east in the Indiana dunelands, where once again she was teased and tormented for her Maine accent.[36]

Eloise later recalled that she left Indiana because she could not find a position to her liking.[37] This is not surprising, given her training. In the latter part of the nineteenth century, when most of the American population lived on farms, one-room country schools were still the primary means of education of rural children.[38] The country schoolteacher had to make do with the barest of necessities in books, and few amenities were provided by the thrifty farmers. The teacher, usually not more educated than the eldest of her pupils, was often responsible for cleaning the schoolhouse by herself, hauling water and wood, and lighting the fire in winter. Winnie Furness wrote in her journal of the country school she attended, "the scholars all huddle around the stove to keep warm, [and] the wind whistles right through the building."[39]

Wayne Fuller, author of a history of country schools, wrote that teachers educated in the normal schools often preferred to teach in graded city schools rather than in the country schools for which they had been trained. To these teachers,

> . . . against the background of a fine, large, centrally heated schoolhouse with rooms filled with the latest school apparatus, encyclopedias, dictionaries, uniform textbooks, and uniform classes, the country school seemed ineffably bleak and backward.[40]

School boards usually changed teachers every term or two, so a teacher had to be constantly on the move—perhaps not such a hardship for a young woman who, as most did, married and quit teaching after a few terms; but not acceptable to a woman who intended to make teaching her lifelong career.

By the end of the summer of 1873, when she turned twenty-three, Eloise had made up her mind to leave Indiana for Minnesota. Many natives of Maine, especially those in the lumber business, had already settled in Minnesota; her family may have had a friend or distant relative there. The Minneapolis school board was advertising positions for teachers in the schools of the rapidly-growing city. Emma Rigby, the hired woman employed on the Furness place, had married a surveyor who was working in Minnesota; Emma's departure to join her husband preceded Eloise's own by only a few weeks. News of teaching jobs may have reached Eloise through newspapers sent back to her by Emma.

On August 31, 1874, Eloise packed her bags, made her farewells, and boarded the train at Furnessville for Minnesota, by way of Chicago. That night Winnifred Furness wrote in her journal: "Ello started for Minneapolis Minn. this evening, where she intends to teach."

Notes

1 Quote from "The Story of Appleton," *Courier-Gazette* [Rockland, Maine], 24 August 1929 (copy in Eloise Butler Papers, Minnesota Historical Society).

2 Theodore L. Brown to author, 7 November 1988 and 20 September 1989; Appleton School *Record Book*, District 7, 1854-1859.

3 Eloise Butler to Gray Memorial Botanical Chapter, Agassiz Association, Division D (eulogy for Cora E. Pease), April 1928, copy in Minneapolis Public Library, Minneapolis Collection.

4 Old and New (women's club in Malden, Massachusetts) *Minute Book* Vol. VII, 10 November 1896.

5 "Story of Appleton," *Courier-Gazette*, 24 August 1929; research of Theodore F. Hall provided by Theodore L. Brown in conversation with author 17 July 1989. A Caleb Butler killed in the Civil War and buried in Miller Cemetery in Appleton may have been an uncle of Eloise Butler.

6 Mary Baker Eddy's career as the founder of Christian Science is considered by some to have begun when she (then Mrs. Patterson) gave a series of lectures on spiritual healing ten miles south of Appleton in the town of Warren, Maine, in 1864; Theodore L. Brown to author, 23 December 1989.

7 Janet Lane, "A Brief History of Lynn" (pamphlet), Lynn Historical Society (1895); James R. Newhall, *History of Lynn* (Lynn: [c.1890]), p. 22; Maria Mitchell lived in Lynn from 1861 to 1865

and after her retirement from Vassar in 1888 (typescript "Maria Mitchell" in files of Lynn Historical Society).

8 Lynn School Committee, *Annual Report*, 1870, pp. 45-48 (46); Butler's teaching of Greek is mentioned in, for example, "Eloise Butler Dies in Woodland She Loved," Minneapolis *Journal*, 11 April 1933.

9 Eloise Butler, unidentified newspaper clipping (c.1869) in Eloise Butler Papers, Minnesota Historical Society.

10 "Ladies to Make Law; Three in Colorado Assembly," unidentified newspaper clipping (Colorado, c.1897) in scrapbook, Martha A. Bushnell Conine Papers at Denver Public Library, Western History Department.

11 Nona Butler Allen to author (February, 1989).

12 Here and next paragraph see Furness *Journal*, September 1869 (see chapter 1, note 13).

13 Appleton School *Record Book*, 18 August 1870. Description of the school by Ray Bartlett, in Cyndi Gonzalez to author, 15 March 1990 and 4 April 1990.

14 Eloise Butler to Gray Memorial Botanical Chapter, Agassiz Association, Division D (1911), copy in *Early History of Eloise Butler Plant Reserve, Theodore Wirth Park*, p. 1 at Minneapolis Public Library, Minneapolis Collection.

15 Barbara Welter, *Dimity Convictions—The American Woman in the Nineteenth Century* (Athens: Ohio University Press, 1976), p. 21.

16 On higher education available to women interested in science in the nineteenth century see Margaret W. Rossiter, *Women Scientists in America: Struggles and Strategies to 1940* (Baltimore: John Hopkins University Press, 1982); on the life of Almira Hart Lincoln Phelps see Lois B. Arnold, *Four Lives in Science* (New York: Schocken Books, 1984), chapter 3.

17 Margaret Rossiter, *Women Scientists in America*, pp. 30-31.

18 Wayne Edison Fuller, *The Old Country School: The Story of Rural Education in the Middle West* (Chicago: University of Chicago Press, 1982), pp. 159-160.

19 Vassar tuition as stated in Vassar College *Catalog* (1870-1871), courtesy Nancy MacKechnie at Vassar College Library. Here and below, Eastern State Normal School, *Catalogue and Circular*, 1870, 1871, 1873 (archives of the Maine Maritime Academy); Eastern State Normal School *Record Book*, 1867-1922 (Maine State Archives, Augusta); and Francis W. Hatch, "Castine, Historic Gem of Penobscot Bay," *Down East* 17 (July 1971), pp. 66-69, 88, 91.

20 Francis W. Hatch, "Castine, Historic Gem of Penobscot Bay," pp. 66-69, 88, 91; Eastern State Normal School, *Catalogue and Circular* (for the year ending May 1870), p. 17.

21 Elizabeth E. Evans, *Laura, An American Girl*, (J.B. Lippincott, 1884), exerpts as printed in "A Castine Summer of the 70s," *Wilson Museum Bulletin* (Castine), Vol. 3 (Fall 1987), pp. 1-4 (2-3).

22 "Eastern State Normal School," *Maine Teachers' Digest*, Vol. 1 (December 1940), pp. 64-65, 75; Paul H. Mattingly, *The Classless Profession* (*American Schoolmen of the Nineteenth Century*), (New York: New York University Press, 1975), p. 62.

23 Here and below, George Wheeler, *History of Castine, Penobscot and Brooksville, Maine* (Cornwall [New York]: Cornwall Press, 1923), pp. 123-125, 429-431.

24 "Exercises of Examination and Graduation at the Close of the Fifth Year of the Eastern State Normal School at Castine, Maine," pamphlet, 21 May 1873 (archives, Maine Maritime Academy).

25 See note 3.

26 Daniel Scott Smith, "Family Limitations, Sexual Control and Domestic Feminism in Victorian America," in *Clio's Consciousness Raised*, ed. Mary Hartman and Lois W. Banner (New York: Octagon Books, 1976), reprint ed., pp. 120-121.

27 George C. Purington, *History of the State Normal School, Farmington, Maine* (Farmington: Knowlton, McLeary & Co., 1889), pp. 23-24; here and below, Richard P. Mallett, *University of Maine at Farmington, A Study in Educational Change*

(*1864-1974*), (Freeport: Bond Wheelwright Co., 1975), pp. 69-70.

28 Joan N. Burstyn, "Early Women in Education: The Role of the Anderson School of Natural History," *Boston University Journal of Education*, Vol. 159 (August 1977), pp. 50-64.

29 Helen Coffin married Daniel Beedy in 1875 when she was thirty-five. She became a leader of Maine's temperance movement, worked for woman suffrage, founded the Dorothea Dix Memorial Association, and wrote a book about remarkable women of Maine, *Mothers of Maine* (Portland, The Thurston Print, 1895). See *Bangor Daily News*, 15 June 1904, p. 7 (obituary); and "Helen Coffin Beedy," *Memorials of Maine*, ed. A. F. Moulton (New York: The American Historical Society, 1916), pp. 285-286.

30 Ethelwyn Pease to Martha P. Pease, 28 May 1948 (courtesy Martha P. Pease; copy in Eloise Butler Papers, Minnesota Historical Society). Town records reveal that a George Sibley, brother-in-law of Oliver Butler's sister Melea, was elected treasurer in March 1872 and is not listed in later censuses of Appleton; Theodore L. Brown to author, 12 August 1989.

31 Esbon Butler became a butter, cheese and egg merchant at Faneuil Hall, Boston, and later in Malden, Massachusetts. He and Maria had six children. In his old age, Esbon is said to have fled a home for the elderly, found a job, and lived independently for two years until a car accident revealed his identity. He was returned to the home, and died in 1939 at the age of 93. Author's interview with Oliver E. Butler (Esbon's grandson) at Melrose, Massachusetts, July 1989.

32 Furness *Journal*, 1 November 1873.

34 Weston A. Goodspeed and Charles Blanchard, ed., *Counties of Porter and Lake, Indiana* (Chicago: F. A. Battey & Co., 1882), pp. 295-296, 743-748. The Pulitzer Prize-winning author, naturalist, and photographer Edwin Way Teale (1899-1980) was the grandson of Edwin and Louisa Furness, and second cousin of Eloise Butler; Furnessville was the setting for Teale's autobiographical *Dune Boy, the Early Years of a Naturalist* (1943).

34 Here and below, Furness *Journal*, 1872-1873.

35 Weston and Blanchard, *Counties of Porter and Lake*, pp. 156-157, 228-229.

36 See note 14.

37 Ibid.

38 Wayne Edison Fuller, *The Old Country School*, pp. 53, 159-163, 189-190, 217, here and next paragraph.

39 Winnifred Furness, *Journal*, 9 January 1873.

40 Wayne Edison Fuller, *The Old Country School*, p. 190.

Eloise Butler as a young teacher, c. 1878. *Grace Butler Smith*.

3

Pioneer Minneapolis Teacher

Dutchman's Breeches

WHEN ELOISE BUTLER ARRIVED in Minnesota early in September 1874, the transformation of Minneapolis from a rough-hewn frontier town, first settled some twenty-six years before, to a leading lumber and flour-milling city was well under way. The citizens of St. Anthony, the older town on the eastern side of the Mississippi River, and Minneapolis, to the west, had voted only two years before to unite as one municipality; the population of the city was about 31,000.[1] Most of the industry was concentrated in a few blocks along the western bank of the river, where, among the dozen or more water-powered sawmills and flour mills, the limestone Washburn "A" mill, just completed, was by far the finest at seven and one-half stories tall. The old sawmills that huddled in low rows above St. Anthony Falls on both sides of the river were sawing the last of the season's logs, and the streets were crowded with lumbermen purchasing supplies and harnessing teams of oxen for the winter's labor in the pine woods to the north.[2]

The city was a striking mixture of old and new. Many vestiges remained of the city's recent pioneer days, though the modest frame homes and storefronts of the early settlers were rapidly being replaced by more durable and ornate buildings of brick and stone, such as Thomas Lowry's mansion, then under construction at Hennepin and Groveland. Neither streetcars nor gas lights were yet in place. Farmers and their families, in wagons piled high with household goods, passed through town, headed for the Red River Valley to stake homestead claims. Townspeople mingled in the streets with miners buying provisions for expeditions in search of gold rumored to be found in the Dakota Territory. The only lake within the city limits was Jewett Lake, on land destined to become Central (later Loring) Park, and the only park was a two-block former cow pasture known as Murphy Square.[3]

That fall, the Minneapolis newspapers followed General Custer's movements in the Black Hills as closely as they did the latest antics of Greased Lightning, an unruly horse that delivered the *Evening Mail*. Pleas went out for rooms in which to board the many new teachers arriving daily from the East to teach in the public schools, along with reminders that cows were prohibited from running at large after the first of November (twenty-five

17

Nicollet Avenue in 1874. *Minneapolis Public Library, Minneapolis Collection.*

were impounded in one day). Lap robes made of wolf pelts and buffalo skins were offered for sale in the dry goods stores. Fires that swept rapidly through the lumber yards and wooden buildings were a common occurrence. The following spring, the Minneapolis *Tribune* would condemn the deplorable condition of the unpaved streets, calling them "rivers of mud," and claiming there was "better traveling anywhere on the open prairie around us, than in the streets of the city."[4]

The youthful city already had cultural institutions for learning and the arts. Entertainment could be had at a number of establishments, including the Pence Opera House and the Academy of Music, where traveling theater troupes, singing minstrels, and burlesque shows were regularly featured. The spelling-match mania was as strong in Minnesota as it had been in Indiana, with teams from Minneapolis and St. Paul pitted against one another to orchestral accompaniment at the Opera House. On Sundays, citizens could choose among a full complement of churches or attend meetings of the Liberal League, forerunner of the Unitarian Society, which sponsored controversial but well-attended lectures on Darwinism.[5]

Thomas B. Walker's private art gallery was open to the public, the movement for the establishment of a free public library was under way, and the University of Minnesota had just graduated its second class. There were over fifty teachers employed in the city's ten public schools, which ranged from a one-room schoolhouse left over from the town's early

days to two large buildings made of stone. The editors of the *Minneapolis City Directory,* aiming to attract new residents, lauded the city's "magnificent business structures, beautiful private residences and numerous mills" and called it "the new city of the Upper Mississippi Valley."[6]

On the strength of her diploma from the Eastern State Normal School, Eloise Butler obtained a position in the Third Ward school of the East Division known as Center School.[7] The school occupied a block along University Avenue between the present Central and East Hennepin Avenues, on the St. Anthony side of town, and faced the Winslow House and the Mississippi River across an open block of land which is the present site of Richard Chute Square. It was an imposing structure, made of limestone quarried from the banks of the river, and had been built only seven years before at a cost of more than $40,000.

There were four classrooms on each of the two lower floors of Center School and a large assembly hall on the third floor that offered a panoramic view of the suspension bridge, the milling district along the river, and the farmland which began only a few blocks to the east. Topped with an elegant Mansard roof and an ornate wrought-iron railing, it was regarded as one of the finest school buildings in the state. The school contained primary, intermediate, grammar, and high school departments, and was home to one male principal, seven female teachers and nearly seven hundred students.[8]

Eloise had reason to be pleased with her

new position in such a modern school, compared to the drafty one-room country schools where she had taught in Maine and Indiana. Her salary of close to fifty dollars a month was a marked improvement over what she had previously earned. The only drawback was that Center School was already overcrowded; students had to attend in morning and afternoon shifts, and high school classes were held in the hallways to free classrooms for more primary students.

At Center School Eloise first taught the grammar grades. Her subjects reportedly included Latin and Greek, which were usually offered in grammar school to students in the seventh through ninth grades who were preparing for college.[9] Her grammar students were divided according to their scholarship, rather than by age, then a progressive notion.

After two years, Eloise was appointed to teach in the high school division, then held in classrooms carved out of the assembly hall on the top floor. Her salary was raised to sixty-five dollars per month. A year later, the Board of Education offered her the Assistant Principalship of Center School, but she declined the appointment, choosing instead to return to teaching in the grammar school with a ten-dollar cut in pay. She may have had her mind set on a position in the grand new Central High School then under construction across the river on Fourth Avenue South between Tenth and Eleventh streets.[10]

When Central High opened in 1878, Eloise Butler was installed as teacher of history

Central High School, 1878. *Minnesota Historical Society.*

and botany.[11] Her joy at assuming her post in the new school was marred just as the term began, however, by news of the death of her younger brother Arthur in a logging accident near the town of Truckee, California, on September 15, 1878. He was twenty-two years old.[12]

Butler taught at Central High for the next twenty-four years, until 1902, then at South High nine more years until her retirement from teaching in 1911. Through her classes passed the sons and daughters of many of the prominent families of the city, as well as the children of the wave of immigrants that arrived in Minneapolis by the thousands in the 1880s and 1890s, many of whom did not speak English. To accommodate the newcomers, the schools added night classes, partitioned auditoriums, and held classes on stair landings until new buildings could be put up, yet overcrowding remained a fact of life all through Eloise Butler's teaching career. Teaching and maintaining order under such conditions must have been difficult.[13]

The women teachers at Central High, especially those who remained unmarried, formed deep, lifelong friendships. They socialized together, traveled together, and formed literary and art history clubs. They often gathered in the Paige mansion on Yale Place which overlooked Central (now Loring) Park, where Emma Paige, a teacher at Central, lived with her brothers Howe and James.[14] Among Eloise's closest friends were younger women who had studied with her at Center School or at Central High, then had gone on to become teachers themselves. One such friend was Esther Friedlander, the first woman to obtain a master's degree at the University of Minnesota, who taught Latin at South High School for thirty-two years. Esther Friedlander recalled Eloise Butler, often carrying her "inseparable tin herbarium," during her years at Central; with her "smoothly combed black hair, her drooping eyelids, and a peculiar sibilant sound" to her voice, Eloise handled frogs "without hesitation" to illustrate the action of the heart and nerves. "One day," recalled Esther, Eloise "dissected a cow's eye in front of the class and by doing so revealed the beauty and order of the human eye."[15]

After her transfer to South High School, Eloise made new friends among the teachers there, as well. With Lela Klampe, who taught German, she discussed literature, and was considered knowledgeable on the subject; and, to Lillian Mathias, the art teacher at South, Eloise brought wildflowers and loaned biographies of artists from her own collection.[16] Among her papers at the Minnesota Historical Society is a lengthy poem in Butler's handwriting, entitled "A Gallinaceous Ode," dedicated to the women teachers of Central High.[17] It appears to have been composed by Butler on the occasion of her transfer from Central to South High in 1902, when Eloise switched schools with her friend Clara Leavitt, who taught botany at South. In the poem, Eloise compared her friends to a "wise brood of hens" who fed their young chicks "classical lore," "etymological crumbs," and "old Latin rules, most excellent food," in order to "nourish their minds [and] make them learned and wise." She honored:

> . . . hens whose wise heads hold all sorts of deep
> lore; Mathematical hens, and hens who know more
> Than the wisest of roosters about bugs and things,
> Astronomical hens who can count Saturn's rings;
>
> Historical hens, who can give every date
> From Adam to William McKinley,—can prate
> Of hydraulics, magnesia, civics, Shakespeare and Burns,
> "Parler" French, "sprechen Deutsch," and analyze ferns. . . .[18]

During her first year in Minnesota, Eloise formed a relationship that was clearly one of the most important in her life, yet about which little is known. Sarah Brackett was teaching the primary grades at Center School when Eloise took up her position. Two years older than Eloise, Sarah had already been in Minneapolis for a year; she came from the same area in Maine (Livermore Falls) as did Dorilus Morrison, first mayor of Minneapolis. Sarah was a talented violinist and was, like Eloise, a lover of art and poetry. Their backgrounds drew them together, although the extent of Sarah's interest in botany is not known. Sarah taught school in Minneapolis for thirty years, mainly at Jefferson and Sumner schools.[19]

Eloise often took rooms at the same boarding houses as did Sarah in the 1870s, returning to stay with her parents in Indiana for the summer and moving into a new boarding house each fall. After 1878, Eloise and Sarah's friendship deepened, although they lived apart for ten years. Eloise found lodgings closer to Central High School. When Eloise was thirty-eight and Sarah forty, they moved into shared quarters—first at a boarding house, later renting an apartment on Portland Avenue—and lived together for the next fifteen years, thereby managing to evade the "dreadful loneliness of heart," the "hunger for home" and lack of "tender ties" decried by Louisa May Alcott as the usual fate of spinsters.[20] Sarah Brackett's final illness forced her resignation from teaching in November 1904, and a year later she returned to Maine to be cared for by her stepmother and sisters. Her death on September 18, 1906, at age fifty-seven, must have been another "great grief" for Eloise Butler. Sarah's bond with Eloise was acknowledged in Sarah's obituary published in the Lewiston [Maine] *Evening Journal* on September 19, 1906: "She had made for herself a home, where, with Miss Butler, another teacher, she lived."[21]

Early on, Eloise made the acquaintance of several persons who might have advised her on the geography and flora of the woods and prairies within easy reach of the city. Besides Emma Rigby's surveyor husband, there was Nathan Butler (no relation), whose sister Mattie taught a term with Eloise at Center School in 1876, and with whose family Sarah Brackett had boarded. Nathan Butler had been in Minnesota for more than twenty years and had made extensive land surveys for the Great Northern Railroad. He was a member of the Minnesota Academy of Science, and knowledgeable about the Indian mounds of the state.[22] Another source of information on the local natural history, and a man who could have provided Eloise an introduction to the botanists, geologists, and naturalists of Minnesota was E. W. B. Harvey, the principal of Center School when Eloise first taught there, and one of the founding members of the Minnesota Academy of Science.[23]

In the 1870s and 1880s, many opportunities for botanizing in and around the Twin Cities were near at hand. The countryside was easily reached, provided one had transportation or sufficient stamina for walking. In 1874 the Minneapolis city limits extended only as far as Franklin Avenue on the southwest edge of the city, and Twenty-seventh Street to the south, with farmland and

prairie beyond. A railroad station at
Minnehaha Falls made the land below the
cascade, which abounded in wildflowers,
accessible to the public, although it was
still privately owned. Tamarack bogs at Lake
Calhoun and Lake Harriet made much of the
surrounding land unsuitable for building,
besides which the lakes were then considered
too remote for city dwellers; Lake of the Isles
was largely marsh. The northern boundary of
Minneapolis was at Twenty-sixth Avenue, and
the eastern edge at Oak Street and Stinson
Boulevard.

Humboldt Avenue was the city's western
edge, past which lay the Oswold and Halloran
farms on the hills outside the city along dirt
roads known as Western Avenue and Cedar
Lake Road. Unbroken stretches of woods and
wetlands extended all the way to Lake
Minnetonka, some ten miles distant, and
beyond. Trains stopped at stations at Cedar
Lake and Wayzata on Lake Minnetonka,
where travelers could catch a steamer to
Excelsior, already a popular summer resort.

Eloise was eager to avail herself of
opportunities for further formal study of
botany. In the summer of 1881, the University
of Minnesota offered its first Summer School
of Science, designed to instruct teachers in
"methods of original investigation and of
teaching from actual specimens" in chemistry,
geology, and botany.[24] One instructor was
Charles E. Bessey, thirty-five, then professor of
natural history at the Iowa State College of
Agriculture at Ames, who had studied at
Harvard under Asa Gray.[25] As head of the
department of botany at the University of
Nebraska from 1884 until his death in 1915,
Bessey would become a leader of the
"transitional period" in American botany
when its emphasis was moving away from the
classification and naming of new species and
toward the study of living plants, their life
cycles and diseases.[26] Bessey's textbook, *Botany
for High Schools and Colleges* (1880), had just
been published, and he was the botanical
editor of the *American Naturalist*, a popular
science monthly. Eloise Butler was among the
group of teachers who took Bessey's course
that summer.

The botany course, held during the
month of July, included a daily lecture
preceded and followed by work with
microscopes at the botanical laboratory.
Bessey brought twenty-five compound

Charles E. Bessey. *University of Nebraska-Lincoln,
Archives.*

microscopes with him from Iowa, to be
used in the course, since the University of
Minnesota had none at the time. It was said
to be the first time microscopes were used in
teaching botany there.[27] The course with
Charles Bessey, who was remembered by
Eloise Butler as "the greatest and most
enthusiastic teacher I have ever met," was
Eloise's first recorded exposure to the delicate
and beautiful structure of plants as magnified
by the lens of a microscope.[28]

Bessey often took his students into the
field to collect living plants for examination.
The group botanized along the banks of the
Mississippi River, above and below the falls of
St. Anthony all the way to Fort Snelling, and
visited many lakes in the vicinity of
Minneapolis.[29] The unspoiled wild places that
she saw in those excursions were recalled years
later by Eloise:

> In the early '80s Minneapolis was a place
> of enchantment—a veritable fairyland.
> Along the river banks grew in profusion
> trillium, bloodroot, wild phlox, anemones,
> Dutchman's breeches, and hepatica; the
> meadows were glorious with Indian paint
> brush, both red and yellow, with gentians,
> purple fringed orchids, and royal clumps
> of blue violets. In the tamarack swamps
> of the suburbs might be seen long vistas of
> our state flower, the showy lady's-slipper,

together with the wild calla, and pitcher plants without number. And who could describe the outlying prairies, rioting in colors far exceeding the brilliancy of tropical flora. A long procession beginning with the pasque flower, "the crocus in chinchilla fur," the rosy three-flowered avens, and the equally profuse bird's-foot violet, that gave way in turn to the more gorgeous blooms of midsummer and early autumn, as the purple blazing stars, giant sunflowers, goldenrods and asters of many species and hues. Various lily-rimmed pools and lakes were teeming with algae, among them microscopic desmids and diatoms of extraordinary beauty, many of which were new to the world.[30]

Pitcher Plant

After the course ended, Eloise went east to visit Cora in Malden, Massachusetts. The sisters had met only twice, briefly, in the previous seven years. Eloise found Cora deeply depressed, listless and apathetic. By then the mother of two small children, Bronson, age five, and Ethelwyn, two, Cora had also taken on the care of Margaretta Butler in her last illness (she died in 1883), and was exhausted.[31] Into this difficult situation came Eloise, fresh from her study with Charles Bessey and bursting with enthusiasm for botanizing.

Cora was prevailed upon to accompany Eloise on explorations of the woods and bogs of the Middlesex Fells surrounding the Pease home, which was built into the side of a steep hill in a still largely-undeveloped suburb of

Boston. These outings provided Cora the much-needed respite which healed her depression and renewed the girlhood bond between the two sisters. Five years later, in an article entitled "The Treasures of the Fells," published in the popular outdoor magazine *Outing*, Cora related the story of her "rambles" with Eloise that summer:

> . . . though we were debarred from making frequent excursions into the woods, our few walks were made most fruitful. Such was our greed for new varieties that we always extended our rambles until, from fatigue, we felt as though we could never reach home. We never returned without something new, and, while I restricted my search to flowering plants, [Eloise] gathered ferns, mosses, lichens, fungi, and dived into every slimy ditch and pool for fresh-water algae. . . . She frequently lamented that this ground had been all gone over by scientists, and nothing was left for her to discover. But one memorable day her diligent search in the slimy water was rewarded, for she found an alga in fruit, so rare as to be almost unknown, and, by sending it to an eminent botanist of Pennsylvania, caused a thrill of joy in his heart, for he had been hunting for it, in vain, for nine long years.
>
> The elves and wood nymphs must have often wondered what sort of creatures had invaded their precincts, for, sometimes, when working our way through closely-grown thickets, we would get separated; then would be heard the cry, something like this: "Oh! oh! oh! Come quick! Do come quick! Here is the biggest find!" Then the reply, "Don't touch it! I am coming. Where? Where?" We always preferred seeing the new plant growing, if possible, and half the pleasure of the discovery was lost if we first saw it after it was broken off. No ledge was so steep and jagged as to be insurmountable, if there was a suspicion of vegetation in the crevices at the top; no bog so miry, and no brook so deep and wide, as to be impassable, if there was a prospect of discoveries on the opposite bank.[32]

The sisters searched for a tract of the Fells in which "trees of the primeval forest" were said to be found; instead, they discovered a hidden, sheltered spot, shaded by sprays of wild clematis draped over the trees and shrubs and protected by blackberry vines, which they named the "Virgin's Bower." A bit further along the same path through the woods lay "a most eerie place," a circular basin enclosed by a thick wild hedge, surrounded by rocky cliffs and carpeted with sphagnum moss, which they called the "Devil's Punch-Bowl" or the "Witches Chaldron."[33]

In the summer of 1882, Eloise attended the second Summer School of Science at the University of Minnesota. The botany course was taught by Joseph Charles Arthur (himself a former student of Bessey), an instructor at the University of Wisconsin who had done postgraduate work at Harvard under Asa Gray and William Gibson Farlow.[34] Arthur was then at work (with Charles Barnes and John Coulter) on his *Handbook of Plant Dissection* (1886) which subsequently became a highly regarded book on laboratory practice.[35] Although the lectures covered material with which Eloise was already familiar, the collecting excursions and hours spent in laboratory work with the hand lens and microscope were invaluable to her.[36]

Eloise incorporated what she had learned from Bessey and Arthur into her own teaching. Besides building an herbarium at Central High by the usual method of exchanging dried and mounted plant specimens with other botanists, she took her students out-of-doors into the countryside to show them living plants in their native environments, and to let them experience the joy of discovery for themselves.[37] She often took her students botanizing in and around the tamarack bogs in Glenwood Park, where as one of her students recalled, "she was in her native element." Her teaching methods apparently met with less than unanimous appeal; the South High Annual of 1906 wryly advised students not to take botany "unless you enjoy ten-mile walks through bog and swamp" looking for "unobtainable" flowers.[38]

Eloise and three other high school botany teachers wrote an essay in the early 1900s which stated the reasons why they regarded the study of botany as important:

> Botany trains the eye to see, the hand to deftness of action, and the mind to an appreciation of the wonderful and beautiful in nature.

Besides the enjoyment of nature, the teachers emphasized the practical usefulness of botany:

> ... it is to the students of plant life that the world looks for the solution of two great problems of the future—the

reforestation of the cut-over timber lands and the feeding of the people. . . .

Even sex-education was hinted at:

> For, through botany, the fundamental facts of physiology are presented, as nutrition and reproduction, which plants and animals have in common, and the natural curiosity of youth in regard to embryology is satisfied and the harmful misconceptions of half-knowledge, surreptitiously acquired, are swept away.

The spiritual benefit of nature study was not ignored, though clothed in humanistic language; botany would convey

> . . . a sympathetic interest in nature that will prove as the years go on an inexhaustible source of unselfish pleasure, solace, and mental health, in the midst of the hurry and nervous strain of modern life.[39]

In a letter to friends, Eloise recalled efforts by herself and other botany teachers on behalf of their subject:

> . . . [I]n the latter part of the last century, our beloved science was at a low ebb. There were but four high schools, each with but one teacher of botany. We called ourselves ironically, "The Big Four." Our superintendents and principals were blissfully ignorant of the subject and indifferent. Botany was considered by them a "sissy" pseudo-science, perhaps suitable for a young ladies' boarding school, and of no practical importance. . . . We hadn't a compound microscope, or even a reference book except those we furnished ourselves. . . . Through persistence we gradually gained good laboratory equipment and reference libraries. . . . We initiated a correspondence with the departments of botany in all our leading cities, sending out a questionnaire to ascertain methods and equipment.[40]

Eloise prided herself on being in the "van of the march of improvement" in the teaching of botany. Despite her strict Baptist upbringing, she embraced the theory of evolution as expressed in Darwin's *Origin of Species* (1859), about which the debate had raged all through her youth; Eloise regarded the concept of evolution as "the greatest contribution to thought in the nineteenth century."[41] The expenditure of one hundred and seventy dollars by the Minneapolis Board of Education in 1886 for the purchase of ten microscopes was likely at her urging; Asa Gray's *Manual of the Botany of the Northern United States*, used in her courses, was, at just over two dollars, the most expensive textbook purchased by the Minneapolis public schools in 1888.[42]

Eloise and the other botany teachers also campaigned for the provision of greenhouses in the schools, so that students had access to living plant material for study during the long Minnesota winters. When a new Central High School was built in 1913, the botany classrooms opened onto a pair of large greenhouses, which Eloise believed to be the first in the country.[43]

Eloise supported the idea of school gardens, where city children could learn about the life cycle of plants from seed to fruit. In the hot and drought-stricken summer of 1910, Eloise had charge of a garden at the Rosedale elementary school, where she was "blistered by the sun and thickly coated every day with grime." Despite the heat, the students raised a fine crop of vegetables; a bed of buckwheat, in flower, was a particular "delight." Eloise was pleased when her young gardeners declared that their own produce "tasted much nicer than any that could be bought of the grocer."[44]

During most of her teaching career, Eloise and her female colleagues bore the indignity of receiving less pay than men who taught the same subjects and often had less experience than the women. Until 1907, salaries in the Minneapolis schools were specified by the sex of the teacher. Notices of vacancies usually indicated whether a male or female replacement was sought.[45] Principalships of the larger schools were reserved for men, and the women teachers were paid up to twenty-five percent less than the men.[46] In 1907 the women teachers in the high schools of Minneapolis, incensed at the inequality in wages and spurred to action by a move on the part of the male principals to gain higher pay for themselves, petitioned the School Board for equal pay. After studying the matter for a year, the board finally adopted a merit system, with substantial raises for the women.[47]

Eloise always felt a mixture of emotions about her profession. On a list entitled "My Hates," made in March 1931, she included strident voices, the scraping of chairs, and the sound of paper tearing, all unmistakably the sounds of a schoolroom.[48] Upon retiring from schoolteaching, Eloise wrote, she "found it blissful . . . to be freed from routine" and declared, despite the obvious pride she took in her accomplishments and the adulation of many former students, that "in my next incarnation I shall not be a teacher."[49]

Eloise Butler's heart was clearly in her own botanical collecting, which she had steadfastly pursued at every opportunity during breaks from teaching. The "eminent scientist in Pennsylvania" to whom she had sent her "alga in fruit" was Francis Wolle, and the story of her association with Wolle and other botanists reveals her dedication and skill as a botanical collector while illuminating the position of women working in science in the late nineteenth century.[50]

Notes

1 Minneapolis Board of Education census reported in Minneapolis *Tribune* 11 October 1874 (WPA Annals of Minnesota files, Minnesota Historical Society).

2 Lucile M. Kane, *The Falls of St. Anthony—The Waterfall That Built Minneapolis* (St. Paul: Minnesota Historical Society Press, 1987), p. 58; Shutter, Marion D., *History of Minneapolis; Gateway to the Northwest* (Chicago: S.J. Clarke Pub. Co., 1923), p. 346. The Washburn "A" Mill blew up in a spectacular explosion on 2 May 1878 that destroyed one-third of the milling capacity of the city and killed seventeen workers.

3 This paragraph based on Minneapolis *Tribune*, 29 August 1874, 6 September 1874, 9 September 1874, and Charles M. Loring, "History of the Parks and Public Grounds of Minneapolis," *Minnesota Historical Society Collections*, Vol. 15 (1915), pp. 599-608 (601). See also "Plan of the City of Minneapolis and Vicinity," *Illustrated Historical Atlas of State of Minnesota* (Chicago: A.T. Andreas, 1874) (reprinted ed. Evansville, Indiana: Unigraphic Inc., 1975), p. 41.

4 Paragraph based on clippings from Minneapolis *Tribune* dated 28 August 1874, 14 November 1874, 24 December 1874 and 4 May 1875 in WPA Annals of Minnesota files, Minnesota Historical Society; and Minneapolis *Tribune*, 1 September 1874 and 6 September 1874. Quote from Minneapolis *Tribune*, 9 April 1875 (copy

in WPA Annals of Minnesota files, Minnesota Historical Society).

5   Paragraph based on clippings from Minneapolis *Tribune* dated 1 January 1875, 23 March 1875, 25 March 1875, and 8 April 1875 in WPA Annals of Minnesota files, Minnesota Historical Society.

6   *Minneapolis City Directory* 1873-1874 (Minneapolis: Tribune Printing Co.), pp. 20-23 (21).

7   Eloise Butler's name first appears in the Minneapolis Board of Education (East Division) *Minutes* on 19 June, 1875, with regard to teachers at Center School: "Miss Eloise S. Butler was re-elected teacher in [room] No. 8." The only recorded teacher's examination taken by Butler occurred two years after she began teaching. On 26 June 1876, she was among ten (of twenty-eight candidates) who passed both the oral and written examinations; Minneapolis Board of Education (East Division), *Minutes*, 27 June 1876. The Minneapolis public schools remained separated into two districts—East and West—until 1878.

8   The school, renamed Winthrop in 1878, was demolished in 1899 to make way for East High School. This paragraph and next based on unidentified newspaper clipping entitled "Historic Associations Cling to the Winthrop School," (20 August 1899), Hennepin County [Minnesota] Historical Society; Minneapolis Board of Education *Annual Report*, 30 June 1878; and Minneapolis Board of Education (East Division), *Minutes*, 22 and 28 April 1874, and 18 June 1875.

9   Records of courses taught by Eloise Butler are incomplete. Her obituaries stated that the first subjects she taught were Latin and Greek; see "Noted Botanist Succumbs at 81," Minneapolis *Tribune*, 11 April 1933, and "Eloise Butler Dies at 81 in Woodland She Loved," Minneapolis *Journal*, 11 April 1933.

10 Minneapolis Board of Education (East Division) *Minutes*, 20 June 1876, 1 August 1877 and 5 September 1877.

11 Central High School remained in its first building until 1913, when the school moved to new quarters at Thirty-fourth Street and Fourth Avenue South. Central High was closed in 1982.

12 Simpson Butler to Cora E. Pease, 26 July 1919, (copy in Eloise Butler Papers, Minnesota Historical Society); conversation with Lucia Fryer McKenzie, July 1988.

13 The crowded conditions at South High School are mentioned in the yearbooks 1902-1911, when a new addition was finally completed.

14 Emma Paige's brothers were both attorneys. James married law student Mabeth Hurd in 1895; Mabeth Hurd Paige was elected to the Minnesota Legislature in 1922, and (with Hannah Kempfer) introduced legislation protecting the showy lady's-slipper and other wildflowers in 1925. Mabeth Hurd Paige's biography is Cora Chapline Aldrich's *Lady in Law: A Biography of Mabeth Hurd Paige* (Chicago: Seymour, c.1950, under pseud. *Darragh Aldrich*).

15 Esther Friedlander, "A Tribute to Eloise Butler, a Pioneer Teacher of Central High, Minneapolis," (c.1940), in *An Early History of the Eloise Butler Wildflower Garden*, typescript, pp. iv-v, archives of The Friends of the Wild Flower Garden, Inc.

16 Lillian E. Mathias, "A Letter from a Reminiscent Friend," (c.1940), in *Early History*, p. vi.

17 Gallinaceous—Latin, having to do with fowl.

18 Eloise Butler, "A Gallinaceous Ode," (c.1902), 2 p. manuscript in Eloise Butler Papers, Minnesota Historical Society.

19 This paragraph and the next based largely on Sarah Brackett's obituaries: Minneapolis *Tribune*, 23 September 1906, 7; Minneapolis *Journal*, 23 September 1906, 6; and Lewiston *Evening Journal*, 19 September 1906.

20 Louisa May Alcott, *Work, A Story of Experience* (New York: Schocken Books, 1977), p. 150. The novel, which portrays the importance of friendship among unmarried working women in the mid-nineteenth century, was first serialized in *The Christian Union* in 1872-73. The word "spinster" is used here in its positive sense (as used by theologian Mary Daly) to mean a woman whose life is not defined in relation to men or children.

21 See also "Well Known Teacher Dead," Minneapolis *Journal*, 23 September 1906. According to her obituaries, Sarah Brackett was born in 1849 in Livermore Falls, Maine. Her mother died when she was very young, and her father remarried. Sarah began teaching in Maine country schools at the age of thirteen. She had three younger half-sisters and a half-brother who remained in Maine. Sarah Brackett was said to be a member of the Unitarian Church in Minneapolis. Among the Eloise Butler Papers at the Minnesota Historical Society are a humorous poem composed by Eloise and Sarah (undated) that refers to Cora's husband, Curtis Pease, that refers to Eloise and Sarah as "your two B's," and is signed "Eloise Brackett;" and a letter from Sarah Brackett to Cora Pease dated 1 December 1889 describing the Tribune Building fire, which she and "Elo" had witnessed the previous night.

22 Nathan Butler read his paper entitled "Progress in the Study of the Mounds of the State" to a meeting of the Minnesota Academy of Science in 1877 or 1878; it was subsequently lost in a fire. *Bulletin of the Minnesota Academy of Sci-*

ence 4 (No. 3, 1910), p. 434.

23   The founders and nearly all of the early members of the Minnesota Academy of Science were men, although women were admitted as early as 1876, when Mrs. F.L. Tinsley, wife of George W. Tinsley, was elected by virtue of having "presented the Academy with thirteen mounted bird skins, which she had herself prepared . . . with artistic skill." Harlow Gale, "Historical Sketch of the Minnesota Academy of Science," ibid., p. 435. Butler's friends Clara Leavitt and Elizabeth Foss, botany teachers in Minneapolis high schools, were members in the early 1900s. There is no evidence that Butler ever joined.

24   University of Minnesota, *Calendar*, 1881-1882, p. 107.

25   Asa Gray (1810-1888) abandoned a fledgling medical practice in 1832 to become a botanist. He was appointed professor of natural history at Harvard in 1842 and by 1850 was the leading botanist in the United States, serving to classify and name much of the new flora of North America. Gray led the American defense of Darwin against Louis Agassiz's opposition. A. Hunter Dupree's *Asa Gray: 1810-1888* (Cambridge, Mass.: The Belknap Press of Harvard University Press, 1968) is the standard biography of Gray.

26   Raymond J. Pool, "A Brief Sketch of the Life and Work of Charles Edwin Bessey," *American Journal of Botany*, Vol. 2 (December 1915), p. 505; and A. D. Rodgers, *American Botany 1873-1892—Decades of Transition* (Princeton: Princeton University Press, 1944), p. 200.

27   Pool, "Charles Edwin Bessey," p. 511.

28   Eloise Butler to Gray Memorial Botanical Chapter, Agassiz Association, Division D, (1911), copy in *Early History of Eloise Butler Plant Reserve, Theodore Wirth Park*, at Minneapolis Public Library, Minneapolis Collection.

29   Charles E. Bessey, ed., "Botany in Minnesota," *American Naturalist* (September 1881), p. 732.

30   Eloise Butler, "Annals of a Wild Garden," unpublished typescript, (c.1926), in archives of the Minneapolis Board of Park Commissioners; a later version is in *Early History of Eloise Butler Plant Reserve*, p. 3-4, at Minneapolis Public Library, Minneapolis Collection.

31   As Cora wrote in 1885: "It has been stated that our insane asylums contain a large proportion of housekeepers . . . and what else can be expected when we consider the number of women who have nothing to divert their minds from household drudgery that never is done though they labor diligently early and late?" She recommended the study of botany as an antidote to the "seasons of depression [that] may come to all housekeepers." Cora Butler Pease, "Recreation for Housekeepers," unidentified newspaper clipping [c.1885], in scrapbook of the Old and New Club, Malden, Massachusetts.

32   Cora Butler Pease, "The Treasures of the Fells," *Outing*, Vol. 7 (October/November 1885), pp. 175-181 (178). By 1885, wrote Cora, she had analyzed "more than three hundred varieties of flowers of the Fells and vicinity." (Ibid., p. 177).

33   Ibid., p. 181.

34   William Gibson Farlow (1844-1919), noted specialist in cryptogamic botany, studied at Harvard, where Asa Gray advised him to "study medicine first because the possibility of gaining a living by Botany was so small that one should always have a regular profession to fall back on." L.W. Riddle, "William Gibson Farlow," *Rhodora*, Vol. 22 (January 1920), pp. 1-8. Many early male botanists were medical doctors or clergymen.

35   Joseph Charles Arthur (1850-1942) was appointed botanist of the Minnesota Geological and Natural History Survey in 1885. He received a Ph.D. from Cornell University in 1886, said to be "the first doctorate in America conferred for conclusive research on the pathological aspects of a plant disease," and spent his career as a professor of botany at Purdue University. Rodgers, *American Botany*, p. 130.

36   The botany course is described in C.E. Bessey, "Botany in Minneapolis," *American Naturalist*, Vol. 17 (January 1883), p. 79.

37   The remnants of Eloise Butler's teaching herbarium, stamped "Central High School" and consisting of 179 mounted specimens collected by others (perhaps acquired by exchange), were donated by the Minneapolis Park and Recreation Board to the herbarium of the Department of Plant Biology at the University of Minnesota in 1988.

38   Quotes from Esther Friedlander, "A Tribute to Eloise Butler" (see note 15) and South High School *Annual* (1906), p. 61.

39   Eloise Butler and four anonymous others, "The Importance of Botany as a Subject of Study in the Secondary Schools," (c.1905), quoted in Eloise Butler to Gray Memorial Botanical Chapter, Agassiz Association, Division D, June 1931, copy in Eloise Butler biography file at Minneapolis Public Library, Minneapolis Collection.

40   Eloise Butler to Gray Memorial Botanical Chapter, Agassiz Association, Division D, June 1931 (under title "Pioneer Teaching of Botany"), Eloise Butler biography file, Minneapolis Public Library, Minneapolis Collection.

41   Quotes from Eloise Butler, ibid., and "The Importance of Botany," (see note 39).

42   Minneapolis Board of Education, *Minutes*, 26 February 1886; Minneapolis Board of Education, *Manual of the Public Schools* (1888-1891). Reference to Butler's use of microscopes in

teaching is made in Cora E. Pease, "About Mushrooms," *Transcript Monthly* (Boston, c. 1890), clipping in scrapbook owned by Martha P. Pease. Laura Linton, head of the science department at Central High School, would also have used microscopes in her zoology course. See note 46.

43 Eloise Butler, "Pioneer Teaching of Botany," see note 40. Besides those at Central, there were greenhouses at North, South, West, Edison and Roosevelt High Schools and at Jordan Junior High. The greenhouses were expensive to maintain and were abandoned prior to World War II. Their function is at least partly served today by the Learning Center at the University of Minnesota Landscape Arboretum.

44 Eloise Butler to Gray Memorial Botanical Chapter, Agassiz Association, Division D, November 1910, in Eloise Butler biography file, Minneapolis Public Library, Minneapolis Collection. The Rosedale School stood on the northwest corner of Wentworth Avenue and 43rd Street in Minneapolis. School gardens and the planting of trees by schoolchildren were promoted by Professor Maria Sanford of the University of Minnesota, and her Minneapolis Improvement League, in the 1890s.

45 See, for example, Minneapolis Board of Education (East Division), *Minutes*, 3 March 1878, "Secretary instructed to procure . . . a male teacher for the 4th ward," and 29 May 1878, "Here a gentleman to be hired at salary not exceeding $1,000." The standard teacher's contract contained a clause which deemed marriage by a teacher during employment grounds for dismissal; see Minneapolis Board of Education, *Minutes*, 26 April 1898.

46 See Minneapolis Board of Education (East Division) *Minutes*, 17 July 1875; Minneapolis Board of Education *Minutes*, 29 May 1878, and 29 May 1894. The case of Laura Linton, for whom the mineral Lintonite was named in 1879, presents an interesting exception. Laura Linton was hired in 1884 and was for ten years head of the science department at Central High School. Two years younger than Eloise Butler and a graduate of the state normal school in Winona, she had also graduated from the University of Minnesota in 1879, had done postgraduate work at M.I.T., and was a member of the American Association for the Advancement of Science. Linton was well paid; by 1890 her salary had risen to $1,400 per year, five hundred dollars above that

of the other senior teachers. After the appointment of John Greer to the principalship of Central High School in 1892 (a man said to have a bent for natural history himself), Laura Linton's salary was cut to $1,200; her request for leave to attend the World Women's Congress in Chicago in 1893 was denied by the School Board. When Linton was offered a salary of only $1,000 per year for 1895-1896, she resigned. See Minneapolis Board of Education, *Minutes*, 2 June 1892; 29 May 1893; 29 May 1894; and 30 April 1895. Laura Linton later became a medical doctor and from 1900 until her death in 1915 cared for mentally ill women at the State Hospital in Rochester, Minnesota. Jean C. Dahlberg, "Laura Linton and Lintonite," *Minnesota History*, Vol. 38 (March 1962), pp. 21-23; and *A Woman of the Century: Biographical Sketches of Leading American Women*, ed. by Frances E. Willard and Mary A. Livermore (Buffalo: Charles Wells Moulton, 1893), p. 463 (copy in Linton file at Olmsted County Historical Society). What sort of relationship Eloise Butler and Laura Linton had is not known. The potential existed for either great friendship or great rivalry.

47 Minneapolis Board of Education, *Minutes*, 13 March 1907, 22 April 1907, and 25 May 1908.

48 Eloise Butler to Gray Memorial Botanical Chapter, Agassiz Association, Division D (entitled "My Loves and Likings [and Hates]"), March 1931, in Eloise Butler biography file at Minneapolis Public Library, Minneapolis Collection. Other things Butler disliked were "nagging, boasting, idle curiosity, . . . discordant colors, . . . [and] the dress of the modern flapper." Ibid.

49 Eloise Butler to Gray Memorial Botanical Chapter, Agassiz Association, Division D, June 1931; Eloise Butler to Gray Memorial Botanical Chapter, Agassiz Association, Division D, (1911), copy in *Early History of Eloise Butler Plant Reserve*, Minneapolis Public Library, Minneapolis Collection. Butler "met with an [unspecified] accident in the performance of her duties" during the school year 1910-1911, which may have been a factor in her decision to retire (she was offered a contract for the following year, but declined it); Minneapolis Board of Education, *Minutes*, 25 April 1911 and 6 June 1911.

50 Quotes from Cora E. Pease, "The Treasures of the Fells," see note 32. The incident described by Cora in which Eloise discovered the "alga in fruit" actually took place in 1883, not 1881.

Eloise Butler at thirty-one with a vial of desmids, 1882. *Martha P. Pease.*

4
Cosmarium Eloiseanum

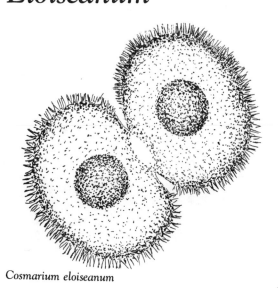

Cosmarium eloiseanum

IN THE MID-NINETEENTH CENTURY, anyone with a bent for natural history might, by self-study and careful fieldwork, make a contribution to the accretion of botanical knowledge. American botanists were primarily concerned with the classification and naming of the flora of North America, and new species could still be discovered by a devoted searcher. The ranks of naturalists included clergymen, physicians, and numerous women of the middle class who, barred from most professions, gained in the study of botany an outlet for their intellectual energies as well as the physical benefits of outdoor exercise.

All aspects of natural history received heightened public attention during the Victorian era, especially after the publication of Charles Darwin's *Origin of Species* in 1859. Every proper drawing room featured an aquarium, fern-case, or a display of rocks, shells or mounted butterflies; lavishly illustrated botanical journals advertised themselves to potential subscribers as unsurpassed "parlor ornaments."[1] Exhibits of exotic flowers or beasts captured in far-off lands drew large crowds on both sides of the Atlantic.[2] The lecture circuit was a source of income for scientists at a time when academic positions were few; in the spring of 1875, the Academy of Music in Minneapolis presented one "professor J. H. Pepper, F.C.S., the eminent Scientist from London," whose series of lectures entitled "Science Popularized" on "Electricity, Light, Sound, Magnetism, &c" was augmented by "thirty-five boxes of apparatus, in all weighing three tons."[3]

The field of botany underwent dramatic changes during the final quarter of the nineteenth century, changes that were mirrored in all of the sciences. With the advent of the land-grant universities after the Civil War, American scholarship in the sciences gradually became concentrated at academic centers. At the same time, as historians of science Margaret Rossiter and Sally Gregory Kohlstedt have shown, botany became increasingly dominated by male professionals who formed fraternal societies which refused to admit (or delegated to second-class status) "amateurs," a term which acquired negative implications as the century progressed and was usually applied to women, regardless of their abilities. The segregation of botanists into the castes of the professional and the amateur was essentially complete by the turn of the century.[1] Of 1,185 women identified by one author as active in botany in the United States prior to the year 1900, only two percent were connected with a college or university, and only fifteen percent managed to have any career at all.[5]

The seriousness with which Eloise Butler approached the study of science, her career as a teacher of botany, and the degree of knowledge that she eventually attained set her apart from those who pursued the natural history fads of her time. Yet her lack of advanced training, her lack of publications (with the exception of two brief notes on desmids) and her sex relegated her irrevocably to the status of "amateur" in the eyes of the profession. Stratification existed even within the category of amateurs, with women largely assuming the role of collectors, while the tasks of analyzing and naming new species, writing up descriptions of the plants for publication in botanical journals, and presenting papers at scientific gatherings were almost exclusively done by males—not surprising, considering that public speaking and even authorship were considered unseemly for women in the

nineteenth century.[6] Although the botanists to whom she sent her specimens were themselves amateurs—Francis Wolle was a clergyman, Frank Shipley Collins a bookkeeper—as males they had access to professional circles and the consequent discourse and recognition that Butler and most other women botanists did not. Despite the obstacles facing all women who sought achievement in the field of botany, Eloise Butler pursued her studies and collecting with a focused determination worthy of note.

It was at the Summer School of Science at the University of Minnesota in 1881, under the tutelage of Charles Bessey with his microscopes carried from Iowa, that Butler was first introduced to the excitement of the search for desmids, tiny freshwater algae that have long fascinated microscopists. Desmids, unicellular plants so named because of their appearance as a pair of symmetrical shapes joined together (the Greek word 'desmos' means bond or chain), are considered to be among the most beautiful of microscopic organisms. As Conway MacMillan, first chairman of the botany department at the

Reverend Francis Wolle, c. 1880s. *Moravian Historical Society.*

University of Minnesota, wrote in 1899, desmids

> are often particularly well-developed in the water of peat-bogs, so that if one goes to the nearest tamarack swamp and brings away a tumbler full of water which he has squeezed out from among the peat-mosses, and sets the tumbler in the window, within a few hours a green film of desmids will be likely to form upon the side of the glass turned toward the light.[7]

With their many-varied shapes resembling pairs of fans, rods, spheres, snow crystals, starfish, and even communications satellites, desmids have attracted the attention of students of morphology (the shapes of cells) but are otherwise little-understood.[8]

In May 1882, Butler wrote a letter to Charles Bessey in which she described a peculiar rotating movement within the desmid *Cosmarium botrytis*:

> Dear Sir:
>
> I have been much interested lately in observing a species of desmid, *Cosmarium botrytis*. When in bright sunlight it has a slow rotary movement, turning successively from right to left and from left to right, with now and then (if my eyes did not deceive me) what might be called a spasmodic jerk. The play of the protoplasm within the plant-body is exceedingly rapid, resembling as some writers say, "the swarming of bees." There seem to [be] three centers of movement among the granules in each half of the desmid; but of this I am not positive. I have never seen the plant revolve except when in the full glare of the sun, even when it gave evidence of being alive by the movement of its protoplasm.
>
> I call your attention to this, because in the few books of reference accessible to me, I find no mention of a *revolving* desmid.
>
> I will send you some specimens of the same, if you wish for them, and can suggest a safe method of transportation.
>
> Yours very truly, Eloise Butler.[9]

Correspondence between botanists was, in the nineteenth century, an important means for the carrying on of scientific discourse. As Beatrice Scheer Smith writes of letters that passed between Lucy Bishop Millington and Charles Peck, State Botanist of New York, in the 1890s:

> By writing letters, information was shared; questions raised between correspondents generated new avenues of inquiry. By exchanging specimens, herbaria were enlarged; ranges and distributions of species, and innumerable other problems, could be studied. . . . The zeal of the participants fueled the process, and the data accumulated.[10]

Charles Bessey, then the botanical editor of the *American Naturalist*, a respected journal of natural history, promptly printed Butler's letter under "General Notes" in the July issue of the journal.[11] Bessey undoubtedly also advised Butler to correspond with Francis Wolle, who was then at work on his reference work *Desmids of the United States* (1884).[12]

Francis Wolle, a Moravian minister in Bethlehem, Pennsylvania, had been publishing articles on freshwater algae in botanical journals since 1876.[13] After his retirement as principal of the Moravian Seminary for Young Ladies in 1881, when he was sixty-four, Wolle devoted himself to the study of freshwater algae and particularly desmids. Francis Wolle is likely to have shared the liberal views of the Moravians towards scientific education for women, and would have been most receptive to an inquiry from a young woman interested in desmids.[14] Butler wrote to Wolle in July 1882. His response was presumably encouraging, for Butler immediately embarked upon the study and collection of desmids which absorbed her energies for much of the decade.[15]

In 1883 and subsequent years, Wolle repeatedly acknowledged Eloise Butler's collecting skill in the papers he published in botanical journals, in correspondence with other botanists, and in his books. Her name first appeared in the seventh of his series of ten articles on fresh-water algae published in the *Bulletin of the Torrey Botanical Club* in February 1883:

> In the appended list of new plants, all those credited to Minneapolis, Minn., were collected and forwarded by Miss Eloise Butler of that place. Miss Butler, first a student under Prof. C.E. Bessey of botanical fame, then a member of the Summer School of Science under Prof. J.C. Arthur of the Iowa Agricultural College, Charles City, has, in her contributions sent me for microscopical investigation, furnished much more that is new than has any other collector this year.[16]

Among the seventeen different species Butler sent Wolle from Minnesota in 1882 were three desmids which Wolle deemed new species, as well as five new varieties (different forms warranting taxonomic distinction) of known species. Wolle bestowed her name upon two of the new desmids, *Cosmarium eloiseanum* and *Staurastrum eloiseanum*.[17]

During the summer of 1883, Eloise traveled again to Malden, where her mother was seriously ill at Cora's home; Margaretta Butler died on August 24. Butler's botanical collecting continued, although somewhat abated. Wolle's annual review of new desmids published the following February mentions five different desmids sent him from Minnesota, three of which Wolle found to be new (one new species and two new varieties). He also noted having received a specimen of alga in fruit which had been collected by Butler in Malden.[18]

Butler not only collected the desmids, but also studied them during long hours at a microscope, probably fitted with an eyepiece micrometer with which the size of the specimen could be measured. She would have kept notebooks of sketches comparing them to known species as described in the scientific literature, and identifying those desmids that were new and different. Those she preserved in vials with a few drops of carbolic acid, or on glass slides, and sent to Francis Wolle for his analysis. Wolle, in turn, sent vials of Minnesota desmids collected by Butler to other botanists in the United States and abroad,

including John Roy of Aberdeen, Scotland, and Otto Nordstedt and V.B. Wittrock of Sweden.[19]

In the summer of 1884, Wolle received from Butler specimens of twenty different desmids, of which seven were deemed new species. Of *Staurastrum xiphidiophorum*, Wolle wrote: "When sending me this beautiful and remarkable little *Staurastrum*, Miss Butler called my attention to 'the little gothic structure,' a very appropriate comparison."[20]

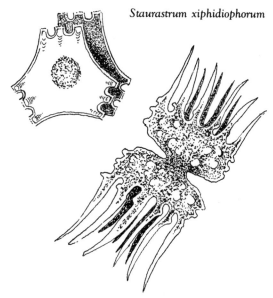

Staurastrum xiphidiophorum

The species names "*minneapoliense*" and "*minnesotense*" were bestowed upon two new *Staurastrum*. And Butler, breaking with tradition and in honor of her mentor, even ventured to name one new species herself: *Staurastrum wolleanum*, of which Wolle wrote, "This species was discovered and identified as new by Miss. E. Butler, who declines to have the name changed."[21]

In October, Wolle wrote to Charles Bessey: "Have made some valuable accessions this summer to the list of desmids—about twenty-five—of which Miss Butler collected some of the finest."[22] Wolle sent specimens of the new Minnesota desmids to John Roy in Scotland, who wrote back to Wolle in 1885: "Thank you for . . . [the] wee bottle safely received some time ago. . . . That is a very fine *Staurastrum* Miss Butler has joined your name to."[23]

The year 1884 also marked the publication of the first edition of Wolle's

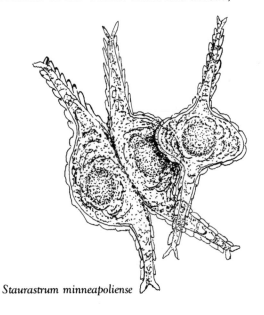

Staurastrum minneapoliense

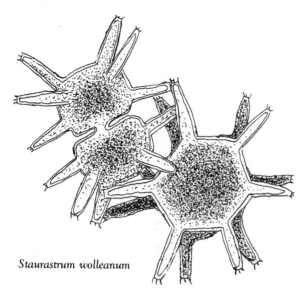

Staurastrum wolleanum

Desmids of the United States. The book represented an enormous amount of labor on Wolle's part, including over a thousand drawings of desmids sketched by him from living plants viewed under a microscope. The fifty-three plates were laboriously hand-colored by a host of Wolle's female relatives working from a colored key prepared by Reverend Wolle. "To overlook their color," he wrote of algae, in the Introduction, "would be to neglect a very striking characteristic. The predominant of the entire class . . . is green; then pink grading off into all the shades of purple, and finally olive, from golden green and bright tawny to black; indeed, there are few if any colors from the most gorgeous to the dullest, but are to be found among the Algae."[24] In his book Wolle acknowledged the contributions of Eloise Butler, who had sent in nearly a third of the 497 desmids described, calling her "a most successful collector of Desmids."[25]

It is not known whether Eloise Butler and Francis Wolle ever met in person. Butler may have stopped to visit Wolle in Bethlehem, Pennsylvania, on her way to or from Malden in 1883. By February of 1884, Wolle knew Butler well enough to refer to her in his annual *Torrey Botanical Club* article as "my friend, Miss Butler."[26]

Butler continued sending specimens of desmids to Wolle through the year 1885, as evidenced by his tenth, and last, article on fresh-water algae in the December issue of *Bulletin of the Torrey Botanical Club*, which

included descriptions of one new variety and one species found for the first time in the United States, collected by Butler.[27] In June 1886 a short article by Eloise Butler, entitled "Desmids," appeared in *Botanical Gazette*:

> Desmids are select and elusive, the result of long tramps, the reward of perseverance, long-suffering, and other kindred virtues. A collector of desmids needs to be provided with a large stock of patience, considerable endurance, and some courage, a pair of rubber boots, and vials *ad libitum.*[28]

Butler told of a "summer's search in Dakota" which had proved "fruitless on account of the alkaline water."[29] And even in writing for a scientific journal, Butler could not supress the joy and excitement found via her microscope:

> When I find sphagnum under water I am jubilant, for it has never failed with me to produce desmids in abundance. They can be stripped from the leaves by the hand, or, better still, the moss can be gathered, being careful to dislodge as little mud as possible, and washed thoroughly in water. When the sediment has settled pour off the superfluous water. Your microscope may show the remainder to be a rich harvest of such inexpressibly rare and beautiful forms as to make one forget all fatigue and vexation.[30]

Before his last illness, Wolle managed to bring out a second edition of *Desmids of the United States* in 1892, which described many additional desmids from Minnesota sent to him by Eloise Butler in the intervening years. Ultimately, Francis Wolle credited Eloise Butler with the discovery of twelve new desmid species and thirteen new varieties of previously known species, as well as numerous species known from Europe not previously found in the United States.[31] His tendency to summarize the range of many desmids as "widely distributed" in his second edition of *Desmids*, rather than by place and name of collector as he had in the first, may be attributed, in part, to the poor health and exhaustion from overwork of his later years— between the two editions of *Desmids*, Wolle had published a two-volume *Freshwater Algae of the United States* (1887), with 117 colored plates and 2,300 figures, followed by his *Diatomaceae of the United States* (1891) with 20 plates and 2,300 figures. Wolle's preface to *Freshwater Algae* acknowledges the contributions of "Miss E. Butler, of Minneapolis, Minnesota" who "made some good finds."[32] It may be assumed that many of the freshwater algae species (in addition to the desmids) noted from Minnesota were collected by Butler, although, as in his second edition of *Desmids*, Wolle gave few details.

In addition to her desmid studies of the 1880s, Eloise Butler actively pursued her interest in the higher plants of Minnesota. She shared her findings with Warren Upham, surveyor and geologist with the Geological and Natural History Survey of Minnesota. Upham's *Catalogue of the Flora of Minnesota* (1884), which listed "all the species that are known to have been found in Minnesota by all observers up to the present time," mentions thirty species of plants collected at Lake Calhoun, Minnehaha Falls, Lake Minnetonka, Stillwater, West Saint Paul, and Redwood Falls by Eloise Butler.[33] In August of 1884, Upham wrote to Butler:

Dear Miss Butler:

Will you be so kind as to send memoranda of plants noted this summer by you. There will probably be some

among them that I would like then to be favored with specimens of for study. It is only after comparing such notes as you would send, or as I would copy from your herbarium, with my *manuscript* that I can be sure in many cases that they are rare or otherwise deserve special examination. . . .

Very Respectfully, Warren Upham.[34]

In compiling his book, Upham used manuscript lists from Eloise Butler as well as numerous other local collectors in making references to the geographic range of species or the localities of rare plants. His preface includes a paragraph which describes Eloise Butler as "another successful student of fresh-water algae, especially of the Desmids."[35]

Butler's desmid collecting slowed after the publication of Wolle's first edition of *Desmids* and came to an end some time before his death in 1893 at the age of seventy-six. By then her interest in the algae had grown beyond the desmids to include other fresh-water species, as well as those of the oceans. Her appetite for botanical collecting had been whetted by her success with the desmids, and by the end of the decade, she was ready to move on to another, greater challenge.

Notes

1 Quote from back cover of the *American Flora*, Vol. 1 (January 1850). The periodical was aimed at "physicians, students, [and] young ladies . . . interested in the science of botany."

2 See Lynn Barber, *The Heyday of Natural History* (Garden City, New York: Doubleday, 1980) for an account of the public passion for natural history in Great Britain during the Victorian era.

3 Minneapolis *Tribune*, 25 March and 28 March 1875, in WPA Annals of Minnesota files, Minnesota Historical Society.

4 Sally Gregory Kohlstedt, "The Nineteenth-Century Tradition: The Case of the Boston Society of Natural History," in *Science and Its Public: The Changing Relationship*, ed. Gerald Holton and William A. Blanpied (Dordrecht, Holland: D. Reidel, 1976), pp. 173-190 (175, 183-186); Margaret Rossiter, *Women Scientists in America*, pp. xvii, 77-78. The thirty-one founders of the Torrey Botanical Club (in 1870) were all male; women were admitted in 1879 beginning with Elizabeth Knight (later Britton). By 1890, female membership had risen to forty percent; the males regrouped and founded the Botanical Society of America in 1893 and mem-

bership was restricted to "professionals" (twenty-five men and one woman—Elizabeth Britton). Rossiter, ibid., pp. 84-85. Women were excluded from the New England Botanical Club, which published *Rhodora*, a respected journal. When an article appeared in *Rhodora* in 1899 claiming that the club was the first of its kind in New England, the botanist Maria Owen indignantly wrote the editor that she and Lydia Shattuck, botany teacher at Mount Holyoke Seminary, had founded a club open to women and men in 1873 called the Connecticut Valley Botanical Society and that the only respect in which the New England Botanical Club was unique was that it was "for gentlemen only." Maria Owen, "The Connecticut Valley Botanical Society," *Rhodora*, Vol. 1 (June 1899), pp. 95-96. See also Beatrice Scheer Smith, "Maria L. Owen, Nineteenth Century Nantucket Botanist," *Rhodora*, Vol. 89 (April 1987), pp. 227-237.

5 Of the fifteen percent who had a career, almost half were elementary or high school teachers; others were authors, illustrators, laboratory assistants, curators, librarians, physicians, and horticulturalists. Emanuel D. Rudolph, "Wom-

en in Nineteenth Century American Botany: A Generally Unrecognized Constituency," *American Journal of Botany*, Vol. 69 (1982), pp. 1346-1355 (1350). A recent paper by Rudolph raised the number of known nineteenth-century women botanists to 1,454; see "Women Who Studied Plants in the Pre-Twentieth Century United States and Canada," *Taxon*, Vol. 39 (May 1990), pp. 151-205. Butler's student Josephine Tilden was one of the two percent who held academic positions in colleges and universities by the end of the nineteenth century. See Chapter 6.

6   Sally Gregory Kohlstedt, "The Nineteenth-Century Amateur Tradition: The Case of the Boston Society of Natural History," in G. Holton and W.A. Blanpied (eds.), *Science and Its Public* (Dordrecht-Holland: D. Reidel Publishing Co., 1976), pp. 173-190 (183-186).

7   Conway MacMillan, *Minnesota Plant Life* (St. Paul: Report of the Minnesota Geological and Natural History Survey, Botanical Series III, 1899), p. 34.

8   Present-day studies of desmids include research on their use as predictors of the level of nutrients in bodies of water as well as indicators of changes in water chemistry. See Alan J. Brook, *The Biology of Desmids*, (University of California Press, Berkeley, 1981).

9   Eloise Butler to Charles E. Bessey, 1 May 1882, in Charles E. Bessey Papers in University of Nebraska—Lincoln Archives. The same species is used in present-day studies of movement in desmids, according to botanist Elizabeth Flint of Christchurch, New Zealand; letter to author, 12 October 1989.

10   Beatrice Scheer Smith, "Lucy Bishop Millington, Nineteenth-Century Botanist: Her Life and Letters to Charles Horton Peck, State Botanist of New York," (unpublished 117-page typescript at Albert R. Mann Library at Cornell University, Ithica, New York, 1989), pp. 77-78.

11   Eloise Butler, "An Active Desmid," *American Naturalist*, Vol. 16 (July 1882), p. 584. The *American Naturalist*, founded in 1867, aimed "to occupy a happy medium between a technical magazine and one in which all science is sacrificed to popularity." (editorial comment in) *American Naturalist*, Vol. 21 (February 1887), p. 163.

12   Francis Wolle, *Desmids of the United States and List of American Pediastrums with Eleven Hundred Illustrations on Fifty-Three Colored Plates*, (Bethlehem, Pennsylvania: Moravian Public Office, 1884). Until the 1960s Wolle's reference book was considered the standard work on American desmids.

13   Wolle's first publication, "Fresh-Water Algae," appeared in the *Bulletin of the Torrey Botanical Club*, Vol. 6 (No. 23, 1876), p. 121.

14   The Moravians established the first Protestant girls' boarding school in America in Germantown, Pennsylvania, in 1742. The curriculum of the Young Ladies Seminary at Bethlehem included Latin, botany, geography, astronomy and mathematics; their science instruction and equipment was considered advanced for the times. See Mabel Haller's *Early Moravian Education in Pennsylvania* (Nazareth, Pennsylvania: The Moravian Historical Society, 1953), p. 230 (note 94), and 248.

15   The present whereabouts of Wolle's extensive scientific correspondence is unknown. At least one letter from Butler to Wolle, dated July 1882, was known to exist as recently as 1949. See Philip Weiss Wolle, "Library List: Correspondents, Herbarium, Note Books [of Francis Wolle]," (1949), unpublished 10-page, typescript at the Moravian Historical Society, Nazareth, Pennsylvania.

16   Francis Wolle, "Fresh-Water Algae. VII," *Bulletin of the Torrey Botanical Club*, Vol. 10 (February 1883), pp. 13-21 (13).

17   Ibid., pp. 16 and 20. New species were usually given the last, not first, names of their discoverers; Wolle apparently made an exception for women. *Cosmarium eloiseanum* was "found in a pond in the vicinity of Minneapolis, Minnesota, by Miss Eloise Butler. The first specimens gathered late in the season [1882] were of a dull yellow, or brown color. Specimens of the following summer were dark green." Francis Wolle, *Desmids of the United States* (1884), p. 85. Eloise Butler either sent Wolle multiple specimens of the same species, or described her observations to him in their correspondence. See note 31 for a list of desmids discovered by Butler.

18   Francis Wolle, *Bulletin of the Torrey Botanical Club*, Vol. 11 (February 1884), pp. 13-17.

19   See note 23.

20   Francis Wolle, "Fresh-Water Algae. IX," *Bulletin of the Torrey Botanical Club*, Vol. 12 (January 1885), pp. 1-6 (5).

21   Ibid., p. 6. All of the Wolle articles are accompanied by sketches of each desmid described.

22   Francis Wolle to Charles Bessey, 3 October 1884, courtesy of Hunt Institute for Botanical Documentation, Carnegie-Mellon University, Pittsburgh, Pennsylvania.

23   John Roy to Francis Wolle, 26 March 1885, quoted in Philip Weiss Wolle, "Library List," p. 34b. Roy added that due to "increasing years," he was "less able than formerly to sit at the microscope far into the night." Eloise Butler may have corresponded directly with John Roy; among her papers at the Minnesota Historical Society is a reprint of Roy's "Japanese Desmids"

(*Journal of Botany*, July & August 1886, pp. 193-196), inscribed "To Miss Eloise Butler with J. Roy's kind regards 1888." The Swedish botanists V.B. Wittrock and Otto Nordstedt distributed Butler's *Staurastrum minnesotense* as No. 818 of their *Algae Exsiccatae* (published set of algae specimens); a slide containing a specimen of *S. minnesotense*, collected in 1884 in Minneapolis, is in the herbarium of the Department of Plant Biology at the University of Minnesota.

24 Wolle, *Desmids of the United States*, p. xii.

25 Ibid. p. vii. Wolle's granddaughter was the American imagist poet Hilda Doolittle (1886-1961), known as H.D. Wolle's life is summarized in "Francis Wolle: Teacher, Inventor, Minister, Scientist," chapter 4 of *A Moravian Heritage* by his grandson, Francis Wolle (Boulder: Empire Reproduction & Printing Co., 1972), pp. 21-27 (copy at Moravian Historical Society, Nazareth, Pennsylvania).

26 Francis Wolle, "Fresh-Water Algae. VIII," *Bulletin of the Torrey Botanical Club*, Vol. 11 (February 1884), pp. 13-17 (15).

27 Francis Wolle, "Fresh-Water Algae. X," *Bulletin of the Torrey Botanical Club*, Vol. 12 (December 1885), pp. 125-129.

28 Eloise Butler, "Desmids," *Botanical Gazette*, Vol. 11 (June 1886), pp. 148-149. *Ad libitum*: Latin, "at pleasure." Butler used the phrase loosely to mean an assortment of jars and vials for collecting pond water.

29 Ibid., p. 149.

30 Quotes from ibid., p. 149.

31 Present authorities on desmids deem that some of the species named by Wolle are growth forms of other species. New desmids discovered by Butler whose identification is still accepted are: *Cosmarium eloiseanum, Cosmarium inflatum, Cosmarium minneapolitanum, Staurastrum minneapoliense, Staurastrum minnesotense, Staurastrum wolleanum*, and *Staurastrum xiphidiophorum*. The species *Cosmarium aculeatum, Cosmarium lobatulum*, and *Staurastrum eloiseanum*, while still listed, are regarded as questionable; *Euastrum nordsteteanum* has been made synonomous with *Euastrum evolutum*, and *Staurastrum cornutum* has been renamed *Staurastrum subcornutum*. The status of many of the desmids believed by Butler and Wolle to be new varieties is still under study. See George W. Prescott, Hannah Croasdale, et al., *A Synopsis of North American Desmids*, Vol. I and Vol. II, Parts 1-6 (University of Nebraska Press, Lincoln, Nebraska, 1972-1983); status of *Euastrum nordsteteanum* courtesy of Dr. Alan J. Brook of Buckingham University, England (Brook to author, 3 July 1990). The original notebooks of Francis Wolle are in the archives of the Phycological Society of America; the present whereabouts of Wolle's desmid herbarium is unknown.

32 Francis Wolle, *Fresh-Water Algae of the United States (Exclusive of the Diatomaceae)* (Bethlehem: The Comenius Press, 1887), p. vi.

33 Warren Upham, *Catalogue of the Flora of Minnesota Including Its Phlenogamous and Vascular Cryptogamous Plants, Indigenous, Naturalized, and Adventive* (Minneapolis: The Geological and Natural History Survey of Minnesota, Part VI of the Annual Report for 1883, 1884), p. 5 (analysis courtesy Beatrice Scheer Smith). Eloise may have collected the plants from Redwood Falls during attendance at a teacher's institute held there, at which she would have taught young rural teachers who could not afford to attend a normal school.

34 Warren Upham to Eloise Butler, 7 August 1884, Eloise Butler Papers at Minnesota Historical Society. Of the thirty-four collectors acknowledged by Upham in his preface, nearly one-third were women. The list includes Sara Manning of Lake City, an accomplished botanist of the Lake Pepin area, and Emily Hitchcock Terry, who painted Minnesota wildflowers in the 1870s. Beatrice Scheer Smith of St. Paul, Minnesota, has made a study of Terry's Minnesota period.

35 Upham, *Flora of Minnesota*, p. 11.

5

Botanizing in Jamaica

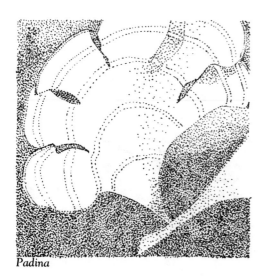

Padina

NO WORDS OF ELOISE BUTLER have survived to tell what sparked her interest in marine algae, living as she did in the Midwest, so far from the sea. Perhaps the memory of tales told in her youth by the old sea captains of South Thomaston, Maine, stirred Butler's desire to travel to foreign shores. Her opportunity to do so came about through her sister Cora's acquaintance in Malden, Massachusetts, with the noted algae specialist Frank Shipley Collins. Collins' botanically-minded wife, Anna Holmes Collins, may well have been the "Mrs. Collins" who was a member of Cora's women's club, the Old and New.[1]

Frank S. Collins was a man of many abilities and interests. His business career was spent as a bookkeeper and "efficiency expert" at the Malden Rubber Shoe Company. He was greatly interested in music, art, languages and theosophy, although his formal education had ended with high school. His interest in algae supposedly began when Anna Collins, with her friend Maria H. Bray, gathered seaweeds along the Massachusetts coast and mounted them on "sea moss" cards, labeled with their botanical names, for sale to Mrs. Bray's boarders. Frank Collins noticed errors in the labeling of the cards and, with his "characteristic efficiency, started to investigate, soon becoming immersed in what was destined to be his specialty."[2] By the age of thirty-three, in 1880, Collins had published his first scientific note on algae; a whole series of articles on New England algae followed.

By 1890, Collins was regarded as one of the foremost algae specialists in America. In addition to his own extensive botanizing along the coast of New England, he was engaged in soaking out, mounting, studying and exchanging with other botanists the considerable collections of algae he received from a large network of collectors, most of whom were apparently women.[3] What became of Anna Collins' interest in algae is not recorded.

Cora Pease's acquaintance with Frank Collins began some time after 1882, when she and Curtis moved to Malden. According to Eloise, her sister assisted in compiling Collins' *Flora of Middlesex County, Massachusetts* (with L.L. Dame), published in 1888. His talk to the Old and New club on January 7, 1890, entitled "Some Curious Beliefs of the Ancient Botanists and Herbalists," was likely at

Cora E. Pease. *Martha P. Pease.*

Cora's invitation (she was then club president). Eloise Butler met Frank and Anna Collins during one of her summer vacations; she later dated the beginning of her own interest in marine botany to "a summer on Buzzard's Bay [Massachusetts]," that of 1890, when she and Cora "collected every available seaweed in the vicinity, and later about Boston." The sisters undoubtedly placed anything of interest into Collins' hands. He included at least one species, *Sargassum vulgare*, which was collected by Eloise Butler in 1890 at Onset, in his *Phycotheca Boreali-Americana*, labeled sets of dried and mounted algae of North America, compiled with Isaac Holden and W.A. Setchell. A hint of the joy the sisters experienced as they botanized together that summer is found in a pencil sketch, owned by Cora's family, of a circle enclosing the inscription "*Memoria in aeterna* [In everlasting remembrance], Onset, Mass., Aug. 17, 1890," surrounding the initials E.B. and C.E.P.[4]

In June 1891, Eloise and Cora set off from Boston on their first of three trips to the island of Jamaica (the later visits were in 1894 and 1900), then a British colony, to collect seaweeds for Frank Collins. Prior to their visits, the marine algae of Jamaica were little known—only thirty-one species, a paltry number, had been reported—and the sisters must have relished the prospect of making a contribution to the field of phycology, and perhaps discovering a few new species along the way. How Cora persuaded her husband to allow her to leave on an expedition of several

weeks' time to Jamaica, leaving behind her two children, is not known.[5]

Some thirty years before the island became known as a tourist resort, the sisters availed themselves of the only means of transportation and booked passage in cramped staterooms aboard a banana steamer owned by the United Fruit Company. In her memoir, "Botanizing in Jamaica," Eloise wrote, "After a day and night of fog, we reached the Gulf Stream, and soon sailed apparently upon a veritable 'sea of glass.'"[6] They passed the time on board by playing whist and pressing out specimens of "sea grapes," *Sargassum bacciferum*, that "stretched out on the surface of the water like beautiful golden brown carpets" that the sailors fished up for them with long hooks.[7]

After landing at Port Antonio, the steamer proceeded around the island, stopping at small harbors along the coast to load bananas before returning to Boston. Where there were no wharves, the steamer anchored offshore. As Eloise wrote:

> In order to go ashore, we were lowered from the steamer's side into a row boat, manned by two or three Negroes and used for bringing bananas to the vessel, the waves tossing the boat so violently that we had to be skilfully caught by the boatmen

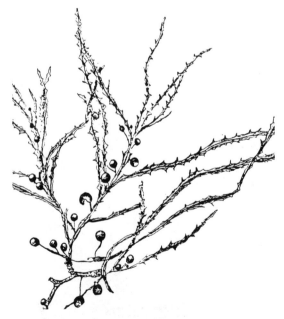

Sargassum bacciferum [S. natans] as sketched by Cora E. Pease to illustrate her article "The Sargasso Sea" in *Popular Science News*, August 1902.

as though we were bunches of bananas. After rowing as near the shore as possible, we were again taken in the Negroes' arms and carried through the shallow water to dry land.[8]

The itinerary of their three visits is recorded in Collins' paper "The Algae of Jamaica," which he presented October 9, 1901, at a meeting of the American Academy of Arts and Sciences in Philadelphia. The paper described the contents of three collections of algae from Jamaica, by far the largest of which (190 species and varieties, three-fourths of the total) was that of Cora Pease and Eloise Butler:

> The first collection was made by Mrs. Cora E. Pease of Malden, Mass., and her sister, Miss Eloise Butler of Minneapolis, Minn. In July 1891, they collected at Port Antonio and points in its vicinity; and some collecting was done at other ports, where the steamer touched for a few hours. In 1894 Morant Bay was visited in July, with a visit to Borden and Annotto Bay the first of August, followed by Orange and Hope Bays and Port Antonio, where the greater part of August was spent. In June 1900, short visits were made to Ora Cabessa, Rio Novo, Runaway Bay, and Rio Bono; June 21 to 27 was spent at Montego Bay; June 29 to July 1 at Kingston; and the time to July 18 was spent at Manchioneal, Port Morant, Hope Bay, Port Antonio, St. Ann's Bay, and Port Maria, in the order named.[9]

The sisters gathered seaweeds at every port, walking along the wharves and beaches, examining the boulders and cliffs and, in bathing dresses, wading into the sea. Butler was fascinated by the "odd, beautiful and fantastic shapes" of the tropical seaweeds, most under a meter in length.[10] Excerpts from a letter written by Cora Pease to Frank S. Collins were printed in *Rhodora* in 1901, under the title, "Collecting Seaweeds in the Tropics:"

> Sometimes the weeds were at long distances from the shore, yet growing in shallow water in eel grass or on coral reefs and ledges. Most of our seaweeding was done from boats rowed by two or three strong experienced boatmen. We would be rowed out to the reefs or to the shallow places overgrown with grass, the water even there being up to our waists; then jump from the boat into the water, to fish about for our weeds. . . . We always wore

bathing suits while seaweeding, and boys' thick hip rubber boots. On the reefs or by the ledges the waves were often strong enough to take us off our feet. Then we would cling closely together, one holding on to the other while she plunged in for the weeds. Even then we would sometimes be washed from our footing. The boatmen would be busy keeping the boat from being dashed on the rocks, and stand ready to assist us back into the boat, often with the greatest difficulty.[11]

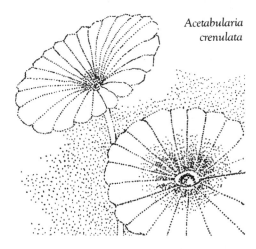

Acetabularia crenulata

In this way they collected species which resembled inside-out "fairy umbrellas," *Acetabularia crenulata*, and "tiny cat-tails," *Dasycladus vermicularis*, in water over their heads.[12] Pease's letter to Collins described the sisters' "happy hunting grounds" on a coral reef below a cliff at Port Antonio:

> The water was extremely shallow out some distance. Perhaps we had half an acre of safe wading. We did not consider it safe to wade where we could not see the bottom, owing to sharks, [and] octopi. . . . We waded out to where the surface was jagged and rocky, the water about to our waists. At this depth we found *Caulerpa clavifera* [C. racemosa] growing like lovely little clusters of green grapes, in big soggy masses. Here also were clumps of all those limy things, *Halimedas, Amphiroas, Galaxauras*, [and] *Cymopolias* . . . with them upon the rocks were those green, warty, potato-ball-like *Dictyosphaerias*. Nearer the shore the water flattened out to nothing, and the bottom was sand, like powdered shells. . . . *Caulerpa ericifolia* [C. cupressoides var. ericifolia] and C. plumaris [C. sertularioides] covered the bottom, as

club mosses grow in the woods. Such a pretty sight! Day after day we searched this reef for the "Mermaid's Shaving Brush" you had told us we would most likely find, but were giving up in despair, and were leaving the water for the last time when just at the shore, the water barely deep enough to cover them, I noticed peculiar little raised mounds in the sand. With my foot I brushed them over and revealed the *Penicillus capitatus*, so long searched for. They grew as abundantly as seedling evergreens in a neglected Maine pasture lot, and we hastily brushed the sand aside and gathered as many as we could carry."[13]

In his paper on Jamaican algae, Collins quoted further from the same letter:

> The conditions under which one must collect algae in the tropics are somewhat different from those for collecting in the North, where we have the rise and fall of the tide at intervals of a few hours, alternately laying bare and covering the algae on the rocks. At Jamaica many weeds grow on rocks so situated as to be alternately bared and covered by the wash of the waves at intervals of a few minutes. Many of the *Polysiphonias*, *Gelidiums*, [and] *Gracilarias* . . . are generally found under these conditions. . . . The finest growth of *Padina* that we saw was at Montego Bay, from a road passing over a bluff, directly on the edge of the sea, down into which one could look and see *Padina* growing like a field of gray morning-glory blossoms set upon stones in the shallow, rather quiet water. Near by were patches of *Zonaria variegata* [*Lobophora variegata*], like red-brown morning glories.[14]

Each day's finds were carried back to their lodgings for washing and drying, which sometimes included the necessity of dislodging colonies of tiny sea creatures that lived among the fronds. It was crucial that the specimens be kept in salt water before mounting, and rinsed in salt water, as well; "fresh water is sometimes instant ruin," warned Collins.[15] The sisters' preservation technique followed pointers given in Collins' article "To Seaweed Collectors:"

> Float out the specimens in some large vessel of clean salt water; remove any dirt or foreign bodies; . . . trim as needed. Let the specimen assume its natural form in the water; if fresh it will do so readily; slide under it a paper of suitable size, lift so that when taken from the water the plant will remain on it, in the same shape

it had in the water. Place the paper on a sloping board to drain for a short time; then lay on drying paper, specimen up; when no more specimens can be placed on the drier, cover all very carefully with a cotton cloth of the same size as the drier. Another drier, more specimens, another cloth, and so on indefinitely.[16]

The whole pile was then pressed, and drying papers changed after an hour and again less frequently as the seaweeds dried. Some of the more delicate algae, such as many of the Jamaican specimens proved to be, were mounted on heavy blotting paper; Collins advised the use of a hairpin, "in emergency," for arranging the specimen on the herbarium sheet. The larger specimens were dried, sprinkled liberally with salt, and packed in crates for the return voyage.[17]

There was no hotel in Port Antonio in 1891. Eloise and Cora stayed two weeks at a local boardinghouse, where they were provided with one small room crammed with furniture and the "missus' things." Upon their return, Cora wrote a humorous article, "Life in a Jamaica Boardinghouse," which described their accommodations.[18] Her account of their first "wretched night" at the boardinghouse is particularly amusing. According to Cora, the sisters slept little, under an onslaught of flying cockroaches and ants, while from just outside their window came frequent "hyena-like" screams that would "freeze the blood in the veins of less courageous women." (The screams were discovered in the morning to have come from a peacock perched on top of the house.)[19] Their microscope and books, propped in a window sill, were imperiled by frequent downpours. Seaweed specimens were washed out on a small folding table and dried on the bed, which Eloise and Cora were obliged to climb over to get to the door. The cloths used in pressing their plants were spread on the grass to dry in the back yard when not in use, while all manner of kitchen refuse was flung out the windows by the servants into the same yard to be eaten by the ever-present "turkey buzzards" (vultures). The women's "Yankee ingenuity," wrote Cora, enabled them to endure the difficult conditions and "preserve such a collection of rare ferns and sea mosses as to make us justly proud."[20]

On later trips their lodgings varied from a "primitive little hostelry" at Annotta Bay to a cottage on the seashore, lent them for a week by an officer of the United Fruit Company, complete with housekeeper and servants. At Manchioneal, they were forced to stay in another "intolerable" place where Eloise had to lie crossways across the bed to keep from falling out, and the air was fouled with the "fumes of the landlady's rum often coming up through [the] floor."[21]

Despite these annoyances, the seaweeding was so successful that the sisters were able to maintain good humor. As Eloise wrote in "Botanizing in Jamaica," she and Cora, ever the intrepid botanists, were not averse to putting their cumbersome Victorian garb to novel use:

> [O]n our second voyage we made an especial trip to Hope Bay to collect specimens of our *Liagora decussata*. We found it in windrows and filled our collecting bag, then inverted our open umbrellas and filled them, and, that not satisfying us, we gathered up our dress-skirts and filled them, going off the beach to the waiting carriage staggering under our loads.[22]

The sisters were apparently not troubled by ill health, despite partaking freely of the local food and water; a Dr. J.E. Humphrey, who collected algae for Frank Collins in Jamaica in 1893 and again in 1897, was not so fortunate. On his second visit, he contracted "island fever," and died two days later.[23]

Eloise found the mountainous island with its jagged coastline to be a "naturalist's paradise," and in later years recalled her trips to Jamaica as high points of her life. "Soil is not necessary on this wonderful island for the growth of vegetation," she wrote:

> The rocks, brick and stone walls, the trunks of trees, the roofs and very doorsteps of dwellings have growing on them mosses, ferns, orchids and very many other forms of plant life.[24]

When not collecting seaweeds, the women took drives into the Blue Mountains, where they visited a coffee plantation and gathered ferns for Cora's window garden in Malden. They found themselves "aghast" at the sight of a Jamaican gardener preparing the ground to plant yams, hacking away at ferns and begonias (the local "weeds") such as they formerly had seen only in conservatories.[25] It was undoubtedly in Jamaica that Eloise learned the knack of sleeping in a hammock,

and the island must have been the source of the machete that she came to favor as a gardening tool in later years.

Only on their third and last visit to the island in the summer of 1900 did Eloise and Cora manage to find any new species. As it turned out, most of the Jamaican algae had been previously described from Puerto Rico, the Canary Islands, Morocco, Europe and North America. Nevertheless, two new species of seaweed were named for them by Collins: *Cordylecladia peaseae*, discovered at Manchioneal, and *Antithamnion butlerae* [*Acrothamnion butlerae*], a small plant of a rich rose color, found at Kingston.[26] Another new species was named *Cladophora intertexta*. Washed up on the beach at Manchioneal, they discovered a black seaweed, resembling "rolled and twisted strings," that seemed to differ from any genus yet described; Collins pronounced it to be a species of a new genus and provisionally named it *Dictyerpa jamaicensis*.[27]

The sisters found the discovery of rare seaweeds as rewarding as finding new ones. The *Liagora decussata* collected so bountifully in their umbrellas and skirts in 1894 had, wrote Eloise, "puzzled the algologists for a long time" when discovered on their first trip:

> They decided it was new to science and were considering what to christen it, when Mr. Collins, in an old French work, stumbled upon a description of *Liagora decussata*, long since dropped out of the books as a freak of the imagination of the author Montagne, no specimen of such a *Liagora* ever having been seen by living scientists. We had the romantic honor of rediscovering a plant and vindicating the veracity of the old, long dead naturalist. This seemed much more interesting than discovering the plant for the first time.[28]

And the third trip yielded, besides the new species, another "great find." Growing on large boulders in rough water at Manchioneal were "large patches of a gloriously beautiful weed of most vigorous growth, and its color varying shades of purple." The plant, *Gracilaria domingensis*, had been noted only once previously, in 1869.[29]

The marine algae collections of Eloise Butler and Cora Pease made a significant contribution to the natural history of Jamaica. Prior to 1901, wrote Collins, the dearth of species of algae known from Jamaica made it "seem as if there must be some special conditions at Jamaica to impoverish the marine flora," but these collections (including those of the ill-fated Dr. Humphrey and a Dr. J.E. Duerden who contributed a few species in 1901) showed "quite conclusively that this is not the case, and that there is every reason to suppose that the flora of the island is in no way inferior to similar regions."[30]

Collins used at least fifty species of the seaweeds collected by Butler and Pease in the *Phycotheca Boreali-Americana*. Impressed with the quality of the algae the sisters had gathered, Collins wrote to his collaborator William Setchell, at the University of California at Berkeley, in August 1900:

> I am working now on a lot of material from Jamaica, brought by Mrs. Pease and Miss Butler, who spent five weeks there in June and July giving special attention to algae. The material is salted, which gives me all but the most delicate in practically the same condition as when they grew, which is interesting to me who have never seen tropical algae in such shape before. I expect to get at least twenty sets for the Phycotheca out of it, perhaps more.[31]

These sets, of which eighty are believed to have been issued between 1895 and 1919, eventually contained more than 2,300 different species of North American algae, and were purchased by many prominent academic institutions and museums in the United States and abroad.[32]

Butler and Pease exchanged seaweeds with other botanists besides Frank Collins, including William G. Farlow of Harvard whom the sisters may have met at the Marine Biological Laboratory in 1893. A number of algae specimens collected in Jamaica by Butler and Pease (in addition to those in the *Phycotheca*) are in the Farlow Herbarium of Cryptogamic Botany at Harvard. A letter dated March 22, 1902, from Pease to Farlow is owned by the Farlow Reference Library at Harvard University. Its self-effacing tone reveals much about relations between amateurs and professionals as well as typifying the modesty obligatory for women. Nevertheless, Pease's challenge to Farlow to give his authority for a statement about the alga *Sargassum bacciferum* [*S. natans*] which contradicted her and Butler's own observations bespeaks the determination to make a serious contribution to botany which motivated both women:

My dear sir,

Some time ago in acknowledgement of some Jamaica seaweeds my sister and I sent you, I received a kind note from you asking me to come to Cambridge some time and select some [sea]weeds I might wish from your duplicates. Instead, I have a favor to ask, and if you are too busy to reply I will readily forgive you. I have read . . . that the *Sargassum bacciferum* is never found otherwise than forever floating. In the Century Dictionary I find it stated under your name that it grows attached and fruited in the West Indies. Can you tell me if you have seen it growing thus yourself, and just where in the West Indies? If *you* have not seen it growing attached and fruited, can you give me your authority? My sister and I searched for it in Jamaica but never found one bit of it excepting as we found it floating in mid-ocean. . . . Most assuredly I will pardon you if you do not think it worth while to take your valuable time to reply, much as I would like to know the facts in the case.

Most respectfully yours, (Mrs.) Cora E. Pease.[33]

Farlow's reply, which referred to a rare fruited specimen collected in Florida, apparently laid the matter to rest.[34]

Eloise and Cora traveled together on many other occasions, always on the lookout for interesting plants. Clippings in Cora's scrapbook refer to visits by the sisters to Maine, Nova Scotia, and Colorado, often followed by newspaper articles or letters written by Cora to the editors of botanical journals, describing interesting plants they had found.[35] In August 1892 the sisters visited Colorado, where their father had settled with his second wife, and their brothers Simpson and Edgar lived with their families. Cora described the Colorado trip in a long, two-part article entitled "Among the Rockies," written for a Maine newspaper the following year.[36] The party (including Edgar Butler, his wife Mary, and their three little girls, Eva, Helen, and Jessie Eloise) had camped in tents at Manitou in the foothills of the Rockies. Cora and Eloise took a stagecoach drawn by mules to the top of Pikes Peak and, on the precipitous road to the summit, were entranced by the sight of a lightning storm below them, then were nearly frozen in a sudden snowstorm at the mountain top.

After several days of hiking in the mountains, the party decided to explore Cheyenne Canyon, the "favorite haunt" of the writer Helen Hunt Jackson, crusader for Indian rights, whom Eloise and Cora greatly admired.[37] With the three children atop a burro, and the two plant-hunters "loaded down with botanical boxes and portfolios for preserving the plants [they] hoped to find," they followed the stream between the rock walls. Once, the inveterate collectors noticed an unfamiliar fern growing high up above their heads. "Diligently we heaped up some stones upon which my sister stepped," wrote Cora, "and availing herself of every little projecting ledge, managed to scale the rock far enough to reach up with her umbrella handle and knock down the precious fern." It proved to be a cloak-fern, *Notholaena fendleri*.

A series of waterfalls plunged into a pool at the end of the narrow canyon, creating a spectacular rainbow. "We felt like worshipping at the foot of the falls forever," wrote Cora, but they pressed on, climbing above the falls to discover a higher valley where stood the remains of a cabin supposedly once occupied by Helen Hunt Jackson. Determined to reach the place where "H.H." was buried, at the top of the canyon wall, Cora and Eloise left the rest of the party behind and climbed still higher, pulling themselves up by the exposed roots of trees. Finally the path reached a meadow filled with goldenrod, purple asters, blue lupine, and wild onions. At the edge of the plateau the sisters found the lonely burial place, but were disappointed to discover that Jackson's body had been removed to a cemetery at Colorado Springs and the cairn of stones left by her friends broken up and carried away by tourists, who had carved their initials onto all the pines within reach.[38]

The decade of the 1890s, when she was in her forties, brought Eloise into contact with an expanded network of women botanists, many of whom were Cora's acquaintances in Boston. In addition to her interest in seaweeds, Cora had become an all-around naturalist who read botanical journals such as *Bulletin of the Torrey Botanical Club* and the *American Botanist*, experimented with beekeeping, and published numerous articles on the birds, mushrooms and wildflowers of New England. Like Eloise, she read and admired Darwin and Thoreau.[39] She belonged to a botany study group of the New England Women's Club in Boston, led by

Cora H. Clarke, expert on insect galls and mosses, who (with Elizabeth Knight Britton) was one of the founders of the National Science Club for Women in 1891; also in the Boston group was Lucretia Crocker, a steadfast advocate of scientific education for women. Another friend was Ellen Swallow Richards, Vassar graduate and professor of chemistry at the Massachusetts Institute of Technology. On her regular trips east during her summer vacations, Eloise would have been welcomed into Cora's circle of scientifically-inclined friends.[40]

Eloise Butler was undoubtedly a supporter of woman's suffrage, as was her sister, although any political tendencies she had were clearly subordinated to botany. She had a subscription (perhaps a gift from Cora) to the *Woman's Journal*, a publication of the Boston-based National Woman Suffrage Association, in the 1880s. Eloise saved one issue, dated 1884, for more than thirty years, then used it in 1916 to wrap a specimen of moss.

In 1893 Eloise and Cora attended the summer session of the Marine Biological Laboratory at Woods Hole, Massachusetts.[41] The laboratory had been founded only five years before as a successor to a sea-side school at Annisquam which combined instruction with research. It was intended to become a national center of marine research and sought the participation of leading biologists and their students from all of the major research centers. Both the Marine Biological Laboratory and its precursor had been supported from the beginning by advocates of the scientific education of women such as the Women's Educational Association of Boston and the Boston Society of Natural History; several of the original trustees and nearly half of the early students and investigators were women.[42]

In 1893, the facilities were still under development and consisted of one two-story frame building, called "Old Main," which stood near the United States Bureau of Fisheries station at Woods Hole and faced Martha's Vineyard across Vineyard Sound in Buzzard's Bay. It had laboratory apparatus for thirty-three investigators who had the use of private rooms on the second floor; the first floor held five general laboratories for the use of students, with twenty tables reserved for researchers from various colleges (including Vassar, Wellesley, and Mount Holyoke). There was a well-stocked library with a large framed placard over the door inscribed with Louis Agassiz's motto, "Study nature not books." Students boarded with residents of the village.

Eloise signed up for the six-week course in marine zoology and microscopical technique for teachers in high schools and colleges, taught by Professor Hermon C. Bumpus of Brown University; Cora took the marine algae course under William A. Setchell (then at Yale). Laboratory work and lectures alternated with collecting trips on the rich waters of Buzzard's Bay in a steam-powered sailing yacht. Evening lectures were offered on various topics, including one by William G. Farlow on the classification of algae.[43]

At Woods Hole, under conditions inclined to foster friendship, Eloise and Cora met more than thirty other women botanists and zoologists who attended the laboratory that season. Eloise wrote that "several friendships . . . were cemented" there.[44] Among the women present were Cornelia M. Clapp, professor of zoology at Mt. Holyoke College, who had attended Louis Agassiz's Penikese Island school some twenty years before, and Harriet Randolph, biology instructor at Bryn Mawr College, who had earned a doctorate degree in 1892 from the University of Zurich. (Five of the seventeen Ph.Ds in botany earned by American women prior to 1900 came from

the University of Zurich, which welcomed female students when most American graduate schools were closed to them.) Also present at Woods Hole that summer were zoologist Emily R. Gregory, who earned a doctorate from the University of Chicago in 1899 and taught at Wells College in Aurora, New York, and Katherine Foot, of Evanston, Illinois, who later published several articles on cellular morphology.[45]

Courses in summer schools, such as those Eloise had attended at the University of Minnesota in the 1880s and at the Marine Biological Laboratory in 1893, were an important means to higher education in the sciences for women in the late nineteenth century. Eloise, who supported herself by teaching and had neither the time nor means to attend regular college courses, eagerly availed herself of every such opportunity to further her formal education. Thus she enrolled at Harvard for a summer chemistry course designed for teachers in 1895 under Mr. Joseph Torrey; her name also appears on a list of special students at the University of Minnesota in the 1893-1894 catalogue, although what additional courses she took there are unknown.[46]

The summer of 1896 brought a change from study and botanizing. Eloise later wrote that she spent that summer in Europe,

Seaweed collecting at the Marine Biological Laboratory at Woods Hole, Massachusetts, in the mid-1890s. *Library of Marine Biological Laboratory.*

"revelling with the old masters in art."[47] In England she made a pilgrimage to the Lake District to visit the homes and gardens of William Wordsworth, a favorite nature poet. Eloise was living with Sarah Brackett at the time; Sarah may have accompanied her to Europe, but few details of the trip are known.

After their final visit to Jamaica in 1900, Eloise and Cora placed the seaweeds gathered there into the hands of Frank S. Collins, who immediately set to work writing his "Algae of Jamaica." There is no evidence that Cora did any further collecting for Collins, although her interest in marine algae continued unabated until her death in 1928 at the age of eighty, when she was said to have completed a manuscript for a book on seaweeds.[48] Eloise was to have yet one more summer seaweeding adventure, this time to the island of Vancouver in British Columbia in the company of some younger botanists who were establishing a center of marine botany at an unlikely place, the University of Minnesota.

Notes

1   The Old and New Club was founded in Malden in 1878 by Harriette R. Shattuck and her mother, Harriet Robinson, both ardent feminists and suffragists. Shattuck was a journalist and expert on parlimentary law who worked for woman's suffrage with Elizabeth Cady Stanton and Susan B. Anthony; she also reported for the *Boston Transcript* on the nearby Concord School of Philosophy led by Bronson Alcott and Ralph Waldo Emerson. Cora was active in the writing group and was sixth president (1888-1890) of the club, whose emblem was the old moon in the arms of the new. See Ruth Kimball Randall (compiler), *Old and New: Recollections of Ninety-Five Years (1878-1973)*, 53-page pamphlet in archives of the Old and New Club, Malden Public Library.

2   W.A. Setchell, "Frank Shipley Collins, 1848-1920," *American Journal of Botany*, Vol. 12 (January 1925), pp. 54-62, (56).

3   Ten of the thirteen persons named as collectors for Frank S. Collins in his obituary in the *American Journal of Botany* were women. Besides Eloise and Cora's collections from Jamaica, the article mentions Miss M.M. Miles, Mrs. A.E. Bush, Mrs. J.M. Weeks and Mrs. M.S. Snyder, who sent him rough-dried algae of the Pacific Coast; Miss Julia Houegger sent him "very considerable collections from the Canary Islands"; Miss C. Messina and Mrs. G.A. Hall collected in Key West and in other parts of Florida; and (with Eloise Butler) Jessie Polley in Minnesota and on Vancouver Island. W.A. Setchell, "Frank Shipley Collins," p. 57.

4   Quote from Eloise Butler to Gray Memorial Botanical Chapter, Agassiz Association, Division D, April 1928 (entitled "Cora E. Pease") copy in Eloise Butler biography file at Minneapolis Public Library, Minneapolis Collection; Collins' talk is described in Old and New *Minute Book*, Vol. 7, January 1890. A dried specimen of *Sargassum vulgare* collected by Eloise Butler in 1890 is in the herbarium of the Department of Plant Biology at the University of Minnesota (Collins, Holden and Setchell, *Phycotheca Boreali-Americana*, Fasc. IV, no. 178). The pencil sketch is owned by Martha P. Pease (copy in Eloise Butler Papers at Minnesota Historical Society).

5   Little is known of the relationship between Cora and Curtis Pease. Curtis Pease was a man of order. He was known for his punctual departures for the Boston train each morning; he worked at the Boston Ice Company for seventy years. Cora, on the other hand, loved wildness—her wild garden at their home in Malden was among her greatest treasures—and chafed at the bonds of female life and domestic responsibility. Relations between Eloise Butler and Curtis Pease appear to have been strained. In a three-page eulogy that Eloise wrote on her sister's death in 1928, the existence of a surviving husband is mentioned only in passing; his name is not given at all. Eloise Butler to Gray Memorial Botanical Chapter, Agassiz Association, Division D, April 1928, (eulogy for Cora E. Pease), copy in Eloise Butler biography file at Minneapolis Public Library, Minneapolis Collection.

6   Eloise Butler, "Botanizing in Jamaica," *Postelsia, The Year Book of the Minnesota Seaside Station* (for 1901) (St. Paul: The Pioneer Press, 1902), pp. 89-131 (89).

7   Cora E. Pease, "The Sargasso Sea," *Popular Science News*, clipping dated August 1902 in scrapbook owned by Martha P. Pease. A specimen of *Sargassum bacciferum* collected by Eloise Butler on her first visit to Jamaica is in the herbarium of the Department of Plant Biology at the University of Minnesota (in Collins, Holden, & Setchell, *Phycotheca Boreali-Americana*, Fasc. XVII, no. 832).

8   Eloise Butler, "Botanizing in Jamaica," p. 96. The term "Negro" did not carry the derogatory connotations in 1901 that now make it an unacceptable way to refer to persons of African

descent.

9   Frank Shipley Collins, "The Algae of Jamaica," *Proceedings of the American Academy of Arts and Sciences*, Vol. 37 (1901), pp. 231-270 (233).

10 Eloise Butler, "Botanizing in Jamaica," p. 129.

11 Cora E. Pease to Frank S. Collins (c.1901), published as "Collecting Seaweeds in the Tropics," *Rhodora*, Vol. 3 (April 1901), pp. 90-91 (90).

12 Eloise Butler, "Botanizing in Jamaica," p. 125.

13 Cora Pease, "Collecting Seaweeds in the Tropics," p. 91.

14 Frank Shipley Collins, "The Algae of Jamaica," p. 237.

15 F.S. Collins, "To Seaweed Collectors," *Rhodora*, Vol. 1 (July 1899), pp. 121-127 (122).

16 Ibid., pp. 122-123.

17 Quote from ibid., p. 123. I am grateful to Dr. Paul C. Silva, curator of the algal herbarium at the University Herbarium, University of California, Berkeley, for a discussion of algal preservation techniques; Silva to author, 27 December 1990.

18 Cora E. Pease, "Life in a Jamaica Boardinghouse," *The Portland Transcript*, Vol. 2, December 1891 (Part I), and 9 December 1891 (Part II); clippings in scrapbook owned by Martha P. Pease.

19 Ibid., Part I.

20 Ibid., Part II.

21 Eloise Butler, "Botanizing in Jamaica," p. 114.

22 Ibid., p. 130. A fragile, dried fragment of *Liagora decussata* collected by Eloise and Cora at Hope Bay is in the herbarium of the Department of Plant Biology at the University of Minnesota (Collins, Holden, & Setchell, *Phycotheca Boreali-Americana*, Fasc. II, no. 89, 1894).

23 Frank Shipley Collins, "Algae of Jamaica," p. 233.

24 Eloise Butler, "Botanizing in Jamaica," p. 112.

25 Cora E. Pease, "Plants as Souvenirs of Travel," *Popular Science News* (February 1901), clipping in scrapbook owned by Martha P. Pease; and "What is a Weed?", *The House Beautiful*, Vol. 38 (July 1915), p. 48.

26 Frank Shipley Collins, "Algae of Jamaica," pp. 255, 259. Status of *Antithamnion butlerae* [*Acrothamnion butlerae*] courtesy Michael J. Wynne, letter to author, 27 July 1990. *Cordylecladia peasae* was included in Collins, Holden and Setchell, *Phycotheca Boreali-Americana*, Fasc. XVI, no. 791 (1900).

27 Ibid., p. 251. *Cladophora intertexta* is in Collins, Holden and Setchell, *Phycotheca Boreali-Americana*, Fasc. XVII, no. 818 (1900). The label of a specimen of *Dictyerpa jamaicensis* in the herbarium at the Department of Plant Biology, University of Minnesota reads "Washed ashore in tangled masses, Hope Bay and Machioneal, Jamaica, July 1900; Mrs. C.E. Pease and Miss E. Butler" (in Collins, Holden and Setchell, *Phycotheca Boreali-Americana*, Fasc. XIV, no. 780). Present-day experts have concluded that the plant was a juvenile form of a *Padina*, a previously known genus, but differ on whether it was a new species (renamed *Padina jamaicensis* (Collins) Papenfuss in 1977 by one authority). Michael J. Wynne to author, 27 July 1990.

28 Eloise Butler, "Botanizing in Jamaica," pp. 127-128. Jean Francois Camille Montagne (1784-1866) was a prolific French naturalist whose accounts of botanical expeditions to Cuba and South America were published in the 1850s.

29 Eloise Butler, "Botanizing in Jamaica," p. 127.

30 Collins, "Algae of Jamaica," p. 233.

31 Frank Shipley Collins to William Setchell, 17 August 1900, in William Setchell Papers at University Herbarium, University of California at Berkeley.

32 Elizabeth M. Fahey and Maxwell S. Doty, "An Alphabetical Index to the *Phycotheca Boreali-Americana*," 37-page typescript, courtesy Michael J. Wynne (copy at Marine Biological Laboratory, Woods Hole, Massachusetts), p. 1. The *Phycotheca* also contains specimens of numerous species collected by Eloise Butler with Jessie Polley at Vancouver in 1901; see Chapter 6. The *Phycotheca* is owned by, among others, the University of Minnesota, Harvard University, the Field Museum of Chicago, the Institute of Jamaica, and Kew Gardens in England. The algae collected by Eloise Butler, Cora E. Pease and Jessie Polley are discussed in the correspondence of Frank S. Collins and William Setchell in the William Setchell Papers, University Herbarium, University of California at Berkeley.

33 Cora E. Pease to William G. Farlow, 22 March 1902, Farlow Manuscripts (Vol. 125 no. 29), Farlow Reference Library of Cryptogamic Botany, Harvard University (emphasis in original).

34 In her article "The Sargasso Sea," Cora Pease wrote: "'Fruiting specimens are among the greatest of algological rarities,' according to Dr. Farlow of Harvard University. He has only one fruited specimen. . . . collected on the coast of Florida. The most eminent authorities in the world doubted the existence of this specimen, but by actually seeing it, they have had to acknowledge it to be a genuine fruited *Sargassum bacciferum*. As found floating it is always infertile, so must increase by branching and subdividing." Cora E. Pease, "The Sargasso Sea," *Popular Science News* (August 1902), clipping in scrapbook owned by Martha P. Pease.

35 Cora's scrapbook is owned by Martha P. Pease; copy in Eloise Butler Papers at Minnesota His-

torical Society. See, for example, Cora E. Pease, "A New Yarrow?," *The American Botanist*, Vol. 8 (May 1905), pp. 90-91, which refers to a visit by Eloise and Cora to Maine and their trip through the White Mountains in August 1904.

36 This and next two paragraphs based on Cora E. Pease, "Among the Rockies," two-part article in *The Portland Transcript*, (c.May 1893), clippings in a scrapbook owned by Martha P. Pease (copy in Eloise Butler Papers, Minnesota Historical Society). Edgar Butler became a grocer in Denver; he died in 1931. Simpson Butler had a career as a grocer in Lynn and later worked for the United States Mint in Denver; he served in the Colorado legislature in 1923-24, and died in 1927.

37 Helen Hunt Jackson (1830-1885) was the author of *Mercy Philbrick's Choice* (1876), said to be a fictional portrait of her friend Emily Dickenson; *A Century of Dishonor* (1881), an historical account of the government mistreatment of the Native American; and *Ramona* (1884), a popular novel about a young Native American woman. She also published poems and sonnets under the initials "H.H."

38 Quotes from Cora E. Pease, "Among the Rockies."

39 Cora was not afraid to disagree publicly with the venerated naturalists on occasion. In her article "Additional Bits of Nature," she took issue with Thoreau's reference to the *Utricularia vulgaris* as a "common bladderwort, a dirty, ill-conditioned flower, like a sluttish woman with a gaudy yellow bonnet." Cora wrote that she had read about the "beautiful" plant in the writings of the botanist Mary Treat, and then discovered it herself near a pond; "Much as I admire Thoreau's keen observations of nature, I cannot easily forgive him for this slanderous attack upon a plant with such a wonderful life-history." Clipping (source for Thoreau quote not given) from the *Ladies' Floral Cabinet*, June 1886, in scrapbook owned by Martha P. Pease.

40 Lucretia Crocker's activities to promote the scientific education of women, and her membership in the Boston club to which Cora Pease belonged, are mentioned in Sally Gregory Kohlstadt, "In From the Periphery: American Women in Science, 1830-1880," *Signs: Journal of Women in Culture and Society*, Vol. 4 (Autumn 1978), pp. 81-96 (93-94). Cora Clarke's botany group is discussed in Anne L. Read, "Cora H. Clarke," *The Bryologist*, Vol. 19 (1916), pp. 73-74. Clarke and Richards belonged to the American Association for the Advancement of Science. Richards' accomplishments are told in Margaret W. Rossiter, *Women Scientists in America*, pp. 68-70, 77. The National Science Club for Women is discussed in Margaret W. Rossiter, *Women Scientists in America*, p. 95.

41 This paragraph based on Frank R. Lillie, *The Woods Hole Marine Biological Laboratory* (Chicago: University of Chicago Press, 1944), pp. 26-42; Margaret W. Rossiter, *Women Scientists in America*, pp. 86-88; and Marine Biological Laboratory *1893 Annual Circular and Annual Report of the Trustees*, pp. 42-45.

42 After 1897, according to Margaret W. Rossiter, control of the Marine Biological Laboratory was wrested from its philanthropic Boston founders by a coalition of male professionals who sought and received large endowments from big business and big foundations "which few women ever penetrated. . . . The women at Woods Hole were after 1897 back on the outside." Margaret Rossiter, *Women Scientists in America*, p. 88.

43 Marine Biological Laboratory, *1893 Annual Circular and Sixth Annual Report of the Trustees*, pp. 29-31, 42-45.

44 Eloise Butler to Gray Memorial Botanical Chapter, Agassiz Association, Division D, April 1928 (eulogy for Cora E. Pease), copy in Eloise Butler biography file at Minneapolis Public Library, Minneapolis Collection.

45 Marine Biological Laboratory, *1893 Annual Circular and Sixth Annual Report of the Trustees*, pp. 7-11; Mrs. M. Burton Williamson, "Some American Women in Science," *The Chautauquan*, Vol. 27 (November 1898), pp. 161-168 (Part I); (January 1899), pp. 361-368 (Part II); and Vol. 28, (February 1899), pp. 465-473 (Part III) contains information about Cornelia Clapp (p. 363); Harriet Randolph (p. 468) and Katherine Foot (p. 469); information on Emily R. Gregory courtesy Emmanual D. Rudolph, letter to author, 9 January 1991. Doctoral degrees in botany earned by women are discussed in Rudolph's "Women in Nineteenth Century American Botany: A Generally Unrecognized Constituency," *American Journal of Botany*, Vol. 69, no. 8, 1982, pp. 1346-1355 (1350).

46 Harvard University *Catalog* (1894-1895); University of Minnesota *Catalogue* (1893-1894).

47 Eloise Butler to Gray Memorial Botanical Chapter, Agassiz Association, Division D (c.1911), copy in *Early History of Eloise Butler Native Plant Reserve*, p. 2, at Minneapolis Public Library, Minneapolis Collection.

48 Cora's obituary stated that she "was about to publish a book on seaweed, she having made an extensive study of the work and was only awaiting the arrival of her sister from Minneapolis to go over it with her, before giving it to the printer." *Malden Evening News*, 29 February 1928. The whereabouts of Cora's manuscript and her herbarium of pressed and mounted Jamaican plants (mentioned in a clipping in a scrapbook owned by Martha P. Pease) are not known.

Laboratory dubbed "the Formalose Club" at the Minnesota Seaside Station on Vancouver Island. *University of Minnesota Archives.*

6

The Minnesota
Seaside Station

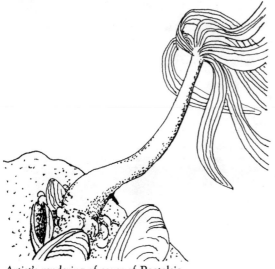

Artist's rendering of cover of Postelsia

HARDLY HAD SHE RETURNED from her final trip to Jamaica in 1900 than Eloise began making plans for yet another seaweeding expedition, this time to the western shore of Vancouver Island where the largely unknown—and very large—algae of the north Pacific flourished. Her former student Josephine Tilden, eighteen years younger than she and, since 1897, a member of the botany faculty at the University of Minnesota, was establishing a new marine station there modeled after the Marine Biological Laboratory at Woods Hole. In her fiftieth summer, Eloise had the honor of attending the inaugural season of the Minnesota Seaside Station.

Eloise Butler and Josephine Tilden offer a classic case of the nineteenth-century female science teacher-student relationships described by historian of science Sally Gregory Kohlstedt in her article, "In from the Periphery: American Women in Science, 1830-1880." The first generation of women in science worked in isolation in the early nineteenth century and were "largely unrecognized," according to Kohlstedt; the second generation, to which Eloise Butler (and her own botany teacher, Helen Coffin) belonged, worked as educators and "disseminators of science," and "provided the foundation that helped gain the third generation [Josephine Tilden] access to advanced training and scientific association."[1]

Eloise Butler's association with Josephine Tilden began in the late 1880s, when Tilden took Butler's high-school botany classes at Central High School in Minneapolis. Tilden's senior year (1890-1891) was framed by Butler's summer of seaweed collecting on Buzzard's Bay and her first trip to Jamaica. One can easily imagine the older botanist imparting her love of plants, and especially the excitement of the search for rare and new species of algae, to her young protege. Certainly Butler shared with her students her experiences in desmid collecting, her plans for traveling to Jamaica to collect tropical seaweeds, and, with one who showed special interest, her impressions of the Marine Biological Laboratory at Woods Hole formed during the summer of 1893.

After graduation from high school, Josephine Tilden enrolled at the University of Minnesota, where she earned a B.S. in 1895 and an M.A. in 1897. Tilden was well aware of the importance, in the academic world to which she aspired, of having scholarly publications. She began writing and publishing articles on her algal studies before she had her undergraduate degree. Her first publication, entitled "List of Fresh-Water Algae Collected in Minnesota During 1893," included many species of desmids.[2] By 1894, she had put together sets of herbarium specimens, with descriptions, of one hundred species of Minnesota algae and was offering them for sale as *American Algae: Century I.* In 1897 she was offered a position as instructor in the botany department at the University of Minnesota, and became the first woman scientist employed there.[3] Eloise followed Tilden's career in botany with great interest and pride as the younger woman joined the ranks of the professionals.

Josephine Tilden early on announced that she wished to make her specialty the algae of the Pacific Ocean. Her study of marine algae began on Puget Sound, where she spent the summers of 1897 and 1898 (along with short visits to the coast of California). Sixty miles north of Victoria, on the rough and rock-bound western coast of Vancouver Island, she found a cove rich in algae. As she later wrote, "the algae covering that exposed shore were beyond my wildest dreams."[4] The shore of the cove was a large sandstone shelf carved by wave action into a myriad of pot-holes lined with pink coralline algae, mussels and many-hued seaweeds. At low tide, the pot-holes offered a close look at the sea anemones, crabs, spiny sea urchins and other marine life trapped within. After four glorious days in

1898 exploring the tide pools, reefs and rocks in which Tilden "spent every daylight moment in collecting algae," subsisting on cold beans and tea doled out by her mother, she was offered, by the owner of the property, four acres of land along the shore for the establishment of a seaside botanical station.[5]

In the summer of 1900 Tilden returned to the site and scouted the beach from a dugout canoe paddled by a local Siwash Indian guide. She selected an ideal spot for the station, sheltered by a high cliff near a place where two freshwater streams flowed into the ocean. Plans were made for the erection of several log buildings and a road to be laid through the three miles of rain forest which stood between the camp and Port Renfrew, the nearest town. In January 1901 a Minneapolis *Journal* article touted the forthcoming birth of the new station, listing the names of about thirty midwestern botanists, including Eloise Butler, who had signed on for the opening session.[6] Conway MacMillan, State Botanist of Minnesota and youthful head of the department of botany at the University of Minnesota who directed the station with Tilden, praised the unique location of the camp which would be "accessible both to sound and ocean waters." MacMillan claimed that its location was superior to those of rival stations on the Atlantic coast, an area he found "hackneyed, stale and uninteresting in botanical lines when compared with the virgin shores of the north Pacific."[7] The station was

Party of botanists en route to Vancouver Island in 1901. Eloise Butler believed to be third from right. *University of Minnesota Archives.*

50

to be privately funded and operated by Tilden and MacMillan, who were given to understand that the University of Minnesota would take over the management and expenses of the station if they could run it successfully for five years.

The group of thirty-three left Minneapolis on the evening of June 15, 1901, in a private rail car (with kitchen) of the Soo Line. Besides Tilden, Butler and MacMillan (and MacMillan's wife and daughter), the party included C. Otto Rosendahl and Frederic K. Butters of the university's botany department; Charles J. Hibbard, photographer of the department, and his wife; Clara Leavitt and Jessie Polley, teachers in Minneapolis high schools and friends of Eloise Butler; Francis Ramaley, a noted taxonomist from Boulder, Colorado; and several students in the department. Also in the party were Tilden's companion (and probable financial backer) Caroline Crosby of the well-to-do Crosby milling family in Minneapolis, as well as Tilden's mother, who (until her death at the age of eighty-seven) accompanied her precocious daughter on all of her botanizing trips, providing much-needed housekeeping and cooking services.

En route to Vancouver, the party studied prairie and mountain plants at every opportunity. Before proceeding through the Canadian Rockies, they stopped at Banff, Alberta, to observe the travertine-forming algae in the sulfur springs; Eloise collected specimens of the algae in small bottles for posting to Frank Collins.[8] A week after leaving Minnesota, the group arrived in Vancouver and boarded a steamer for the city of Victoria, and took another through the Strait of Juan de Fuca to the logging town of Port Renfrew. This was followed by a difficult four-hour hike along a trail through the ancient cedars, moss-covered hemlocks, yews and giant ferns of the rain forest. The large Saratoga trunks some of the women had brought were delivered three days later via canoes paddled by Siwash Indians who "braved the surf."[9]

Upon arrival at the camp, the party found ready for occupany two log buildings facing the snow-capped Olympic mountains across the Strait of Juan de Fuca. There was a large two-story bunkhouse (dubbed "the Sea Palms") containing beds of spruce and balsam on the upper floor, with separate rooms for the men and women; below were quarters for cooking and dining, and a large assembly room with a stone fireplace. Microscopes and other laboratory equipment were set up there, as well as in the smaller building, called "the Formalose Club."

Daytime botanical work at the station focused primarily on the seaweeds, with every low tide bringing new discoveries. Josephine Tilden collected plants for inclusion in her own series of exsiccatae, *American Algae*, which she issued between 1894 and 1909.[10] Eloise Butler, with her friend Jessie Polley, set about collecting seaweeds for Collins. Seventy-five of the one hundred thirty-two species collected that summer by Butler and Polley are described in Collins' paper "The Marine Algae of Vancouver Island" published by the Canada Geological Survey in 1913. Many of them were also included in the *Phycotheca Boreali-Americana*; the rest of Butler and Polley's specimens went into Collins' personal herbarium, now owned by the New York Botanical Garden.[11]

The atmosphere of a holiday camp seems to have prevailed that first summer, rather than the regular schedule of courses and lectures that were instituted at the Seaside Station in later years. Impromptu lectures, took place along the tide pools and on the beach as the need arose; talks were given in the evenings around the fireplace. Josephine Tilden presented a paper on the five months in 1899 that she and Caroline Crosby had spent botanizing in the Hawaiian Islands; one evening, Eloise Butler shared tales of her adventures in seaweed collecting with Cora in Jamaica. These talks were later published in *Postelsia* (the scientific name of a palmlike kelp found on the rocks of the Vancouver coast), a yearbook of the Minnesota Seaside Station intended to be issued annually but which appeared only twice, in 1902 and 1906.[12]

Brochures for the station in later years advertised a "freedom and unconventionality which cannot be found at any of the Eastern laboratories."[13] Certainly the women were at ease, scrambling over the rocks wearing hob-nailed, high-topped bicycle shoes and relatively short skirts (twelve inches from the ground). As Josephine Tilden advised,

> "Good" clothes are not even desirable since the work is rough and one must be ready at all times during the day or evening for a tramp over the rocks or through the woods. Much of the

Tea party at the Minnesota Seaside Station, Vancouver Island, 1901. Eloise Butler standing behind the table (white blouse). Caroline Crosby is to her left, and Josephine Tilden is seated (in kimono) at the far left. *University of Minnesota Archives.*

restfulness comes from the absence of "competitive dressing."[14]

Social life at the camp featured clam bakes on the beach, skits based on "the mysterious and savage rites of the Hodag founded upon ancient Siwash superstitions," a Japanese tea party with Josephine Tilden and Caroline Crosby in kimonos, and a midnight ceremony of the Order of Energids, "held in a surf cavern on a stormy night," which dramatized the phenomenon of mitosis (cell division) in the plant and animal cell (Tilden and Crosby served as "Wardens of the Astrospheres").[15] It was an unforgettable trip for all who were there.

The Minnesota Seaside Station continued for six more years. Altogether, according to Josephine Tilden, more than two hundred biologists and graduate students attended the camp, and over ninety publications on algae resulted from their work there.[16] Despite the success and unique location of the station, the University of Minnesota regents ultimately refused to assume its sponsorship, reportedly because they felt it unwise to own land in a

foreign country. The regents ordered all books and microscopes belonging to the university returned after the 1906 season. Enraged, Conway MacMillan resigned from the university, moved to Philadelphia and is said to have gone into advertising. Josephine Tilden kept the station open for one more summer, then bitterly closed it for good in 1907.[17]

Tilden never forgave the university for failing to support the Seaside Station. The abandonment of her and MacMillan's "visionary project," according to phycologist Paul C. Silva at the University of California at Berkeley, caused the University of Minnesota to lose a "golden opportunity" to play a "key role in the development of phycology in the Pacific Northwest."[18] Nevertheless, Tilden had a long and productive career as a phycologist at the University of Minnesota. She made thirteen collecting trips, including five to the South Pacific, collecting and classifying algae from Hawaii, Tahiti, Australia and New Zealand in addition to those of Vancouver and Minnesota. She wrote numerous articles for scholarly and popular journals, published an illustrated monograph on the blue-green algae of North America (*Minnesota Algae*, 1910) and compiled an ambitious card index of the marine, freshwater, epiphytic and parasitic algae of the world (*Index Algarum Universalis*, 1915-1930).[19] Her textbook, *The Algae and Their Life Relations* (1935) was still widely used at her death in 1957. Tilden joined or was elected to many professional organizations, including the American Association for the Advance of Science (A.A.A.S.) and the Botanical Society of America. She was known for her advocacy of the wider use of seaweeds as food for the human race, and early on warned of the dangers of oil spills to marine life.

Like Butler, Josephine Tilden never married. She received an enormous amount of support from her mother, Mrs. Henry Tilden, who spent several evenings each week and Saturdays helping her at the Botany Department, and with whom Josephine lived. After her mother's death in 1919, Tilden moved in with her long-time traveling companion, master's student and laboratory assistant Caroline Crosby, and lived at Crosby's Minneapolis mansion for many years.[20]

Tilden never publicly acknowledged mentorship by Eloise Butler. While her announcement in 1896 that she wished to study marine algae had raised eyebrows in the land-locked midwestern university, it is not surprising in light of the interests and accomplishments of her first botany teacher, Eloise Butler. When asked by a journalist how she became interested in the algae, Tilden in her old age told a story about having been in Conway MacMillan's botany class and that, when MacMillan had found a kitten outside the zoology building, he walked over and dropped it into her lap. Thus, she implied, was her interest in algae born.[21] It is more likely that Tilden, in her determination to be respected as a scientist, felt she could not acknowledge the old-fashioned naturalist and "amateur," Eloise Butler, and preferred to attribute her start in botany to a professional—and male—university professor. The only comment Eloise Butler is known to have made on the matter, in describing the accomplishments of the high school botany teachers of Minneapolis, was that "several of our pupils chose botany as a major subject in

the university and are now known as specialists in the subject."[22]

Frederic King Butters, another former botany student of Butler, was also in attendance at that first session of the Minnesota Seaside Station. After graduating from Central High in 1895, Butters went on to graduate from the University of Minnesota, where he joined the faculty as a botany instructor in 1901. He obtained a doctorate at Harvard in 1917. While his later interests spanned a wide range of topics, Butters' early efforts, like Tilden's, were in the study of algae, with his first paper, "Observations on *Rhodymenia*," published in 1899.[23] At the Seaside Station, he served as the mock High Priest in the mythical Hodag cult and ferried microscopes in a dugout canoe from the steamer anchored offshore to the buildings of the station.[24]

Eloise Butler left no record of her impressions of the Seaside Station, other than to recall her sojourn there in 1901 as among the most memorable events of her life.[25] It must have been deeply rewarding to Butler to be surrounded by botany-loving friends and former students, encamped on a beach on the

Josephine Tilden, Professor of Botany at the University of Minnesota, 1926. *Minneapolis Public Library, Minnesota History Collection.*

wild coast of Vancouver with a fantastic array of seaweeds exposed by each low tide, and to be present at the founding, by her student Josephine Tilden, of the new Minnesota Seaside Station. No doubt these memories moved her, thirty years later, to include on a list of things she loved "mountains," "the boundless expanse of ocean," "a storm at sea," "high waves" and "tides."[26]

Her trip to the Minnesota Seaside Station appears to have marked the end of Eloise Butler's algae collecting period. With

professionalization of the science of botany much advanced, and new developments in the field occurring mainly among the younger generation trained in the graduate schools of academic institutions, Eloise may have wondered what further contribution an old-fashioned naturalist like herself might make. Wizened by her years of botanical observation, study and collecting, she may have felt, as once did Thoreau, ready to embark on some "great work," yet uncertain what that might be.

Notes

1 Sally Gregory Kohlstedt, "In from the Periphery: American Women in Science, 1830-1880," *Signs: Journal of Women in Culture and Society*, Vol. 4 (Autumn 1978), pp. 81-96 (82, 96). The mentoring of younger women scientists by older ones in the nineteenth century is "rarely recorded," according to Emmanuel Rudolph, "Women Who Studied Plants in the Pre-Twentieth Century United States and Canada," *Taxon*, Vol. 39 (May 1990), pp. 151-205 (204).

2 Josephine Tilden, "List of Fresh-Water Algae Collected in Minnesota During 1893," *Minnesota Botanical Studies*, Vol. 1, Part I (16 January 1894), pp. 25-31.

3 Josephine Tilden had planned to work for her Ph.D. at the British Museum, but her plans fell through when her traveling companion, Caroline Crosby, became ill. As Tilden wrote, "President Northrop finally persuaded [her] to begin the Pacific program at once," promising that if she did, he would see that she was made Professor of Botany (a title that she received in 1911), which would be "better than the Doctor's degree." Josephine Tilden biographical file, University of Minnesota Archives.

4 Clipping from *Minnesota Chats* (April 1937) in Josephine Tilden biographical file, University of Minnesota Archives.

5 Ibid.

6 "A Seaside Station—Botanical Department of the U. Plans to Open One on the West Coast of Vancouver Island," Minneapolis *Journal*, 26 January 1901 (Pt. II, p. 1).

7 Conway MacMillan, "Pacific Botanical Station," Minneapolis *Journal*, 18 May 1901. As Frank S. Collins wrote to William A. Setchell, "One has to scratch pretty close to find new marine algae in New England now." Frank S. Collins to William Setchell, 17 August 1900, in William Setchell Papers at University Herbarium, University of California at Berkeley.

8 Frank S. Collins to William A. Setchell, 12 January 1902, in William Setchell Papers, at University Herbarium, University of California at Berkeley.

9 The planned road to the station apparently was not completed. Accounts of the first season of the Minnesota Seaside Station are found in "Minnesota Botanists Study at the Seaside," Minneapolis *Journal*, 3 August 1901, p. 20; Conway MacMillan's "The Minnesota Seaside Station," *Popular Science Monthly*, Vol. 60 (January 1902), pp. 193-209; and "A Marine Biological Station on the Straits of Fuca," *The Journal of Geography*, Vol. 1 (June 1902), pp. 263-271. Station rules forbade trunks in subsequent years, and instead recommended the use of satchels or packsacks which could be portaged over the trail. An account of the season of 1904 is given in Charles Bessey's "Life in a Seaside Summer School," *Popular Science Monthly*, Vol. 67 (January 1905), pp. 80-89; other materials are in the Minnesota Seaside Station file, University of Minnesota Archives.

10 Josephine Tilden's *American Algae* was issued in sets of one hundred specimens each. Specimens in Century I (1894) were Minnesota algae; Century II (1896) were from Yellowstone Park, where Tilden spent the summer of 1894; Century III (1898) were from Utah, California and Washington; Century IV (1900) were from Washington and Vancouver Island; Century V (1901) were from Hawaii; Century VI were from Hawaii and Vancouver Island; Century VIIa were from Guatemala, Texas, and Minnesota. Tilden later issued a similar collection entitled *South Pacific Algae*, with specimens collected in Tahiti, Australia, and New Zealand. Josephine Tilden biographical file, University of Minnesota Archives.

11 Frank S. Collins, "The Marine Algae of Vancouver Island," *Victoria Memorial Museum Bulletin*, Vol. 1 (1913), pp. 99-137. As Collins

wrote to Setchell on 21 September 1901, "Miss Butler, who has contributed so many things from Jamaica, went to Vancouver the past summer with the Minneapolis crowd, and we shall have probably quite a number of sets as a result." A list of 132 species entitled "Algae collected by Miss E. Butler and Miss Jessie M. Polley, Minnesota Seaside Station, Vancouver, July 1901" in the handwriting of Frank S. Collins is in the William Setchell Papers at the University Herbarium, University of California at Berkeley. Butler is not known to have contributed any specimens to Tilden's *American Algae*; Tilden did not want her subscribers (who also bought Collins' sets) to have to "pay twice for the same thing." Josephine Tilden to Frank S. Collins, 28 February 1902, Frank S. Collins Papers, Library of the American Philosophical Society, Philadelphia.

12 *Postelsia, The Year Book of the Minnesota Seaside Station* (for 1901) (St. Paul: The *Pioneer Press*, 1902).

13 Minnesota Seaside Station, 1903 *Annual Announcement*, p. 4, University of Minnesota Archives.

14 Minnesota Seaside Station, 1905 *Annual Announcement*, pp. 10-11, University of Minnesota Archives.

15 Quotes from "Minnesota Botanists Study at the Seaside," Minneapolis *Journal*, 3 August 1901. The Energids ceremony and the Hodag rites are discussed in Sheri L. Bartlett, "The History of the Department of Botany, 1889-1989, University of Minnesota" (1990) copy at University of Minnesota Archives.

16 Clipping from *Minnesota Chats* (April 1937), in Josephine Tilden biographical file, University of Minnesota Archives.

17 Josephine Tilden to J. Islay Mutter, 24 November 1948, copy in Josephine Tilden biographical file, University of Minnesota Archives; "Conway MacMillan," in Harry B. Humphrey, *Makers of North American Botany* (New York: The Ronald Press Co., 1961), pp. 159-160. The tide pool shelf is still known locally as Botanical Beach, and is visited by marine biologists, students and tourists. A portion of the beach was purchased by the Nature Conservancy in 1983 and donated to the Canadian Government for a park; the rain forest has been clear-cut to within a mile of the beach. The moss-covered outlines of the buildings of the station are reportedly still visible, and an ancient cedar overlooking the beach bears a plaque commemorating the station. See Janet Pelley, "The Minnesota Seaside Station," James Ford Bell Museum of Natural History (University of Minnesota), *Imprint*, Vol. 2 (Spring 1985), pp. 5-7; information about the commemorative plaque courtesy of Penelope Krosch, University of Minnesota Archives.

18 Paul C. Silva to author, 17 January 1991.

19 Josephine Tilden, *Minnesota Algae*, Vol. 1 (the Myxophyceae of North America and adjacent regions including Central America, Greenland, Bermuda, the West Indies and Hawaii), (Minneapolis, 1910).

20 After her retirement in 1937, Josephine Tilden moved to Lake Wales, Florida, where she founded a colony for retired academics ("Hesperides," named after the garden in Greek mythology), began work on a book about her 1934 voyage around the world, and continued her botanical work until her death in 1957. See Josephine Tilden biographical file at University of Minnesota Archives. Tilden's interesting and unconventional life is certainly deserving of a biography. Caroline Crosby became known for her social work in Minneapolis, and several unmarried social welfare workers lived in her home; after her death in 1950, her heirs established a scholarship fund in her name at the University of Minnesota for students of botany. Letters from Tilden and Crosby to Frank S. Collins are in the Collins Papers at the Library of the American Philosophical Society in Philadelphia.

21 "Golden Bough Authoress Begins Work on Nine Books," *Lake Wales News*, Lake Wales, Florida, (c.1953), courtesy Janet Pelley.

22 Eloise Butler to Gray Memorial Botanical Chapter, Agassiz Association, Division D, June 1931, copy in Eloise Butler biography file, Minneapolis Public Library, Minneapolis Collection.

23 Frederic King Butters, "Observations on *Rhodymenia*," *Minnesota Botanical Studies*, Vol. 2 (29 December 1899), pp. 205-213.

24 More details of Butters' interesting life can be found in Ernst C. Abbe, "Frederic King Butters, 1878-1945," *Rhodora*, Vol. 50 (June 1948), pp. 133-144.

25 Eloise Butler to Gray Memorial Botanical Chapter, Agassiz Association, Division D, (c.1911), copy in *Eloise Butler Native Plant Reserve*, p. 1, at Minneapolis Public Library, Minneapolis Collection.

26 Eloise Butler to Gray Memorial Botanical Chapter, Agassiz Association, Division D, March 1931, copy in Eloise Butler biography file at Minneapolis Public Library, Minneapolis Collection.

February 22 , *1902*

Spent the morning with
Miss Lillie in Riverside Park.
Saw three flocks of evening
grosbeaks, one flock feeding
on maple fruits still attached
to the tree. The birds paid no
attention to us, so busily were
they engaged. Bluffs decked
with ice sheets and pillars
toward Spirogyra in pools
formed from a flowing
spring. Surface snow in some
places in forms of filmy
lace. Saw two ash trees covered with galls formed in
the flower buds, also an
interesting bird's nest made
of sprangly twigs resembling
a circlet of thorns. Thought
it might be the cedar waxwing's.
Beautiful day, clear and bright.
February is as pleasant as May.

stump, or rock and tree, by their pretty
trails. They evidently travel for adventure and to hear the news, as well as for
food. They know that the foxes and
owls are about, and they keep pretty
close to cover."

Lastly, there is a group of common little animals that avoid the ills and famine
of winter by hibernation. Such are the
bats in caves, hollow trees, and garrets;
certain of the mice, like the jumping deer
mouse; and especially the woodchuck or
ground-hog, who retires to his grass-lined
underground chamber early in the fall
and rarely is seen until March.

There is, perhaps, no reason why a bird
should not be able to pass the winter in
dormancy as well as a mouse or a bat, but
as a matter of fact none does, most of
them migrating each autumn to the
warmer South. Nevertheless, we in the
colder parts of the country are not left
without the companionship of these most
delightful of our out-door friends, in regard to which I shall have an opportunity
to speak again at the close of the year.

"Sunny hill-sides," as I wrote once,
"the wooded banks of creeks, the hedge-
rows and brier-grown fences along the
country roads, are all favorite places for
the winter birds. Here come the sparrows and finches, the winter wren and
rare cardinal, skulking about the thickets,
hopping through the dead fern brakes,
threading the mazy passages of the log

February 23   Each day, clear, cloudy, or stormy, and
each season has its charm, if our eyes are
opened to see it.

Heard to day a very sweet bird note and
was surprised to find it come from the English
sparrow. 1903:— At Minnehaha, Feb. 22nd.
Saw crows, nuthatches, brown creepers,
chickadees, blue jays, red squirrels. Saw
real bladder nut (Staphylea)
shrubs in the glen. A lovely day.

A page from Eloise Butler's diary. *Minnesota Historical Society.*

7

The Quiet Years

Yellow Violet

THE SIX YEARS THAT PASSED between Eloise Butler's trip to the Minnesota Seaside Station and her founding of the Minneapolis Wild Botanic Garden were outwardly quiet ones. Her days were ordered by the rhythm of the school calendar, with regular visits to her sister's household during the summer months. Entries in a diary kept by Eloise in 1902 and 1903 offer a rare glimpse of her activities in those years. The diary consists of notes made in her sharp, rapid scrawl in the wide margins of a book entitled *Nature's Calendar*, designed for use as a record of observations of natural history. Eloise Butler did not commit to paper intimate details of her personal life; she despised "idle curiosity" and valued her privacy. Nevertheless, the diary offers a fascinating, if brief, record of the observations of a devoted naturalist in search of a new focus for her collecting passion. Perhaps it would be birds.

Eloise wrote her first entry on February 22, 1902:

> Spent the morning with Miss Lillie [a Minneapolis teacher] in Riverside Park. Saw three flocks of evening grosbeaks, one flock feeding on maple fruits still attached to the tree—The birds paid no attention to us, so busily were they engaged—Bluffs decked with ice sheets and pillars. Found *Spirogyra* [a filamentous pond algae] in pools formed from a flowing spring. Surface snow in some places in forms of filmy lace. Saw two ash trees covered with galls formed in the flower buds, also an interesting bird's nest made of sprangly [sic] twigs resembling a circlet of thorns. Thought it might be the cedar waxwing's. Beautiful day, clear and bright. February "is as pleasant as May."[1]

The next day she wrote:

> Each day, clear, cloudy, or stormy, and each season has its charm, if our eyes are opened to see it. Heard today a very sweet bird note and was surprised to find it came from the English [house] sparrow.

Eloise, often accompanied by her friend "Miss Lillie," went on many birding outings in the spring of 1902. They took the streetcar to St. Paul to visit Indian mounds, as well as to Como Park; the parks of Minneapolis, including Riverside, Washburn (along Minnehaha Creek between Lyndale and Nicollet Avenues) and Minnehaha were favorite destinations, as was Lake Calhoun. A

THE WILD GARDENER

typical entry is dated March 8, 1902:

> Spent the morning with Miss Lillie at Minnehaha. The buds of the red-berried elder begin to show their green. Elm flower buds are visibly swelling. Heard the crows cawing and saw them flying. A red squirrel chattered angrily at us—Found his nest, a hole in the ground between the roots of a butternut tree. The ground about the nest was strewn with fully two quarts of butternut shells. Each nut had one side broken away, with mathematical precision, the central partition remaining intact. Knocked down what we supposed to be a waxwing's nest, shavings of bark, strings and rags were woven into it —

Eloise noted on March 18 that she was enjoying reading *Idle Days in Patagonia* (London, 1893), an account by the English naturalist William Henry Hudson of his travels in the Argentine pampas, and observations of the brilliantly colored birds found there. March 24 was the occasion of a visit to local ornithologist Dr. Thomas Roberts' home to see his "large collection of Minnesota birds"; Eloise noted that she "spent most of the time on the sparrows and warblers." On another visit, May 12, 1902, she wrote: "While looking at the collection of Minn[esota] birds in Dr. Roberts' attic, we heard the shrill shriek of the night-hawk, and looking out of the window saw him on the flat roof of a neighboring house."[2] An entry for March 28 conveys the delight she took in watching birds:

> A robin stood on the door mat of my boarding-house piazza this morning. I watched him from the sidewalk until someone opened the door. He changed his mind about making a call and flew to the nearest tree—Went to Como again. Saw from the car a flock of tree sparrows. We sat on a bench in the sun at the park—a fox sparrow perched on a tree close by and burst into his wonderful song. Observed him carefully through the glass. He is rightly named, for his tail is fox red—a moment after a phoebe favored us in like manner—what a dear little quakeress she is. Got a splendid view of a bluebird standing in a path—What a wonderful blue it is! Saw several mourning cloak butterflies—Went on to Minnehaha. The air was full of minute insects—a kingfisher sounded his hoarse rattle, flew across the creek, settled on a fence post, gazing steadily into the water. We stayed there

15 minutes, and left him still watching for his prey.

As did many botanists, Eloise owned a Wardian case, a closed glass container designed for growing plants indoors, and often used it for observations of living flora. She noted on April 8, 1902:

> Collected March 29 Hair-cap moss with the antheridial hinds just forming—Planted them in my Wardian case. They were nicely developed today, the spermatozoids in full activity. Found in some pond stuff collected at Washburn Park a quantity of Cyclops, the females having but *one* large egg mass attached to the abdomen, instead of the usual paired egg masses.

On May 3, 1902, Eloise and her friend took a train to the Spring Park station and walked two miles to the Chapman House, a resort on Lake Minnetonka, to begin a week's vacation. In her diary she wrote:

> Saw on the way prothonotary warblers and lark sparrows. At the Mounds, the flicker, red-headed woodpecker, hairy woodpecker, loon, chipping sparrow, robin, purple martin, bluebird, Baltimore oriole, catbird, cowbird, phoebe, red-winged blackbird with the brown streaked female, rusty blackbird (female plain slate color), myrtle warbler, yellow warbler, great bittern, crow, vulture, hawk, belted kingfisher, English sparrow, white throated sparrow, [and] song sparrow. The English sparrows are fortunately few in number—The Mounds are beautifully situated, and abound in leafy coverts for the birds, and the roadsides, fields, meadows and the great lake each yield a harvest.

Crane Island was visited the next day:

> We rowed two miles to Crane Island, the great heronry of this part of the world—The island is the sole abode of the great blue herons and the hooded cormorants—The trees covered with the nests [are] like large brown flower clusters. The movements of the herons are ludicrous when settling on their perch—They seem to have some difficulty in managing their long legs—While the birds are sitting on the nest, the males (I suppose) sit on the end of the branch containing the nest as sentinels, rigid as graven images. It is said to be dangerous to visit the island when there are young birds. The old birds fly upon intruders and peck out their eyes.

By the end of the week's stay, wrote Eloise on May 11, she had seen "in all 81 species of birds—This makes nearly a hundred that I have seen since I began the Calendar."

On another visit to the Chapman House a few weeks later, Eloise watched a redstart beginning to build a nest, and found a yellow warbler's nest as well. An entry dated June 1, 1902, shows Eloise to be a dedicated birder:

Raining hard, but I went into the woods—It was my last day here, and I wanted to see how the nests were coming on. The redstart's nest was fully completed, and beautifully built—I thought it would take longer to construct it—The yellow warbler's nest had four eggs in it, proving that the bird lays an egg each day—The eggs were white, and covered with spots, with a wreath of spots around the larger end . . .

Eloise knew the mushrooms as well as the higher plants, and her records reveal many occasions on which she found and feasted on delicious varieties. Her entry of June 1 concludes:

Found a large quantity—all I could carry—of oyster mushrooms growing on a stump, great white over-lapping shell-like growth—Had them cooked for supper—They were very nice.

On another occasion, her taste for mushrooms attracted unwanted attention. As she wrote on May 20, 1902:

I espied today a quantity of mushrooms growing around the base of a tree [by the] side of the street. I inverted my open umbrella and filled it nearly full—Was nearly a block away when I heard some one running and calling behind me, "O, Missus, you're not going to eat those mushrooms are you? They're poison—A lady saw you picking them and told me to tell you not to eat them!" I told the breathless maid that I surely should eat them, and said impressively, "I know them. They are fine specimens of *Coprinus Micaceus.*" I had gone but little farther when another scene took place—I saw an unfamiliar bird fly to a nest, and a robin drive it away. Trying to make out the bird, I stepped from the sidewalk onto a lawn and stood peering into the trees—I heard a commotion but paid no attention, so intent was I on the bird—When the bird was out of sight, I found that a little [black] girl had been shrieking to me with all her might to get off the grass.

An entry of two days later recalls her visit to Minnetonka and reveals how birding was often done in the days before the availability of good binoculars and color-illustrated field guides:

While at Minnetonka I was one day alone in a wood in a rain storm. Espied two cowbirds sitting together on a branch. When they saw me, they began to fly around me in a large circle of which I was the center. They were joined by a third. This they kept up for some little time making a sound very much like sleigh bells. At Lake of the Isles to-day, a man driving past noticed my opera glasses, [and] got out of his carriage, bringing to me a bird to look at, which he had just shot. He judged from my glasses that I was studying birds. It was a female indigo bird—it resembles the male only in form and carriage, and a dark streak in the middle of its under bill. Its underparts are light gray, the back brownish; the tail has a peculiar grayish, greenish-blue tint.

Eloise made regular entries in the diary for a period of sixteen months. To celebrate Thanksgiving Day in 1902 she went sailing on Lake Calhoun with Charles Hibbard, photographer for the botany department at the University of Minnesota who had attended the 1901 session of the Minnesota Seaside Station, and his wife. "The wind was fresh," wrote Eloise, "but it was great fun, and a memorable event on account of the lateness of the season." Other entries noted "innumerable blue birds" at Como Park in St. Paul on March 21, 1903; her rapture at the "most wonderful song" of the chewink (rufous-sided towhee), "an indescribable, joyous bird medley"; and many other observations of bird and animal life.[3] Only once did Eloise lift her gaze from the natural world, to take note of the supernatural, in an entry dated April 9, 1903:

Attended this evening a materialization séance. Some seventeen or more ghosts, all sizes and shapes, dressed in gauzy white, except one man who appeared in officer's uniform. Some dissolved in air and seemed to sink through the floor—Spoke in a husky whisper—Wonderful, if a fake, more wonderful still, if not.

Butler's regular entries in the diary ceased abruptly in June of 1903. Perhaps she simply lost interest in recording the names of all of the birds that she saw, or sadness in her personal life may have intervened. The years before the garden were marked by the deaths of Eloise's father and of her dear friend Sarah Brackett. The death of Oliver Butler in Colorado on November 7, 1902, came soon after a late summer's visit to Maine by Eloise and Cora; her diary fails to mention whether Eloise attended her father's funeral in Denver. By the fall of 1904, Sarah Brackett, who had been ailing for some time with heart disease, was so troubled by ill health that she had to leave her teaching position at Sumner School. She remained with Eloise at the apartment they shared on Portland Avenue—what burden of care Eloise must have assumed can only be imagined—until a year later when, suffering from partial paralysis, Sarah returned to Maine to the home of her brother to be cared for by her mother and sisters until her death on September 18, 1906.

After Sarah's death, Eloise moved into the home of Eugenia Wheeler Goff, an accomplished maker of historical maps and a former normal-school teacher, on Clinton Avenue. Her energies no longer absorbed in caring for and worrying over Sarah, and perhaps to occupy her grieving mind, Eloise began actively working to realize her vision of making a public garden of Minnesota wild plants. She had been dreaming of such a garden for years.

Who can say when the idea for the garden first germinated in the mind of Eloise Butler? The thought of having a garden of any sort must have seemed, for most of her adult life, an impossibility; her teacher's salary was never enough to enable her to purchase land. Cora had a garden filled with wildflowers, tangled vines, and untrimmed shrubbery at her home in Malden, to which Eloise sent many plants from Minnesota. Her visits to "Wild Corner," as Cora's home was called, must have left Eloise yearning for a garden of her own to tend.

The practice known as "wild gardening" had originated in England in the nineteenth century. Eloise would have read *The Wild Garden* by the popular British garden writer William Robinson, first published in 1870 and reprinted many times. The book recommended the abandonment of formal beds of annuals in favor of "wild gardens" comprised of naturalistic plantings of hardy native and exotic perennial flowers, shrubs and trees. It contained a chapter advocating the use of native wildflowers and trees not commonly grown in gardens. Plants in a wild garden, wrote Robinson, were "more charming than any [formal] garden denizen" and were "usually surrounded by some degree of graceful wild spray—the green above, and the moss or grass around." And the wild garden, wherein plants were said to "flourish without further care or cost," supposedly required less labor than the formal garden.[4]

The English garden writer Gertrude Jekyll approved of Robinson's suggestions but urged caution in wild gardening, lest the countryside become spoiled and overrun by carelessly placed and out-of-place hardy exotics. "No kind of gardening," she wrote in her *Wood and Garden* (1899), "is so difficult to do well, or is so full of pitfalls and of paths of peril." Jekyll, who possessed a remarkable sensitivity to color harmony, preferred the use of native plants, lest a "hillside already sufficiently and beautifully clothed with native vegetation be made to look lamentably silly by the planting of a nurseryman's mixed lot of exotic Conifers."[5]

The idea of a public wild garden in Minneapolis took shape against the background of a growing movement in America for wilderness preservation. Among the earliest voices raised for the cause had been those of Henry David Thoreau and George Perkins Marsh, author of the classic *Man and Nature* (1864). Eloise may have read John Muir's impassioned accounts, published in eastern newspapers in the 1870s, of the Sierra Nevada mountains; by 1890, due largely to Muir's efforts, 1,500 square miles of the Sierras were brought within the protection of Yosemite National Park. Two years later, the Sierra Club was born.[6] Another important figure in the movement was Charles Sprauge Sargent, director of the Arnold Arboretum in Boston, which Eloise often visited and greatly admired. Sargent called for forest protection, as did the writer Aldo Leopold. The succession of Theodore Roosevelt to the Presidency in 1901 brought the first conservationist into the White House; during his seven and one-half years there, Roosevelt created fifty-three wildlife preserves by executive order.[7]

In Minnesota, too, a call for forest conservation was heard toward the end of the nineteenth century, over the din of sawmills which had turned millions of acres of pine forest into so many board feet of lumber for the rapidly developing state. A leader in the cause of forest management was Minnesotan Christopher Columbus Andrews, who, while serving as United States Minister to Sweden in the 1870s, became convinced of the importance of "perpetual forests."[8] Itasca State Park was created in 1891, and, after extensive campaigning by Andrews, Maria Sanford and the Minnesota Federation of Women's Clubs (among others), the Minnesota (now Chippewa) National Forest was established in 1902.

Naturalists of the late nineteenth century were alarmed by the reduction or entire disappearance of many species of native plants from the woodlands of the eastern United States. An occasional editorial appeared in the newspapers of New England urging citizens to refrain from purchasing mayflowers (trailing arbutus) in Boston streets in the spring or to refrain from gathering holly and mountain laurel at Christmastime. Maidenhair and other ferns were dug wholesale in the countryside for sale to florists in large cities for use in bouquets. While vegetation quickly covered the sides of newly cut roads and the disturbed ground around buildings, it was not the delicate native bog and woodland plants that grew but rather the more vigorous and aggressive alien species from Europe which took their place. In Minneapolis, Eloise Butler and the other botany teachers found themselves forced to travel increasingly long distances in order to acquaint their students with the native flora, especially the orchids and other bog plants fast disappearing under the spread of development.

Eloise Butler (left) and friends studying a natural graft in Glenwood (now Theodore Wirth) Park, c. 1900.
Minneapolis Public Library, Minneapolis Collection.

Eloise Butler's sister provided her with a model of a conservationist in action. Cora was a zealous advocate of wildflower preservation; she had been active in the movement in the 1880s, led by Boston businessman Elizur Wright, to establish a forest preserve in the Middlesex Fells in Malden. The ancient hemlocks that she and Eloise had sought in 1881, according to her "Treasures of the Fells," had been cut down for lumber by 1890, wrote Cora in her article "Lost Treasures of the Fells"; a rubber factory had been built on a marsh where the fringed gentian once grew. The 2,000-acre Middlesex Fells Reservation was made part of the Boston metropolitan park system in 1894; it included about half of the "Five Mile Wood" in which Cora and Eloise had botanized.[9]

Clubs for the protection of wildflowers and other native plants existed in Europe and formed in America around the turn of the century. A club called L'Association pour la Protection des Plantes had been founded in Switzerland in 1883, and alpine wildflower gardens existed in Switzerland, Austria and Germany prior to 1900. The movement in America gained momentum when Dr. William Trelease, Director of the Missouri Botanical Gardens at St. Louis, called for the protection of native plants and the organization of societies for that purpose in an address before the American Association for the Advancement of Science at New York in June 1900.

Two groups organized on the east coast: the Society for the Protection of Native Plants in Boston in 1900 and the Wild Flower Preservation Society of America in New York in 1902. The Boston group was comprised of several Harvard botanists as well as members of the Boston Society of Natural History. Its notices and minutes were published in the botanical journals *Rhodora* and *Plant World*.[10] The Wild Flower Preservation Society of America, led by the well-known botanist Elizabeth Knight Britton and her husband, Dr. Nathaniel Lord Britton, director of the New York Botanical Garden, was the more active and long-lived of the two groups.

Elizabeth Britton was largely responsible for the national momentum of the American wildflower preservation movement in the early twentieth century. She was the leading authority on mosses of the United States and the West Indies and author of over three

Elizabeth Knight Britton (1858-1934). *Library of the New York Botanical Garden, Special Collections, Bronx, New York.*

Both of the American groups had similar goals: to educate the public about the need for conservation; to prevent the rapid extermination of wildflowers through excessive picking and digging of rare plants by picnickers, children, and nurserymen; and to urge the passage of laws protecting certain specified wildflowers that were in danger of extinction. Concern was expressed about the destruction of native flora by city expansion, although little would be done to address the problem. The Boston group, although short-lived (it became inactive some time after 1906), presciently called for "the setting apart, for the public, of spots of woodland, where natural conditions can be maintained." Not until 1920 did the Wild Flower Preservation Society of America (the Washington D.C. chapter) begin to urge the establishment of such preserves.[13]

It is not a great leap from the idea of a preserve to the idea of a garden, where desired plants are deliberately introduced. As a botanist, Eloise was, of course, familiar with botanic gardens, collections of living plants grown for some useful or educational purpose. The earliest known European botanic gardens, established in Italy in the 16th century, contained medicinal plants described in the ancient herbals. Numerous botanic gardens, usually associated with colleges and universities, had existed in the United States since the mid-eighteenth century, when John Bartram developed an extensive collection of native and exotic plants on his farm on the Schuylkill River (now in Philadelphia). The plants in botanic gardens were typically grown in conservatories or arranged in outdoor formal beds laid out according to their classifications. Some had native plant sections; besides Bartram's (which eventually contained many exotics acquired by exchange abroad), one such garden was established by botanist Lydia White Shattuck at Mount Holyoke College in South Hadley, Massachusetts. During her tenure there (1851-1889), Shattuck developed an outstanding herbarium and planted many native wild plants of the area, collected on her excursions into the surrounding countryside, in a botanical garden near the science building. Shattuck had attended Louis Agassiz's Penikese Island school along with Butler's normal school teacher Helen Coffin in 1873, was a co-founder (with Maria Owen) of the Connecticut Valley Botanical Association, and was a member of

hundred botanical papers. From 1901 until her death in 1934, she organized numerous chapters of the Wild Flower Preservation Society of America (incorporated in 1915), lectured tirelessly on wildflower preservation, and authored thirty-two articles on the subject. Also among the founders of Britton's group was Eloise Butler's former botany teacher, Charles E. Bessey, who served as president of the association from 1904 until 1907.[11]

Eloise Butler kept abreast of activities of the two groups through their notices and minutes which were carried in the natural history journals, as well as her personal connections. She appears not to have been an official member of either group except for a brief period in the 1920s when she helped found a Minnesota chapter of the Wild Flower Preservation Society of America, Inc. (see chapter 9). At least one Boston acquaintance, her sister's friend Cora H. Clarke, was a member of the Boston Society for the Protection of Native Plants. Cora Clarke won second prize in the first annual essay competition sponsored by the Caroline and Olivia Phelps Stokes Fund for the Preservation of Native Plants at the New York Botanical Garden in 1902 with her essay "New Missionary Work."[12]

the Woods Hole Biological Laboratory Corporation; Butler may have known of, and perhaps even visited, Shattuck's garden.[14]

Some unnamed visionary in Minneapolis, perhaps Eloise Butler herself, had proposed the establishment of a botanic garden within the city park system in the year 1898. The park board maintained a zoological garden of sorts at Minnehaha Falls, and, it was urged, "the wonders of the vegetable world are as great and numerous and as important in education as those of animal nature." The proposal was poorly received; William Folwell, president of the Board of Park Commissioners, was wary of the expense such an institution would require. He felt that it was a more fitting project for the state university and declared:

> For the immediate future, it will be sufficient if along with our little collection of animals, kept as mere park attractions, there be gathered and maintained examples of exotic plants for the primary purpose of park decoration and incidentally to instruct."[15]

No more was heard by the Board of Park Commissioners on the matter of botanic gardens until April 1, 1907, when the board received a formal petition asking that it set aside a portion of the large, undeveloped Glenwood Park on the city's west side for a "natural Botanical Garden for the instruction of students of botany and for the enjoyment of all lovers of nature." William Folwell had been replaced as president of the Park Board by Jesse Northrup the previous January. The new Swiss-born park superintendent, Theodore Wirth, had been on the job barely a year and was not likely to object to the plan, so long as it did not divert funds from improvements at the city's lakes and the grand boulevards being constructed around them. Just as Charles Sprague Sargent and Frederick Law Olmsted had resorted to a petition drive to sway the Boston city council when their plan for city support of the Arnold Arboretum had faltered, so, during the winter of 1906-1907, had Eloise Butler lined up support for a proposal she intended to make to the Minneapolis Park Board. Drawing upon the principles of forest conservation and wildflower preservation, she had combined them in a novel way with her own passion for plant collecting and wild gardening and conceived the idea for a wild botanic garden of Minnesota plants. And she knew just the right place for the garden.[16]

Notes

1 Eloise Butler, *Diary*, 22 February 1902 (written in pages of Ernest Ingersoll, *Nature's Calendar* [New York: Harper & Brothers, 1900]) in Eloise Butler Papers at Minnesota Historical Society. "Miss Lillie" may have been any of four women listed in the Minneapolis *City Directory* for 1902-1903, three of whom were teachers. It was common for women friends to address one another by their title "Miss" or "Mrs." and last name in the nineteenth and early twentieth centuries.

2 Dr. Thomas Roberts (1858-1946) graduated from Central High School in 1877, the year before Butler began teaching there. In 1902 he was obstetrician and pediatrician to the prominent families of the Twin Cities (Caroline Crosby was among his patients). Roberts curtailed his medical practice in 1915 to teach ornithology at the University of Minnesota and by 1919 was director of the zoology museum (now the James Ford Bell Museum of Natural History). His beautifully-illustrated work, *The Birds of Minnesota* (1932), is considered a classic. See *Shotgun and Stethoscope: Journals of T. Sadler Roberts* (1991), Penelope Krosch, ed., Bell Museum of Natural History.

3 Eloise Butler, *Diary*, 11 July 1902.

4 William Robinson, *The Wild Garden, or the Naturalization and Natural Grouping of Hardy Exotic Plants with a Chapter on the Garden of British Wild Flowers*, 4th ed. (London: John Murray, 1894), p. 4.

5 Gertrude Jekyll, *Wood and Garden: Notes and Thoughts, Practical and Critical, of a Working Amateur* (London: Green & Co., 1899), p. 269. For a discussion of nineteenth-century landscaping and garden design see Christopher Thacker, *The History of Gardens* (Berkeley: University of California Press, 1979), pp. 248-251, 263-265.

6 The nature writers of the late nineteenth century are described in Paul Brooks, *Speaking for Nature: How Literary Naturalists from Henry Thoreau to Rachel Carson Have Shaped America* (Boston: Houghton Mifflin Co., 1980).

7 Stephen Fox, *John Muir and his Legacy: The American Conservation Movement* (Boston: Little, Brown & Co., 1981), p. 129.

8 For an account of early forest conservation in Minnesota see Theodore C. Blegen's *Minnesota, A History of the State* (Minneapolis: University

of Minnesota Press, 1963), pp. 404-407 (404); and Christopher C. Andrews *Recollections: 1829-1922* (Cleveland: The Arthur H. Clark Co., 1928), pp. 293-294.

9   Cora E. Pease, "The Lost Treasures of the Fells," Boston *Evening Transcript*, clipping dated 20 January 1890, in scrapbook owned by Martha P. Pease. A history of the Fells is Ellen Levin and Thomas Mahlstedt's *Middlesex Fells Reservation Historical Land-Use Study*, Cultural Resource Management Study Series No. 1 (Metropolitan District Commission, Boston, Massachusetts, 1990).

10 See "Meeting of the Society for the Protection of Native Plants," *Plant World*, Vol. 9 (May 1906), pp. 119-121. Eloise Butler (as do modern conservationists) preferred the term "native plants" because it includes all species.

11 See Percy L. Ricker, "A History of the Wild Flower Preservation Movement," Part I, *Wild Flower*, Vol. 14 (April 1937), pp. 26-30; Part II, *Wild Flower*, Vol. 14 (July 1937), pp. 49-53; and C. Stuart Gager, "Elizabeth G. Britton and the Movement for the Preservation of Native American Wild Flowers," *Wild Flower*, Vol. 17 (July 1940), pp. 135-140. The July 1940 issue of *Wild Flower* was designated a memorial issue for Britton (1858-1934).

12 Cora H. Clarke, "New Missionary Work," *The Journal of the New York Botanical Garden*, Vol. 3 (1902), pp. 62-69.

13 "Meeting of the Society for the Protection of Native Plants," p. 119; Percy L. Ricker, "Methods and Aims in Protecting Wild Flowers," *Wild Flower*, Vol. 17 (July 1940), pp. 123-128 (126).

14 Bartram's garden is described in D. Roger Mower, Jr., "Bartram's Garden: Where it all began in Philadelphia," American Association of Botanical Gardens and Arboreta, *Bulletin*, Vol. 19 (January 1985), pp. 20-24; Lydia Shattuck's botanical garden is mentioned in *Notable American Women 1607-1950* (Cambridge, Mass.: The Belknap Press of Harvard University Press, 1971), pp. 273-274. (I am grateful to Beatrice Scheer Smith for calling Shattuck's garden to my attention.) Early American botanic gardens are discussed in U.P. Hedrick, *A History of Horticulture in America to 1860* (Portland: Timber Press, 1988 reprint edition), pp. 421-430. On the role of the botanic garden as a conservator of biodiversity (in the form of germplasm), see V.H. Heywood, "The Changing Role of the Botanic Garden," *Botanic Gardens and the World Conservation Strategy* (London: Academic Press, 1987), pp. 5-18. An "American Garden" installed by landscape architect Jens Jensen existed in the 1890s in Union Park in Chicago; the garden was comprised of trees, shrubs and beds of herbaceous plants native to the Chicago area. Other early American advocates of landscaping with native plants were Warren Manning and Ossian Cole Simonds. I am grateful to Bonnie Harper-Lore and Robert Griese for calling my attention to their work.

15 Quotes from President William W. Folwell's address to the Minneapolis Board of Park Commissioners, *Sixteenth Annual Report*, 1898, p. 21.

16 Quote from 1911 petition in Eloise Butler file, Minneapolis Park and Recreation Board Archives. A similar, but unsuccessful, attempt was made in St. Paul at about the same time to save Battle Creek Park as a "botanical preserve," according to Marion Gold, who wrote: "The contrast between what has been done in Minneapolis and the destruction wrought since in Battle Creek Park speaks for itself." Marion Gold, "A Wilderness Sanctuary," *Minnesota Conservationist*, No. 35 (April 1936), pp. 4-5 (5).

8

The Wild Botanic Garden

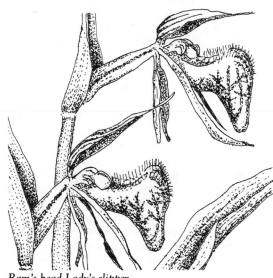

Ram's-head Lady's-slipper

IF EARTH IS A LIVING BEING, as the Gaia hypotheses suggest, then surely water—of oceans, rivers, lakes, ponds and springs—is a medium of contact between the human sphere and Gaia. The bit of earth upon which Eloise Butler chose to bestow her protection had a long watery history, having been submerged first on the floor of a vast prehistoric ocean for millenia, and later in the bedrock valley of a rushing tributary of the ancient river that we call, in its present location several miles to the east, the Mississippi. The terrain of the bedrock valley was completely altered ten thousand years before by the deposit of more than two hundred feet of glacial drift which, contoured by enormous, slowly melting blocks of ice left behind by the last retreating glacier, gave the land its present "knob and kettle" topography.[1]

The tamarack bog that evolved in one depression among the hills was no different, centuries ago, from millions of acres of wetlands that stretched across the land beyond the limits of an eagle's sight. The birds that visited on their annual migrations and the wild animals—bear and mastodon, beaver, otter and deer—shared the land with small bands of aboriginal people who hunted and drank freely of the clear, cool ground water that flowed out of the many natural springs. The gods of the Dakota Indians, descendants of the early aborigines, endowed all of nature with "medicine." Spirits resided in rocks, trees, winds, streams, and in the Great Medicine Spring near the bog, a few miles west of the city of the white settlers which grew up around the sacred falls of St. Anthony.[2]

In the summer of the year 1851, the Dakota tribes signed the Treaties of Traverse des Sioux and Mendota which ceded most of what is now southern Minnesota to the United States government. The ceded land included the Great Medicine Spring and the nearby tamarack bog which lay nearly a mile outside the northwestern boundary of the Fort Snelling reservation. The government surveyor who walked the section lines in the vicinity of the bog two years later found "heavy timber" of elm, linden, ironwood, bur and black (red) oak with undergrowth of oak and hazel thickets to the east and "thinly planted" stands of bur and black oak, linden, aspen and elm on rolling, "second-rate" soil to the south and west. To the north he found more tamarack, osier (willow), and nettles. The

65

Eloise Butler in the early 1900s. *Martha P. Pease.*

swamps he pronounced "unfit for cultivation." In closing his report, the surveyor noted that "the land in this Township is all claim[ed] some of it by at least ½ dozen claimants."[3]

Killian and Eva Schickling, recently naturalized immigrants from Bavaria who had spent six years in Ohio before heading west, were the first settlers to lay claim to eighty acres of rolling hills, spongy meadows and marshes west of the John Halloran farm and just southeast of a wagon trail that passed between Highland Lake and the Great Medicine Spring on its way to Fort Ripley. The parcel contained the tamarack bog, nearly encircled by high hills in its northwest corner; between the north end of the bog and the trail lay wet meadows and more tamarack.

According to an affidavit signed with an "X" and filed in support of their claim by their son Frederick, the Schicklings and their six children had taken possession of the land on April 22, 1855, by erecting a "log building 15 x 20 feet in size, double pitch bark roof, board floor nailed down, one door and one glazed window." They had fenced and planted about five acres in crops that summer, swore

the son, thus fulfilling the requirements for making a preemption claim. On August 12, 1855, upon payment of one hundred dollars ($1.25 per acre), Killian Shickling received a certificate entitling him to a patent for the land.[4] Within thirty days, the Schicklings sold the parcel; the rapid sale suggests that the "settlers" may have participated in a sham transaction on behalf of investors interested in the property (such schemes were common when the lands acquired in 1853 were first opened for sale). The property changed hands several times during the next decade. By 1867 the original price had quintupled, when the parcel was acquired by Samuel and Susan Gale.[5]

Samuel Gale was a lawyer who had come to Minneapolis from Massachusetts in 1857. Active in civic affairs, he was among the founders of the Academy of Science, the Minneapolis Society of Fine Arts, and the Athanaeum, and served on the School Board. Gale ran a real estate office and made a fortune in land speculation, buying and selling choice parcels in the path of city expansion. It mattered nothing to Gale that the land was unfit for cultivation, for he had house lots in mind, and bogs were easily filled; the rolling hills and nearness to Cedar Lake would make the property desirable to those seeking the cleaner air and slower pace away from the center of town. In 1883, Gale's and neighboring property joined the city of Minneapolis as Saratoga Springs Addition in the same annexation that brought in Cedar Lake, Lake Calhoun, Lake Harriet and Lake of the Isles; two years later, Gale sold out to developer Thomas W. Wilson for forty thousand dollars. No doubt the proceeds helped defray the cost of the elegant stone mansion that the Gales built soon after on Central (now Loring) Park.[6]

As once the bog had been no different from many others in Minneapolis, now it was slated to share the fate of all the rest, its waters drained, its graceful tamaracks felled and sawed into telegraph poles and fenceposts, and its delicate flora replaced with sod and pavement. The land was surveyed once again and platted into narrow house lots and streets to be named Florence Avenue and Aonian Avenue. Twenty-seven lots occupied the heart of the bog; Abbott Avenue would cut a wide swath through the marsh and meadows toward Keegan's (formerly Highland) Lake to the north. Lots sold rapidly, many to out-of-state investors. The city's insatiable hunger for land was well on its way toward devouring these particular wooded hills and bog when action by the Minneapolis Park Board in February 1889 brought development to an abrupt halt.

A group of residents in the city's Fourth Ward petitioned the board to purchase land in the Saratoga Springs Addition for use as a park. The land included a pond ringed with birches, called Devil's Glen (later Birch Pond), and the tamarack bog to the northeast. The petitioners, whose property adjoined the proposed park, offered to bear the cost of the land themselves. The fledgling Park Board, only six years old and perennially strapped for acquisition funds, eagerly accepted the offer and arranged for the purchase of sixty-four acres between Western Avenue and Superior Avenue (now Glenwood Avenue and Interstate Highway 394) for the sum of $100,000, payable in annual assessments of the benefitted property over ten years.[7] The new park was at first called Saratoga Park; its name was changed after a year to Glenwood Park.

Little was done by way of improvements to Glenwood Park in the early years, save laying a roadway connecting Western and Superior Avenues to provide access, and a bit of mowing and clearing of brush by a part-

Eloise Butler botanizing in the Quaking Bog, in Glenwood (now Theodore Wirth) Park in 1911. *Minneapolis Public Library, Minneapolis Collection.*

time parkkeeper. The land remained undisturbed as the onrush of development simply split where the park lay in its path like an island in a stream and pushed westward beyond. The wild park was an oasis for the birds and animals that fled the surrounding woods being cut and wetlands being drained and filled; an oasis, too, for nature lovers and botany teachers who found that it abounded in wild plants once present throughout the area and which now could be found only in far-outlying prairies and bogs. After 1891, when a streetcar line was opened along Western Avenue as far as Penn Avenue (to within one-half mile of the park), Eloise Butler was a frequent visitor, as were her friends and former students Clara Leavitt, teacher of botany and zoology at South High, and Elizabeth Foss, who taught botany at North High, along with Julia Clifford, the botany teacher at East High.[8]

Eloise condemned the loss of native flora to the "rapid growth of the city" in her essay, "Annals of a Wild Garden:"

> The shy woodland plants are fast dying out on our river banks; the tamarack swamps have been drained, and with the drying up of the water have disappeared the wondrous orchids and the strange insectivorous plants; the pools with the desmids and diatoms have been filled in and houses built over them; and the prairies have been plotted into building lots. The land has been ruthlessly stripped of the exquisite features that Nature, the greatest landscape gardener, has wrought through the ages, and "all the king's horses and all the king's men" can never make the place the same again. . . . Cottagers on the suburban lake shores have fettered ideas of planting that are more appropriate for city grounds, and condemn their neighbors, who strive to preserve the wildness, for a lack of neatness in not using a lawn mower, and in not pulling down the vine tangles in which birds nest and sing—apparently dissatisfied until the wilderness is reduced to a dead level of monotonous, songless tameness. What does one go into the wilderness for to see? A reed shaken by the wind, if you please; but surely not geometric flower beds, nor mounds of the ubiquitous canna and castor bean.[9]

The four botany teachers, led by Eloise, agreed that a place convenient to the city was needed where native plants could be tended and protected, where, as Eloise wrote, "representatives of the flora of our state" could be induced to flourish. The hoped-for botanic garden would serve "as a depot of supplies for the schools; as a resort for the lovers of wild nature; and to afford an opportunity to study botanical problems at first hand."[10] The garden would be different from all other botanic gardens—it would be wild:

> A paramount idea is to perpetuate in the garden its primeval wildness. All artificial appearances are avoided and plants are to be allowed to grow as they will and without any check except what may be necessary for healthful living. . . . Each [plant], when procured, is to be given an environment as similar as possible to that from which it came, and then left to take care of itself, as in the wild open, with only the natural fertilizers furnished by decaying vegetation.[11]

For the site of the garden Eloise and the other teachers chose the undrained tamarack bog lying northeast of Devil's Glen in Glenwood Park. "Most lovers of wild plants are bog-trotters," she wrote, "and find in the depths of a swamp an earthly paradise."[12] While botanizing there alone, years before, Eloise had once nearly drowned in the bog. She later told a reporter that she fell into a "pool of quicksand" and sank up to her armpits. As she recalled,

> It was no use shouting because nobody was within hearing distance. So I finally managed to wiggle myself out like an inch worm, all dripping wet and covered with mud. Next day I went back and measured it with a stick and it was 27 feet deep. No one ever would have known what happened to me, as I had meant to go to St. Paul that day, and had told my friends so before I left the house.[13]

Sheltered on three sides by high wooded hillsides lushly carpeted with ferns and spring wildflowers, the bog closely resembled the landscape of Eloise Butler's childhood in Maine. A path said to have been made by the Indians along the northwest edge of the bog led to the Great Medicine Spring (whose Indian name was by then largely forgotten) over the hill. The teachers hoped that city ownership would assure the perpetual protection of the garden by the Park Board,

and there was plenty of room in Glenwood Park for the arboretum, traditional botanic garden, and children's museum also envisioned by them."[14]

A petition was prepared, stating the teachers' "desire to preserve intact all the wild and natural features of the place," and requesting that they be given permission to supervise the garden. Its signers included the principals of all the high schools of the city, University of Minnesota president Cyrus Northrup, and university faculty members Henry Nachtrieb (German naturalist and curator of the zoological museum), entomologist O.W. Oestlund, geologist C.W. Hall, and botanists C.O. Rosendahl and Josephine Tilden. Even William Watts Folwell, previous opponent of a botanic garden in the park system, looked favorably upon the proposal for a "natural botanic garden" that would cost the Park Board nothing but the price of a fence to enclose it.[15]

The Park Board granted the petitioners' request. On April 15, 1907, Park Superintendent Theodore Wirth was instructed to "select the proper place and make such minor improvements in the way of paths and fencing as may be necessary at an expense of not to exceed $200."[16] A three-acre portion of the bog, along with meadows and hillsides to the south and west, was soon fenced, and the enclosed area proclaimed a botanic garden. "Opened today the 'Natural Botanical Garden,' " Eloise wrote on April 27, 1907, in her diary that had lain neglected for four years, "by planting two pitcher plants, which I had kept over winter."[17] On May 7, 1907, the Minneapolis *Journal* applauded the opening of the new garden in an article entitled "Shy Wild Flowers to be Given Hospice."

The jubilant teachers immediately began taking a census of the flora indigenous to the garden.[18] The botanists explored every foot of their preserve, and Eloise listed the plants by their Latin scientific names in her *Garden Log*. According to Eloise, "the indigenous flora was found to be captivating."[19] Within the enclosure they found growing sixteen species of trees. White and yellow birch were abundant; there were white and red elm, basswood, hackberry, box elder, and four species of oak. Crows nested in the moss-draped tamaracks, the predominant tree in the garden, whose shallow roots grew entwined in a thick mat of sphagnum moss which made the ground in the bog spongy to walk upon. Red-osier dogwood ringed the bog, and twenty-seven other species of shrubs were noted, including pagoda dogwood, several willows, wild rose, sumac, blackberry, blueberry, raspberry, highbush cranberry, hawthorn, prickly ash, black currant, wolfberry, and chokeberry. Among the ten different species of ferns were especially luxuriant growths of maidenhair, while cinnamon ferns were prominent among the tamaracks; a hillside covered with a dense growth of the interrupted fern was deemed by Eloise "the most spectacular feature of the garden." Eight mosses, two liverworts, and several grasses were also noted.[20]

During the last week of May, Butler identified seventy-six species of wildflowers indigenous to the "Minneapolis Wild Botanic Garden." Marsh marigolds carpeted open stretches of the bog with mounds of yellow flowers. The woodland floor was sprinkled with the delicate white blossoms of rue anemone and the nodding yellow flowers of large-flowered bellwort. In sunny openings among the trees were patches of meadow blue violets and early meadow rue. Sweetly-scented white violets and goldthread bloomed along the edges of the bog. Nodding trillium, wild lily-of-the-valley, and jack-in-the-pulpit were in bud. In the swamp Eloise noted coral root, dwarf cornel, cattails, the native iris (blue flag), and water dock, as well as spotted jewelweed, swamp milkweed, and horsetail. On the hillsides she found red baneberry and spreading dogbane, wintergreen, and false Solomon's seal; and the delicately-scented, trailing twinflower (*Linnaea borealis*), a favorite of the Swedish botanist Linnaeus and also of Eloise Butler, was happily noted.[21]

In mid-summer Eloise made her customary visit to Cora's home in Malden. While there she collected and packed, for shipment to the garden, many wild plants including an aromatic shrub called spicebush, two buttonbush shrubs, and a large quantity of a plant she supposed to be fireweed, whose showy purple spires Eloise thought would be striking against a background of tamaracks. She continued her census in Minneapolis on September 6. She counted fifty more species indigenous to the wild garden, mainly the later-blooming plants of open meadows such as blue vervain, Culver's root, coneflower, turtlehead, and wild bergamot. Five species of

asters sprinkled the meadows with drifts of purple, blue and white, and sunflowers and six species of goldenrod added bursts of yellow to the early autumn palette. More grasses were discovered, including wild rye and bottle-brush grass. Eloise also noted the presence of showy ladyslippers, although her trip to Malden had prevented her witnessing their bloom. The sticktights, stinging nettle, poison ivy and poison sumac already resident in the preserve were allowed to remain for "the instruction of the unwary."[22]

Planting began at once as the teachers made the rounds of their favorite "haunts" to dig plants for transplanting into the garden. The two pitcher plants first installed by Eloise came from Mahtomedi, near White Bear Lake. From a peninsula on the lake came large yellow lady's-slipper, clintonia, wild calla, and royal ferns. A wooded glen below Minnehaha Falls became a perennial source of hepatica, dutchman's breeches, wild ginger, skunk cabbage and maidenhair ferns, while a prairie above the falls furnished pasque flower and bird's-foot violet (*Viola pedatifida*). Visits to Mound yielded showy orchis and Adam-and-Eve orchis, and sensitive ferns were found near Excelsior. Clumps of spring beauty and vines of Virginia creeper and greenbriar were gathered along the banks of the Mississippi River under the Lake Street bridge, and moonseed vines were dug from a ravine along Minnehaha Creek between Lyndale and Nicollet Avenues. The vines were planted along the fence, to which the indigenous wild grape, bittersweet, honeysuckle, ground nut and hop vines were also moved. Planting continued through November 5 when Eloise returned from a last visit to Minnehaha Falls with tall blazing-star (*Liatris pychnostachya*) and a shrub called wahoo, or burning-bush, for the garden.[23]

Within a year of its founding, the garden was expanded, more than doubling in size. "Longing eyes were cast upon a marsh overgrown with willows on the eastern side of the bog," wrote Eloise; the marsh (called the "Treeless Swamp") and an adjacent wet meadow and hillsides were soon purchased by the Park Board and added to the garden.[24] A spring-fed stream, named "Lullaby Brook," threaded through the marsh and joined in an open meadow to the north of the garden with "delicious" water that flowed from a bubbling spring on the eastern boundary. A moss-

covered earthen dam was constructed where
the stream left the garden, forming a pool for
aquatic plants and desmids. Along the banks
of the stream in the heart of the garden grew
the insectivorous sundew plants so fascinating
to children. The new meadow was home to
grass-of-Parnassus and the lovely blue fringed
gentian, which Eloise named, after *Linnaea*, as
the "chief pride of the garden."[25]

At the base of the eastern hillside, above
the marsh, reigned an ancient white oak
favored as a nesting place by the barred owl.
Butler believed the tree, at eight and one half
feet in circumference, to be the largest of its
kind in Minneapolis; she estimated its age at
seven hundred years. In 1912, she called in a
tree surgeon, and, as she later wrote, "in
obedience to the scriptural injunction, his dead
limbs were cut off and cast away;" the
partially-decayed trunk was reinforced with
concrete. Butler revered the aged oak, whose
spirit she evidently regarded as male. She
called him "Monarch," and planted a bed of
violets at his feet.[26]

Monarch, 1926. *Minneapolis Park and Recreation Board.*

Butler gave names to all the parts of her
domain. In Monarch's entourage were a
seven-boled clump of yellow birch called "the
Seven Sisters," which grew in the marsh below,
and an eight-boled clump of white birch just
beyond "Wormwood Gulch" on the hillside
above. A place where puff-balls grew was
named "Puff-Ball Flats," and a spot where
Eloise was charged by a swarm of hornets
came to be known as "Roaring Camp." A
mature white elm near the fernery in the
original enclosure formed the "Inner Guard."
Atop a hill just outside the northwest corner
of the garden stood the "Lone Sentinel," an
elm "flat-topped like the stone pines of Italy."[27]

During the first three years of the garden's
existence, Eloise spent two months or more of
each summer at Cora's home in Malden. In
the summer of 1908, the sisters visited relatives
in Appleton, Maine, where Eloise obtained
dwarf ginseng. They paid a special visit to New
Brunswick, Nova Scotia, to appraise a "rival
garden" which they had read about in the
Boston *Transcript.* Eloise wrote that she had
believed the idea for her garden to be "purely
original" until reading about the one in
Canada established on private land by a Dr.
George Hays near the town of St. John some
years before. Eloise found the garden "of vivid
interest," while nevertheless pronouncing her
own wild garden "superior," as it was larger
and open to the public, and Dr. Hays' plants
were often swept away at floodtimes by a
brook.[28]

While away from the garden, Eloise
hunted for plants for the new collection with
all the passion and pride formerly given to her
desmids and seaweeds. In Nova Scotia, she and
Cora gathered Christmas ferns, oak ferns and
two species of beech ferns that grew prolifically
in the woods near Evangeline Beach.[29]
According to an account by Cora published in
the Needham *Chronicle,* the two "adventurous
botanists" also hunted that summer for the
beautiful fringed polygala, a low perennial
with a single, rose-purple flower, native to
Minnesota and rumored to grow near
Rosemary Pond in Needham, Massachusetts.
Storms and the loss of a handbag and its
contents did not deter the plant hunters, and
the search proved successful. The fringed
polygala was planted in the garden by Eloise
on her return in September, along with the
wild ginseng and ferns.[30]

Cora was an enthusiastic supporter of the

new garden. In the fall of 1907 her article "A New Botanical Garden" appeared in the *American Botanist*. "A Wild Botanic Garden having many distinctive features has been established within the past year by the teachers of botany in the city of Minneapolis," she wrote. After summarizing the indigenous flora of the garden, she added:

> The teachers of botany in Minneapolis have certainly undertaken a most fascinating and important work if only they succeed in saving in a natural condition the wild things already established within the garden. One can hardly comprehend the result of extending its flora until it includes that of the whole State. Not only the young people passing through the schools . . . will be incalculably benefitted, but it will be of great pleasure and profit to mature citizens also; for a bit of natural growth is a source of greater delight to the true nature lover than the most beautiful and most highly cultivated formal garden could ever be.[31]

Among Cora's many interests were spiritistic phenomena, including phrenology and mediumship. One day during Eloise's stay Cora invited a medium to visit the house. Eloise, who professed to having "no belief in such phenomena," was told during a sitting with the medium that the reason she always found the plants she searched for was that she had two ghostly friends, botanists, who put their hands on her shoulders and guided her steps in the right direction.[32]

As the transplanted "fireweed" of the previous summer had proved, when it bloomed, to be a less attractive species of willow herb already too abundant in the garden, Eloise was determined to collect it again on her trip east in 1908. Prior to leaving Malden, she returned to the place where she and Cora had picked "great bouquets" of fireweed all during the previous week. She was greatly disappointed to find the field "burned over, ploughed and harrowed" and that a tethered cow had eaten every scrap of the plant at another place where it grew, so she was obliged to depart without it.[33]

Returning to Minnesota along the northern route through Canada in 1908, Eloise Butler's train met with an accident. "My train was wrecked (fortunately without loss of life) in the wilds of Ontario," wrote Eloise; to her great delight, she found herself marooned in

the midst of a large stand of the coveted fireweed (*Epilobium angustifolium*) and other "rarities," which she busied herself collecting during the delay. Wishing also to find sweet gale, Eloise called upon her two "ghostly botanist" friends and walked "aimlessly" until she stumbled into a patch of it; using the same method, she found the eastern yellow round-leaved violet (*Viola rotundifolia*). The "spoils of the accident" were packed in her suitcase," regardless of the rights of clothing," and duly planted in the wild garden upon her return.[34]

In the season of 1909, many species of trees and wildflowers were added to the garden. A pinetum was established in May on a western hillside overlooking the swamp. It contained white and Norway pines, junipers and yews (in 1911, along both sides of the brook, Eloise planted a grove of eastern hemlock). May also marked the installation in the Wild Botanic Garden of squirrel corn, a fragrant, white-flowered plant closely related to the cultivated bleeding heart. In search of the plant, Eloise and her friends went to Big Island in Lake Minnetonka, where, after "a long journey by water and pathless woodlands," they found that the wild land where it grew had been surrounded by a high fence topped with barbed wire. Undaunted, the teachers scaled the fence using long poles covered by a "thick waterproof, recklessly sacrificed to the cause." The coveted plants were at last gathered, and the teachers, flattened to the ground, made their escape through a hole where a sewer was being dug, to emerge "dusty and triumphant."[35]

During the months of July and August 1909, Eloise went East on a grand collecting expedition. After a visit to Malden, she went on to Maine and revisited the bogs and woods she had roamed as a child to gather barrels full of plants for the garden. From the edge of a pond in Appleton she gathered yellow-eyed grass (*Xyris torta*) and water lobelia, with its flowers of pale violet held above the water on thin stalks. In the woods on Appleton Ridge she collected painted trillium and bishop's cap. From the banks of Round Pond, near where her great-grandfather Phineas Butler had built his cabin one hundred thirty years before, Eloise collected the purple fringed orchid, *Platanthera psychodes*.[36] The results of her summer's plant hunting, no doubt most of it in league with Cora, were recorded in the

Garden Log on September 4, 1909. Nearly sixty species of wildflowers, ferns, vines, shrubs, and grasses had been collected in Massachusetts and Maine. Most were plants native to Minnesota for which Eloise did not have local sources.

Eloise Butler had no known church affiliation as an adult, despite her strict Baptist upbringing, yet her writings convey a reverence for the natural world that is deeply spiritual. Eloise was fond of quoting Bible verses memorized in her childhood but with subtle changes which gave the words a decidedly pantheistic slant. Thus, Acts 17:28, *"In Him* we live and move and have our being," became, for Eloise, "I live and move and have my being in and for the *Wild Botanic Garden.*" To Jesus' rebuke to the crowds, concerning John the Baptist, in Matthew 11:7—"What did you go out into the wilderness to behold? A reed shaken by the wind?"—Eloise breathed an unequivocal *yes.* Her spiritual center was, simply, the natural world, of which she regarded herself an inseparable part. She felt no need of church pew or minister when she spent her days in an "earthly paradise," priestess of her own sacred grove.[37]

Eloise Butler wrote of the wild garden and her adventures in plant hunting as though deliberately making myth. Her classical education and wide reading made her familiar with ancient history; among her best-loved authors was Homer, whose *Iliad* is a primary source of Greek mythology. The myths, wrote Edith Hamilton in the introduction to her *Mythology* (1942), "lead us back to a time when the world was young and people had a connection with the earth, with trees and seas and flowers and hills, unlike anything we ourselves can feel," at a time when "[t]he imagination was vividly alive and not checked by the reason, so that anyone in the woods could see through the trees a fleeting nymph, or bending over a clear pool to drink behold in the depths a naiad's face."[38]

Butler may have chosen, whether consciously or not, the Greek goddess Artemis as an archetype for the inner pattern of her life. Artemis was the "Lady of Wild Things," virgin goddess of the Hunt and the Moon, according to Hamilton. Her sisters were Aphrodite, goddess of love, and Athena, goddess of war; Artemis was the "lover of woods and the wild chase over the mountain," who roamed the wilderness with her band of young nymphs (dieties of mountains, woods, and streams) dressed in an unencumbering tunic.[39] Jungian analyst and psychiatrist Jean Shinoda Bolen, in her book *Goddesses in Everywoman* (1984), writes that Artemis was a protector of young women. Artemis and her band of nymphs "were unconstrained by domesticity, fashions, or ideas of what women 'should' be doing, and were beyond the control of men or of masculine preferences. They were like 'sisters.' "[40] Butler's tendency to befriend younger female students and botany teachers is evocative of this aspect of Artemis.

According to Bolen, "when a woman senses that there is a mythic dimension to something she is undertaking, that knowledge touches and inspires deep creative centers in her."[41] Butler's accounts of her adventures in plant-hunting display the bravado of which myth is made. Her tales (written for her botanical correspondence club), with titles such as "The Quest of the Walking Fern," are sometimes reminiscent of the "swashbuckling adventure stories" that she favored.[42] Like the poet Emily Dickenson, Butler's meek appearance belied a rich and passionate inner life. To some, she was a placid and rather eccentric old maid; to herself, she was the Wild Gardener.[43]

After 1909, Eloise could no longer bear to be away from the garden during the growing season. She spent the months of April through October of 1910, and of every year thereafter until her death in 1933, immersed in her labor among the plants of the wild garden. Gaia was evidently pleased with her ways, and the garden flourished under her loving care.

Notes

1   The Gaia hypothesis (named for the earth goddess of the ancient Greeks), as stated by its originator, British scientist James Lovelock, holds that "the Earth's living matter, air, oceans, and land surface form a complex system which can be seen as a single organism and which has the capacity to keep our planet a fit place for life." James Lovelock, *Gaia: A New Look at Life on Earth* (Oxford: Oxford University Press, 1979), p. vii. This paragraph and below based, in part,

on a conversation with Gary Meyer of the Minnesota Geologic Survey, St. Paul, 19 December 1990; and George M. Schwartz and George A. Thiel, *Minnesota's Rocks and Waters: A Geological Story* (Minneapolis: University of Minnesota Press, rev. ed., 1976), pp. 3-52.

2   The Great Medicine spring apparently was the spring that is located southeast of the intersection of Theodore Wirth Parkway and Glenwood Avenue in Theodore Wirth (formerly Glenwood) Park in Minneapolis. Indian use of a spring believed to have medicinal qualities "about two miles from the city on Western [now Glenwood] Avenue, on the land of Mr. Wales," is mentioned in a clipping from the Minneapolis *Tribune* dated 26 September 1874, in the Annals of Minnesota file, Federal Writers' Project, Minnesota Historical Society. The water was thought to be of great value, particularly in cases of consumption (tuberculosis), and the Indians were said to come great distances to use the spring. The "Great Medicine spring, an old resort of the Indians" is referred to in a chapter entitled "The Geology of Hennepin County" by N.H. Winchell in the *Geological and Natural History Survey of Minnesota 1882-1885*, Vol. 2 (St. Paul: Pioneer Press Co., 1888), p. 308 (the spring is treated separately from the nearby Glenwood and Inglewood Springs); the "Big Medicine spring" is mentioned in Isaac Atwater's *History of the City of Minneapolis, Minnesota*, Part II, (New York: Munsell & Co., 1893), p. 807. Jack Babcock, a former resident of the area, found Indian relics there, including arrowheads and a grinding bowl and pestle, according to his granddaughter Jean Rorbaugh.

3   Surveyor's field notes for Minnesota Range 24, Township 29, Vol. 166 (27 and 28 July 1853; survey completed November 18, 1853), archives of Minnesota Secretary of State, St. Paul.

4   Preemption certificate No. 428 dated 12 August 1855 (Record Group 49, Cash File 428), National Archives, Washington, D.C. The location of the Schickling's cabin is not given, but a former resident of the area recalls the rotting remains of a log cabin that lay on a hilltop just southwest of the intersection of Chestnut and Xerxes Avenues in the 1920s (author's interview with Lloyd Teeuwen, 29 January 1991). Highland Lake, later known as Keegan's Lake and Glenwood Lake, is now called Theodore Wirth Lake.

5   The patent from the United States to Killian Schickling, dated 30 November 1885 (titles were not secured until the end of lengthy pre-emption litigation in which Samuel Gale was involved as attorney), is recorded in Deed Book 181, p. 152, at the office of the Hennepin County Recorder, Minneapolis. The Schicklings' warranty deed to subsequent purchasers Herbert M. Carpenter and Thomas Moulton, dated 15 September 1855, is recorded in Deed Book C, p. 138; see also warranty deeds from Henry (illeg.) to Susan D. Gale dated 28 September 1866 (Deed Book 11, p. 418), and from Charles W. Pierce to Susan D. Gale dated 11 February 1867 (Deed Book 14, p. 188); Samuel C. Gale and Susan D. Gale to Thomas W. Wilson, warranty deed dated 30 November 1885 (Deed Book 176, p. 431); and plat map of Saratoga Springs Addition to Minneapolis dated 1 March 1886. Sham land transactions are mentioned in Theodore C. Blegen, *Minnesota: A History of the State* (Minneapolis: University of Minnesota Press, 1963), p. 364.

6   This paragraph based on Isaac Atwater, *History of Minneapolis* (New York: Munsell Pub. Co., 1893), pp. 234-236.

7   Minneapolis Board of Park Commissioners, *Minutes*, 9 February, 9 March, 3 August, and 31 August, 1889. The original petition appears not to have been preserved and the names of the original petitioners on behalf of Saratoga Park are, unfortunately, not known.

8   The teachers called themselves the "Big Four" —see Chapter 3. Clara Leavitt had attended the 1901 session of the Minnesota Seaside Station with Eloise Butler; Leavitt and Foss were elected to membership in the Minnesota Academy of Science on 3 April 1906. Minnesota Academy of Science, *Proceedings*, Vol. 4 (Bulletin III, 1906-1910), p. 325.

9   Eloise Butler to Gray Memorial Botanical Chapter, Agassiz Association, Division D (c.1926), copy (under title "Annals of a Wild Garden") in *Early History of Eloise Butler Plant Reserve*, pp. 3-4, at Minneapolis Public Library, Minneapolis Collection.

10   Eloise Butler, "The Minneapolis Wild Botanic Garden," *School Science and Mathematics*, Vol. 10 (March 1910), pp. 229-234 (229) (reprint in Eloise Butler biography file at Minneapolis Public Library, Minneapolis Collection).

11   Ibid., 231.

12   Eloise Butler to Gray Memorial Botanical Chapter, Agassiz Association, Division D (c.1926), copy (under the title: "Annals of a Wild Garden") in *Early History of Eloise Butler Plant Reserve*, p. 5, at Minneapolis Public Library, Minneapolis Collection. The word "bog" in Butler's day referred to a wet, "boggy" area and was used interchangeably with "swamp." Modern ecology defines a bog as a community of herbs and shrubs growing on soggy peat carpeted with sphagnum moss; the presence of alkaline spring water (as opposed to a more acidic environment in bogs filled only by rainwater) would provide more nutrients, supporting a richer flora more akin to a fen, sedge meadow, or swamp. Butler sometimes distinguished parts

of the original garden as the "tamarack bog," "wet meadow," and the "treeless swamp," and they appear to have had distinct vegetation. Most often, she used "bog" to refer to the wetland portion of the garden generally, and such usage is followed here.

13 "Neighbors Don't Know She Exists, but Botanic Garden Curator is Famous Over America," unidentified clipping (c.1924) in Scrapbook III, p. 13, Archives of The Friends of the Wildflower Garden, Inc.

14 Only once did Eloise Butler take credit for the idea of the wildflower garden; usually she modestly attributed it to the botany teachers as a group. See Eloise Butler, "The Minneapolis Wild Botanic Garden," *School Science and Mathematics* (1910). As Elizabeth Foss recalled in 1942, "my part during the years since 1906 was just stimulating interest among Minneapolis people so that Miss Butler could carry on." Elizabeth Foss to Varl Vitz, 27 July 1942, in Eloise Butler biography file at Minneapolis Public Library, Minneapolis Collection.

15 The signed petition, adopted 15 April 1907, is in the archives of the Minneapolis Board of Park Commissioners.

16 Minneapolis Board of Park Commissioners (Report of Standing Committee on Improvements), *Minutes*, 15 April 1907.

17 Butler gave at least two other dates for the opening of the garden. The first entry in her *Garden Log*, typed at a later date from handwritten notes, is dated 29 April 1907; it notes "planted in bog two pitcher plants from Mahtomedi." In her paper entitled "The Wild Botanic Garden in Glenwood Park, Minneapolis," presented 5 April 1910, at the Minnesota Academy of Science, Butler stated that the garden was opened on 20 April 1907.

18 A list of plants indigenous to the garden, compiled from Eloise Butler's records, is on file at the garden and at the Minneapolis Park Board.

19 Eloise Butler to Gray Memorial Botanical Chapter, Agassiz Association, Division D (1926) copy (under the title: "Annals of a Wild Garden") in *Early History of Eloise Butler Plant Reserve*, p. 5, at Minneapolis Public Library, Minneapolis Collection.

20 Quote from Eloise Butler to Gray Memorial Botanical Chapter, Agassiz Association, Division D, June 1915, copy (under the title: "Ferns in the Wild Garden") in *Annals of the Wild Life Reserve*, p. 3, at Minneapolis Public Library, Minneapolis Collection.

21 Eloise Butler, *Garden Log*, 29 April, 25 May and 31 May, 1907.

22 Quote from Eloise Butler, "The Wild Botanic Garden in Glenwood Park, Minneapolis," Min-

nesota Academy of Science *Bulletin*, Vol. 5 (September 1911), p. 19-24 (22).

23 This paragraph based on entries in Eloise Butler's *Garden Log* dated April through November 1907. Scientific names of plants not on Eloise's indigenous plant list (on file at the Minneapolis Park and Recreation Board Archives and in the garden) may be found in the *Garden Log* and on cards in Butler's *Index Card File* (copies at Minneapolis Park and Recreation Board).

24 Eloise Butler to Gray Memorial Botanical Chapter, Agassiz Association, Division D (c.1926), copy (under the title: "Beginnings in 1907") in *Early History of Eloise Butler Plant Reserve*, p. 5, at Minneapolis Public Library, Minneapolis Collection.

25 Quotes from Eloise Butler to Gray Memorial Botanical Chapter, Agassiz Association, Division D, (1926), copy (under the title: "Annals of a Wild Garden") in *Early History of Eloise Butler Plant Reserve*, p. 6, at Minneapolis Public Library, Minneapolis Collection; and Eloise Butler to Gray Memorial Botanical Chapter, Agassiz Association, Division D (1915), copy (under the title: "Notable Features of My Wild Garden") in *Annals of the Wild Life Reserve*, p. 22, at Minneapolis Public Library, Minneapolis Collection. The "bubbling spring" was capped off some years ago by the Park Board. A wonderfully detailed description of the early garden is contained in W.P. Kirkwood, "A Wild Botanic Garden," *The Bellman*, Minneapolis, 3 May 1913 (clipping in Eloise Butler Papers, Minnesota Historical Society).

26 Quote from Eloise Butler to Gray Memorial Botanical Chapter, Agassiz Association, Division D (c.1926), copy (under the title: "A Tree Census"), in *Early History of Eloise Butler Plant Reserve*, p. 8, at Minneapolis Public Library, Minneapolis Collection.

27 Butler's use of these names occurs throughout the *Garden Log*; the places to which they refer are described in W.P. Kirkwood, "A Wild Botanic Garden." Quote from Eloise Butler, "Annals of a Wild Garden," (c.1914), unpublished 6 page typescript in Eloise Butler file, Minneapolis Park and Recreation Board Archives.

28 Quotes from Eloise Butler, "The Wild Botanic Garden," (1924), 4 p. unpublished typescript (p. 4), and "A Wild Botanic Garden," (c.1911), 10 p. unpublished typescript (p. 6), in Eloise Butler file, Minneapolis Park and Recreation Board Archives. Another early native plant garden was established at the Brooklyn Botanic Garden in 1912. The plants were laid out in rectangular beds in "systematic family order;" the garden featured a concrete-lined basin filled with bales of sphagnum moss for bog plants. It

became overgrown and was abandoned; the garden was restored after 1930 with naturalistic plantings. See Henry K. Svenson, "The Wild Garden of the Brooklyn Botanic Garden, I," *Wild Flower*, Vol. 14 (July 1937), pp. 42-45.

29 Cora E. Pease, "Notes on the Acadian Flora," *The American Botanist*, Vol. 14 (August 1908), pp. 70-71.

30 Cora E. Pease, *The Needham Chronicle*, clipping dated 22 August 1908, in scrapbook owned by Martha P. Pease; Eloise Butler, *Garden Log*, 6 September 1908. An account of the collection of fireweed is found in Eloise Butler, "A Wild Botanic Garden," 10-page unpublished typescript (c.1911), pp. 5-6, Eloise Butler File, Minneapolis Park and Recreation Board Archives.

31 Cora E. Pease, "A New Botanical Garden," *The American Botanist*, Vol. 13 (September 1907), pp. 3-5 (5).

32 Eloise Butler to Gray Memorial Botanical Chapter, Agassiz Association, Division D, (c.1916), copy (under the title: "Occult Experiences of a Wild Gardener") in *Annals of the Wild Life Reserve*, p. 30, at Minneapolis Public Library, Minneapolis Collection.

33 Eloise Butler, "A Wild Botanic Garden," 10-page unpublished typescript (c.1911), p. 5, Eloise Butler file, Minneapolis Park and Recreation Board Archives.

34 Ibid; and Eloise Butler, "Occult Experiences of a Wild Gardener," pp. 31-32 (see note 32).

35 Eloise Butler, "A Wild Botanic Garden," pp. 5-6 (See note 33). Butler wrote that "closely related plants like squirrel corn and dutchman's breeches have been set side by side in the hope that they might hybridize"; Eloise Butler, "The Native Plant Reserve," *Bulletin of the Garden*

Club of America (January 1924), pp. 61-62 (62).

36 Eloise Butler, *Garden Log*, 4 September 1909.

37 Biblical quotations from Revised Standard Version. Quotes from Eloise Butler to Gray Memorial Botanical Chapter, Agassiz Association, Division D, (c.1911), copy in *Early History of Eloise Butler Plant Reserve* ("live and move and have my being"), p. 1; and (1926) ("reed shaken by the wind"), p. 4. I am grateful to Patricia McKernon for pointing out the biblical origin of the latter.

38 Edith Hamilton, *Mythology* (Boston: Little, Brown & Co., 1942), pp. 3-4. Butler included on a list of her favorite literature "genuine poetry, particularly Wordsworth's; Walter Pater's writings—*Marius the Epicurean* is my ideal—the *Meditations* of Marcus Aurelius, Homer, Plato, [and] the old Greek plays." Eloise Butler to Gray Memorial Botanical Chapter, Agassiz Association, Division D, March 1931, copy in Eloise Butler biography file at Minneapolis Public Library, Minneapolis Collection.

39 Edith Hamilton, *Mythology*, pp. 31-32.

40 Jean Shinoda Bolen, *Goddesses in Everywoman: A New Psychology of Women* (New York: Harper and Row, 1984), p. 50.

41 Bolen, *Goddesses in Everywoman*, p. 6.

42 Eloise Butler to Gray Memorial Botanical Chapter, Agassiz Association, Division D (March 1931), copy in Eloise Butler biography file at Minneapolis Public Library, Minneapolis Collection.

43 As Butler wrote across the top of a pamphlet on the garden, sent to a friend—"With compliments of the Wild Gardener." I am indebted to Martha P. Pease for sending this to me, and thus providing the title of this book.

Eloise Butler's "Lodge in the Wilderness." *Minneapolis Park and Recreation Board.*

Eloise Butler in the wild garden in 1921. *Minneapolis Public Library, Minneapolis Collection.*

9

The Wild Gardener

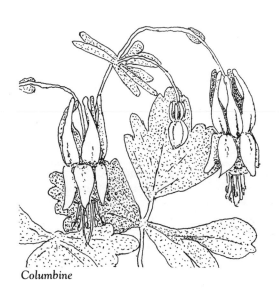

Columbine

A BOTANIC GARDEN or arboretum, to be successful, requires a dedicated leader to develop its plant collection and shape its identity, as well as financial support for the furtherance of its mission. One can hardly imagine Boston's Arnold Arboretum without Charles Sprague Sargent and the support of Harvard University, the Missouri Botanical Gardens without William Trelease and the substantial estate of Henry Shaw, or the Minnesota Landscape Arboretum without Leon Snyder and the University of Minnesota.

Four years after its founding, when she was nearly sixty, Eloise Butler was appointed curator of the Minneapolis Wild Botanic Garden. She became one of those rare persons whose lives completely express their calling. Her life's work became the promotion of the appreciation and conservation of native plants through development of the garden. She served as curator until her death in 1933 at age eighty-one.

Ownership of the garden by the city's Park Board provided the continuity for which Butler had hoped but required that the garden compete for funds with other projects desired by an increasingly recreation-oriented administration. Butler never managed to secure the funds necessary for optimal operation and maintenance of such a large and ambitious garden, nor to bring the garden under the sponsorship of the botany department at the University of Minnesota, to which she appealed for help near the end of her lifetime. Her age, sex, and position on the periphery of modern botanical science no doubt led some to dismiss her efforts as amateur or frivolous. Nevertheless, working alone and with the help of a few loyal friends, Eloise Butler managed to develop a wild botanic garden with a native plant collection that was truly impressive, even by today's standards.

Butler's appointment as curator was made by the Park Board in response to a petition brought by the Conservation Committee of the Minneapolis Woman's Club in the spring of 1911 upon her retirement from teaching. A preamble to the petition urged "that a curator be appointed to take charge of the garden and carry it on," and stated that, "inasmuch as the success of the garden up to this time has been due almost entirely to the gratuitous efforts of Miss Eloise Butler, we ask that she be appointed curator."[1] A three-page document entitled "Concerning the Wild Botanic Garden in Glenwood Park" accompanied the petition. The document, unsigned but obviously authored by Butler, set forth the many needs of the young botanic garden that would be met by the appointment of a curator. Among them were listed the collection and culture of six hundred species of Minnesota plants still to be obtained; labeling the plants with their common and botanical names; and the keeping of extensive records, including a topographical survey, with the location of plants and their history to be indicated on cards in a card-catalogue. Other duties would include conducting visitors through the garden during regular hours, preparing lists of plants in bloom for publication in the local newspapers, giving talks about the garden, conducting plant and seed exchange with other parks, and the making of an herbarium. Eloise Butler's plan was a well-thought-out and professional approach to the management of a true botanic garden. Perhaps most importantly, the appointment of a curator would give official stature to what had been a "labor of love" since 1907.

That most of the labor, as well as love, of those early years had been supplied by Eloise was known to everyone familiar with the garden. Just to be sure the park commissioners understood the depth of her commitment, Eloise included a summary of her efforts in the Wild Botanic Garden:

> Besides what the other teachers of botany have done, Miss Butler has given all her spare time for four years to the work. During vacations, she has collected many hundreds of plants in Massachusetts, Maine, Nova Scotia, and different parts of Minnesota, cared for them pending transportation, packed and planted all except the larger species. She has spent many days of arduous labor in clearing up the grounds and has expended over $150 for plants, expressage, cataloguing, and wages to boys. This is not regretted by her, and would not be mentioned except to make clear some of the requirements in the management of a wild garden.[2]

The documents also cited the publicity given the garden in the form of widely-circulated articles written by herself and her sister, an exhibit held at the Minnesota State Fair in 1910, and eleven lectures on the garden. It closed with the query, "In view of the general interest manifested, and the time, labor, and money expended, should the work be allowed to lapse?" The commissioners agreed it should not, granted the petition, and accepted an offer by the Minneapolis Woman's Club to pay half the curator's salary of $50 per month for the first season.[3]

The following year, Eloise found "cause for congratulation" when a large area was added to the garden, increasing its size to more than twenty acres. The area annexed in 1912 included the open northern and western slopes of the west hillside, known as "Promontory Hill," as well as a boggy meadow containing stands of tamarack, which skirted the base of the hill to the north and west. At the top of the hill, the highest point in the garden, grew the flat-topped elm known as the "Lone Sentinel," surrounded by Eloise's juvenile pinetum. An equestrian trail led to a lookout at the summit, where the views were extensive, across tamaracks toward Glenwood Lake to the north, and toward the buildings of downtown Minneapolis to the northeast. After the 1912 expansion, Eloise referred to the older part of the garden as the "Inner Court."[4]

"The highland supports a prairie flora, and the meadows are brimful of treasures," wrote Eloise of the annexed land in 1912. A moss bank covered the northern slope of the hill; the meadow below, called simply the "North Meadow," contained pitcher plant, large stands of showy lady's-slipper, and turk's cap lily, as well as nodding ladies'-tresses and rose pogonia. Through the meadow flowed a winding stream, formed where Lullaby Brook joined with water from the bubbling spring on the eastern boundary that Eloise drank from daily. In the western meadow, called "Gentian Meadow," grew the fringed gentian and white closed gentian. Among the plants found within the new meadows and not formerly growing in the garden were prairie clover, phlox, the rare marsh arrow grass, *Triglochin palustris*, and false asphodel, *Tofieldia glutinosa*.[5]

Promontory Hill soon came to be known as "Old Andrew's Mount." Eloise wrote that shortly after the hill was added to the garden, she heard the sound of "ghostly" woodchopping coming from the remains of a cave-like shelter on the western slope where a hermit called Old Andrew had lived—and had been murdered—years before. Seeking the source of the chopping sounds, Eloise found nothing but an old boot lying on the ground.

She laid the ghost to rest, she wrote, by burying the boot and planting hepatica, violets, maidenhair ferns and wild ginger above it.[6]

After her appointment as curator, Eloise established regular hours for the garden. She met visitors on Tuesday and Thursday mornings as well as Saturday and Sunday afternoons at the streetcar terminus at the corner of Sixth and Russell Avenues North, about one-half mile away. The tiny botanist, her face at sixty deeply lined by years spent outdoors, led her visitors on a hike through Glenwood Park to the place where the bubbling spring fed a pool filled with watercress. Hand-painted signs announced entry into the unfenced Wild Botanic Garden and warned visitors to stay on the paths and not to pick the flowers. Walking single file along narrow grassy footpaths, Eloise led the group through the garden along a path that skirted the edge of the bog to the south entrance gate, where visitors coming by automobile were met an hour later. She led the group around the garden, explaining the features of the various plants, telling their history and medicinal uses, and sometimes carefully removing leaves and brush used as camouflage to conceal from vandals the location of prized plants during their flowering time. To botanize with Eloise in her "deep, tangled wildwood" was a rare treat for all who experienced it.

Eloise wrote in 1911 of her belief that "the most important and valuable of the plants are those that are indigenous to the place." Chief among the splendors of the garden was the showy lady's-slipper, *Cypripedium reginae*, state flower of Minnesota. A secluded trail through the new north meadow became "Lady's-Slipper Path," as Eloise added generously to the indigenous clumps of the regal pink and white flower. Along the path she also planted other species of lady's-slipper obtained from meadows along the Minnesota River near Savage and bogs near Anoka and Minnetonka. The path's location was revealed only to her most trusted visitors. As Eloise wrote in 1932:

> The showy Lady Slipper . . . is the crowning glory of the Preserve. It is endemic and has increased from year to year, so that there are now hundreds in large clumps making vistas of beauty through a marsh containing a few scattered tamaracks. Frequently a stalk bears two flowers, and often three. . . . Visitors are so enraptured with the display in my garden that they feel like falling on their knees to worship them. This *Cypripedium* is . . . considered by many the most beautiful flower in the world.[7]

Butler was well aware of the importance to a botanic garden of carefully kept records. She maintained an alphabetical index card file of all species established in the wild garden, as well as a log of every species found or planted there (noting her sources for the transplants) between 1907 and 1933, the latter in two closely-typed, black loose-leaf notebooks called the *Garden Log*. Her records of plants already growing in the garden when it was founded include over four-hundred species of fungi, mosses and liverworts, ferns, grasses, sedges, rushes, and other herbaceous flowering plants, shrubs, woody vines, and trees; they constitute an "excellent record of past vegetation in a local, rather diverse spot in the Twin Cities area," according to botanist Gerald B. Ownbey.[8] The records, especially the *Garden Log*, which only recently came to light, are of great interest to botanists at the Natural Heritage Program of the Minnesota Department of Natural Resources. When analyzed, they are expected to shed new light on the historical distribution of native plants around the Twin Cities.[9] Butler's records also may yield useful information about the changes in plant communities, over many years, in an urban bog preserve.

Butler's ambition was to establish in the garden specimens of all of the flora of Minnesota, including both native species (plants present in the state before white settlement) and naturalized ones (species from Europe that had accompanied settlement and become established in the state). Chief among her sources for information on plants of Minnesota was Warren Upham's *Catalog of the Flora of Minnesota, Including it's Phaenogamous and Vascular Cryptogamous Plants, Indigenous, Naturalized, and Adventive* (1884), to which Butler had contributed more than twenty years before; she also consulted C.O. Rosendahl and F.K. Butters, *Guide to the Ferns and Fern Allies of Minnesota* (1909).[10]

In the years following Eloise Butler's appointment as curator, an enormous amount of planting was accomplished, largely by her own hands (trees were planted by Park Board workmen under her direction). Butler's annual

Eloise Butler in the Wild Botanic Garden. *Minneapolis Public Library, Minneapolis Collection.*

letters to Theodore Wirth and her contributions to the bulletins of her botanical correspondence club listed the notable additions and summarized the number of species and total of plants installed each season. By 1911, she wrote, "already the trees of the state, with the exception of the black oak and shell bark hickory, and nearly all of the ferns and the most notable shrubs and herbs have been established." The collection of ferns was said to include forty species by 1913.[11]

The peak of planting occurred in 1914 and 1915, when nearly twenty-five hundred plants were added each season. By 1914, reported Butler in her annual letter to Wirth, the collection had grown to include 607 species of herbaceous plants, 66 species of trees, and 101 species of shrubs; in the following season, 94 new species were added. Planting continued unabated through 1918, when nearly two thousand plants were set out. After that, according to Park Board *Annual Reports*, the

level of planting remained at well over one thousand individual plants each season throughout most of Butler's tenure as curator. During her last few years, when advanced age took its inevitable toll on her physical abilities, around 750 plants each season were installed by local boys hired by Butler and paid from her own wages. By the end of her lifetime, according to Eloise Butler, her living plant collection contained 1,137 species established in the wild garden, 710 species of which she had planted there.[12]

Whether all of the species included in Butler's count were actually established and growing at the same time, as she implied, is now impossible to determine. Some, such as pitcher plant, pasque flower, and rose pogonia, were renewed annually with transplants. Butler wrote that her method of noting the "necrology" of those that failed to survive was removal of the index card from her card file. That no cards are found for many species of orchids she is known to have repeatedly attempted and failed to establish, such as ram's head lady's-slipper, dragon's mouth, adder's mouth, and the large purple fringed orchid (*Platanthera fimbriata*), lends credibility to her claim.[13] It was, by any measure, an astounding feat of wild gardening.

Always cognizant of the plant life around her, Eloise seems to have been incapable of alighting from a streetcar or passing a railway crossing or bridge without scouring the sides of the tracks and river banks for more finds. Her *Garden Log* is replete with records of plants salvaged from vacant lots, school grounds, cemeteries, bus and streetcar terminals, under bridges, and along the roadsides, ditches, creeks and ponds of Minneapolis.

In the early years of the garden, few nurseries sold wildflowers or offered advice on their culture. Butler gladly patronized those that did exist. Some plants were obtained by exchange; Butler once traded one hundred maidenhair ferns to a woman from Bemidji, Minnesota, for a clump of the rare ram's head lady's-slipper. Of necessity, however, most of her plants came from the wild. As Butler wrote in 1911, "I have dug up in the wilderness the greater number of plants I introduced into the garden"; in later years, she added the qualifier that the wild land where she obtained the plants was slated "to be made over for so-called improvements."[14] Her mission to preserve native plants and to discourage others from digging rare species in the wild clashed with her collector's instinct as she sought to build and sustain her ambitious plant collection; more often than not, the needs of the garden prevailed. She gathered plants freely in the public parks of the Twin Cities (perhaps with the permission of Theodore Wirth) as well as from the Middlesex Fells Reservation near Cora's home in Malden, apparently untroubled by the irony of depleting stands of wild native plants in order to save them in her garden. Undoubtedly, she felt justified in doing so because the plants on display in her garden could be enjoyed by the public rather than remain hidden from view, unappreciated and unprotected, in a remote or inaccessible place.

Eloise had a few favorite "hunting grounds" that she returned to year after year. A patch of prairie at Fort Snelling and the banks of the Minnesota River below the fort were visited several times each season. The wild land at the confluence of the Minnesota and Mississippi rivers was especially rich in ferns and spring wildflowers; Eloise called it "Happy Valley," perhaps because of the memories it evoked of her botanizing there with Charles Bessey in the early 1880s. Close by were the prairie and "fairy land" woods at Minnehaha Falls, one of the first places Eloise visited each spring upon her return from Malden where she spent winters with Cora after retiring from teaching.[15] In Eden Prairie, Eloise botanized with her friend Clara M. Schutt who lived with her family on forty acres near where Purgatory Creek flowed into the Minnesota River.[16]

One place that Eloise especially loved was a hidden tamarack bog west of Birch Pond in Glenwood Park, within easy walking distance of the wild garden. She called it the "Quaking Bog" and visited it year after year for sods of sphagnum moss containing rose pogonia, pitcher plants, and bog rosemary. A photograph taken in 1911 shows Eloise, clad in a long skirt and wearing a hat piled high with silk flowers, precariously crossing a log over a stream surrounding the bog. She is said to have kept a "secret garden" of ferns and wildflowers in a sheltered swale where the stream entered the bog.[17]

Despite her claims to the contrary, Eloise Butler took great pains in cultivation of the wild plants of her garden. The widely varying conditions of light, moisture and soil available

Eloise Butler, c. 1917. *Minnesota Historical Society.*

in the garden allowed her to fit plants into their native surroundings as closely as possible. Soil from their original location was often imported with transplants, especially those "suspected of root parasitism," such as Indian paintbrush. "Sand and lime are imported for species requiring an excess of that diet," wrote Eloise; "and tannic acid and ammonium sulphate for greater acidity"; horsemint thrived, she found, on coal cinders.[18] Plants taken from the Anoka sand plain were placed in a spot where sand heaped up for the construction of Glenwood Parkway had washed into the garden. In 1926, Eloise wrote to friends of her efforts to grow the white flowered lance-leaved violet, rare in Minnesota, in a special sand tank:

> I have finally induced *Viola lanceolata* to live over the winter, blossom, and go to seed. For years I have tried various supposably [sic] suitable spots to no avail and imported a quantity of its native soil. Last fall the contrary violet was planted in a water tank that had been

filled with sand. The sand is kept moist by water seeping up from a subterranean spring. I could hardly believe my eyes to see the plants in blossom this spring.[19]

Other plants such as the round-leaved sundew, butterwort, and creeping snowberry were also tried there. A "bed of calcareous earth" was prepared for the reception of the walking fern in 1908; specimens obtained in later years were carefully pressed into the crevices of a limestone boulder. The rock fern, common polypody, was "bribed to take root in the garden by a diet of ground rock and a bed of sunken stones."[20] Eloise's cherished twinflower, obtained from northern Minnesota, was planted into an acid peat bed where she had tried for years to establish trailing arbutus. When the trailing arbutus had failed to grow there, she planted the delicate creeping evergreen under a white pine in the Pinetum, and mulched it with pine needles.

The efforts Eloise made for the sake of golden saxifrage, a low-growing plant found in springheads and other cold, wet places, were related in an article entitled "A Wild Botanic Garden" which appeared in *The Bellman*, a Minneapolis periodical, in 1913:

> The saxifrage is an importation to the garden, though native to the state. At first all efforts to get it to grow in the garden were futile. It seemed to resent being transplanted. Something was lacking. Then Miss Butler, the curator, on a plant-hunting expedition to the Wisconsin cliffs of the St. Croix River, found a thin limestone slab, like a large piece of heavy strawboard. This, by train and by trolley and by hand, she carried to the garden. Under two or three inches of soft soil at the water's edge below the dam she placed it, and over it she again planted her saxifrage. This time it took root, and it is now in its fourth year.[21]

Three years later, Eloise wrote to her botanical correspondence club about the same plant:

> The golden saxifrage is a wonder. Years ago I planted it in the swamp, but it refused to grow. Then I tried it in the open in a marshy place below my dam, placing it over a thin slab of limestone. It took root there, formed a good-sized mat, but was nearly choked out by sand several times at the annual repairing of the dam. Two years ago I reinforced it by another mat from Osceola, Wisconsin, where I had first obtained it. A few days ago I found in

> a marsh formed from the overflow of my boiling spring large dense mats of golden saxifrage—the finest I ever saw. Query: have they been there from the first?[22]

Eloise's legendary green thumb was perhaps due, in part, to her love for the plants which she regarded as her children. Like Demeter, she anxiously waited for the return of Persephone from the Underworld each spring. "Still harping on my daughter, as you see—will write about something else later," she penned across the top of a pamphlet about the garden sent to friends. Her friend Elizabeth Foss wrote in 1942 that Butler's writings, compiled by Foss and others after her death, "give but a faint idea of the effect of Miss Butler's love for plants on their successful transplanting and growth."[23]

Like any mother, Eloise was sometimes annoyed by her charges. Of the skunk cabbage, planted in 1907, she noted its first bloom in 1916 with thinly-veiled irritation: "Skunk cabbage blossomed for the first time in the garden swamp. It is not indigenous to the garden, is late in coming to time, and has been a number of years about it."[24] Plants which obstinately failed to flower were liable to receive a "good talking-to"; her scoldings were often followed by profuse bloom.

Eloise Butler had a special fondness for wild orchids, of which she attempted nearly forty species. She found the orchids, with few exceptions, to be "uncertain, coy and hard to please." Among the exceptions was the small white lady's-slipper. Eloise wrote that it had "responded nicely to cultivation when planted on tussocks surrounded by water. A sod of this species so treated increased from ten blooms to seventy-two, growing in a dense mass. I have seen nothing to equal it elsewhere."[25]

Eloise experimented with growing many species of wildflowers from seed, evident from numerous references throughout her *Garden Log*. She scattered the seeds where she wished them to grow but did not use seed-flats as she thought they would spoil the wild appearance of the garden. The results of the seed sowing are largely unknown. It is likely that Eloise's monthly contributions to the round-robin bulletins of the Gray-Memorial Botanical Chapter of the Agassiz Association, a botanical correspondence club to which she belonged for twenty-five years beginning in 1908, contained much information about the culture of wildflowers gleaned from her work in the wild garden. Unfortunately, only a small number of the bulletins are known to exist.[26]

About eight percent of the 1,650 species and varieties of plants known in Minnesota before 1900 and described in Upham's *Catalogue of the Flora of Minnesota* were non-native, often undesirable plants "such as follow civilized man, and grow in his cultivated fields and gardens, in spite of all efforts to banish them."[27] Only a few of these aliens, called adventive species, had gained a foothold in Glenwood Park before the garden was founded; less than one percent of the plants noted by Butler in the beginning were aliens, such as dandelion and sheep sorrel. In the years that followed, wind-borne seeds of others floated into the garden, and some arrived, unnoticed, in the soil of transplants. Yellow goat's beard, burdock and lady's thumb were among the immigrants. Queen Anne's lace, chicory, and ox-eye daisy were some of the attractive European plants naturalized in Minnesota that Butler purposely planted in the garden.[28]

Butler wrote in 1910 of her "inviolate rule of admitting only native or naturalized Minnesotan plants" into the garden; perhaps it was the nonconformity, which led her to found the garden in the first place, that prompted her on many occasions to ignore her own rule.[29] In 1908 she collected in Ontario a specimen of purple-flowering raspberry, *Rubus odoratus*, an eastern shrub. In her annual letter to Theodore Wirth six years later, Butler proudly reported the first flowering of the transplanted shrub, whose "large rose-colored blossoms and maple-like leaves . . . would attract attention in any garden. It is not listed among the native plants of Minnesota," she explained, "but a root of it pulled up by the railroad in Ontario . . . was given refuge in the wild garden." Under the mistaken belief that eastern hemlock was not native to the state, Butler planted a grove of the graceful trees along the brook. "Hemlock has not been listed among Minnesota plants," she wrote, "but it has been sneaked in, contrary to rule, with the idea that it may sometime break across the Wisconsin border."[30]

Although Eloise never amended her official description of the plant collection, her records reveal numerous other examples of the importing of species neither native to nor naturalized in Minnesota, usually personal favorites from the East. Still present in the garden are the purple-flowered *Trillium erectum* and the popular forget-me-nots, *Mysotis scorpioides*, planted by Eloise along the brook.[31] Her special fondness for the rein orchis, such as the large purple fringed orchid, *Platanthera fimbriata*, abundant in the Maine woods of her childhood, led her to experiment repeatedly with many of them. With no private land of her own, Eloise could not resist including them in "her" wild garden in Glenwood Park. Not surprisingly, few of the foreigners survived for long.

The unpredictable behavior of the "inmates" of the garden was a constant source of amusement to Eloise, who wrote, "In quirks, in whimsies, and in sheer contrariness a wild garden surpasses Mistress Mary." In 1915 she wrote to Theodore Wirth:

> The wild garden has been true to its name and nature in behaving contrary to rule and precedent. Plants sometimes have refused to grow where conditions seemed favorable, and have perversely appeared in unlikely places. *Aster multiflorus*, a prairie plant, has taken to the bog, and meadow gentians have been found on the dry hillside. The small, pale-blue dog violet, *Viola conspersa*, and the interesting little twayblade, *Liparis loeslii*, carefully planted on one side of the swamp, have developed more thrifty colonies on the extreme opposite side; and the royal fern, *Osmunda regalis*, set out on the edge of the swamp, has lodged itself in the center.[32]

Eloise's initial resolve to let plants "grow as they will" without interference was soon abandoned, as she found herself refereeing disputes between species competing for the same turf. A few that would not behave were expelled from the garden. By 1912 she was "exterminating pestilent weeds like poison ivy, Canada thistle, burdock, and *Lappula* [beggar's lice]" and "grubbing out the excess of prickly ash and sumach," permitting only a few of the "vegetable pariahs" for educational value. Eloise refused to use "poison" (herbicides) and, for control of the offenders, preferred old-fashioned pulling or simply pitting more aggressive species against one another. Maidenhair ferns, wild roses, asters and goldenrod were planted to "dispossess" wood nettle; wild cucumber seeds were sown in a patch of quack grass, and wild mint and common tansy were enlisted "to head off Creeping Charlie."[33]

One notable alien, imported from a nursery in Vermont, was purple loosestrife, *Lythrum salicaria*, which Eloise planted along the brook in 1916. She admired the plant's tall spires of purple flowers, familiar from the wetlands of Maine where it was well established in the days of her grandparents. *L. salicaria* was commonly planted in gardens, promoted by landscape designers, and naturalized by American beekeepers as a honey plant. The disastrous tendency of purple loosestrife to dominate wetlands to the near-total exclusion of native vegetation was not realized until the 1930s. *L. salicaria* eventually became a nuisance in the garden and is now being extirpated.[34]

As curator, Eloise needed an office in which to keep the records, receive visitors, and take shelter on cold and rainy days. In 1915 a small, shingled wooden cabin resembling Thoreau's hut on Walden Pond was built to her design on a natural plateau overlooking the bog. A sign which read "Office of Curator, Wild Botanic Garden" was posted by the door and wild roses planted on both sides of the entrance. Vines of clematis, honeysuckle, and dutchman's pipe were trained on a pergola on the front of the cabin. Inside, Eloise kept her microscope and botanical books; the walls were covered with pictures of birds. Natural objects found in the garden, such as wasp's nests, bird's nests, and mushrooms, were displayed on counters and shelves. A kerosene heater provided warmth on cold days, and a

hammock furnished rest on sultry afternoons. Eloise called the office her "lodge in the wilderness." Visitors to the garden would often find her there, dressed in riding breeches or brown overalls and high-laced black leather boots, or digging in the bog wearing a beekeeper's veil and scented with citronella oil used against the hordes of mosquitoes that were "withstood only by grim endurance."[35]

The birds that frequented the wild garden were close companions of Eloise Butler's days. Each spring she noted in the *Garden Log* the return of the sparrows and warblers and recorded, at various times, a pair of bald eagles, osprey, and nesting pheasants. Wrens and phoebes built nests and reared their young under the eaves of her office. Once she found in a stand of cattails five nests of red-winged blackbirds; she found the eggs a "beautiful blue, scrawled with dark purple Runic inscriptions."[36] In 1914, Eloise wrote of the birds in the wild garden:

> I have stroked baby crows, too young to be timid, followed the whip-poor-will in his short flights through the swamp, seen bluebirds chase out the long-eared owl, the great bittern stiffen like a stick when he heard my footsteps, and a pair of the rare crested wood ducks swimming in my little pond. The red-shouldered hawks have nested and reared their young in the garden, and just the other day a covey of nine bobwhites were found in their retreat in the meadow.[37]

An entry in the *Garden Log* dated June 3, 1917, noted simply: "A young grosbeak just out of the nest came directly to me in the swamp, and huddled under my skirt."[38]

Eloise's encounters with the various small animals of the preserve, such as snapping turtles, woodchucks, and snakes, were also noted in the *Garden Log* or in a diary that she sporadically kept. In 1915 Eloise encountered a muskrat on the earthen dam she had built across the brook:

> He stood motionless, as did I. Then he turned and faced me, baring his teeth. "Why do you grin at me?" I asked him pleasantly. Whereupon, he slid through the wild balsam into the brook.[39]

Two years later, Eloise made note of a visit from a woodchuck:

> Found a woodchuck perched on a stone set against the boles of an ironwood beside

the broad path. There he sat motionless while a crowd gazed at him. When a camera was trained on him, he sprang away, ran over the hillside and darted into a large hole just dug in which to set a tree. The workmen could not persuade him to budge until they filled in the hole with the sod they had just removed. Later he ran by other workmen who were resetting a tree on the edge of the northwest meadow; was rediscovered standing stock still in the pathway below Prickly Ash Arbor. This time he did not move and allowed a long-time exposure of the camera. An hour later a dog caused him to take refuge in the fork of a small elm. There he hung all night and the next day in the same position.[40]

Early one morning Eloise found a fat young pig asleep on the hillside below her office. She wanted to name him Endymion, after the slumbering shepherd loved by the Moon in Greek mythology, but the son of the family with whom she boarded insisted on calling him Rip, she wrote, "because his ear has been ripped on a barbed wire fence, and he sleeps like Rip van Winkle."[41]

The lack of a fence to define the garden area and protect the valuable plant collection was a continuing source of distress to Butler. Aside from the original enclosure of three acres, quickly outgrown, the wild garden remained unfenced until 1924. Picnickers picked the flowers, made campfires in the midst of violet beds, and left rubbish strewn about. Thieves stole clumps of lady's-slippers in full bloom and once walked off with a hive of Italian bees. Marauding dogs dug holes in pursuit of woodchucks, and horseback riders strayed from the bridle paths in Glenwood Park and rode through the preserve, heedless of the precious plants. Butler once came upon a "hobo" washing his socks, with soap, in the birdbath. The secluded road to the garden was known to locals as "Lovers' Lane"; Butler, armed with a broken-off machete she used as a gardening tool and wearing a park watchman's star pinned to her chest, was forever running out "spooners" whom she suspected of trampling the wildflowers.[42]

Butler repeatedly raised the need for a fence with Park Superintendent Theodore Wirth, but her pleas went unheeded as the Park Board poured funds into developing the golf course, bath house, ski facilities, and building an ill-advised artificial waterfall (the

Loring Cascade) in Glenwood Park. Butler lobbied for a fence in a newspaper column she wrote on Minneapolis public gardens (including the wild garden) in 1919:

> Now that their day of glory has gone by, it may be safe to mention the showy ladies'-slippers [sic]. Never have they been more beautiful—the most wonderful sight in the flower world. It is a pity that all could not have enjoyed this sight. But it must be denied to the general public until the garden is fenced in and protected from vandals. When these flowers are picked, the plants are destroyed, because they do not put out more leaves, and are . . . unable to prepare food for next year's growth.[43]

A formal request for fencing of the garden, made by Mrs. E. Naftalin on behalf of the Minneapolis chapter of the Wild Flower Preservation Society of America, was denied by the Park Board in 1923. Impatient of standing by while her life's work was threatened, Butler hired a man to put up a fence in 1924 at a cost to herself of nearly $700. She could not afford to fence the entire garden; only about five acres of the North Meadow, including Lady's-Slipper Path, were enclosed, and the northwest Gentian Meadow had to be left out entirely. After the fence was installed, Wirth surprised Butler by offering to reimburse her for its cost, according to a letter she wrote to friends from Malden in November.[44]

Tamaracks and birches in the swamp, c. 1915. Most of the trees were lost to the tornado of 1925. *Minneapolis Public Library, Eloise Butler file.*

Eloise Butler considered the wild garden a success from the beginning. She had fulfilled her goals of securing the preservation of the bog and providing a place where students of botany could study living plants, and she felt she was well on her way toward her goal of collecting all of the native plants of Minnesota. Specimens of each of the trees and shrubs in the garden bore labels with their common and Latin scientific names. "The garden has become an efficient aid to young botanists in determining difficult species, since it is easier to learn type characters from living, growing plants than from dried herbarium specimens," she wrote in 1914.[45] A professor of botany at the University of Chicago, to whom she had sent an article she wrote on the wild garden, wrote back with praise for her efforts, adding, "the time will come when Minneapolis teachers of botany will 'rise up and call you blessed'."[46]

Articles about Butler and her remarkable garden, with titles such as "Botanists All Over U.S. Visit Glenwood Wildflower Garden" and "Neighbors Don't Know She Exists, but Botanic Garden Curator is Famous Over America," ran regularly in the local newspapers, stating that many botanists from other parts of the country traveled to

Minneapolis expressly to visit the garden; members of the general public came each season by the "thousands," estimated Butler.[47]

The name "Wild Botanic Garden" proved misleading to some visitors who expected to find beds of showy flowers. After 1920, Eloise called the garden the Native Plant Reserve, the Wild Garden, or simply "the Preserve." Theodore Wirth preferred the name "Wild Flower Garden," but Eloise felt that the other plants—the trees, shrubs, ferns, grasses, mosses, fungi and algae—were just as important as the lady's-slippers and trillium which attracted more attention. In 1929 the Park Board formally changed the name to the Eloise Butler Wild Flower Garden in recognition of Butler's achievement in "establishing in the garden as complete a collection of hardy plants as there is to be found anywhere in the great Northwest."[48] A speech given by a representative of the Park Board honored Eloise, who, "with the loving aid of the great god Pan and the universal Mother Nature . . . has been from the first the Good Spirit of this 'garden of the Lord'."[49] Eloise felt gratitude at the recognition accorded her but persisted in calling the garden the Native Plant Reserve or the Wild Garden until her death.

Notes

1   The original petition is in the Eloise Butler file, Minneapolis Park and Recreation Board Archives.

2   Eloise Butler, 3-page unpublished typescript entitled "Concerning the Wild Botanic Garden in Glenwood Park," filed with Woman's Club petition of 1911 in Eloise Butler file, Minneapolis Park and Recreation Board Archives.

3   Minneapolis Board of Park Commissioners, Minutes, 19 June 1911. Butler's salary of $50 per month was less than half that paid to head gardeners and nurserymen employed by the Park Board in 1911; from 1919 until her death in 1933, she received $60 per month.

4   The precise size of the garden after the 1912 annex is unclear, but appears to have been at least twenty acres. Butler gave the acreage at various times as 20, 25 and 27 acres. A newspaper article entitled "How the Park Board Plans to Improve Glenwood Park" indicated that the northern boundary of the wild garden in 1914 was Western (now Glenwood) Avenue (Minneapolis Tribune, 28 June 1914).

5   I am indebted to Lloyd Teeuwen and Maynard Erickson for aid in interpreting the records of Eloise Butler with regard to the area and features of the early garden. An artist's map of the early garden faces the title page. Some plants indigenous to the 1912 annexation were mentioned in Eloise Butler to Theodore Wirth, 8 November 1912, published in Minneapolis Board of Park Commissioners, Thirteenth Annual Report, pp. 61-63 (63); quote from Eloise Butler, "Annals of a Wild Garden" (c.1914), unpublished 6 page typescript, p. 2, in Eloise Butler file, Minneapolis Park and Recreation Board Archives.

6   Ibid.; also Eloise Butler, Garden Log, 9, 22, and 26 September 1912 and 7 October 1912.

7   Quotes from Eloise Butler to Theodore Wirth, 3 November 1911, published in Minneapolis Board of Park Commissioners Twenty-ninth Annual Report, pp. 66-68 (68); and Eloise Butler, "Orchids in Native Plant Preserve, Minneapolis, Minnesota," in Gray Memorial Botanical Chapter, Agassiz Association, Division D "Orchid Special" April 1932, pp. 16-18 (32-page photostat booklet in Eloise Butler Papers at Minnesota Historical Society).

8   Gerald B. Ownbey to author, 24 January 1991. A list of the flora indigenous to the garden is on on file at the garden and at the Minneapolis Park Board. As curator, Butler also wrote a letter to Theodore Wirth each winter, reporting on the plantings and other events of the previous season. Wirth published seven of these interesting letters (for the years 1911-1914, and 1930-1932) in the Minneapolis Board of Park Commissioners' *Annual Reports*; sadly, none of Butler's original letters appear to have been preserved.

9   Welby Smith to author, 15 February 1991.

10   Eloise Butler to Gray Memorial Botanical Chapter, Agassiz Association, Division D, September 1919, copy in Eloise Butler biographical file, Minneapolis Public Library, Minneapolis Collections; Warren Upham, *Catalogue of the Flora of Minnesota, Including its Phaenogamous and Vascular Cryptogamous Plants, Indigenous, Naturalized, and Adventive* (Minneapolis: Geological and Natural History Survey of Minnesota, 1884); C.O. Rosendahl and F.K. Butters, "Guide to the Ferns and Fern Allies of Minnesota," *Minnesota Plant Studies*, Vol. 3 (1909), pp. 1-23.

11   Quote from Eloise Butler, "A Wild Botanic Garden" (c.1911), unpublished 10-page typescript in Eloise Butler file, Minneapolis Public and Recreation Board Archives, p. 3; number of ferns mentioned in Eloise Butler to Theodore Wirth, 1 January 1914, published in Minneapolis Board of Park Commissioners, *Thirty-First Annual Report*, pp. 47-48 (48). There are fifty-eight true ferns native to Minnesota (Gerald B. Ownbey to author, 18 February 1991).

12   Figures supplied by Eloise Butler on plantings made during each season were printed in most *Annual Reports* of the Minneapolis Board of Park Commissioners between 1907 and 1933. Final figures taken from Butler's handwritten corrections (c.1930) to an undated pamphlet entitled "Wild Flowers in their Garden at Glenwood Park," copy in Eloise Butler Papers at Minnesota Historical Society.

13   Quote from Eloise Butler to Gray Memorial Botanical Chapter, Agassiz Association, Division D, (1926), copy (under the title: "Beginnings in 1907") in *Early History of Eloise Butler Plant Reserve*, p. 7, at Minneapolis Public Library, Minneapolis Collection; Butler's efforts to grow wild orchids are described in her "Orchids in Native Plant Reserve" (see note 7).

14   Quotes from Eloise Butler to Theodore Wirth, 3 November 1911, published in Minneapolis Board of Park Commissioners, *Twenty-Ninth Annual Report*, pp. 66-68 (68); 2-page typescript, dated 18 April 1928, of talk given by Eloise Butler to the staff of the Minneapolis Public Library (p. 2), in Eloise Butler file, Minneapolis Park and Recreation Board Archives.

15   Quotes from Eloise Butler, *Garden Log*, 5 May 1927 and 10 April 1915.

16   Author's interview with Elizabeth Schutt, 17 May 1988. Caroline Crosby purchased the Schutt property for use as a summer house in 1914, according to Elizabeth Schutt.

17   I am grateful to Maynard Erickson for details of Eloise Butler's secret garden. The quaking bog was seriously invaded by buckthorn and purple loosestrife, and is presently under restoration by the Minneapolis Park and Recreation Board.

18   Quotes from Eloise Butler to Gray Memorial Botanical Chapter, Agassiz Association, Division D, (c.1916), copy (under the title: "Garden Experiences") in *Annals of the Wild Life Reserve*, p. 27, at Minneapolis Public Library, Minneapolis Collection; Eloise Butler to Gray Memorial Botanical Chapter, Agassiz Association, Division D, (1926), copy (under the title: "Beginnings in 1907") in *Early History of Eloise Butler Plant Reserve*, p. 7, at Minneapolis Public Library, Minneapolis Collection; and Eloise Butler to Gray Memorial Botanical Chapter, Agassiz Chapter, Agassiz Association, Division D, February 1931, copy in Eloise Butler biographical file, Minneapolis Public Library, Minneapolis Collection.

19   Eloise Butler to Gray Memorial Botanical Chapter, Agassiz Association, Division D, October 1926, copy in Eloise Butler biographical file at Minneapolis Public Library, Minneapolis Collection.

20   Quotes from Eloise Butler, "The Quest of the Walking Fern" (1908), unpublished 2-page typescript (p. 1), and "Annals of a Wild Garden" (c.1914), unpublished 6-page typescript (p. 5), both in Eloise Butler file, Minneapolis Public Library, Minneapolis Collection.

21   W.P. Kirkwood, "A Wild Botanic Garden," *The Bellman*, Vol. 14 (3 May 1913), pp. 559-562 (560), (copy in Eloise Butler Papers, Minnesota Historical Society).

22   Eloise Butler to Gray Memorial Botanical Chapter, Agassiz Association, Division D, May 1916, copy in Eloise Butler biographical file, Minneapolis Public Library, Minneapolis Collection.

23   Quotes from Butler's handwritten note across top of "The Minneapolis Wild Botanic Garden," reprinted from *School Science and Mathematics* (1910), in Eloise Butler biography file at Minneapolis Public Library, Minneapolis Collection; and Elizabeth Foss to Carl Vitz, 27 July 1942, in Eloise Butler biography file, Minneapolis Public Library, Minneapolis Collection.

24   Eloise Butler to Gray Memorial Botanical Chapter, Agassiz Association, Division D, May 1916, copy in Eloise Butler biographical file, Minneapolis Public Library, Minneapolis Collection.

Pond carpeted with green duckweed in the wild garden, 1926. *Minneapolis Park and Recreation Board.*

25   Eloise Butler, "Orchids in Native Plant Preserve," p. 16 (see note 7).

26   The club had members in many states; one member was botanist Lycurgus R. Moyer (1848-1917) of Montevideo, whose life is told in Edmund C. Bray's "Surveying the Seasons on the Minnesota Prairies," *Minnesota History*, Vol. 48 (Summer 1982), pp. 72-82. (Selections from Butler's contributions to the club's monthly bulletins are reprinted at pp. 153-184 as "Annals of a Wild Garden.")

27   Warren Upham, *Catalogue of the Flora of Minnesota*, p. 15 (see note 10).

28   Eloise Butler, *Garden Log*, 10 September 1929, 9 August 1915, 13 June 1923.

29   Eloise Butler, "The Minneapolis Wild Botanic Garden," p. 234 (see chapter 8, note 10).

30   Quotes from Eloise Butler to Theodore Wirth, 1 January 1915, published in Minneapolis Board of Park Commissioners, *Thirty-Second Annual Report*, pp. 38-40 (38); and Eloise Butler, "Annals of a Wild Garden" (c.1914), unpublished 6-page typescript in Eloise Butler file, Minneapolis Park and Recreation Board Archives, p. 4. Eastern hemlock (*Tsuga canadensis*) is native to Minnesota, although rare.

31   Eloise Butler apparently planted what she

thought was *Mysotis laxa*, the Minnesota native, that she obtained from wild land in Massachusetts in 1909. A list of plants made by Butler in 1931 lists *M. scorpoides*, a naturalized European species common in the East (see list filed with C.O. Rosendahl to Eloise Butler, 14 October 1931, in correspondence files of Department of Plant Biology, University of Minnesota Archives); *M. scorpoides* is the species now present in the garden. Butler's card file indicates that she discovered a specimen of mountain laurel (*Kalmia latifolia*), "perhaps planted by park nurseryman," in bloom in the wild garden in 1924.

32   First part of quote from Eloise Butler to Gray Memorial Botanical Chapter, Agassiz Association, Division D (c.1916), copy (under the title: "Garden Experiences") in *Annals of the Wild Life Reserve*, p. 27, at Minneapolis Public Library, Minneapolis Collection; indented quote from Eloise Butler to Theodore Wirth, 1 January 1915, published in Minneapolis Board of Park Commissioners, *Thirty-Second Annual Report*, pp. 39-40.

33   Eloise Butler to Theodore Wirth, 8 November 1912, published in Minneapolis Board of Park Commissioners, *Thirtieth Annual Report*, pp. 61-63 (63); Eloise Butler to Theodore Wirth,

3 November 1911, published in Minneapolis Board of Park Commissioners, *Twenty-Ninth Annual Report*, pp. 66-68 (67); Eloise Butler, *Garden Log*, 13 October 1921, 9 August 1923, 30 May 1925, 10 June 1930, 23 September 1930, and 10 October 1932.

34   Daniel Q. Thompson, Ronald L. Stuckey, and Edith B. Thompson, "Spread, Impact and Control of Purple Loosestrife (*Lythrum salicaria*) in North American Wetlands" (Washington, D.C.: U.S. Department of the Interior, Fish and Wildlife Service, 1987). *Lythrum salicaria* was designated a noxious weed in Minnesota in 1987; it is now illegal to sell or transport the plant in the state.

35   Eloise Butler, "A Native Plant Preserve," *Wild Flower*, Vol. 1 (1 October 1924), p. 27.

36   Eloise Butler, *Garden Log*, 1 June 1931.

37   Eloise Butler to Gray Memorial Botanical Chapter, Agassiz Association, Division D, June 1914, copy (under the title: "Animal Life in the Wild Garden") in *Annals of the Wild Life Reserve*, p. 1, Minneapolis Public Library, Minneapolis Collection.

38   The bird was probably a rose-breasted grosbeak, which nests in Minnesota.

39   Eloise Butler, *Garden Log*, 16 July 1915. Wild balsam is a synonym for jewelweed.

40   Eloise Butler, *Diary*, 19 May 1917 (in Eloise Butler Papers, Minnesota Historical Society).

41   Eloise Butler to Gray Memorial Botanical Chapter, Agassiz Association, Division D, May 1916, copy in Eloise Butler biographical file, Minneapolis Public Library, Minneapolis Collection.

42   Eloise Butler, *Garden Log*, 22 October 1912, 21 August 1922; Eloise Butler, "Frequent Occurrences in the Unfenced Native Plant Reserve," 1-page unpublished typescript (c.1924) in Eloise Butler file, Minneapolis Public Library, Minneapolis Collection; Minneapolis Park and Recreation Board Archives; unidentified clipping (c.1923) in Scrapbook III, p. 10, Archives of The Friends of the Wild Flower Garden, Inc.

43   Eloise Butler, unidentified clipping (c.1919) in Scrapbook II, p. 25, Minneapolis Park and Recreation Board Archives.

44   Minneapolis Board of Park Commissioners, *Minutes*, 6 June 1923, and 5 September 1923; Wirth's offer to reimburse Butler for the fence is mentioned in Eloise Butler to William H. and Martha Crone, 29 November 1924, Martha Crone Papers at Minnesota Historical Society.

45   Eloise Butler to Theodore Wirth, 1 January 1915, published in Minneapolis Board of Park Commissioners, *Thirty-Second Annual Report*, pp. 38-40 (39).

46   Otis W. Caldwell to Eloise Butler, 5 January 1910, in Eloise Butler file at Minneapolis Public and Recreation Board Archives.

Grey-headed Coneflower, *Ratibida pinnata*, in wild garden in 1915. *Minneapolis Public Library, Minneapolis Collection.*

47   Unidentified clippings (c.1920s) pasted in Scrapbook III, pp. 3 and 13, at Archives of The Friends of the Wild Flower Garden, Inc.

48   Minneapolis Board of Park Commissioners, *Forty-Seventh Annual Report*, 1929, p. 57.

49   Typescript of speech entitled "The Eloise Butler Wild Flower Garden" (c.1929) in Eloise Butler file, Minneapolis Public Library, Minneapolis Recreation Board Archives. In 1986 the name of the garden was changed to the Eloise Butler Wildflower Garden and Bird Sanctuary.

Pergola for native vines in the Wild Garden. *Minnesota Historical Society.*

Eloise Butler, wearing a bee veil against mosquitoes, and Monarch, c. 1920s. *Friends of the Wild Flower Garden, Inc.*

10

The Friendship of Nature

Showy Lady's-slipper

ELOISE BUTLER'S EFFORTS on behalf of native plants were not limited to her labor in the garden. She wrote articles, gave talks and held numerous exhibits to promote the appreciation of wildflowers and native plants by the public. Her activities attracted the attention of like-minded souls who joined an ever-widening circle of friends and admirers.

In 1911, Eloise was invited by the Minneapolis *Tribune* to write a weekly article on wildflowers in the garden. Her articles, extolling the virtues and beauties of native plants and pointing out the bad habits of some of the "tramps from foreign lands," were lavishly illustrated with photographs taken in the garden by her former student, Mary Meeker. Her aim in writing the articles, she explained to her botanical correspondence club, "was to interest people in nature who had but little botanical knowledge, and to coat the pill of information, so that it could be easily swallowed." Another member of the club added to the round-robin bulletin: "Miss Butler's articles [are] so charming, I should enjoy a whole bottle of such 'sugar-coated pills' at once."[1]

In 1919, Eloise was employed by the Minneapolis *Tribune* and the Minneapolis *Journal* to cover the flowers blooming in the Rose Garden at Lake Harriet and in the Armory Gardens at Lyndale Avenue and Kenwood Parkway, as well as those in the wild garden. Her serviceable listing of the various hybrid teas in the Rose Garden and "all the usual standbys of the season" in bloom in the Armory Gardens were followed by rapturous descriptions of the "riot of color prevailing in the Wild Garden," whose meadows, she wrote, were "ravishing harmonies of pink, white, gold and blue," with gentians of "rare and wondrous beauty"; the "little Indian pipes in ghostly white" lent "a glamour of mystery to the scene." Eloise's dislike of the exotic canna lilies in the Armory Gardens was barely concealed as she wrote, "we shall be summoned to court-martial if we do not stand at attention before the canna, General Merkel, in a blazing uniform of crimson-orange edged with gold."[2]

Eloise overcame a professed phobia of public speaking to gain friends for the garden, giving talks to students, civic organizations, and factory workers on wildflowers. In 1910 she addressed a meeting of the Minnesota Academy of Science and presented a paper on the Minneapolis Wild Botanic Garden. After describing the founding and the plants of the wild garden, she again urged the establishment of an arboretum in Glenwood Park:

> Why can we not duplicate in Minneapolis the Shaw Gardens [now the Missouri Botanical Gardens] of St. Louis, the Bronx Gardens of New York City, or the world-famous Arnold Arboretum of Boston? Barring the primeval hemlock grove, Glenwood park has more natural advantages, as water supply, fertility and variety of soil, than the Arnold Arboretum. Such a garden would add greatly to the fame and attractiveness of Minneapolis, and would be second only to the public library in its educative and refining influences.[3]

At a meeting of a literary society in Minnetonka, Eloise pled for forest conservation and decried the "wasteful and improvident" habits of Americans. "We have snatched at our treasures with both hands, and flung them to the winds," she warned. In her talk, Eloise made what must have been, in 1910, one of the first appeals in the state for the recycling of paper products to spare the trees.[4] In a *Garden Log* entry dated April 8, 1915, Eloise wrote: "Talked to girls at Loose-Wilds Biscuit Co. factory, at their noon hour."

The photographs of native plants taken by Mary Meeker were used in the Wild Botanic Garden exhibit, held annually from 1909 through at least 1918 in the Horticultural Building at the Minnesota State Fair. The exhibit, which won a blue ribbon in 1910 in the wildflower competition sponsored by the Minnesota Horticultural Society, featured a display of wildflowers arranged in crockery vases and a mushroom table with a foul-smelling stinkhorn fungus kept in a tightly-capped bottle.[5]

According to a clipping pasted into her scrapbook, an agent of an English seed house paid a call at Butler's exhibit in 1915 and went away bearing seeds of the fringed gentian; he pronounced its blue the "most perfect in the entire plant world." He added that "this collection prepared by Miss Butler is one of the finest I have ever seen," and stated that "a city which makes provision for such things in its parks indeed is to be complimented."[6]

Other exhibits were held as well. A display of wildflowers at the 1913 annual

The Wild Botanic Garden exhibit at the Minnesota State Fair in 1910. *Minneapolis Park and Recreation Board.*

meeting of the American Florists and Ornamental Horticulturalists held in Minneapolis was said to include "seventy-five varieties"; Butler hoped to interest the members in the "fragility, delicacy and artless grace of the wildings," reminding them that "all cultivated plants are, or were once, wildings somewhere." She promised to display, "depending on conditions of moisture and temperature, whatever wild flowers fickle Nature may choose to bestow at the time in the neighborhood of the city [that] will modestly droop their heads to the stately exotics in the great exhibit held . . . at Armory Hall."[7]

Eloise also maintained annual native plant exhibits at the Minneapolis Public Library from 1918 through 1923 and held one exhibit in the display window of the Minneapolis *Journal* Travel Bureau in the 1920s, saying she would "spare no effort" to teach the people of Minneapolis to love and conserve wildflowers.[8] The exhibits were updated every few days with fresh, living material from the wild garden—ferns, mosses, wildflowers and branches of blossoming trees and shrubs. One can envision Eloise, carrying baskets filled with the wild plants of her garden as she climbed the steps of the stately old library building that stood on Hennepin Avenue, giving a nod of silent greeting to the statue of Minerva, Roman goddess of wisdom (Athena to the Greeks), which stood in a niche above the main entrance.[9]

Eloise Butler was not, by nature, a joiner of organizations; there is little evidence of her affiliation with groups, even botanical ones. In her later years she was a member of the Sullivant Moss Society (founded by Elizabeth K. Britton and her sister's friend Cora H. Clarke) and received their journal, *The Bryologist*. In 1923, apparently with the primary motive of gaining a fence for the garden, she helped found a Minnesota chapter of the Wildflower Preservation Society of America. Butler was put in charge of membership and publicity; she wrote leaflets on the need for restraint in picking wildflowers. In 1923 she wrote to Elizabeth Britton, then serving as secretary-treasurer of the organization, informing her of the existence of the new Minnesota chapter and apologizing for her delay in answering a previous letter: "I have absolutely no leisure, and my correspondence accumulates for a rainy day," she wrote. Britton wrote back:

> I . . . am so glad that you have such an excellent start and have already such a large collection. You must have considerable and interesting variety of soil and location to be able to grow so many. . . . You certainly are fortunate in the number and variety of your orchids, and there are a good many rare plants on your list that are not here in the New York Botanical Garden.[10]

Britton sympathized with Butler's wish for a fence, pointing out that "Kew Garden[s] in England have all their special and best things fenced in." A month later, Butler wrote to Britton, enclosing a list of plants in the garden:

> Our Reserve contains at present about twenty-seven acres in the midst of a 700-acre park. You may imagine my state of panic during the time of rare blooms, with but one policeman, who is on duty only afternoons and evenings, and is in demand at the . . . bath houses, the picnic grounds, and the golf links. I am grateful for your sympathy. Only those who are in the work can understand the situation.[11]

Butler's article about the garden, entitled "A Native Plant Reserve," was published in *Wild Flower*, the official organ of the society, in 1924.

One goal of the Minnesota chapter, whose "field marshals" were Professors C.O. Rosendahl and William S. Cooper of the University of Minnesota botany department, was the passage of a state law barring the picking or digging of any wild orchids, trillium, and other protected plants. Passage of the bill,

introduced by Hannah J. Kempfer and Maybeth Hurd Paige in the House of Representatives, was accomplished in 1925, and Minnesota joined six other states that already had such legislation. After 1925, Eloise sharply increased her purchase of protected plants from nurseries in Wisconsin and on the East Coast.[12]

When Elizabeth K. Britton stepped down from her work at the national headquarters of the Wild Flower Preservation Society of America in 1925, Percy L. Ricker, head of the Washington D.C. chapter, took over leadership of the group. Eloise Butler wrote to Ricker at once, informing him of the existence of her garden in Minneapolis and stating that it was probably the first such preserve in the country. Ricker wrote back claiming precedence for a sixty-acre private preserve on the Potomac River in Maryland established in 1901 by an all-male club of biologists to which he belonged. His response seems to have annoyed Butler to such an extent that she had nothing further to do with the organization. Ironically, in January 1939 the front cover of its publication, *Wild Flower*, began carrying the motto: "Dedicated to the establishment of Wild Flower Sanctuaries as the only practical means of real Wild Flower Conservation."[13]

Friendships and correspondence based on a mutual love of wild plants enriched Butler's years in the garden. "Isn't the communion of friends on 'God's Out of Doors' one of the choicest privileges the world can offer?" she wrote in 1927.[14] Dr. Thomas S. Roberts, ornithologist and curator of the Minnesota Natural History Museum at the University of Minnesota, visited the garden for the many birds that found shelter and food there. Roberts brought Butler wild orchids, such as calypso and striped coral root, gathered on his visits to Lake Itasca. The Minneapolis Audubon Society met in the garden in 1915, its first year of existence.[15] Clara Leavitt, Elizabeth Foss and other former students who remained close to Butler as the years passed by were frequent visitors; together, the paths of the garden were trod round again and again, in "space shaped by the movements of white-haired women and ringing with the laughter of old lady friends."[16]

Another friend was Frances Hutchinson, president of the Illinois chapter of the Wild Flower Preservation Society of America. Mrs. Hutchinson and her husband, a wealthy

Chicago banker, owned a seventy-acre wooded bird and wildflower sanctuary at Lake Geneva, Wisconsin, called "Wychwood" for the witch hazel that grew wild there. Their aim was to protect the native plants of Wisconsin and to plant fruit-bearing shrubs as a "berry garden" for the birds. Eloise Butler and Frances Hutchinson exchanged plants and knowledge about wildflower culture. The Hutchinson property, eventually acquired by the University of Chicago (the Hutchinsons intended that it be used for botanical field work), was sold to developers in 1958.[17]

In 1923 Eloise Butler wrote to the editor of the *Garden Magazine*, offering to furnish some herbs about which another reader had inquired. Her letter, printed under the heading "A Generous Offer of Oldentime Herbs," elicited many letters to Butler from readers seeking information about the cultivation of wild or neglected plants.[18] One who wrote to Butler, initiating a friendship of equals, was Fannie M. Heath, the "flower woman" of North Dakota. Fannie was born in Wykoff, Minnesota, in 1864 and had gone with her husband to homestead a farm near Grand Forks in the 1880s. Fannie had learned to know the plants of Minnesota from her father, who is said to have learned them from the Indians. During her years on the treeless prairie, she gathered and planted on the farm hundreds of native plants as well as hardy ones from abroad, while studying botany alone. She wrote many articles for publications such as the *American Botanist* and *Nature Magazine*, and her horticultural knowledge was nationally recognized. Her special affection for native plants and experience with their culture led to correspondence and friendship with Eloise; the *Garden Log* lists numerous plants Fannie sent to Eloise from North Dakota. After Fannie Heath's death in 1931, her extensive wildflower gardens were abandoned, but the trees and shrubs she planted still surround the old farmstead where she lived.[19]

After living three years, from 1912 to 1915, with her friend Jessie Polley in south Minneapolis, Eloise began boarding in 1916 with the family of John ("Jack") and Susan Babcock. The Babcocks lived in a large house on Xerxes Avenue (just north of Chestnut) at the eastern edge of Glenwood Park. Although not a working farm, it had the feel of a country place with a barn, a windmill, an apple orchard, and several log cabins that stood on the property. The household was large and active, similar to the extended family in which Eloise had spent her own childhood. Still at home were Bessie and Vernon, two of the Babcock's three children; their daughter Viola's little girl, Jean, was a frequent overnight visitor. Susan Babcock did the cooking and cleaning with the help of Swedish servants, leaving Eloise free for her botanical work; Eloise often spent summer evenings sitting on the screened porch, typing the records of the garden. Her bedroom on the second floor overlooked the orchard and the back gate, which opened onto a path that led through a deep glen of elms to the wild garden.

Jack Babcock owned an engraving business and was an avid hunter and naturalist. The walls of the Victorian house were hung with hunting trophies and Indian relics that Jack had found on the property and in Glenwood Park. On his hunting expeditions to northern Minnesota, Jack found and brought back many wild plants for the garden. He often took Eloise botanizing; locations near Minneapolis were visited for an afternoon, and on longer trips, with one of the Babcock children along, they stayed overnight in tourist camps at Lake Kabekona and other places "up north." The Babcocks had a large library, and Jack and Eloise, who shared a birthday (August 3), often sat up late talking of books or of Eloise's travels abroad (she spent the winter of 1913-1914 touring botanic gardens and museums in Greece and Italy with Cora and her husband). Butler's vivid descriptions of places she had visited in Europe inspired one of the Babcock girls, Bessie, to become a teacher.[20]

Foremost among the friends Eloise made in the garden was Martha Crone, forty-three years her junior and a self-taught naturalist who visited often with her husband, dentist William H. Crone, and their daughter, Janet. Members of the Minnesota Mycological Society, the Crones shared an interest in mushrooms with Eloise and knew well the bogs and sand dunes of Anoka from their mushroom-hunting excursions. On camping trips to northern Minnesota, the Crones gathered wild plants sought by Eloise for the garden.

Dismayed, no doubt, by the fact that Martha Crone's formal schooling had ended with the eighth grade, Eloise gradually came to

Martha Crone (right) and Mrs. A.R. Nelson with giant puffball in 1929. *Minnesota Historical Society.*

trust the young woman who came bearing clumps of pasque flowers and wild orchids and seeking knowledge about native plants. "You really should know her," Eloise remarked to her friend, Gertrude Cram; "she's a wildflower crank like you."[21] Eloise accompanied the Crones on botanizing trips in Anoka, and they stood below the still-agile botanist as she scrambled up steep hillsides in search of rare plants. She led them, in turn, to the quaking bog in Glenwood Park where the Crones gathered cranberries and mushrooms. A portion of the garden which received the plants from northern Minnesota was dubbed "the Crone plantations," and Martha built a rockery (called "Little Sahara") in the garden in 1930 for native cacti.[22] When Eloise gave tours of the garden, she often asked Martha to come along to make sure no one picked the flowers. Six months before her death in 1989, at the age of ninety-four, Martha Crone recalled her relationship with Eloise Butler in the words: "I was her best guard."[23]

Eloise wrote to the Crones from Malden, where she spent most winters with Cora's family. Her existing letters, which date from 1923 to 1933, hint at the heavy nursing and housekeeping duties Eloise shouldered there as she cared for her ailing sister, as well as her brother-in-law Curtis, her brother Esbon, and Cora's daughter, Ethelwyn, who were ill, at turns, for long intervals. "For to do their duty cheerfully under adverse circumstances is the metier of spinsters," Eloise had written in 1911 of the showy wildflower called bouncing bet (or old maid's pinks) which thrived on a "hard bed and a crust of earth"; no doubt she was also expressing dissatisfaction with the plight of unmarried women, who were expected to be at the beck and call of everybody and often had to depend on the kindness of relatives for a home. "I am longing to be in Minneapolis again where I can be out of doors all day," Eloise wrote to "the Cronies" in 1927, adding that the sun parlor at Cora's house "isn't equal to the great open."[24]

Eloise often mailed to Martha Crone boxes of plants collected in the East, asking that they be "heeled in" for the winter for planting in the wild garden in the spring. In the fall of 1930, Martha and Bill Crone discovered a stand of the American lotus lily by tracing the origin of some undigested seeds found in the crop of a pheasant shot near Shakopee. The seeds were embedded into clay balls and tossed into Birch Pond, which Eloise considered "an adjunct of the Garden." "I never heard of such a wonderful snoopin'!" wrote Butler to the Crones, upon receiving their account of the adventure. "It reads like a fairy tale or a story out of *Arabian Nights.*"[25] That year, Eloise gave Martha a small book with a gold-embossed cover from her own library—Mabel Osgood Wright's *The Friendship of Nature: A New England Chronicle of Birds and Flowers* (1894).

After a long illness that left her bedridden for more than a year, Cora died in Malden on February 29, 1928, at the age of seventy-nine. In April, Eloise wrote a eulogy for her beloved sister. Cora had "led an intellectual life," spending her later years "in laborious study," wrote Eloise; she had taken courses in philosophy, law and literature at Harvard University Extension School and other colleges about Boston until poor health put an end to her studies only one course short of a degree.[26] Cora was buried in Forest Dale Cemetery in Malden. Its orderly rows of nearly identical tombstones and closely-cropped lawn must have been anathema to Eloise, who laid plans in 1931 to bombard the pools on the grounds

Cora E. Pease. *Martha P. Pease.*

with lotus seeds sent by the Crones. As for herself, Eloise had no intention of being laid to rest in such a place. Among her papers she kept a copy of a letter printed June 13, 1916, in the New York *Globe*, headed "The Behest of Dr. Frank Crane," to which she had added, "and also of Eloise Butler":

> . . . Please have my body cremated. Take the ashes and enclose them in an earthen urn. Keep them until there comes a warm sunshiny day in spring or summer. . . . Then when evening falls let some one open the urn, and taking my ashes in handfuls, let him sow them in silence to the winds, so that some shall fall on the earth, and some on the flowers and trees, and some be blown away. So when [people] ask for my grave it shall be said, "Earth, meadow, and all living things are [her] grave. You will find [her] spirit in sunny days."[27]

By her eightieth birthday in 1931, Eloise's health was declining. She could no longer walk the one thousand miles in a season logged on her pedometer in 1928. She was troubled by neuritis and suffered from burns received in 1929 when an electric heating pad caught fire while she was asleep. "I have been ill for the last three years and will never be able to do anything worthwhile," she wrote in 1931 to friends, turning to osteopaths, chiropractors and herbalists rather than the medical establishment for relief from her ailments.[28] Butler relied more and more on others to do the necessary planting, grateful for the assistance of Martha and William Crone and

the neighbor boys, Lloyd and Leroy Teeuwen.

A matter of great concern to Eloise Butler in her final years was the fate of the garden after her death. Realizing she could not "carry on much longer," in 1931 Butler proposed to C.O. Rosendahl at the University of Minnesota that the botany department "assume the permanent supervision of the Preserve, and appoint an assistant for the curator before she is compelled to relinquish her position." She restated her long-held belief that the university should also establish an arboretum in Glenwood Park. She believed the wild garden to be "an excellent field for the study of and experiments in ecology," and wrote that it was "equipped with office building, reference books, card index, records of the preserve, photographs, lantern slides, furniture, tools, and a few paintings taken from life." She gave Rosendahl a list of numerous species that were "abundant in the preserve."[29]

Rosendahl's reply was politely negative. He saw "no right nor legitimate reason" for the botany department to support the garden. The grounds given for the university's refusal to become involved with the garden were that plants could not be taken for field work by students and, in words eerily echoing language used by the regents in denying support for Josephine Tilden's Minnesota Seaside Station on Vancouver Island twenty-five years before, that it would be inappropriate to devote university funds to "the care of property wholly outside the jurisdiction of the university." Rosendahl suggested that any further attempt to press the proposal would "only cause us embarrassment."[30] Butler's disappointment must have been keen, but she remained hopeful that the "impasse" with the university could eventually be resolved.[31]

In 1932, her last full season in the wild garden, Butler supervised the excavation of a pool for aquatic plants near Lady's-Slipper Path in the northern section of the garden. A pond (formed by the dam) in the southern section had proved too shady for the water lilies and other aquatics desired by Butler, and for more than twenty years she had dreamed of—and lobbied Theodore Wirth for—the new pool. An unemployed man was found to dig the pool for a low sum, and Butler commissioned Lloyd Teeuwen to build her a "rustic bridge" over one end and to forge a small water wheel to throw a spray on nearby

Eloise Butler crossing the rustic bridge over Mallard P[ool] 1932. *Courtesy Minnesota Historical Society.*

rocks. In her annual letter to Wirth, written from Malden the following winter, Butler expressed her joy over the new "Mallard Pool:"

> The greatest pleasure in all the years of my curatorship was the installment of the pool for aquatics, where two small streams converge in the sunlit marsh of the north enclosure. This bids fair to be one of the beauty spots of the park and a sanctuary for all of our choicest native water-loving plants. The pool is about fifty feet long and has a charming, irregular contour. It is crossed by a neat, rustic bridge made of unpeeled tamarack, above which the pool is like a winding river that widens below the bridge into a miniature pond. At the narrow head has been inserted a water-wheel of galvanized tin, about six and a half inches in diameter. The purpose of the wheel is to throw a mistlike spray over plants like the butterwort that grow on dripping rock. The chugging of the wheel can be heard from a distance, and a word has been coined to describe the place—the jolly "Spin[d]rift." From the bridge the

pool is seen to great advantage, and with the distant setting of shrubs and trees is a scene of enchantment.[32]

The pool was named when a mallard duck with four young ones was seen by a workman during the excavation.

Eloise spent the rest of the summer and fall planting the borders of Mallard Pool. She went first to the Quaking Bog for snake-mouth orchids and grass pink and moved turk's-cap lily from elsewhere in Glenwood Park. Wild calla, pale-spike lobelia and other plants were [trans]planted from the banks of Lullaby Brook [to the] border of the new pool. Her friend [Gertrud]e Cram sent hooded ladies-tresses, [?] bastard-toadflax and rosettes of the [?]ed saxifrage from Isle Royale, [?] [M]artha and Bill Crone contributed [?] milkwort and lance-leaved violet [?]nd fetched cardinal flower from [?] the St. Croix River near [?]. [Eloi]se left for Malden in [?] with the planting unfinished and [?] [frie]nds, "Even now, at the beginning [of the wor]k, the place with its setting is truly [charm]ing, and I have to tear myself away [from] it. I shall dream of it all winter and [conj]ure up the futurity of the plantings."[33] [Butl]er wrote to Theodore Wirth of her [in]tention to add thirteen species of aquatic plants to the pool and more than eighty to the sunny border in the following spring.[34]

Butler's friend Fannie Heath had died in 1931. In the fall of 1932, Heath's daughter, Pearl Frazer, a writer and photographer, contacted Theodore Wirth to suggest that she be employed by the Minneapolis Park Board for a season to document Eloise Butler's pioneering work with wildflowers. Butler, mistakenly thinking that Frazer sought to be her successor in the garden, wrote to the young woman at Wirth's request:

> For several years I have been trying in vain to find an understudy for the Native Plant Preserve, as I have fully realized that I would not always be able to "carry on." . . . My aims are only to secure the preservation and perpetuity of The Preserve, as well as its helpfulness to students of Botany and lovers of wild life. When these aims are assured, I am ready to fade out of the picture and will promise that not even my ghost will return to haunt the premises. . . . Are you willing to accept this position for your life work? . . .

Eloise Butler in the wild garden. *Minnesota Historical Society.*

Pardon my brutal frankness. You have a child to care for. You are young. If you are a widow, you may marry again, however firm any present determination not to do so. In that case what would be the fate of the Preserve? The hours are long. . . . Working by yourself in the woods, far from a telephone, you might not be able to endure the loneliness.[35]

Frazer wrote back to Butler, attempting to clarify her plan:

Your work has been with your hands and with your heart. The millions who come after you will have only the evidence shown in your garden for the years of experience, priceless to others if it could be printed. The countless experiments of my mother have to a large extent been lost to the public. . . . I know positively from what I saw while in your park that it is going to be the same in your case. It was to preserve on paper for future generations . . . the result of your experience and knowledge that I wanted to get *with you*, not to take your place. . . . Almost in an instant [my mother] was struck down. Never from the moment she was taken ill was she able to give us one word of

suggestion or information about her garden. Forgive me—it may be the same with you.[36]

Wirth and the park commissioners declined the offer made by Frazer, who wrote to Butler that she could not afford, in "these terrible times," to travel to Minneapolis at her own expense to work on the project: "For the present, my dream must go. Perhaps some day the fates will swing me to you again and I may work out my ideas."[37]

During the winter, Eloise made a half-hearted attempt to sort through her twenty-six years of notes and writings on the garden. Annetta Thwing, an employee of the Park Board who admired Eloise, had urged her to make a start toward a long-planned book to be called *Annals of a Wild Garden*, even offering to help write the book if Eloise would provide the drafts she had begun over the years. Eloise planned to offer the serial rights to *Nature Magazine*.[38] Little progress was made on the project, however. Eloise wrote to her friend Lulu May Aler, a birding enthusiast who sent Eloise snapshots of the newly-erected feeder in the hemlock grove, that she longed to "fly to the garden."[39]

Eloise Butler in her seventies. *Minneapolis Park and Recreation Board.*

Eloise returned by train to Minneapolis at the end of March 1933, and settled into her room at the Babcocks' house. She telephoned Lloyd Teeuwen, asking him to fetch his wheelbarrow to carry her books and microscope down to the office. Lloyd accompanied the frail, eighty-one-year-old "Miss Butler" as she slowly made the rounds of the garden, exclaiming at the yellow catkins and tiny red flowers of the hazelnut and stroking the soft grey aments of the pussy willows. She examined the buds on the highbush cranberry and the flowers of the silver and sugar maples, which had grown into fine large trees from the saplings planted in the early years of the garden. Eloise paused on the east path to greet Monarch, where a pair of barred owls awaited the hatching of four eggs in a cavity of the old oak. Her gaze took in with pleasure the mosses and grey-green lichens on fallen logs and the trunks of trees. She bent to carefully brush away the leaves covering the blooming snow trillium, and smiled at the sight of bloodroot and hepatica blossoming on the woodland floor. In the bog, she bid hello to the skunk cabbage pushing up toward the warm spring sun through the peaty soil. She was filled with joy at the annual "spring resurrection" under way in her garden.

On April 8, according to the last entry in her *Garden Log*, Eloise resumed the planting of Mallard Pool with six roots of yellow swamp candles (*Lysimachia terrestris*), a native of Minnesota bogs and swamps. On April 10,

with a light rain falling, she set out alone for the garden in the early afternoon. The boys who usually escorted her down the muddy paths had gone ahead to clear brush. She made her way as far as the spring on the eastern edge of the garden, where she collapsed, apparently stricken with a heart attack. She was found "leaning on a stump" by a workman, according to one account. Efforts were made at the Babcock home to revive her, but she died a short while later.[40]

In accordance with Eloise's wishes, her body was cremated and her ashes scattered in the wild garden. This was done on May 5, 1933, when the park commissioners and Butler's friends gathered near the office, amid the blooming violets and trillium and under the gaze of the baby owls in Monarch, and planted a young oak in her memory. A year later, a bronze plaque anchored to a boulder was placed nearby. The inscription on the tablet, framed by lady's-slippers, reads:

> In loving memory of Eloise Butler, 1851-1933. Teacher of botany in Minneapolis schools, founder and first curator of this native plant reserve, this oak has been planted and this tablet erected by a grateful public. To this sequestered glen Miss Butler gathered from all sections of our state, specimens of its beautiful native plants and tended them with patient care. This priceless garden is our heritage from her and its continued preservation a living testimony of our appreciation.

Eloise Butler's eightieth birthday party, August 3, 1931. *Minnesota Historical Society.*

Dedication of memorial plaque on May 5, 1934. Left to right: Elizabeth Foss, Clara Leavitt, Park Superintendent Theodore Wirth, Audrey Kelly, Park Commissioner F.A. Gross, Dolores Hoiby, and Jennie Hall, Science Supervisor of the Minneapolis Public Schools. *Courtesy Minneapolis Public Library, Minneapolis Collection.*

Notes

1   Eloise Butler to Gray Memorial Botanical Chapter, Agassiz Association, Division D, October 1911, copy in Eloise Butler biographical file, Minneapolis Public Library, Minneapolis Collection.

2   Undated clippings (c.1919) from Minneapolis *Tribune* and Minneapolis *Journal* in Scrapbook II, pp. 25-27, in Eloise Butler file at Minneapolis Park and Recreation Board Archives, and Scrapbook III, pp. 1-6, Archives of The Friends of the Wild Flower Garden, Inc.

3   Eloise Butler, "The Wild Botanic Garden in Glenwood Park, Minneapolis," *Bulletin of the Minnesota Academy of Science*, Vol. 5 (September 1911), pp. 19-24 (24).

4   "Eloise Butler Gives Talk on Trees" (c.1910), unidentified newspaper clipping in Eloise Butler file, Minneapolis Park and Recreation Board Archives.

5   Eloise Butler to Theodore Wirth, 3 November

1911, published in Minneapolis Board of Park Commissioners, *Twenty-Ninth Annual Report*, pp. 66-68 (68). A wildflower competition was featured at the State Fair prior to 1920, with premiums awarded to the best bouquets. A number of photographs and glass slides of wildflowers, probably those used at Butler's State Fair exhibits, are owned by the Minneapolis Park and Recreation Board. Butler always sent to the State Fair the enormous mushroom clusters, *Grifola frondosa* (called *Polyporus frondosus* in her day), that grew each summer at the base of Monarch.

6   Unidentified clipping (September 1915), in Scrapbook II, Eloise Butler file, Minneapolis Park and Recreation Board Archives.

7   Quotes from "Urge Organization for all Florists," Minneapolis *Journal*, 21 August 1913; and Eloise Butler, "Native Wild Flowers of Minnesota to be Shown to Hundreds of Visiting Florists This Week," Minneapolis *Tribune*, 17

August 1913.

8 Unidentified clipping "Floral Exhibit at Library Includes Spring Harbingers" (c.1923), in Scrapbook III, Archives of The Friends of the Wild Flower Garden, Inc., p. 7. Butler's plant exhibits at the Minneapolis Public Library and the Minneapolis *Journal* Travel Bureau are described in unidentified clippings in Scrapbook III, pp. 6, 7 and 10, Archives of The Friends of the Wild Flower Garden, Inc. Butler wrote a detailed description of the 1918 library exhibit to her botanical correspondence club in 1929 (Eloise Butler to Gray Memorial Botanical Chapter, Agassiz Association, Division D, January and March 1929), copy in Eloise Butler biographical file, Minneapolis Public Library, Minneapolis Collection.

9 The seven-foot-tall statue, sculpted by Jakob Fjelde, was moved to the new library building at Fourth and Nicollet when the original building was demolished in 1961.

10 Eloise Butler to Elizabeth K. Britton, 15 September 1923, and Elizabeth K. Britton to Eloise Butler, 20 September 1923, in archives of the Wild Flower Preservation Society of America, Inc., Library of the New York Botanical Garden, Special Collections, Bronx, New York.

11 Eloise Butler to Elizabeth K. Britton, 8 October 1923, in archives of the Wild Flower Preservation Society of America, Inc., Library of the New York Botanical Garden, Special Collections, Bronx, New York.

12 The Minnesota statute forbids the purchase and sale of "the state flower (*Cypripedium reginae*), any species of lady's-slipper (*Cypripedieae*), or any member of the orchid family, trillium [sic] of any species, lotus (*Nelumbo lutea*), gentian (*Gentiana*), arbutus (*Epigaea repens*), or any species of lilies (*Lilium*)" gathered on public or private land without the written consent of the Commissioner of Agriculture and for scientific and herbarium purposes, unless upon private land registered with the Commissioner as a commercial nursery (M.S. 17.23 effective 1925). Minnesota's endangered and threatened species are protected under the State Endangered Species Act (M.S. 84.0895) as amended in 1981, and regulations promulgated in Commissioner's Order Number 2204 issued by the Department of Natural Resources (1985). It is not known whether the Park Board reimbursed Butler for her plant purchases; there is no record of any expenditures for plants for the wild garden in the published *Proceedings* of the Minneapolis Board of Park Commissioners between 1907 and 1933 (expenditures for the Rose Garden and other parks are noted).

13 The 1925 exchange of letters between Butler and Ricker is referred to in P.L. Ricker to Martha Crone, 3 December 1953, Martha Crone Papers, Minnesota Historical Society. Most of the preserve of The Washington Biologists' Field Club on the Potomac was taken in 1958 by the United States government for highway construction. The twelve-acre Plummer's Island was spared and is still used by the club under the jurisdiction of the National Park Service. The story of Plummer's Island is told in "The Members and History of the Washington Biologist's Field Club" (1984), courtesy of club archivist Karl V. Krombein, Dept. of Entomology at the Smithsonian Institution, Washington, D.C.

14 Eloise Butler to Gray Memorial Botanical Chapter, Agassiz Association, Division D, January 1927, copy in Eloise Butler biography file at Minneapolis Public Library, Minneapolis Collection.

15 Eloise Butler, *Garden Log*, 9 August 1915; 12 August 1915; 9 July 1920.

16 Quote from Susan Griffin, *Woman and Nature: The Roaring Inside Her* (New York: Harper and Row, 1978), p. 169.

17 The Hutchinson's preserve is described in Frances Kinsley Hutchinson, *Wychwood* (Chicago: Lakeside Press, 1928); and "Mrs. F. Hutchinson, Summer Resident, Dies in Chicago Mon." in *Lake Geneva Regional News*, 2 April 1936, p. 11.

18 Eloise Butler to editor, *Garden Magazine*, Vol. 35 (April 1923), p. 48.

19 A 150-page typescript of Fannie M. Heath's writings, entitled "Gardening in North Dakota" (with 40 of Heath's ink and water color drawings), compiled by her daughter, Pearl Frazer, is in the Archives of the State Historical Society of North Dakota, according to the introduction to "Flower Gardens on the Plains" by Fannie Heath, *Plainswoman*, Vol. 6 (October 1986), pp. 7-9.

20 Interviews with Bessie Babcock Johnson, 17 and 20 August 1988, and Jean Rohrbaugh, granddaughter of Jack and Susie Babcock, 16 August 1988; and unpublished essay on Jack Babcock by Dianne Hermes (1958), copy in author's files.

21 Gertrude Schill Cram to Martha Crone, 23 April 1933, in Martha Crone Papers at Minnesota Historical Society.

22 Author's interview with Martha Crone, 27 May 1988; Martha Crone, *Diary*, 2 June 1930 (courtesy Judy Prevey).

23 Author's interview with Martha Crone, 11 May 1988.

24 Eloise Butler, "Tramp Plants, Migrants from Foreign Lands, Thrive in Minnesota," Minneapolis *Tribune*, 6 August 1911; Eloise Butler to Martha and William Crone, 9 January 1927, Martha Crone Papers at Minnesota Historical

Society. Cora's daughter, Ethelwyn, studied music at the Royal Academy in London and became an accomplished pianist and violinist; she had music studios in Boston and Malden. Ethelwyn never married; she died in 1948 at the Pease home in Malden at age 70. Cora's son, Bronson, a postal worker, died in 1962 in San Francisco.

25 Eloise Butler to Martha and William Crone, 28 October 1930, Martha Crone Papers at Minnesota Historical Society; see also Minneapolis Board of Park Commissioners, *Forty-Eighth Annual Report* (1930), p. 45. The seeds planted in Birch Pond apparently failed to germinate; Martha Crone wrote to Theodore Wirth in 1933 that she was still gathering and planting the seeds, first "treating them with acid." Martha Crone to Theodore Wirth, 22 June 1933, copy in Martha Crone Papers, Minnesota Historical Society.

26 Eloise Butler to Gray Memorial Botanical Chapter, Agassiz Association, Division D, April 1928 (eulogy for Cora E. Pease), copy in Eloise Butler biographical file, Minneapolis Public Library, Minneapolis Collection.

27 One-page typescript courtesy Martha P. Pease (copy in Eloise Butler Papers, Minnesota Historical Society) (gender changed for clarity). The page also contained, in Butler's handwriting, Thomas Moult's poem "Testament" (from *Down Here the Hawthorn*, New York: George H. Doran Co., 1921, p. 14), which reads in part:

... take my ashes where the sunshine plays
In dewy meadows splashed with gold and white,
And there ... let the wind scatter them. And on the days
You wander by those meadow pools again,
Think of me as I then shall be, a part
Of Earth—naught else ...

28 Eloise Butler to Gray Memorial Botanical Chapter, Agassiz Association, Division D, June 1931, copy in Eloise Butler biography file, Minneapolis Public Library, Minneapolis Collection. Butler's interest in the medicinal uses of herbs, and that she had loaned a book on the subject to "a Herb Doctor with whom she was dealing," is mentioned in a letter from Martha Crone to Theodore Wirth, 22 June 1933, in Martha Crone Papers at Minnesota Historical Society. Butler's notes at the Minnesota Historical Society contain many references to poisonous plants, as well.

29 Eloise Butler, "Native Plant Preserve, Glenwood Park, Minneapolis" (c.1931), three-page typescript filed with C.O. Rosendahl to Eloise Butler, 14 October 1931, in correspondence files of Department of Plant Biology, University of Minnesota Archives.

30 C.O. Rosendahl to Eloise Butler, 14 October 1931, in correspondence files, Department of Plant Biology, University of Minnesota Archives.

31 In a letter to Fannie Heath's daughter, Pearl Frazer, the following year, Butler wrote: "A year ago I thought I had found the solution of the problem, but was confronted by an impasse which I still hope can be broken down." The letter, dated 29 September 1932, is in the Eloise Butler Papers, Minnesota Historical Society.

32 Eloise Butler to Theodore Wirth, (c. December 1932), published in Minneapolis Board of Park Commissioners, *Fiftieth Annual Report*, pp. 36-37 (36).

33 Eloise Butler to Gray Memorial Botanical Chapter, Agassiz Association, Division D, (fall 1932), copy in *Annals of the Wild Life Reserve*, pp. 13-18, at Minneapolis Public Library, Minneapolis Collection.

34 See note 32.

35 Eloise Butler to Pearl Heath Frazer, 29 September 1932, Eloise Butler file, Minneapolis Park and Recreation Board Archives.

36 Pearl Heath Frazer to Eloise Butler, 28 December 1932, Eloise Butler Papers, Minnesota Historical Society (emphasis in original).

37 Ibid.

38 Eloise Butler to Annetta Thwing, 10 November 1932, Eloise Butler file at Minneapolis Park and Recreation Board Archives.

39 Butler's last letter to Aler is referred to in "A Letter from One of Many Friends Formed in the Wild Flower Garden" by Lulu May Aler, (c.1938), in *An Early History of the Eloise Butler Wildflower Garden* compiled by The Friends of the Wild Flower Garden, Inc., Archives of The Friends of the Wild Flower Garden, Inc.

40 Quote from "Eloise Butler Dies in Woodland She Loved," Minneapolis *Journal*, 11 April 1933; see also "Noted Botanist Succumbs at 81: Developed Preserve in Glenwood," Minneapolis *Tribune*, 11 April 1933. The cause of death is listed as "apoplexy" on Butler's death certificate.

11

Epilogue

Wild Rose

ELOISE BUTLER'S WILD GARDEN continues to delight and instruct visitors more than eighty years after its founding. Its location, once on the outskirts of town, is now near the center of the far-flung metropolitan area. As the wild places of the suburbs and countryside are irrevocably altered by encroaching development, Butler's unique garden and its treasures become more precious with every passing year. The garden is visited by numerous school and university classes, scouting troops, herbalists, and persons seeking to learn about the cultivation of native plants in home gardens. Bird watchers report nearly a hundred species sighted in the garden each year (the designation "bird sanctuary" was added to the garden's name in 1986). The garden remains the sanctuary for people that it was in Butler's day. Walking the well-tended paths covered in white cedar shavings through a deep glade of ferns or through chest-high stands of big bluestem prairie grass in the upland section, one feels the tangible presence of great love—that Bryant's "holy peace that fills the air of those calm solitudes, is there."[1] No wonder the garden has been the scene of sacred rituals, including weddings and the scattering of ashes, not always officially sanctioned. A guest book kept at the shelter reveals how highly the garden is valued by its devotees: "Our 37th year of enjoyment here," noted a retired couple, while the children of one young family found the garden "an enchanted forest." One visitor expressed the feelings of many when she called the garden, simply, "a woman's blessing."[2]

Each season brings a variation in bloom and relative abundance of wildflowers, affected by diverse factors such as the depth of the previous winter's snow and the amount of spring rain, the shade in the garden, the level of ground water, and the work of the garden's keepers. Serendipity continues to play a role, as it has from the first. Monarch no longer reigns over the garden (the tree was damaged by storms in 1925 and finally removed in 1940), but another aged white oak across the bog has inherited the title of largest of its kind in the city.[3]

Since Eloise Butler's time, the garden has been tended by a succession of devoted caretakers, beginning with Martha Crone, who served as curator from 1933-1958. Crone was recommended to the Park Board by Theodore Wirth and by Butler's friends as Butler's successor. Her long association with Eloise Butler and intimate knowledge of the wild garden made her ideally suited for the position. Crone became known as the "wildflower lady," rescuing plants from land slated for development and moving them into the preserve, sometimes working into the night by the light of her car's headlights. She discouraged a proposal made by Theodore Wirth in 1933 that the hillsides east of the garden be turned into an ampitheater for musical concerts, on the grounds that the crowds would "put the birds to flight."[4]

Martha Crone made a valiant effort to maintain Butler's plant collection and continued her work in educating the public about native plants and their culture. She gave away wildflower seeds and directed people to the few nurseries that specialized in native plants. She led tours of the garden and gave hundreds of lectures on wildflowers, illustrated with her superb collection of color slides. During her tenure as curator, Crone also made an herbarium of the flowering plants of the garden.[5]

After Butler's death, Martha Crone continued planting the borders of Mallard Pool as the plants Butler had ordered the previous winter arrived from nurseries. For five more years Crone planted lady's-slippers, fringed gentians, violets and other species in the northern portion of the garden. After 1938, that section, including Mallard Pool and Lady's-Slipper Path, became overgrown and gradually fell into disuse.[6]

In the mid-1930s a benefactor appeared in the person of Clinton Odell, a former botany student of Eloise Butler at Central High School. Odell was president of the Burma-Vita Company, maker of Burma-Shave and originator of the well-known billboards that lined the highways of America. Since building his headquarters a few blocks away in the nearby Bryn Mawr neighborhood, Odell often took lunchtime walks through the garden, where he sought refuge from his business concerns. He found Martha Crone overwhelmed with the work of caring for the large garden without assistance and the garden overrun with jewelweed which, he felt, had destroyed many of Butler's plantings. Determined to help save the garden, Odell worked alongside Crone, removing jewelweed and nettles and maintaining the trails.

In 1944, Clinton Odell made a proposal to the Minneapolis Park Board. He offered to contribute $3,000 of his own funds toward the clearing and fencing of some upland hills southeast of the garden for the establishment of "open field and hilltop flowers." Odell also urged the abandonment of the northern part of the garden, which he considered a "swampy area" that "never should have been enclosed."[7] The Park Board accepted his proposal, and Odell arranged for two men to work full time under his and Crone's supervision, battling the jewelweed and clearing sumac and trees from the new upland section. Odell also successfully lobbied the new superintendent, Charles Doell, to raise the curator's salary and saw that piping was laid in 1948 for provision of a regular water supply.

In 1952, Clinton Odell and Martha Crone founded The Friends of The Wild Flower Garden, Inc., a non-profit organization which supports projects that benefit the garden. Odell served as president until his death in 1958. In 1969 the Friends built a rustic shelter with fireplace, southeast of the spot and now paved with flagstones, where Butler's original office had stood. Members of the Friends and other volunteers staff the shelter, named for Martha Crone, during the season. *The Fringed Gentian*, a quarterly publication of the organization, carried news of the garden and information on wildflower culture; Martha Crone was editor from its beginning in 1953 until 1971.

The addition of the upland section, planted with prairie grasses and wildflowers that bloom profusely from mid-summer until frost, fixed the fenced area of the garden at its size in 1991 of 13.8 acres. In 1964 the Park Board declared a wide belt of parkland surrounding the garden a "native conservatory," to be left in its natural state, providing a buffer zone of protection for the garden itself.[8]

One of Eloise Butler's chief aims in founding the garden was the preservation of the wild plants already growing there. A plant survey made in 1986 by botanist Barbara Delaney located approximately fifty-four percent of the trees, ferns, wildflowers, grasses, rushes, sedges, shrubs and woody vines once present in the original garden area, as noted in Butler's records.[9] Most of the indigenous ferns and trees (except for the tamaracks) are still present, as are the more robust wildflowers and shrubs. The marsh marigolds still bloom in such abundance that, as Butler once wrote, "cartloads could be removed without apparent loss."[10] The chief losses in the indigenous flora have occurred among the wildflowers and shrubs of the bog. No longer present are bog dwellers such as three-leaved false Solomon's seal, cranberry, sundew, cotton grass, sweet white violet, and the rein orchids; and neither grass-of-parnassus nor fringed gentian, once abundant in the spring-fed meadow added in the garden's second year, have survived there. Also among the losses are swamp birch, hawthorns and willows, and the twinflower, *Linnaea borealis*, of which Butler wrote, "to conserve this flower alone is a sufficient reason for the perpetuation of the place."[11]

The changing composition of the plant life in the garden is due to a complex web of natural and human factors. Bogs form a stage in the natural succession from lake-edge to forest; they have a tendency to become drier, a process that began with the withdrawal of the last glaciers. The oxidization of the soil by drying supports a different mix of plants. Bogs and swamps fill in with shrubs, trees, and, eventually, may progress to a hardwood forest; the process may be accelerated or delayed by disturbances such as fires and floods. Eloise Butler observed that the bog was noticeably drier after a tornado uprooted most of the tamaracks in 1925, decreasing the shade and hastening evaporation. Her death in 1933 was followed by a severe drought that lasted two years and wrecked havoc on the ferns and wild orchids, in particular. The showy orchis was said to have disappeared for a period of ten years.[12] Other factors affecting the habitat are the lowering of the water table by urban use, accompanied by a change in the chemistry and nutrients of the water in the garden as chlorinated city water is used in place of water from the mineral springs, now largely dry, that once fed the bog. Disease, too, has taken a toll; many large elms succumbed to Dutch elm disease in the 1970s, and the oaks are presently threatened by oak wilt. Recent plantings have included young tamaracks and birches.

An imported species whose rampant growth eventually became a nuisance is alder buckthorn (*Rhamnus frangula*), thought by Eloise Butler to have been shipped by a nursery in South Carolina in place of the native *R. alnifolia* that she had ordered and planted in 1913.[13] In 1922, Butler wrote to C.O. Rosendahl at the University of

Minnesota, enclosing cuttings from "an alien shrub that I have just discovered in the Wild Garden. . . . It has grown up among chokecherry and gray dogwood into a beautiful bush about twelve feet high, much branched from two main stems." She asked Rosendahl to help determine the species, adding "I wish that you could find time to come to see the interloper."[14] The buckthorn multiplied rapidly and (along with common buckthorn, *Rhamnus cathartica*) overran the formerly open, sparsely-wooded hillsides and meadows and shaded out some of the less vigorous wildflowers. The buckthorn is now being extirpated in the garden.

As with the indigenous plants, some of the species introduced by Butler fared better than others over the years. Among native Minnesota wildflowers in the present garden which may be descended from the original plantings of Eloise Butler are large-flowered white trillium that she planted by the hundreds, wild calla, wild ginger, May apple, skunk cabbage, and Virginia bluebells. Her fern grove is as lovely as ever, and a mature stand of eastern hemlock, planted by Butler more than seventy years ago along the sides of the brook, still graces the garden. Several rare native species established by Eloise Butler and still present in the garden are considered endangered, threatened or of special concern by the Minnesota Department of Natural Resources. Rarest among the garden's three species of trout lily is the dwarf trout lily (*Erythronium propullans*). The tiny spring ephemeral, with mottled leaves and a drooping, pale pink flower, grows only in southeastern Minnesota and is listed as federally endangered. Butler obtained the plants near Cannon Falls, Minnesota, in 1909; the garden is one of the few places it has been successfully cultivated outside of the wild. Other rare species established by Butler and still present are golden-seal (*Hydrastis canadensis*), snow trillium (*Trillium nivale*), shooting star (*Dodecatheon meadia*), the marginal shield fern (*Dryopteris marginalis*) and Goldie's fern (*Dryopteris goldiana*).[15]

Many native ferns and wildflowers that Butler planted in the garden have not survived. Of the ferns, once said to number more than forty species, sixteen were evident in 1986. Among the wildflower species formerly "abundant" in the garden, according to a list made by Butler in 1931, were white

Martha Crone. *Minnesota Historical Society.*

lady's-slipper, squirrel corn, and spring beauty.[16] At this writing, the horticulture department of the Park Board has drawn plans and is seeking funds for restoration of the garden. Plans for the first phase of the project include dredging the pool in the bog, extending the north fence to include the abandoned Mallard Pool, the entire hemlock grove planted by Butler, and replanting many species that formerly grew in the bog.[17]

Prior to the founding of the Minnesota Landscape Arboretum in 1958, the garden served as a showcase for wild plants that could grow in Minnesota's climate. During Martha Crone's tenure as curator, the stated scope of the plant collection was enlarged and experiments were made growing southern and mountain species. "The object is to bring together all the native plants hardy in this latitude, also to experiment with plants introduced from other areas," wrote Crone.[18] Besides the many Minnesota native species Crone added—the upland section of prairie plants was largely her creation—she and

Clinton Odell planted azaleas, rhododendrons, and ginkgo trees in the garden, as well as yellow trout lilies and oconee bells from the Smoky Mountains; in 1956, Crone wrote that she had managed to raise the blue columbine (*Aquilegia coerulea*), state flower of Colorado, from seed.[19] According to Kenneth Avery, who served as head gardener from 1959-1987, only species native to Minnesota have been placed in the garden since 1959.[20]

The position of curator was abolished at Crone's retirement in 1959, and the former duties of the curator divided among various employees of the Park Board. A full-time gardener (presently Cary George) is in charge of the planting and maintenance, in consultation with the Park Board's horticultural staff. A number of part-time naturalists lead educational programs and give tours of the garden.

Public interest in native plants has grown tremendously since Eloise Butler's time. Many wildflower sanctuaries and native plant collections now exist throughout the United

States, ranging from small tracts maintained by garden clubs to the forty-five-acre Garden in the Woods, a botanical garden of native plants begun in 1930 in Framingham, Massachusetts, now owned and operated by the New England Wildflower Society. Mrs. Lady Bird Johnson founded the National Wildflower Research Center in Austin, Texas, in 1982, to promote the use and preservation of native plants. The Minnesota Landscape Arboretum contains an area of woodland wildflowers (the Grace B. Dayton Wildflower Garden) as well as a section of restored prairie. A growing number of nurseries sell or specialize in native plants and seeds, and organizations like the Minnesota Native Plant Society are active in more than thirty states. Preservation of the genetic diversity of native plant species threatened by development around the globe is a priority of groups such as the Nature Conservancy.

Eloise Butler was an early, unsung heroine in the movement to preserve and promote native plants. Her wild garden remains as her legacy to us, a place where we and our children might find "an earthly paradise" and there discover and grow to love, as she did, the wild plants of the bogs, woods, meadows and prairies of Minnesota—for love of nature is the first step on the path to preservation.

Martha Crone. Minneapolis *Star Tribune*.

Notes

1   Quote from William Cullen Bryant's poem, "Oh Fairest of the Rural Maids," in *Poems* (New York: Hurst & Co., 188-), p. 115.

2   Entries in guestbook owned by The Friends of the Wild Flower Garden, Inc. dated 2 September, 21 July, and 13 September 1990.

3   The white oak, 104" (8.75 feet) in circumference at a height of four and one-half feet, stands near station 21 along the west path. Other Heritage Trees in the garden are eastern hemlock (*Tsuga canadensis*), black cherry (*Prunus serotina*), pin cherry (*Prunus pensylvanica*), Siberian crabapple (*Malus baccata*), and mountain maple (*Acer spicatum*); see Cary George, "Notes from Our Gardener," *Fringed Gentian* (September 1990), p. 2.

4   See Patricia Deweese, "A Winter Evening with Martha Crone," *The Fringed Gentian*, Vol. 28, (Winter 1978), pp. 1-2; Theodore Wirth to Martha Crone, 15 August 1933, and Martha Crone to Theodore Wirth, 25 August 1933, in Martha Crone Papers at Minnesota Historical Society.

5   The herbarium is mentioned in a letter from Martha Crone to Theodore Wirth, 27 November 1934, copy in Martha Crone Papers at Minnesota Historical Society. Crone wrote to Superintendent Charles A. Bossen in 1937: "The collection of more than 1,000 pressed specimens of plants was used extensively for identification purposes by students and interested visitors." (Martha Crone to C.A. Bossen, 10 December 1937, copy in Martha Crone papers at Minnesota Historical Society). The whereabouts of Crone's herbarium is not known; it may have been part of the 1,172 mounted specimens of native plants that were transferred into the University of Minnesota herbarium from the Minneapolis Public Library (where Martha Crone worked winters in the Academy of Science Museum) in 1939.

6   Muskrats apparently ate many of the lilies and other aquatic plants in Mallard Pool. Martha Crone's records indicate that she transplanted numerous showy and white lady's-slippers from the abandoned northern area into the present bog section after 1945.

7   Quotes from Clinton Odell to Minneapolis Board of Park Commissioners, 22 June 1944, copy in Martha Crone Papers at Minnesota

Historical Society; Clinton Odell, *Diary*, 19 October 1946, courtesy Moanna Beim.

8   Minneapolis Board of Park Commissioners, *Minutes*, 19 August 1964. According to former gardener Kenneth Avery, the buffer zone extends from Theodore Wirth Parkway on the west to Xerxes Avenue on the east, and from Glenwood Avenue on the north to U.S. 394 on the south, encompassing about eighty acres, including the garden.

9   The 1986 plant census found a total of 490 species, 205 of which were noted as indigenous by Butler. The census is on file in the Horticulture Division of the Minneapolis Park and Recreation Board. The percentage given in the text was calculated after first deducting from Butler's total the sixteen indigenous species noted by her whose identity is uncertain. This list is also available at the Gardens.

10   Eloise Butler to Gray Memorial Botanical Chapter, Agassiz Association, Division D (c.1915), copy (under the title: "Notable Features of My Wild Garden") in *Annals of the Wild Life Reserve*, p. 22, at Minneapolis Public Library, Minneapolis Collection.

11   Eloise Butler, Minneapolis *Tribune*, 2 July 1911, p. 35.

12   Martha Crone to C.A. Bossen, Park Superintendent, 12 February 1944, copy in Martha Crone Papers, Minnesota Historical Society.

13   Eloise Butler, *Garden Log*, 14 June 1922. Another invasive species introduced by Butler was purple loosestrife (*Lythrum salicaria*); see Chapter 9.

14   Eloise Butler to C.O. Rosendahl, 15 June 1922, in correspondence files of the Department of Plant Biology, University of Minnesota Archives.

15   Barbara Coffin and Lee Pfannmuller, editors, *Minnesota's Endangered Flora and Fauna* (Minneapolis: University of Minnesota Press, 1988) contains descriptions of these plants.

16   Eloise Butler, "Native Plant Preserve, Glenwood Park, Minneapolis," 3-page typescript enclosed with C.O. Rosendahl to Eloise Butler, 14 October 1931, correspondence files, Department of Plant Biology, University of Minnesota Archives.

17   Minneapolis Park and Recreation Board, *Natural Resource Development Project Proposal: Eloise Butler Wildflower Garden and Bird Sanctuary (Phase I)*, March 1989.

18   Martha Crone, "Function of the Wild Flower Garden," *Fringed Gentian*, Vol. 14 (January 1966), p. 3.

19   Rhododendrons and azaleas mentioned in *Fringed Gentian*, Vol. 8 (April 1960), p. 8; blue columbine in *Fringed Gentian*, Vol. 4 (July 1956), p. 11.

20   Conversation with Ken Avery, 14 April 1989.

Part II

Botanizing
in Jamaica

Eloise Butler's article, "Botanizing in Jamaica," was printed in Postelsia (1902), a publication of the Minnesota Seaside Station at Vancouver, which contained papers given at the station in the 1901 session. Other papers in the 1902 issue included "Uses of Marine Algae in Japan" by K. Yendo, from Tokyo; "Algae Collecting in the Hawaiian Islands" by Josephine E. Tilden and "The Kelps of Juan de Fuca" by Conway MacMillan of the University of Minnesota. Misspelled botanical names in the original have been corrected and modern botanical names in brackets supplied by phycologist Paul C. Silva, curator of the algae herbarium at the University of California at Berkeley.

A STRONG DESIRE TO STUDY tropical vegetation resulted in my embarking with my sister from Boston on a Monday evening in June 1891, on a banana steamer accommodating a few passengers bound for Port Antonio, Jamaica. After a day and night of fog we reached the Gulf Stream and soon sailed apparently upon a veritable "sea of glass." The smooth, glassy waves were occasionally spread with carpets and streamers of golden brown seaweed, *Sargassum bacciferum* [*S. natans*], and frequently schools of flying-fish with silvery wings rose a foot or more from the water and gracefully floated in the air some distance before dropping again into the sea. As we had read that these fish did not use their wing-like fins to direct their flight, but simply gave a flying leap into the air, we were interested to see that often one turned in its course. This action seemed to prove that the fish did really fly somewhat as a bird does. We also saw for the first time the Portugese-men-of-war gliding rapidly over our "sea of glass" like large soap bubbles driven by gentle winds and reflecting rainbow hues in the sunlight. We watched the changing clouds, occasionally a dark curtain falling between sky and water somewhere off in the distance, and we were informed "there is a shower over there." We gazed into the wonderful deep blue sea of the tropics, a blue so intense as to seem almost tangible. We played whist, or read seated upon the hurricane deck. We fed the Mother Carey chickens with crumbs from the table and pressed specimens of *Sargassum* which the sailors kindly fished up for us by means of long boat hooks. The specimens varied as regards the length and width of the fronds, and they have been classified as *Sargassum bacciferum* [*S. natans*] and *S. bacciferum* forma angustum [*S. natans* forma angustum].

On Saturday we saw the first land since leaving Boston. San Salvador came into view as a mere speck on the horizon. We watched this speck most intently until we were enabled to make out a lighthouse on a long, low strip of land far away to our right. Then we again watched it recede from view, recalling all we could remember and imagine of Columbus' wonderful experiences on that first momentous voyage to the new world when this island came into view to cheer his despairing men and to reward his unparalleled faith and courage. The excitement of seeing San

111

Salvador had barely subsided when we were informed that we were about to cross the Tropic of Cancer. It was intensely interesting to realize the moment we were crossing that imaginary line, and we marveled that man had been enabled to formulate accurate rules by which sailors could locate their position at any time upon the trackless deep. After a most gorgeous sunset, with such forms of clouds and such brilliant colors as can never be witnessed elsewhere than far out at sea, darkness following soon without the lingering twilight of the North, we were gazing for the first time upon the Southern Cross. Poets and writers of romance had so inflamed our imaginations regarding this constellation that, we must confess, it did not quite meet our expectations. But we may have seen it at a disadvantage, as it was very near the horizon.

Sunday morning the mountains of Cuba appeared like clouds over the sea, but soon we were sailing close by the eastern shore and could distinguish the scanty vegetation upon the sides of the mountains, most curiously terraced and grooved by deep ravines.

Monday morning we awoke to find ourselves gliding into one of the most beautiful small harbors in the world, and our eyes were feasting upon tropical scenery. And the half of its marvellous beauty and fascinating interest had never been told.

Our second voyage was in 1894, at about the same season of the year. But, though now the Fruit Company's steamers were much larger and swifter, and the accommodations for passengers were not so limited, the time spent at sea was much less enjoyable, as, owing to continuous rainy weather, we never saw the sun from the beginning to the end of the voyage. Moreover, our state-room sprang a leak, and we were drenched in our berths; yet our ardor for studying plant life in Jamaica was not in the least dampened, for we had no sooner returned from this trip than we began to plan for a third; but, there were so many difficulties to surmount, the summer of 1900 arrived before we were enabled to spend another four weeks on the island. This last sea voyage in a steamer, yet again so much improved as to seem impossible for the Fruit Company to do any more for the comfort of its passengers, was varied by days of rain and of sunshine, the latter predominating.

The fruit steamers always enter at Port Antonio, then sail along the coast west to

Lucea, or east to Morant Bay, sometimes rounding the eastern point and continuing along the southern shore to Kingston, stopping at numerous little harbors between these ports to take on bananas, and usually returning to Port Antonio to clear. It was our custom to remain aboard the steamer while it was sailing about the coast; and, during the loading of bananas, we went ashore to search the beaches for seaweeds or to stroll through the streets of the little villages to note the different varieties of fruits and flowers by the wayside and in the gardens of the Negro cabins. In this way we had opportunities to make collections at many places besides those at which we made lengthened stops for that purpose.

There being no wharfs excepting at a few of the larger ports, in order to go ashore at some places, we were lowered from the steamer's side into a row boat, manned by two or three Negroes and used for bringing bananas to the vessel, the waves tossing the boat so violently that we had to be skillfully caught by the boatmen as though we were bunches of bananas. After rowing as near the shore as possible, we were again taken in the Negroes' arms and carried through the shallow water to dry land. These . . . stevedores were most picturesque creatures; they were invariably clothed in rags, tied and fastened on in most ingenious ways. Patches of all hues and shapes were attached here and there among the tatters. Their headgear also was particularly interesting. Gaudy bandanas, straw and felt hats in every stage of dilapidation, brimless crowns and crownless brims, caps of various materials, one even of fur, were among the head coverings we noted. The women often wore flower and ribbon-trimmed hats over turbans.

Whenever the conditions were not favorable for us to go ashore, we never ceased to be amused by watching the loading from the vessel's deck. The streets and footpaths leading from the surrounding hills and mountains to the little coast village near which our vessel was anchored were sometimes thronged with carts of fruit drawn by single mules and pairs of mules or oxen, or donkeys with deep panniers hanging from each side, a Negro woman or child perched on top guiding the animal with a single rope fastened about its nose, and pedestrians, men and women, also loaded with bananas, the men carrying bunches in their hands and the women invariably carrying them on their heads. The women carried all their burdens on their heads, from a spool of thread, or vial of medicine, to a full calabash of water, or heavily loaded basket. Row after row of these grotesquely garbed Negro men, women and children, all chattering, laughing or scolding, making a perfect babel, marched down into the water, often waist deep, to deposit their bunches of bananas in the waiting boats, which, as soon as filled, were rowed off to the steamer, where the fruit was passed up to other . . . men standing at openings in the hold of the vessel. Every bunch as it was handed up was counted by a man whose especial duty it was to keep the tally, and his

> "Banana one,
> Banana two,
> Call this one three,
> Banana four,
> Call this one tally-o-o-o!"

rang out in his musical voice as a cheering song.

The limits of this sketch will not permit me to more than allude to a few of our many interesting experiences. There was no hotel at Port Antonio in 1891, and the only available place for the accommodation of strangers was at a lodging-house, standing on a steep bluff overlooking the harbor, conducted by a handsome, dark Creole. Colored servants, big and little, were numerous. Everything was done for our comfort and happiness in the peculiar way the mistress and servants had of doing things. Fresh from New England homes, we were much interested in noting the differences between Creole and Yankee housekeeping.

We arose at daybreak and went to the bath-house, which was provided with a large stone swimming tank, supplied with water from a mountain stream. The cold morning bath is absolutely necessary in the tropics to keep the system in tone. After being served with coffee, we started on our collecting tour, remaining out until about ten, when we returned to take another bath and attire ourselves in fresh garments for breakfast. This second bath and entire change of clothing was always necessary after collecting, whether we went wading in the ocean, or walking in the woods, for we were always wet and muddy whichever course we took.

While exercising in the tropics one

perspires very profusely. Then showers are so frequent that the soil and rank vegetation are reeking with moisture. We always carried an umbrella to protect us from the sun or from the showers. Though we could not long exercise in the sun's direct rays, beneath the shelter of our umbrellas the heat was more easily endured than when botanizing many summer days at the North. Jamaica is in the line of the cool trade winds, so when in the shade, one is very comfortable. Moreover, the temperature is never so high in Jamaica as it is in our hottest summer weather, the thermometer ranging from the sixties (Fahrenheit) to about ninety as the highest.

After breakfast we usually worked upon our morning collections until time to dress for five o'clock dinner, another light lunch of cake and fruit being brought to our room between one and two o'clock. Dinner was much like the breakfast, with the addition of a usually delicious, strangely concocted soup and a dessert. About eight in the evening we were served cake and tea in our rooms, or in the drawing room, wherever we might be. The general cooking at this house was done by two or three old witch-like [black women] over an open fire in a dark cavern in a precipice forming the boundary wall to one side of our yard.

Our room was small and crowded with "missus' things," which were not removed for our accommodation. A large bed with one starched sheet and an indescribably hard mattress, a big wardrobe, a bureau, a washstand and our two large trunks so filled the room that one could scarcely stand between the bed and surrounding furniture. All the drawers and various boxes under the bed also contained "missus' things," and the big cockroaches rattled around in them all night, to the disturbance of our slumbers. We had to use the bed by day for a work-table, having also a little folding table that we carried with us, which we could tightly squeeze between bed and bureau, and upon which we washed out our seaweeds for mounting. It was very ludicrous, when using this folding table, to have to scramble out over the bed covered with specimens to get to the door, or to close our jalousied windows when a heavy shower came beating in.

Little maids came in every morning while we were off collecting and scrubbed the floor, using a dark colored tea made of mangrove bark, the scrubbing brush being a cross section of a coconut gathered before ripening. We also saw floors polished with sour oranges cut in halves, and with a tea made of *Momordica charantia L.*, a pretty little vine bearing a yellow flower, which the natives called "Cerasee Tea." The floors everywhere received more attention than any other part of the dwellings. To our knowledge, cobwebs and dust were never removed from their usual lodging places on windows, mopboards, etc.

While upon household matters, I will briefly relate our boarding experiences elsewhere when revisiting the Island. In 1894 we disembarked at Annotta Bay, a little, low-lying village between the mouths of two sluggish rivers, and said to be the most unhealthy place in Jamaica. We passed the first night at "The Army and Navy," an imposing name for a primitive little hostelry. We were given a large room having two single beds, each provided with the one stiff sheet, but we carried sheets with us after our first experience. At breakfast we were served first a saucer of oatmeal and milk. This looked homelike, but one taste was sufficient, for it was simply saturated with smoke. Bacon and eggs came next with the same result, and so on to the fruit. This we could eat, but we were surprised to see the waitress take our plates, throw their contents out of the open window and return them for us to eat our fruit from. All refuse is disposed of in this simple manner. Turkey buzzards [vultures], called "Jim Crow" birds, sit perched on the roofs, or near-by tree tops, on the alert to fly down and gobble up every scrap of waste food thrown out. These birds are protected by [the] government for scavengers.

On rising from the table, we passed to the window and gazed down upon an enclosed yard in which was a little cook-room made of rough boards, roofed over, and on the four sides beneath the roof was a broad open space, out of which poured dense clouds of smoke. In the center of this room stood an iron cook stove, the only one we saw on the island, and the stove was provided with the usual pipe, which neither entered a chimney nor provided from any aperture, but simply left off about a yard above the stove. It was certainly no less than a miracle that any human being could stand and cook in such an atmosphere, but the flavor of the food was no longer a mystery.

One of the officers of the Fruit Company stationed at this port called on us early in the day; and, as he was to be away with his family, he asked us to accept the use of his cottage, housekeeper and retinue of servants while we were to stay in Annotta Bay. We accepted his exceedingly generous offer and a week of great enjoyment followed.

Our time here, and elsewhere, was spent much as at Port Antonio but, instead of being cramped in one little room, the whole house was ours, the housekeeper and servants, living in little cabins at one side of the large back yard, coming into our cottage only to serve our meals and to tidy the rooms. The cottage stood on the pebbly seashore, thus being very convenient for our seaweeding. Our housekeeper . . . served us the most delicious meals we had yet eaten in Jamaica. But, had we given the preparation of the food much thought, our stomachs would have rebelled. From our dining-room we could look out upon the large yard enclosed by a line of tall cocoanut palms, and, if our meal was in preparation, see several Negroes, big and little, stooping over little wood fires between three bricks arranged in a triangle. In basins on these fires were steaming the various concoctions later appearing on our table in regular courses as fragrant soups, made dishes, strange native vegetables, fish, meat, desserts, etc. If the time of looking out happened after a meal, we would see the servants stooping over basins of cold water, washing the dishes, which were never wiped, but laid on the ground to dry, knives, forks, spoons, cups, saucers, plates,—everything. We would also see in that yard, frolicking in and out and over the drying dishes, numbers of little half-naked [children], a goat and two kids, dog and five pups, and a flock of hens and chickens.

One day while [there] we drove many miles into the interior along the bewitchingly zigzag course of the wag water, to Castleton Gardens, the Arnold Arboretum of the tropics. Here we saw noble specimens of every species of palm on the globe, and many marvellous growing, blooming things that still haunt our memories. The bamboos everywhere charmed us, standing in clumps, gracefully bending like groups of Prince of Wales feathers. Another interesting tree was the banyan, introduced from India. The seed of the banyan, when lodged on another tree, takes root, grows rapidly and strangles its host. Branches grow down to the ground and also take root, a single tree thus forming a miniature forest.

After leaving Annotta Bay, we boarded two weeks at Morant Bay, in a delightful old Spanish mansion, an ideal tropical home on a steep hill with higher hills rising to the right towards the distant Blue Mountains towering among the clouds. In front and to our left, we overlooked banana and coconut plantations intersected by winding rivers emptying into the bay, which bounded our horizon at a distance of three or more miles. We were accorded the use of the "trap" and a driver to take us to the shore when we wished to seaweed; but the water was always so tempestuous in this bay that our algae collections were not so abundant here as elsewhere. We took long drives to the mountains for ferns, once going to Atalle Gap in the Blue Mountains, a place famous for its coffee plantation. The Blue Mountain coffee is considered by epicures the best in the world, and the whole supply is shipped to London. This drive was one of the red letter days of our experience. We gathered most lovely ferns, gold and silver, and others remarkably rare and beautiful, and saw many wonders in scenery and plant life.

Another remarkable drive was to Bath, where is the famous hot sulphur spring boiling out of the mountain, side by side with a stream of cold water. Both the hot and the cold water are conveyed by pipes into a near-by building provided with stone tanks for bathing. Here sufferers from rheumatism and all cutaneous diseases are speedily cured by the hot baths. During our last trip we boarded a week at the village and took the baths, to our great delight. The hot sulphur water soothed tired nerves and muscles, and cured an eruption on face and hands caused either by a vegetable poison, or by getting over-heated.

In the neighborhood of the hot spring flourished a great variety of rare ferns. The scenery all about was exceedingly lovely, diversified, as everywhere in Jamaica, by rivers gliding rapidly over rocky beds, and cutting their way to the sea through mountains, thus forming many narrow valleys, which are often constricted to deep gorges with perpendicular walls. These walls are always draped with tangled vines, drooping ferns and orchid-covered trees wherever a root can take foothold. Soil is not necessary on this wonderful island for the growth of vegetation. The rocks, brick and stone walls, the trunks of

trees, the roofs and very doorsteps of dwellings, have growing upon them mosses, ferns, orchids and very many other forms of plant life.

At Bath we had a charming temporary home at the lodgings of Mrs. Duffy, who is widely known and appreciated by all travelers in Jamaica.

Perhaps the neat, home-like attractions of Mrs. Duffy's lodgings would not have impressed us so forcibly if we had not come to them from a week at Manchioneal, where our accommodations at the only house open to strangers were intolerable. The lodgings (a name applied to the small hostelries throughout the island, there being no hotels, excepting at a few of the larger settlements) were admirably situated for our work, close to the shore at the head of the little harbor. Our seaweeding was so successful here that we were willing to endure even greater hardships. The mistress of the house, when not lying in a drunken sleep, maundered aimlessly about the rooms, carrying on a monologue in a most peculiar, high-pitched, whining tone. The food was scanty, unpalatable and poorly served.

We had the entire first floor to ourselves, the family occupying the basement, the fumes of the landlady's rum often coming up through our floor. My bed was far the worst I had yet encountered. Our sheets and pillow cases we saw washed, starched and ironed after our arrival, though we had telephoned for our rooms several days before. Two immensely heavy mattresses filled with something hard and lumpy were piled on a bedstead without springs. These mattresses were so much thicker at one side than at the other that to keep on the bed I must lie crossways, my head on the sill of a little jalousied window, against which the bed stood, and my feet hanging over the front edge. Perhaps I might have enhanced my comfort by reversing the mattresses, but I feared to touch them, as they were unclean and the probable abode of centipedes and scorpions. With a proper mistress this might have been an ideal resort, as the house was pleasant, the surroundings charming and the air cool, the prevailing winds coming from off the bay.

When ready to leave Manchioneal we started out to see if we could find a banana cart to take us to Bath, and succeeded in getting the promise of a cart and driver to be at our lodgings at precisely half-past eight in the morning. Strange that, with the experience we had had in waiting for the movements of the natives in all parts of the island, we should get impatient as the minutes passed, then hours, until it was eleven o'clock, and no cart. I would wait no longer, but hastened off to learn why our equipage did not appear. I found the cart broken, and no attempt made to repair it, or to inform us of the mishap. I indignantly turned away and went in search of another cart, and was so far successful that I was promised one as soon as a man could go to the pasture and drive up the mules. Again I returned to the lodgings to sit and wait. In the vicinity of two o'clock the cart arrived. It was a two-wheeled affair, much like our ordinary tip-cart, drawn by a mule harnessed with ropes into the thills, and a little donkey tied on the left front corner to assist. The cart was too narrow to hold our one trunk crossways, so it was pushed in at one side of the back, the hand baggage occupying the space at the side of the trunk. Two small chairs were put in front for us to sit on. But there was not room enough for us to sit side by side, so one was bolstered against the driver and the other against the trunk with her feet beneath the other's chair. We presented such a ludicrous spectacle that we longed for some one with a camera to take our picture to send the friends at home. We laughed until we ached, with the tears streaming down our cheeks, and held on with both hands to keep from being jolted out. As the mule and donkey trotted and cantered up hill and down, our cart rattled and joggled so that we could scarcely hear each other's voices. No wonder that when we arrived at Mrs. Duffy's after being "drawn in a cart" three hours we were charmed with our new home.

Again we took a cart back to Manchioneal to connect with the mail coach for Port Antonio, driving part of the way along the coast and stopping at every available place to seaweed. We found the coach was not due until three o'clock in the morning, and after much demurring decided to go to bed to get some sleep. It happened that I had just dropped my watch and broken the main spring. No one in the neighborhood owned a timepiece. We asked the landlady how we should know when it was time to be ready for the coach. She replied "O, you will know all right. At eleven the roosters will crow a little, and again at twelve; at about half-past two

they will crow some more and at dawn they will have the big crow—the whole lot crowing all together." Well, we must lie awake to listen for the cock crowing. It was not difficult to lie awake, for, after a week's comfort at Mrs. Duffy's, my sister could not drop to sleep on her Manchioneal bed; so after a brief hour of endurance she exclaimed, "Come, the rooster has crowed. It is eleven, and I am going to dress and sit up the rest of the night to watch for the coach." So we both dressed, got our luggage ready and sat by the open door to keep our vigil. Though common sense, taking the place of a timepiece, told us that it was not three o'clock, the waves beating on the rocky shore every few moments sounded like the coach tearing along over the street, and we would snatch up our hand bags, a plant press filled with specimens, a large basket of unmounted seaweeds and our umbrellas and rush down the steps onto the street to hear nothing in either direction but the beating waves, the croaking of lizards and the many insect voices of a tropical night. Then we would return with our bundles to our chairs to repeat this performance many, many times before the coach actually appeared.

We had a remarkable ride with our monkey, jumping-jack driver, in the early dawn, through a picturesque region, much of the way skirting the seashore. At first we were rather terrified at the reckless driving up and down steep hills, through dark woods and across rivers without bridges, the water often rising to the body of the coach. The driver continuously lashed the mules, first on the right, then on the left, the whip lash circling rapidly to and fro, the performance being occasionally diversified by his dashing down beneath the fender, the mules still on the jumping canter, to catch and refasten an unhooked trace, but always coming up all right on his seat again, though we feared every disappearance over the fender would be his last. As we approached a village, our driver, without seeming to cease for a moment his antics with the mules, would whisk out a horn and blow an ear-splitting blast which reverberated through the surrounding woods and hills, with the result that when we tore up to the little wayside cabin labelled postoffice the mail was always ready.

At Port Antonio there is now one of the finest hotels in the world, at least the most enjoyable at which we ever tarried, built and managed by the Fruit Company. Here we lived in luxury until we were ready to embark for home.

On our third trip to Jamaica we left the steamer at Montego Bay, an interesting old town with many of the buildings with massive stone and brick walls dating back to the Spanish possession, and fewer of the usual little board and bamboo-woven cabins.

Our lodgings here were most beautifully situated on a high bluff overlooking the town with its background of wooded hills, and the little semi-circular bay with its circling arms of land buried in luxuriant tropical foliage. From the sea our Roman villa-like lodgings loomed up very imposing, but, truly, distance lent enchantment. For, though the house was large, the rooms airy and pleasant and the situation most desirable, shiftless housekeeping and monotonous fare spoiled much of the charm.

From Montego Bay we took the steam cars across the western end of the island to Kingston, stopping off for a day or two at Mandeville, a hill resort with an ideal climate and reminding one of a village in rural England. From Kingston we returned by the new railway across the eastern end of the island to Port Antonio, stopping on the way at Bog Walk, far famed for its rare ferns.

Columbus in describing Jamaica to Queen Elizabeth is said to have crushed a piece of paper tightly in the palm of his hand, and on releasing it exclaimed: "There is Jamaica!" Certainly, a true description of the island, which is entirely made up of mountain chains and peaks with intervening narrow, steep valleys. The coast is scalloped all about with little bays with usually bold shores. Annotta Bay is the only village I recall having any extent of level land.

As there is no perceptible tide at Jamaica, our seaweeding was conducted rather differently than at the North. The seaweeds found upon the beaches were dashed up by unusually high waves after a storm; therefore collections made from the wrack were apt to be fragmentary. At Port Antonio, from the shore at one side of the bay, extended a large coral reef over which the water was shallow. Here, wearing our bathing suits, we could wade out and gather quantities of "Mermaid's shaving-brushes" (*Pencillus capitatus* Lamarck), *Caulerpa, Udotea, Halimeda, Corallina*, etc., rooted in the sand after the manner of terrestrial plants, and *Galaxaura,*

Dictyosphaeria, Cymopolia and various others on the rocks. At other ports such seaweeds as *Dictyota, Gelidium, Turbinaria, Sargassum, Padina, Amansia, Laurencia*, etc., grew on rocks off bold shores, down which we could not clamber; other species in muddy eel-grass flats far out from land, so that our seaweeding had to be done from boats. Two or three . . . boatmen rowing us wherever we desired to go, we jumped overboard (wearing bathing dresses and long-legged rubber boots), and fished about for the weeds. Where the algae grew on rocks the water was usually very rough and we were often in danger of being washed off our feet; but we would cling to each other, one steadying the other while she dived for a desirable specimen. In this way at Annotta Bay we gathered quantities of "fairy umbrellas" (*Acetabularia crenulata* Lamour) and "tiny cat-tails" *Dasycladus clavaeformis* [Roth] Ag [*D. vermicularis*] growing together on small stones and completely covering them, in water over our heads. The boatmen kept as near as possible to render assistance if we should meet with disaster.

The water was so muddy over the eel-grass flats that we had to dredge for our specimens with our fingers down among the roots. Of course we feared various stinging things, the water being plentifully supplied with them, but we never received any injury worth considering. One day, when dredging off Montego Bay, we were continually stepping on something that felt through our rubber boots like drowned kittens. At last we had the temerity to reach down and bring up one of the objects, and to our great joy and surprise it proved to be an unfamiliar seaweed (*Avrainvillea longicaulis* [Kutz.] Murr., and Bood). The plant was a most disgusting fleshy, hairy, dark brown thing, each specimen harboring colonies of small sea animals, causing us much trouble to cleanse the plant for preservation.

At Manchioneal we made a "great find," among other valuable collections. One day we brought our boat up among some big boulders close inshore, beneath the bank of the village street. We clambered out to reach the sides of the boulders and were rewarded by finding large patches of a gloriously beautiful weed of most vigorous growth, and its color varying shades of purple. We instinctively felt that it was new to science, and we were eager to place it in the hands of the authorities on algae. The plant proved to be *Gracilaria domingensis* Sond, which had been noted but once before, in 1869.

But this is not our only experience of this kind. On our first trip to Jamaica, on our sail up the coast before leaving the stream, we picked up, while ashore a few moments at Hope Bay, a bit of seaweed like a piece of stiff, greenish-gray fringe. This puzzled the algologists for a long time. They decided it was new to science and were considering what to christen it, when Mr. Collins, in an old French work, stumbled upon a description of our *Liagora (decussata)*, long since dropped out of the books as a freak of the imagination of the author Montagne, no specimen of such a *Liagora* ever having been seen by living scientists. We had the romantic honor of rediscovering a plant and vindicating the veracity of the old, long dead naturalist. This seemed much more interesting than discovering the plant for the first time. But this honor, too, was in reserve; for, on our last trip, we found several new species, also a plant in fruit, never before found in that condition, and a species never before found outside the Red Sea, also several Australian species.

Unlike the huge algae of the northwest Pacific, the seaweeds of Jamaica rarely attain a meter in length, *Liagora decussata* Mont, *Sargassum* and *Turbinaria* being the largest species. Neither do brilliantly colored specimens abound. The deficiency in size and bright coloring is counterbalanced by the odd, beautiful and fantastic shapes, as exemplified in the genera *Penicillus, Caulerpa, Udotea, Padina, Anadyomene, Chamaedoris,* [and] *Acetabularia*. The proportion of lime-encrusted forms is large, as species of *Liagora, Halimeda, Galaxaura,* [and] *Corallina*.

The fresh-water algae, as far as I have observed, are not as abundant as in the North, or widely different from northern species.

All other vegetation is extremely varied. The forests are not made up of many trees of one sort, but at every turn different species are encountered.

Many of the marine algae are local in distribution. For instance, on our second voyage we made an especial trip to Hope Bay to collect specimens of our *Liagora decussata*. We found it in windrows and filled our collecting bag, then inverted our open umbrellas and filled them, and, that not satisfying us, we gathered up our dress-skirts and filled them, going off the beach to the waiting carriage staggering under our loads. This we found at no other place, although diligently searched for.

Jamaica is truly the naturalists' paradise. It is a paradise for the entomologist as well as for the botanist. Insects abound. A kind of ant met us in swarms everywhere. Big, shiny, light brown cockroaches dropped eggs like black beans with a comb-toothed edge about our rooms. Ticks, jiggers and another infinitesimal little creature tormented us somewhat, but we had soothing remedies to allay the discomfort caused by their bites. Lizards darted about our rooms and everywhere through the shrubbery. But, best of all, there is no serpent in our Paradise. There never were any harmful snakes in Jamaica, and the few harmless ones have been exterminated by the mongoose, imported from East India to destroy the rats in the cane-fields. Centipedes and scorpions are said to be present, but though we searched for them beneath rocks and fallen decayed tree trunks, we never saw any except those preserved in alcohol. We were assured that we could penetrate to all parts of the island and never meet with any harm from man or beast.

Pasque Flowers at Easter Time
Proclaim Yearly Spring
Miracle   April 16, 1911

HOWEVER EARLY EASTER SUNDAY IS
in the calendar, the bells of the pasque flower
proclaim the yearly miracle. Or, to change the
metaphor, nearly four weeks ago, on sandy,
southern slopes of the virgin prairie, the
"goslings," as the children call them, thrust
their downy heads above the brown, bare
earth, undismayed by succeeding snows and
frosts, all the way from Wisconsin to the
Rockies.

    In exposed situations they lie huddled on
the ground; but, under the stimulus of

Pasque Flower

Wild Plants
of Minnesota

*From April through September 1911, her first
season as official curator of the Wild Botanic
Garden, Eloise Butler wrote a weekly column on
common wild plants of Minnesota (native and
naturalized) for the Sunday Minneapolis
Tribune. The articles were illustrated with
photographs taken by Butler's former student
Mary Meeker. Butler's references to Gray's botany
are to B.L. Robinson and M.L. Fernald, Gray's
Manual of Botany (7th ed.), 1908. Modern
scientific names are as supplied by Gerald B.
Ownbey, David J. McLaughlin and Thomas
Morley of the Department of Plant Biology,
University of Minnesota, according to
authoritative sources.*

increasing warmth, they will peep out from the
stretch above the brooding mother earth, from
day to day, throughout the month of April.

    The scientific name of the pasque flower,
according to the seventh edition of Gray's
botany, is *Anemone patens var. wolfgangiana*
[*Pulsatilla nuttalliana*]. It is called a variety
because the pasque flower of Europe was first
named. None but a botanist would note the
difference between the European and
American forms. Britton calls the plant
Pulsatilla hirsutissima. Under this name it is
known to pharmacists, for it has medicinal
properties. The leaves when bruised exhale a
pungent odor, which has given rise to other
popular names, as hartshorn and headache
plant.

119

Mrs. Helen Hunt Jackson, perhaps better known as "H.H.," has thus recorded her first impressions of this exquisite flower in *Bits of Travel at Home* [Boston, 1878]:

> The first Colorado flower I saw was the great blue wind-flower, or anemone. It was brought to me one morning, late in April, when snow was lying on the ground, and our strange spring-winter seemed to be coming on fiercely. The flower was only half open, and only half way out of a gray, furry sheath some two inches long; it looked like a Maltese kitten's head, with sharp-pointed blue ears—the daintiest, most wrapped-up little blossom. "A crocus, out in cinchilla fur!" I exclaimed.
>
> "Not a crocus at all; an anemone," said they who knew.
>
> It is very hard, at first, to believe that these anemones do not belong to the crocus family. They push up through the earth in clusters of conical gray, hairy buds, and open cautiously, an inch or two from the ground, precisely as the crocuses do; but, day by day, inches at a time, the stem pushes up, until you suddenly find, some day, in a spot where you left low clumps of what you will persist, for a time, in calling blue crocuses, great bunches of waving blue flowers, on slender waving stems from six to twelve inches high, the blossoms grown larger and opened wider, until they look like small tulip cups, like the Italian anemones.
>
> A week or two later you find at the base of these clumps a beautiful mat of leaves, resembling the buttercup leaf, but much more deeply and numerously slashed on the edges. These, too, grow at last, away from the ground and wave in the air; and, by the time they are well up, many of the flowers have gone to seed, and on top of each stem flutters a great ball of fine, feathery seed plumes, of a green or claret color, almost as beautiful as the blossom itself.

Eloise Butler was a great admirer of Helen Hunt Jackson, novelist and crusader for Indian rights. See Chapter 5.

Anemones, Hepaticas and Buttercups Prominent in Crowfoot Family Here   April 30, 1911

A NUMBER OF THE EARLY flowering plants are members of the crowfoot family [*Ranunculaceae*], [such] as the anemones and buttercups. In the divided leaves of a crowfoot, as some of the buttercups are called, the early botanists saw a resemblance to a bird's foot. The buttercups of Minnesota are not so much in evidence as the tall European buttercup—the pest of the hay fields—farther east.

One early species, *Ranunculus abortivus*, has so small a flower that a novice would scarcely notice it, and is surprised to hear it named a buttercup. Neither would a child be likely to apply the time-worn test of holding the flower to your face to learn if you love butter. This lowly buttercup blooms sparsely on the prairie with the pasque flower. The specific name

Hepatica

rhomboideus [prairie buttercup] indicates the shape of the leaf. The low, tufted *R. fascicularis* [early buttercup] has a larger flower, but is not conspicuously massed. Our two prettiest buttercups are aquatics—one with shining, yellow petals; the other with smaller white flowers and long, trailing stems; and both bearing finely dissected leaves.

The large crowfoot family is without strongly marked characters. Its plants have usually an acrid taste; the leaves are generally more or less cut or divided; the corolla is often wanting, and, when this is the case, the calyx is colored like a corolla; the stamens are numerous; the pistils vary in number from one to several; and all the parts of the flower are distinct or unconnected.

All these points may be verified in the hepatica, or liverleaf, now in bloom along the river banks. It seems somewhat incongruous to associate a name so musical and a flower so beautiful with anything so prosaic as the liver. Yet hepatica is liver in Greek, and some herbalist, long ago, made the comparison, when he saw the three-lobed leaf. The leaves endure through the winter and their rich tints of bronze and purple garnish the tuft of lovely flowers varying through all shades of blue and lilac to white. The lighter tones are found in the older and more exposed flowers.

Just under the flower, and separated from it by a very short stem, are three green leaves or bracts, as leaves on flower stems are technically named—which exactly imitate a calyx, thus fooling the unwary. When the flowers go to seed, new leaves appear. Several plants get their flower work done early, before they are shaded by the leaves, which unfold later to prepare the food for the next year's flowers and seeds.

The hepatica is closely allied to the anemones. Two species are found in Minnesota—one with sharp-lobed [Hepatica acutiloba] and one with round-lobed leaves [Hepatica americana]. The sharp-lobed species, only, is indigenous to Minneapolis; but both have been planted in the wild garden in Glenwood Park.

Bloodroots, Marsh Marigolds, Adder's Tongues and Dutchman's Breeches Among Spring Blooms That Delight Eye and Heart   May 7, 1911

WITHIN THE LAST FORTNIGHT the red swamp maple [Acer rubrum] has glorified the lowlands with its flowers of brilliant hue, forming a pleasing contrast with the ash-gray stems. It is strange that this tree is not more often used for decorative planting, for it will adapt itself to drier sites, and would well take the place of the much admired red-bud growing farther south. The flowers of the maple are succeeded by the scarlet wings of the pendulous fruit, and, before the summer is over, the leaves will take on more gorgeous tints than the autumnal colors of other trees.

When the red maple blooms, here and there along the river, we find a shrub still bare

of leaves, but covered with tiny yellow flowers. This is the leatherwood, Dirca palustris. If you strip down the bark and try to pull it from the stem, you will understand the significance of the common name and its value to the Indians, who use the bark for thongs.

Now is the time that we are enticed to buy from children on the streets big bunches of the cheerful marsh marigold [Caltha palustris]. For she always sits with her feet—roots—in the water, and only barefooted boys are likely to reach her, although "Enough for everybody and to spare" is her motto. The plant is wrongly called "cowslip." The true cowslip is a European primrose and resembles the marsh marigold only in color.

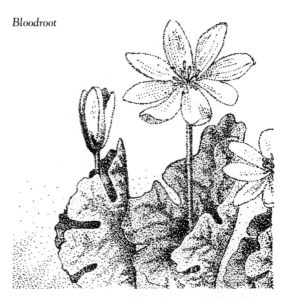

Bloodroot

Wordsworth's Peter Bell would have stopped to pick the young leaves of the marsh marigold for greens—something more substantial than mere yellow flowers. Both the marsh marigold and the primrose are familiar flowers in Europe, and both are named in [English poet] Jean Ingelow's "Songs of Seven."

With the advance of May, Mother Nature's spinning wheels whir faster and faster, and the earth-carpet—the most lovely product of her looms—is woven with intricate designs of flowers in bewildering profusion. But from them all we single out the dogtooth violet or adder's tongue [trout lily, genus Erythronium] for special admiration. The latter name, due to the tongue-shaped, brown-bloched leaf, is more appropriate, for the plant is a species of lily and of no kin to a violet. It has two shining leaves which spring from a deeply buried bulb. Between the leaves arises a beautiful cream colored bell slightly tinted with mauve at the base. The yellow flowered adder's tongue [yellow trout lily, *Erythronium americanum*] is common in the Eastern states. A smaller species [dwarf trout lily, *Erythronium propullans*] with a rose colored flower is also found in Minnesota. This genus flowers best in alluvial soil.

Far more common is the Dutchman's breeches [*Dicentra cucularia*]. Everyone is familiar with the pretty pale pink or yellowish flowers arranged along a slender stalk. The divergent nectaries of the flower have given rise to the ludicrous common name. The single pale green leaf, finely divided into many segments, adds to the delicate beauty of the plant. On Big Island, Lake Minnetonka, protected from marauders by an unclimbable barbed wire fence, grows another member of the same genus, the squirrel corn (*Dicentra canadensis*), similar to Dutchman's breeches except that the flowers are usually white and shaped like those of another relative, the bleeding heart of the gardens. The squirrel corn is developed from subterranean tubers, round and yellow like grains of Indian corn.

Many will not observe the flower of the wild ginger [*Asarum canadense*], although they cannot fail to see the large round leaves. But when one has learned the habit of the plant, he will stoop to look between the leaves for the purplish-red flower-bell bent down to the ground and tricked out with three slender horns. The enigma is easily interpreted: if the curious should lift up the flower to gaze upon it, the horns would protect it from the "evil eye"! With closer approach one perceives another charm—the delightful aromatic odor. Some persons carry about with them a piece of the thick rootstalk as a specific for bodily ills.

Who does not know the bloodroots [*Sanguinaria canadensis*]—babes in the wood— each closely wrapped in the swaddling blanket of a quaintly fashioned grayish-green leaf? As the leaf unrolls the flower bud is disclosed, ensheathed in two thin, pale yellowish green sepals, which fall as the snow white corolla expands. The petals, some eight to twelve, are also evanescent and will not endure rough handling or a long journey. Hence let us leave them to light up the woodland. The flower passes quickly from infancy to maturity.

Presently nothing is left but the seed pod. But the leaf continues to grow lustily. It is an attractive feature with its odd lobation and prominent reddish veins. The red fleshy subterranean stem is the origin of the name bloodroot. The relationship of the bloodroot to the poppy is shown by the two sepals which fall so easily.

Plum Blossoms, Skunk Cabbage, and Modest Jack-in-the-Pulpit among May Arrivals That Please Lover of Life in the Woods   May 14, 1911

FROM A DISTANCE thickets of the thorny, still leafless, wild plum [*Prunus americana*] now seem covered with snowflakes, the illusion being due to myriads of white blossoms. We find the resultant red and yellow, somewhat puckery fruit not unpalatable, if the birds do not forestall us in harvesting it.

And the hard or sugar maple [*Acer saccharum*] becomes conspicuous by reason of its drooping sprays of cream colored flowers, swaying on threadlike stems. The hard maple is certainly our finest deciduous tree. When grown in the open it forms a compact domelike head, which affords refreshing shade from summer's heat. The leaves usually turn a bright yellow in the autumn. This tree will prove an ornament of stately beauty for the street or lawn, and a beneficent testimonial to the wisdom of the planter, calling forth the gratitude of countless passersby, long after he is dust.

To turn to herbs, the skunk cabbage [*Symplocarpus foetidus*] is one of our earliest spring flowers, for it literally thaws through the soil of the icebound marshes. You will have a greater respect for Dame Nature's ability as a packer if you take apart the leaf bud made up of many leaves tightly rolled one within another and smaller and smaller in the center. The bud expands into a clump of large leaves, from which the name cabbage is derived. The disagreeable odor is attractive to flies, which find a shelter from the cold within its purplish-red, hoodlike spathe and pay rent by pollinating the flowers. The spathe—the showy part of the inflorescence—is merely a large leaf enwrapping numerous minute flowers set on a fleshy axis.

It is always well to get at the roots of things. If you dig deep down into the muck you will discover a stout subterranean stem, from which spring many roots ringed like angleworms. These roots have contracted like muscles, thereby forming the rings and giving the stem a deep, safe anchorage in the earth. This is only one of the many instances of self-burial by a "pull on the stem."

More agreeable and better known members of the *Arum* family are Calla [*Calla palustris*] and Jack-in-the-Pulpit [*Arisaema triphyllum*]. In the case of the Jacks, the upper part of the fleshy flower axis is naked and is used as a support of the roof of the pulpit, or spathe. The small, simple flowers at the base of the axis are without floral leaves and are

Jack-in-the-Pulpit with Two Jacks

usually separated, namely, some of the Jacks bear only pollen producing flowers, and others, which in the course of time will develop seeds. The leaves of the Jacks are branched and made up of three leaflets. The seed-producing Jack usually bears a pair of these branched leaves in place of the one carried by the pollen-bearing Jack.

. . . The individual producing the seed must manufacture food for storage in them as well as in the onion-shaped, subterranean bulb, which gives another name—Indian turnip—to the plant. The Indians used the turnip, after pressing out the poisonous sap, as a farinaceous food. Jack-the-Jester . . . has, of course, the reputed wisdom of former times;

but you'll get no drippings of it, unless you frequent the sanctuary of the wilderness. But even as a preacher, he cannot refrain from some foolish pranks. No one would be astonished to find, as is sometimes the case, two Jacks fraternally occupying the same pulpit; but an observer was doubled up with laughter to see a Jack holding forth in two united pulpits. Only the student, or one versed in wood lore, would recognize Jack, when he first pricks through the ground, in the form of a slender, slightly curved, sharp-pointed bud, with a protective sheath mottled like snake skin. Again, but few connect the last stage of seed-bearing Jack with the crowded bunch of bright red berries so common in late summer.

It is a far cry from the Arum to the Portulaca family [*Portulacaceae*], to which the much beloved spring beauty (*Claytonia virginica*) belongs. The spring beauty is local, but it brightens large patches of low woodlands, which it chooses for an abiding place. Spring beauty of Minneapolis is a low, slender plant with narrow leaves which come from a dark brown triangular tuber imbedded in the earth. The flowers are dainty white bells striped with pink, and in masses thickly carpeting the earth are a joy to the eye.

Beautiful Large-Flowered Trilliums Grace Minnetonka Wood in May; Violets, Forest, Hillside and Prairie Varieties Flourish Near Minneapolis   May 21, 1911

IN SOME FAVORED PLACES about Lake Minnetonka may be seen during May profuse growths of the beautiful large-flowered trillium (*Trillium grandiflorum*). So highly is this plant esteemed by the English that they have imported large quantities of it from this country for plantations in their private parks. The petals, at first pearly white, turn pink in age, as does also the seed vessel.

The trilliums are closely related to the lilies. All have a thick underground stem, bearing a single aerial stem, which supports a whorl of three large leaves varying somewhat in size and shape in different species. Above the leaf whorl arises the lovely flower, with or without a stalk; erect or drooping; white, red, purple or pink striped, according to the species. The flower is also on the plan of three green sepals, three colored petals, six stamens in two rows, and one pistil made up of three united carpels. The name trillium probably comes from the three leaves. The plant has a number of local names—wake robin [and] bath flower; . . . "way down East," the pink-striped or painted trilliums are called "wild pinies"—meaning peonies.

A cute little species and one of the earliest to blossom is the dwarf trillium [snow trillium, *T. nivale*], much smaller as the name implies. The most common trillium about Minneapolis is *T. cernuum* [nodding trillium], lovely but

Large-Flowered Trillium

less showy than the large flowered form.

Another ally of the lilies is the large-flowered bellwort (*Uvularia grandiflora*), bearing a slender, drooping yellow bell at the extremity of each fork of the leafy stem. In this species the leaves are perfoliate, that is, the stem seems to pass through the base of the leaf. In another pretty species of bellworts [sessile-leaved bellwort, *U. sessilifolia*]—a smaller plant with cream colored bells—the leaves are sessile.

The following . . . species people often bunch indiscriminately together as May flowers, or anemones. The false rue anemone (*Isophyrum biternatum*), with branched leaves and a few white flowers, stars the woods about Minnehaha. The fibrous roots of this plant are thickened at intervals; the seed vessel has two or three seeds instead of one, as in the anemones. The rue anemone of oak woods [*Anemonella thalictroides*] has a cluster of bright pink flowers on stalks set like the sticks of an umbrella above a whorl of leaves. Another leaf, similar to that of the false rue anemone, arises directly from a cluster of three or four fleshy roots like miniature sweet potatoes.

A genuine anemone—the one-stalked grove anemone [wood anemone, *Anemone quinquefolia*]—bears, above a whorl of branched leaves, a single flower, white and daintily flushed with pink when it first appears, but turning white as it matures. This plant has a slender, horizontal root stalk.

These are all members of the crowfoot family. In all the petals are absent but the sepals are brightly colored. It is a rule in botany to call the outer floral leaves sepals, however bright their color; and if but one set of leaves is present, to consider that the petals are absent.

But the violets are pre-eminently the flowers of May, and is it not true that of all flowers they are the most beloved, not excepting the rose? At least nine sorts of violets can be readily distinguished by the novice in the vicinity of Minneapolis.

Violets may be classed under two heads— the leafless and the leafy-stemmed. The leafless species have only a subterranean stem, while the other class have also a stem above ground. To the first class belong the common blue meadow violet [*Viola nephrophylla*, *V. praticola*, and *V. sororia*]. One is rapturously happy when he chances upon a meadow tufted with clumps of these violets. No wonder at such a time one supposedly guiltless of "dropping into poetry" was heard crooning over and over to himself, "I would rather know where violets grow than a good many other things!"

The bird's-foot violet of the prairies [*V. pedatifida*] has a finely divided leaf. The flower is pale lilac with a lighter eye like a small pansy. The larkspur violet [hybrid between *V. pedatifida* and a common blue meadow violet], also a prairie form, has a flower similar to that of the meadow violet, but a dissected leaf. The arrow-leaved violet [*V. sagittata*] growing on low land usually has leaves with an arrow-shaped base, but it may vary considerably in shape. The flower is a bright purple.

Often associated with this violet, on the sandy shores of ponds, is the white, lance-leaved violet [*V. lanceolata*], its leaves slender as grass blades—not at all like the typical, more or less rounded, violet leaf. Another favorite is the small, white violet of the bogs [*V. macloskeyi var. pallens*], much prized on account of its exquisite fragrance.

In the second class are the common yellow violet of rich woodlands [*V. pubescens*], the small very pale dog violet of wet meadows [*V. conspersa*], and the Canadian violet [*V. canadensis*]. The last named has the same habit as the yellow, but the petals of the flower are white and blotched with purplish pink. Besides pleasing the eye, the flowers are fragrant, and, in open places, bloom throughout the season, like its aristocratic sisters the cultivated pansies.

Over twenty species of violets are found within the borders of the state, but the characters of some of these are based upon features that can be determined only by experts.

Violets are in the habit of producing besides the beautiful flower, so called secret, bud-like flowers, that are without color and never open. These secret flowers mature seeds through self-fertilization; while the showy flowers are dependent upon insects for pollination. The expert on violets must ascertain the number, form and color of the seeds made by the hidden or secret flowers. The insect-pollinated flower is fitted to the insect, and the insect to the flower, as a key to its lock. In sucking the nectar from the hollow spur on the lower side of the violet flower, the insect—a bee, for instance—is obliged to take such a position as to become smeared with the pollen, which it transfers unconsciously to the sticky part of the pistil of the next violet that it visits. The insect is further directed by the nectar guides, where to insert its tongue, as they converge toward the nectary, or spur.

Therefore, when flowers are pollinated by insects, the color, fragrance, spots, streaks and irregularities in the shape of the flower, are all for the purpose of furthering the production of seeds. But from these attractive features, for utility only in the flower, arbitrarily assumed, we derive our purest pleasure.

Geum, Early Meadow Rue, Lousewort, Phlox, and Hoary Puccoon Are Described as Wild Beauties in Miss Butler's Weekly Article May 28, 1911

NEARLY CONTEMPORANEOUS WITH the pasque flower, and likewise on the prairie, grows the Avens, or three-flowered Geum [purple avens or prairie smoke, *Geum triflorum*]. It bears a tuft of fern-like, interruptedly pinnate leaves, each leaf consisting of divided leaflets arranged along the stalk like the parts of a feather, interspersed with still smaller leaflets. The plant has a single flower stalk with three branches at the top, each terminated by a rosy,

Purple Avens

pensile bell, looking like a flower bud, decorated with slender, recurved bracts. One would wait in vain, however, for these debutantes to appear otherwise. "Buds" they will seem to be throughout their season. Opening the five closed petals you will find attached to them five creamy petals and many stamens. In the center of the flower are innumerable pistils, which finally form a lovely claret-colored ball of gossamer plumes, each serving to waft through the air the little seed-like fruit. The Geum belongs to the Rose family, the family containing the most esteemed cultivated fruits of the temperate regions, as the strawberry, peach, cherry, pear—a long list. At the head of this list should be placed the apple, which—tame, wild and crab—has within the past week gladdened the eye with its pearly, rose-tinted clouds of bloom.

Along with the Geum will be seen in abundance another plant, the lousewort [*Pedicularis canadensis*]; or, if you prefer a more euphonious name, the wood betony. The former name was given by farmers, who fancied that cattle feeding upon the plant were infested with one of the Egyptian plagues. The pinnately divided leaves of betony are arranged in a rosette. The pale yellow flowers are bilabiate, with the laterally compressed upper lip arched over the stamens and the pistil and are densely crowded in the leafy spike. This plant belongs to the Figwort family [*Scrophulariaceae*], in which the flowers are usually two-lipped—like the snap dragon—and are ingeniously adapted to insect pollination.

Another prairie flower of brighter yellow is the hoary puccoon [*Lithospermum canescens*], popularly called Indian pink, perhaps because the roots afford a beautiful red dye much used by the Indians. Slender leaves thickly clothe the stem, which bears at the top a good-sized cluster of the brilliant flowers, tubular at the base and spreading abruptly into a flat border. Such a flower is called salver shaped. The tube serves to enclose the stamens and hold the nectar. The puccoon shows its relationship to the heliotrope in the shape of the flower and in the way in which the flower cluster uncoils as the buds expand.

It is not uncommon in Maying parties to hear the exclamation, "Oh, what a pretty fern!" as the attention is attracted to the delicate many-branched leaf of the early meadow rue [*Thalictrum dioicum*], one of the crow-foot family. The leaf stalk of the meadow rue is branched four times into three divisions, so that it bears in all eighty-one leaflets. The leaf is as pleasing as that of a fern and adds an airy fern-like grace to a bouquet. Ferns, by the way, have three characters by which they may be distinguished from other plants—a coiled leaf-bud which unrolls at the base when the leaf expands, displaying a forked venation (a second peculiarity of the fern); and, later, some brown or yellowish dots usually on the under side in which are developed spores. Ferns have neither flowers nor seeds, while one individual of the early meadow rue has a spray of tiny pollen-bearing flowers, and another the seed-producing flowers. These separated flowers are pollinated by the wind.

A much admired genus of the crowfoot family is the columbine, which has one representative in Minnesota [*Aquilegia canadensis*]. All the columbines make a brave showing, from the cultivated ones of different hues to the peerless large [blue-]white species [*A. caerulea*], the state flower of Colorado. But our species holds its own among them all, bourgeoning in red and yellow in rich relief against the background of gray rock, as it nods from boulder crevices. The columbine has both calyx and corolla and both are colored. The long spurred petals gorged with nectar for the entertainment of insect guests have given rise to the name honeysuckle which, to avoid confusion, would better be kept for the true honeysuckle in no wise related to the columbine. The foliage of the columbine is fern-like as is the meadow rue and others of the same family.

In the meadows may also be seen an early composite, the golden ragwort [*Senecio aureus*]. In the composite family what seems to be a flower, at a careless glance, is in reality a flower cluster, composed of small closely crowded flowers, with buds or tubular flowers in the center that might be mistaken for stamens and pistils, and surrounded on the outside by whorls of green leaves called bracts that exactly imitate a calyx. The foliage of the ragwort is more or less cut or parted, hence the name.

Near the Hill seminary [St. Paul Seminary] lies a fairyland, carpeted in May with flower mosaics, pink, white, yellow and blue. The spring beauty forms the pink vistas of this woodland; the false rue anemone, the white; marsh marigold, ragworts and buttercups, the yellow; violets and phlox, the blue. In this flower elysium cares fly away, and all alike are happy children reveling with the flowers. But one is shocked to see traces of the slimy serpent in this paradise. It has been desecrated by dumps of old tins and other rubbish, and it is rumored that it is the intention to cut a road through the place. By next summer, no doubt, it will exist only in memory. The confines of the wilderness are becoming more and more restricted under the resistless march of settlement.

The low phlox [wild blue phlox] (*P. divaricata*) of this region runs the gamut of colors from white, blue to lilac. It is readily transplanted and blossoms freely, and will flourish in sun or shade. There is no better plant, wild or cultivated, for edgings or borders, as it tones harmoniously with other flowers. The world is indebted to America for the splendid cultivated phloxes which have developed, one and all, from various native species.

Hawthorn of World Fame through Poetry and Prose of England, Virginian Waterleaf, White Lily, and Geranium Featured in June June 4, 1911

MANY ARE THE ALLUSIONS to the hawthorns of England in poetry and prose. Indeed, the very name, England, calls up to the observer of plants a mental picture of hawthorn thickets and hedges. It is pertinent to ask why writers neglect to extol the American species [genus *Cratageus*]. For our hawthorn trees or shrubs are of extreme beauty, when covered with their snowy fleece of bloom, or when glowing with the sweet tasting, stony bright red "thorn apples." The leaves of the hawthorn may have margins varying from toothed to lobed or divided. The thorns may be long and stout, or few and feeble; thus belying the name.

Of all the botanical mazes, that of the hawthorn is the most intricate. In Gray's seventh edition, no less than sixty-five species of the genus are described, as well as many varieties.

Some botanists go so far as to affirm that every individual is a distinct species. When the ordinary student wearies of cudgeling his brain over minute differences of stamen, nutlet or whatnot, he ignominiously names the species "*Crataegus sp.?*" or passes on the puzzle to the greatest authority, Professor [Charles Sprague] Sargent, the director of the renowned Arnold Arboretum of Boston. Those desirous of extending their acquaintance of hawthorns may see grouped together in this arboretum the largest collection of both native and foreign species known to the world.

At this time hydrophyllum [*H. virginianum*], the Virginian waterleaf, makes a profuse growth in rich woodlands. It may be recognized by the pinnately divided leaf, often blotched with white, and the somewhat showy flower cluster made up of lavender colored bells to which a touch of fragile grace is added

by the slender protruding stamens.

Close by the waterleaf may be seen some of the smilacinas, or false Solomon's seal, as the star-flowered [*S. stellata*] with sparsely flowered raceme of small white blossoms; *Smilacina racemosa* [false spikenard], stouter, with larger, coarser and smaller and more numerous compactly clustered yellowish flowers; *S. trifolia* [three-leaved false Solomon's seal], similar to and equally beautiful, but of lower habit than the leafy stemmed *stellata* and affecting bog lands; last of all, the two-leaved *Maianthemum canadense*, the lowliest and lovliest—often called wild lily-of-the-valley [Canada mayflower]. The latter species is not classed with the *smilacinas* because it has four

Solomon's Seal

floral leaves and four stamens instead of six. All of these species are decorative in fruit as well as in flower, for they have red berries.

Fortunately, those who are interested may see growing by the side of the smilacinas the real Solomon's seal [genus *Polygonatum*] similar in habit to *Smilacina racemosa*, but with a few drooping, elongated, green flower bells above the leaves, all along the stem, succeeded in time by dark purple berries. Why called Solomon's seal, do you ask? Burrowing in the earth will disclose a fleshy underground stem scarred at intervals with rounded, shallow pits that have been likened to seals—a seal for each annual, aerial stalk. "Venerable is Solomon" you will exclaim, if you attempt to trace their number.

In the same vicinity is the baneberry, more noticeable in fruit than in flower. One species [*Actaea rubra*] bears large red berries, and another white, on short red stalks [*Actaea pachypoda*]. The flowers are inconspicuous and white; the leaf, large and branched, composed of many small leaflets.

Few are unable to name the wild geranium [*Geranium maculatum*] when they observe the form of the leaf, the flower cluster, and the flower. This geranium enlivens large expanses of woodlands with its purplish flowers. The significance of another name—cranesbill—is seen when the blossom goes to seed, forming a bird-like beak, from the base of which uncurl fine little seed-like fruits.

Wild Roses Know When It Is June, According to Miss Butler, Who Describes Blossoms That Delight the Rambler Out-of-Doors   June 11, 1911

ONE UNFAMILIAR WITH the native flora is surprised to learn that the superb large-flowered Pentstemon (*P. grandiflorus*) is not an exotic. A hillside covered by this plant, with its large, showy, five-parted, two-lipped bells of delicate, varying shades of blue, lilac and lavender, once seen, can never be forgotten. Attached to the inner base of the corolla are five curved stamens, the origin of the scientific name, *Pentstemon*. One of these stamens has, instead of the usual pollen sacs, a close tuft of hairs. This bearded stamen, partially closing up the throat of the corolla tube, and thus facilitating insect pollination, has given rise to the common name, beard-tongue. The thickish even-margined, grayish green leaves . . . are arranged in opposite pairs. They are covered with an evanescent bloom, like the leaves of the cabbage and pea, or the fruit of the plum.

The Pentstemon is but one of the many native flowers as remarkable for size, color and beauty as many that are laboriously cultivated in gardens or greenhouse, and with the elusive, individual charm rarely retained by plants torn from their natural setting.

Another beautiful flower, often cultivated, and like the beard-tongue, a

frequenter of sandy soil, is *Tradescantia virginiana* [*T. bracteata* in Minnesota], commonly called spiderwort, from the slender, keeled leaves stretching out like the legs of a spider. This plant is closely allied to the lilies. The flower is on the plan of three—having three green sepals, three bright reddish or bluish purple petals, six stamens and a pistil usually made up of three united carpels. The stamens are a distinctive feature of the flower, with their yellow pollen sacs against the purple petals. The stalks of the stamens are densely fringed with purple hairs, whose beauty has a depth "that is deeper still" under the armed eye of the microscope. The hairs, when magnified, are seen as branching chains of exquisitely tinted spherical and cylindric, bead-

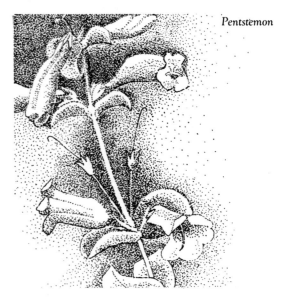

Pentstemon

like cells, within which pulsate circling streams of protoplasm—the living substance—endowed with the same properties in the humblest and in the highest forms of life.

Many plants of the pea or pulse family are now in bloom. Among them the lupine [*Lupinis perennis*] will easily rank first, by reason of its showy spikes of blue or purple butterfly-shaped flowers, and beautiful palmately divided leaves. The lupine also grows in sandy soil, to which it is adapted by a tap root penetrating to a depth that will tire out the most persistent digger who may intend to obtain a specimen for transplanting.

A search in bogs and low rich woodlands will be rewarded at this time by the lovely dwarf cornel [bunchberry, *Cornus canadensis*].

What seems like four white petals in this flower are bracts—as the leaves on flower stalks are technically named—and no integral part of the blossom, but grouped about a cluster of small flowers, which develop later into a rounded bunch of bright red berries, toothsome to children, although of cloying sweetness. One would not at first sight connect this lowly herb with its relatives, the dogwood shrubs, one species of which [C. stolonifera] is favored for hedges on account of its attractive white, flat-topped flower clusters, its white or sometimes purple fruit, and especially for the vividly red stems that give the needed touch of color to the winter landscape.

Although not flowers, we cannot pass without a glance the denizens of decaying logs and stumps. To students of fungi and epicures, these forms of vegetation may be of more interest than the flowering plants. The . . . edible oyster mushroom, *Pleurotus ostreatus* . . . is somewhat shell-like in shape, and the individuals overlap one another like oysters attached to some substratum in the sea. The under surface is covered, too, with gills, not for breathing, as in oysters and fish, but for bearing spores or reproduction cells.

How do the roses know that it is June? With the advent of the crowning month of the year, gardens, wild wood and prairie are ever redolent with the fragrance and glorified with the supernal loveliness of the rose.

Strange to say, a cult exists, slowly increasing in numbers, that considers single flowers—yes, even single roses—more lovely than the double ones, transformed by man from beautiful utility to useless beauty. For, with the multiplication of the velvety petals disappear the stamens and pistils which are the essentials for the formation of the seed—the purpose of the flower in nature. We may marvel at the skill of the florist in producing a cabbage-like double-dahlia and chrysanthemum; but we linger over and dearly love the single forms of these flowers. Banks of single roses in large gardens of double ones compel admiration and seem more decorative than the artificially produced double ones, to these possibly-mistaken few.

Painted Cup Notable among Wild Flowers Found near Minneapolis; Bog-Trotter's Zeal Repaid by Orchids and Other Swamp Blossoms   June 18, 1911

AN ACCOUNT OF THE NOTABLE wild flowers of Minneapolis would be incomplete without some mention of the painted cup [Indian paintbrush], *Castilliea coccinea*. In the latter part of May, the meadows favored by this plant are visions of delight. Painter's brush is by far the better name for it, as only the tips of the floral leaves of the compact spike flame in scarlet, or, less frequently, in yellow, thus suggesting a brush dipped in the pigments of an artist's palette. It is the leaves (bracts) among the flowers that are colored vividly. The tubular calyx has but a narrow rim of brightness and the slender, greenish corolla is, contrary to rule, the least conspicuous of all.

The reckless enthusiast now plunges wildly into mire and willingly pays toll to myriads of mosquitoes. He must needs be a bog-trotter in order to see the carnivorous plants and orchids found only in undrained tamarack swamps. Imbedded in bog mass, whorls of curiously constructed, lurid-veined leaves, arched and hollow, and filled with water, greet his eyes. It is the pitcher plant, *Sarracenia purpurea*—a plant that lives partially on insects.

A fly seldom escapes from one of these leaf traps when she visits it for a sip of water. For, if she succeeds in crawling up the inner slippery surface, she will encounter a margin of stiff, downward pointing hairs that will hinder further progress. As the insects decay, they are absorbed. In this way the plants obtain the nitrogenous food, more or less necessary for all plants, as shown by the use of fertilizers.

But what is novel about the insectivorous plants is that they capture living insects. They can thereby get a living from poorer soil and with feebler roots than can other plants. The flower also has a striking appearance. The calyx is dark red purple. The fiddle-shaped petals of rich wine color are folded over a genuine umbrella—the stigma of the pistil, which not only serves the usual purpose of pollination, but also keeps the pollen and nectar dry—an umbrella in use long before man thought of making one.

We have but one pitcher plant in this latitude. Another species is a native of the southern states, and still another of the Pacific coast. Others again are found in the old world and in the tropics. All these may be recognized by the pitcher leaf, but the plants vary considerably, for "nature repeats herself with a difference." The southern species has a yellow flower; the pitcher of the Pacific states has an arching roof and a lurid, fish-tail appendage; and some of the tropical pitchers are on vines, and are filled with digestive fluids, protected by motile lids that close automatically over the struggling captives.

The greatest prize of the swamp is our state flower, the showy cyprepedium [C. reginae], the pink and white lady's-slipper, a member of the orchid family. No flower, wild or cultivated, is more magnificent than this.

Indian Paintbrush

The plant is the tallest of the genus and has the broadest leaves and the largest and most beautifully tinted flowers, often bearing two on one stalk. Only North American Indian ladies wear slippers of this style, and the precise always call them moccasins. Goddesses, also, must have approved of this kind of footgear, for the scientific name, cypripedium, means Venus' boskin.

Six cypripediums are native to Minnesota—the showy [C. reginae], the small white [C. candidum], the two-leaved pink [stemless, C. acaule] and the small and rare ram's head [C. arietinum, and two varieties of the yellow lady's-slipper, C. calceolus.] All but the [ram's head] may be seen in their season in the wild garden in Glenwood park. The

ram's head is a comical little boskin, with two horns that readily suggest the popular name. . . .

Of extreme interest are the twayblades, cousins of the cypripediums. They have been introduced into the wild garden in Glenwood park and have blossomed faithfully for two successive years. . . . The flowers are bits of fairy gossamer. In one species [L. loeselii] they are green; in the other [L. liliifolia], they are a trifle larger and of an indescribable shade of mauve. They belong to the genus Liparis. Another genus of twayblades is Listera, not yet represented in the wild garden.

The tropics abound in orchids of bewildering forms and hues, many of them air plants; but we are grateful for those we have, although they are hidden for the most part in the cool recesses of bogland. A tree in the tropics is a garden in itself, when covered with trailing ferns, orchids and other air plants. Some of these orchid flowers simulate gay butterflies in shape and coloring; one, called the "flower of the Holy Ghost," resembles a dove sitting on its nest. The fantastic shapes are conformations to the insects that pollinate the flowers. For information on this fascinating subject, the student may be referred to [Hermann] Müller's *Fertilisation of Flowers* [London, 1883] and William Hamilton Gibson's *Our Native Orchids* [New York, 1905].

Also, when floundering in the bogs, we come across the wild calla [Calla palustris], a flower just as lovely, though smaller, as the well-known cultivated calla imported from Africa. This species has a creeping stem and heart-shaped, glossy leaves. It belongs to the Arum family, which includes, as you may remember, the skunk cabbage and Jack-in-the-pulpit. Like them, too, the showy part of the inflorescence is a large bract or spathe enwrapping a dense cluster of small flowers.

Blue Flag, Native Minnesota Iris, Classed as Richest of Lilies; Early Meadow Rue and Larkspur Treated by Miss Butler July 2, 1911

Born in the purple, born to joy and pleasance,
Thou dost not toil nor spin,
But makest glad and radiant with thy presence
The meadow and the lin.

The wind blows and uplifts thy drooping
    banner,
And round thee throng and run
The rushes, the green yeomen of thy manor,
    The outlaws of the sun.

Thou art the Iris, fair among the fairest,
    Who, armed with goldenrod
And winged with the celestial azure, bearest
    The message of some god.

O flower-de-luce, bloom on, and let the river
    Linger to kiss thy feet!
O flower of song, bloom on, and make forever
    The world more fair and sweet.

THUS SANG LONGFELLOW [in "Flower de Luce," 1896] of the iris, most fitting emblem of France, the leader in refined taste and art. "If eyes were made for seeing," we do not need to be poets in order to note the grace of the recurved petals, the stately pose of the flower and the choice reserve that withholds, except under close inspection, the delicate finish of etched lines and blendings of color.

The flower is richer than other lilies by reason of the pistil terminating above in three leafy divisions colored like the petals. Behind them are artfully concealed the three long stamens in exactly the right position for the insect guest to be powdered with the pollen.

An ardent lover of flowers has dreamed of a garden devoted entirely to [irises] from all quarters of the earth and including the hybrids produced under cultivation—[irises] of every conceivable shade and combination of color, ranging from dwarfs to splendid grenadiers, and with a succession of bloom throughout the growing season. Among them our native iris [Iris versicolor], or "blue flag," would have an honored place.

The early meadow rue [Thalictrum dioicum] is one of the most common woodland flowers of early May. In June, the much showier late and tall meadow rue, Thalictrum polygamum [T. dasycarpum in Minnesota], is a charming feature of the low lands. Its white, feathery masses of bloom, swaying in response to the gentlest breeze, cannot fail to win admiration.

No less lovely and growing in the same habitat or on drier soil is the dainty northern bedstraw, Galium boreale. The flowers are very small but so compactly massed that the tract so fortunate as to be starred with them can be detected from a distance. This plant has the same effect in bouquets as the much esteemed exotic, Gypsophila. One species of Galium, very similar to the one under consideration, is cultivated under the name "baby's breath." The entire genus is characterized by small leaves arranged in whorls on slender, four-sided stems and tiny three or four parted corollas. Some of the species are covered with hooks which grip everything at hand, and the roots of some afford a red dye, thereby accounting for the other popular names, cleavers and madder.

Whoever sees a rocky hillside lit up with the tall candles of the white larkspur [prairie larkspur, Delphinium virescens] will decide that they outrank with their ethereal beauty the great blue larkspurs in the formal garden of

Blue Flag Iris

royal pedigree. Burly bumblebees flock about the plants, clasping each flower in turn upon the wandlike stalks and thrusting their long tongues into the upturned spurs to extract the sweets within.

It seems necessary to write a word in favor of what are usually called weeds, which may be defined as plants out of place, growing where we wish something else to grow. The cow parsnip [Heracleum lanatum] shows fine decorative possibilities. A rampant growth of this herb gave character to a certain roadside. Barely an hour after a photograph was taken, the plants were mown down and nothing left in their place but monotonous stubble. A plea is offered for the next season: O scytheman, spare this weed! It is harmless, and does its

best to make glad the waste places. It is named
for the god Hercules on account of its massive
bulk. Compare it with the castor bean
occupying the central post of honor in an
ornamental mound of flowers. Has it not as
vigorous a growth; are not the leaves as large
and finely formed and the flowers as beautiful
as that of the favored imported canna?

Turning from the sturdy habit of the
Heracleum to the Linnaea we are reminded
that it is proverbial that goodness and
sweetness are concentrated in small masses.
For the twin flower [*Linnaea borealis*] is a
trailing, small-leaved evergreen studded with
pairs of little white flowers striped with pink.
It was a favorite with its namesake, [Carl]
Linnaeus [1707-1778], and that it becomes of
every one who once enjoys its exquisite
delicacy and fragrance. The wild garden in
Glenwood park is the only place where it may
be found in Minneapolis. To conserve this
flower alone is a sufficient reason for the
perpetuation of the place.

Milkweed Flowers Much in Evidence during July; Harebells, Ox-Eyes, and Water Lilies Also Bloom in Abundance   July 9, 1911

AT PRESENT THE FLOWERS most in
evidence are the milkweeds. About a dozen
species of them are indigenous to Minnesota.
Every one knows the tall, rank, common
milkweed [*Asclepias syriaca*] and probably
admires more than the large umbels of pale
purplish flowers the rough, gray seed pods,
that, splitting down one side, disclose a
wondrous freight of closely packed, brown
seeds. A gust of wind quickly twirls these out;
for each seed, in place of a magic carpet, is
provided with a tuft of white, silky down to
transport it to some distant place.

The first milkweed to appear was the
oval-leaved, white-flowered species of the
prairies [*Asclepias ovalifolia*]. This has been
succeeded by another species [*A. verticillata*]
with smaller white blossoms and thread-like
leaves. Meadows and treeless swamps are gay
with large masses of a rose colored milkweed
[swamp milkweed], *Asclepias incarnata*, and
sandy banks and roadsides are fairly ablaze
with the red and orange *A. tuberosa*, which has

been successfully transferred to gardens. It is
rightly named butterfly weed, not only because
the flowers attract hosts of butterflies, but
because they vie with them in gorgeous
coloring. Another name, pleurisy root, recalls
the alleged medicinal properties of the
milkweeds that gave rise to the scientific name
Asclepias—a modification of the name of the
ancient physician Aesculapias [a figure in
Greek mythology, son of Apollo and the
mortal Coronis, who became a legendary
healer].

Most of the milkweeds, as the term
implies, are furnished with a copious, milky
juice. Crawling insects are likely to be covered
and impaled by this sticky fluid, which exudes
from wounds made by their sharp claws, as

Common Milkweed

they scale the stems of the plants, and thus
prevents them from rifling the nectar provided
by the flowers for the pollen-distributing,
hairy-bodied flying insects.

Wonderful are the adaptations of the
flower to desirable insect guests. Above the
petals is a crown of five hoodlike nectaries,
each bearing within a slender, inverted horn.
The center of the flower is designedly slippery.
When an insect alights on this slimy surface to
sip the abundant nectar, her feet slip and are
tightly caught in crevices, also of fell design.
When she extricates her toes, so to speak, she
drags out attached to them a dangling pair of
pollen masses—pollinia, a part of which is sure
to adhere to the pistil of the next milkweed
flower she visits. Insects have been caught at

this season with stalks of these pollinia attached to every one of their six feet.

In contrast with the robust milkweed, peeps out from rocky, wooded banks the drooping, purplish blue harebell [*Campanula rotundifolia*], swaying on its slender stalk. It is identical with the bonny bluebell o' Scotland, so often alluded to in Scottish literature. One might wonder on seeing the slender, attenuated leaves why the plant is called *Campanula rotundifolia*. The rotund leaves are the first comers, and generally die away before blossoming time.

Particularly under cone-bearing trees may be found the false wintergreen [shinleaf], or *Pyrola*. The somewhat round and thick leaves of this plant do not rise far above the ground; the sweet, waxy white or pinkish flowers are arranged in wandlike racemes. To think of this plant in its native haunts sets the gypsy blood a coursing for a tramp in the wild to breathe the air from the pines and to crush their needles under foot.

After the pasque flower, our most conspicuous anemone is the canadensis [Canada anemone, *A. canadensis*], once known as the pennsylvanica. On account of a similarity of leaf it is often taken for a white geranium. The flower, however, has an entirely different structure from that of the geranium. The anemone, for instance, has no corolla; the white floral leaves are sepals. The *Garden Magazine* for July has a paper on anemones, especially recommending this species for plantings, and emphasizing the value of white flowers for harmonizing discordant colors and for toning down the hot and violent reds and yellows and outrageous magentas.

The meadows and copses are now gilded with the ox-eye (*Heliopsis*), much like the wild sunflowers, and distinguished from them only by the specialist in a few details. The ox-eye is a forerunner of the golden seas of bloom that characterize the waning summer. It is to be commended for its profuse growth and for its adaptability to varying conditions.

For coolness, rest and peace go to the lakes encircled and islanded by the refreshing white lilies serenely resting on the surface of the water among the large, round leaf pads. These lilies of the water toil not, neither do they spin. They are, indeed, lotuses with power like those of the Nile to induce dreams and visions. The flowers are closed at night. At sunrise, if one chances to be at a lily pond, he will be entranced to see the flowers burst open all at once under the influence of the sun—a sudden transformation of the dark water into a scene of enchantment.

The pond lily of this vicinity [white water lily, *Nymphaea tuberosa*] has but little fragrance compared with that of the East. The stout, subterranean stem scarred with the evidence of former leaf and flowerstalks has also tubers which break off to propagate new plants. The pond lily is of special scientific interest because it illustrates Goethe's theory that all the parts of a flower are modified leaves. The green sepals merge into the white petals, and they, in their turn, into broad yellow stamens, which become narrower toward the center.

Somewhat stiff and coarse by the side of the white lily is the yellow cow lily [yellow water lily, *Nuphar luteum var. variegatum*], a plebian, if you please, but a pleasing foil to the patrician beauty. Nevertheless anyone would admire the flower of the wee cow lily [*N. luteum var. pumilum*], measuring less than an inch across. This species is common in Nova Scotia and New Brunswick and has been reported in Minnesota.

Lily Declared Crowning Wild Flower near Minneapolis in July; Miss Butler Describes, Also, the Blossoms That Kept It Company   July 16, 1911

DOUBTLESS EVERYONE WOULD select as the crowning wild flower for the calendar months of the growing season in Minneapolis the pasque flower for April, violets for May, roses for June and lilies for July.

Of our . . . native lilies the Turk's-cap [*Lilium michiganense*], although not the lily of Palestine, may be said to surpass the glory of Solomon, as it is arrayed in recurved orange-red petals flecked with spots of purple. Sometimes as many as forty blossoms are borne on a single plant.

Beautiful, also, are the yellow swamp lily [species unknown], with floral leaves spotted with brown and less recurved than those of the Turk's-cap, and the wood lily, *Lilium philadelphicum*, with an erect, cup-like flower of deep, glowing red. The vivid colors of all these lilies were developed in crucibles fired by summer's fiercest noon-tide heat.

Troops of black-eyed Susans boldly stare at roamers over the hillsides. As we return Susan's unblinking gaze we see that her eyes are a velvety, purplish brown instead of black. This cone-flower, *Rudbeckia hirta*, is a composite. The "eye" is made up of many small, tubular flowers, and each yellow eyelash is also a flower.

Another composite adorned with yellow ray petals and towering in splendor above its competitors in rich, alluvial soil, is the cup plant, *Silphium perfoliatum*. The large leaves, arranged in pairs along the stem, are united at the base to form a deep cup for holding water. This may serve the double purpose of tiding the plant over a dry spell and of keeping

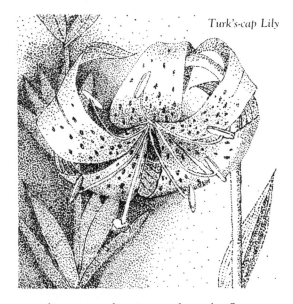

Turk's-cap Lily

unwelcome, crawling insects from the flowers. People in the tropics use a similar means, to keep the ants from the food by inserting the legs of the dining tables in dishes of water.

The interesting rosin, or compass plant of the prairie [*Silphium laciniatum*] is of the same genus as the cup plant. Its leaves are cut edgewise and point due north and south. Persons lost on a trackless, uninhabited prairie might find their bearings by this vegetable compass. An army officer stationed on the western plains, the first observer of the plant, thought the leaves must have the properties of the magnetic needle. Failing to prove this theory by experiments, he forwarded specimens of the *Silphium* to Dr. Asa Gray, the American Darwin, who suggested that the

peculiar position of the leaves was for the purpose of avoiding the direct rays of the sun in order to check too great a loss of water by transpiration.

Since that time "polarity" has been observed in the leaves of many other plants growing in drought regions or in exposed situations, as the eucalyptus trees of Australia. Such trees, of course, afford no shade. The habit may be noted in the roadside weed prickly lettuce, and in some degree even in the garden lettuce.

To subdue the brilliant orange and reds of the lilies and composites, Mother Nature has planted among them with [a] judicious and generous hand various white flowers, as *Veronica virginica* [*Veronicastrum virginicum*], with feathery spires of bloom, some branched like candelabras, topping slender stems, clothed at intervals with whorls of narrow, pointed leaves. It is popularly called Culver's root, or Culver's physic, because one of that name extracted a specific from the root.

The shrublike *Ceanothus* [*C. americanus*], or New Jersey tea, seemingly covered with sea foam and mist, has drifted from the Atlantic to the valley of the Mississippi. This plant has historic interest as well as refined beauty. It is well that it grows in prodigal masses in wide distribution. For, after the Boston tea party, a brew of the leaves of the *Ceanothus* plenished the teapots of our revolutionary forebears.

Who pictures a swamp without the familiar cattails and red-winged blackbirds flying in and out piping their cheerful notes? In an aesthetic craze a few years ago, the cattails, or flags, were the popular decoration of the home, filling large jardineres or embroidered or painted on screens and lambrequins. Though of inherent decorative value they have fallen into "innocuous desuetude" by reason of overuse. It is a warning to "avoid the obvious." Individuality, not too pronounced or extreme, should be expressed. Why, for instance, because a neighbor has a beautiful plant on his premises should every one in the vicinity straightway fill his grounds with the same in monotonous reiteration? Among the hosts of ornamental plants may not something else be selected besides hydrangea, scarlet rambler, canna and golden glow to prevent satiety? If a plant is "all the rage," it is the very best reason why one should fall out of line and imitate nature in her endless variety.

The flower cluster of the cattail [*Typha angustifolia* and *T. latifolia*] is made up of innumerable blossoms of two sorts, without nectar, fragrance or bright color, because they are pollinated by the wind. The slender spike at the top bears the pollen-producing flowers. These after doing their work wither away and disappear, while the flowers of the stouter body below ripen into tiny, seedlike fruits that are converted by tufts of fine hairs into aeroplanes that will take a long flight through the air before they settle down to propagate new plants.

Cattails are still in fashion with children, who carefully store them for a gala time, when they are dipped in kerosene to use for torches in Halloween processions.

Mint, Abundant in Minnesota, Delights the Senses; Miss Butler Tells of Wild Flowers in Glenwood Park Garden   July 23, 1911

THERE ARE MANY KINDS OF gardens. Those are most interesting that have an individual flavor and express, as pleasure grounds should, within the bounds of good taste, the owner's personality. Some persons aim to have strictly an old-fashioned garden, loving best the delightful old-time favorites rooted deep in memory. Again, there are literary gardens, devoted to the flowers mentioned by some author, as Keats or Shakespeare; while more, perhaps, make a specialty of a few beautiful plants, and with solicitous care become experts in raising them.

Mrs. Mable Osgood Wright, in her *The Garden, You and I* [New York, 1910], describes a fascinating garden designed by an invalid lady, in which nothing was admitted but plants with fragrant flowers or leaves. In such a garden, the mints would abound, and among them would be *Monarda fistulosa*, the wild bergamot, that now enlivens the borders of woods and meadows with large clumps of bright lavender bloom. Abundant as it is, we are never ready to cry "Hold! Enough!" For, besides its delicate perfume, it delights the eye as well. This plant will at once remind one of the cultivated, red-flowered bee balm or Oswego tea (*Monarda didyma*). The mints may be recognized by their square stems, two-lipped

flowers, and usually aromatic odor.

The *Tofieldia* [*T. glutinosa*], or false asphodel, is an attractive little lily. Its compact raceme of feathery, small, white flowers forms the larger part of the plant, surrounded by plants that one would trudge miles to see—wild buckbean, orchids, the pitcher plant, and just now a marsh harebell with a bluish white blossom poised on the frailest imaginable stalk.

In wet meadows the white flowers needed to offset the garish yellow are supplied by the water parsnip (*Sium*) and the spotted cowbane [water hemlock] (*Cicuta*), both poisonous, alas! to man and beast. Cattle generally know instinctively that they are inedible and avoid them. But children should be taught not to

Wild Bergamot

taste unknown plants. The leaves of the water parsnip are uni-pinnate, while the leaves of the cowbane are twice or thrice compounded. The poison hemlock (*Conium*), a relative of theirs naturalized from Europe, furnished, according to tradition, the poison by which Socrates was put to death.

The parsley family, to which these dangerous plants belong, together with, strange as it may seem, several food plants, as caraway, parsnip, carrot, [and] celery, may be recognized in the main by the flat-topped flower clusters with stalks arranged like the sticks of an umbrella, each bearing a like bunch of smaller stalks crowned with a tiny flower. Such clusters are called compound umbels.

The blue vervain (hoary vervain, *Verbena*

stricta), a weed common in neglected, vacant lots, is well worthy of attention. It stands up bravely among ignoble surroundings, old tins, broken bottles and ash heaps, which it attempts to mask. Large, downy leaves thickly clothe the stem. The flower spikes are long and slender, having close rows of seed pods at the base with a ring of bright blue flowers above and tapering at the tip with the still unopened buds. The garden *Verbena*, unlike this weed, has the lazy habit of lying with its elbows on the ground and getting covered with dirt. Another weed *Verbena*, the *hastata* [blue vervain], of slenderer habit, but showy in the mass, is abundant in lowlands; also the white verbana [*V. urticifolia*], slenderer still and with still smaller flowers.

Regiments of clover hussars (*Petalostemum*) bivouac on the prairies with shakos of violet red or of white. Three species respond to muster roll in Minnesota. [Actually four *Petalostemums* are native to Minnesota— purple prairie clover (*P. purpureum*), white prairie clover (*P. candidum*), silky prairie clover (*P. villosum*) and *P. occidentale*, discovered since Butler's time.] All are armed with very slender leaf blades and all reek a pungent odor.

The amorphas—camp followers of their military cousins, the petalostemums—have pale, hoary, pinnate leaves and narrow flower spikes. The typical flower of their tribe—the pea—is butterfly shaped, with five petals: the broad standard, or banner, two slender side petals, the wings, and two partially united petals, the keel, arched over the stamens and pistil. The amorphas have but one of these petals, the standard, the purple color of which contrasts pleasingly with the yellow stamens. Amorpha leaves are used in hard times as a substitute for tea. Farmers call the smaller species of the genus "shoestrings" because the roots thickly interlace the soil and make plowing more laborious. The tall *Amorpha* [*A. fruitcosa*] is often cultivated and is an esteemed ornament of parks.

One of our finest native, yellow-flowered plants is the great St. John's wort, *Hypericum ascyron* [*H. pyramidatum*]. It may be seen in rich lowland about Minnehaha. It is tall and sturdy, a profuse bloomer and interesting in bud and in fruit. The multiplicity of the stamens gives a lightsome grace to the flowers of this family. The flower of this species is large, measuring some three inches across. The petals, when aging, roll up lengthwise, forming a spidery appearance, which adds variety to the inflorescence, together with the striking buds and seedpods. We can but wonder that with all its merits this plant has not been seized upon for cultivation. In the wild garden in Glenwood Park, it is well established in two colonies.

Flowering Spurge Graces Roadside and Prairie in Late Summer; Varieties of Yellow Blooms Classed as "Sunflowers," Confusing July 30, 1911

ON DRY OR SANDY SOIL by the roadsides and on the prairies, throughout the rest of the season, will be found the flowering spurge, *Euphorbia corollata*. On account of its white, filmy, lace-like inflorescence, it is much used by florists to set off other flowers in bouquets.

What seem to be petals in the flower cluster are colored bracts. The flowers themselves are inconspicuous. The euphorbias form a large family of highly specialized plants, including the small-leaved, pestiferous weed-mats, poinsettas and trees in the tropics. One of the characters is a milky sap, which is, in the rubber tree, now indispensable to man. A wild species [*E. marginata*], with leaves about the flowers deeply margined with white, is cultivated under the name of mountain snow. The painted leaf [*E. cyathophora*], a quaint little native euphorbia, a new-comer in the wild garden, is like a miniature poinsettia, the bracts being blotched with red. Often trained against the wall in greenhouses is a tropical species, a stout vine covered with cruel thorns [crown-of-thorns, *E. milii*]. One might well believe that from this was plaited the crown that symbolizes the agony of the world.

Very confusing are the many varieties of yellow blooms which the amateur is likely to class as sunflowers. The green involucre under the head of the sunflower is made up of several unequal rows of leaves overlapping each other like shingles on a roof; while the ox-eye, mentioned in a previous article, has nearly equal rows of bracts, and the cup plant may be known by the large leaves united to form a cup. All the sunflowers [genus *Helianthus*] are natives of North America, and . . . about fifteen are found within the borders of the state. When this country was discovered, the huge-flowered species was cultivated by the Indians, the seeds affording food and oil and the stalks textile fibers. The size of the flower makes apparent an obeisance to the sun, a feature not peculiar but common to the leaves as well and to other plants to get needful exposure to light.

Dusky glens are illuminated by the starry campion, *Silene stellata*, thus refuting the poet who says that the night has a thousand stars and the day but one. The poignant beauty of the flower is due to the delicate white-fringed petals that cap the green calyx bell. Some of the silenes are catch-flies and are active assistants in the campaign against the malignant germ carriers, slaying innumerable

Flowering Spurge

hordes by glutinous hairs.

All the food of animals is directly or indirectly prepared from the elements of earth, water and air by green plants. Plants without leaf-green (chlorophyll) are, like ourselves, consumers instead of producers. Among them is the dodder, *Cuscuta*, an annual belonging to the *Convolvulus* [Morning-glory] family. The seed germinates in the ground. But as soon as the plantlet can stretch to neighboring vegetation the connection with the earth dies away and it twines closely around its hapless host, drawing out the life-sap with countless, toothlike roots. It is merely a yellow, leafless, thread-like stem, which, in the course of time, will wreathe its victim with a beautiful garland of compact, small white flowers. . . .

The dodder is pernicious in the garden and on the farm. A very inferior quality of flower or fruit, if any at all, would be produced by plants attacked by it. It is called love vine. A less demonstrative and less self-seeking affection is certainly to be preferred. We allow the dodder to grow in the wild garden in order "to point a moral and adorn a tale," but strive to keep it under restraint.

We will reserve our admiration for plants that make their own living, as the sweet basil or mountain mint [*Pycnanthemum virginianum*]. It needs no other charm than its sweet fragrance, although the flat-topped flower clusters have a cool gray, artistic tone.

To this agreeable list we may add another mint, wild anise [fragrant giant-hyssop, *Agastache foeniculum*], which has long, whorled spikes of blue flowers. The leaves are white beneath. When bruised, they exhale an odor like that of anise.

Tramp Plants, Migrants from Foreign Lands, Thrive in Minnesota; They Often Pre-empt Ground, Crowding Out Native Citizens of Soil   August 6, 1911

MOST OF OUR VEGETABLE TRAMPS, like the human ones, are of foreign birth. These migrants from the old world, where the land has been cultivated from times immemorial, inured through fierce competition, have become adaptable and fit to cope with hard conditions. Hence, when brought by design or accident to a new country, they pre-empt the land, wherever they can gain roothold, and crowd out other plants. Our native plants can hold their own on virgin soil. But more than seven evil spirits (weeds) enter into land once cultivated, and then neglected, and dwell there, and the last state of that field becomes worse than the first. The best remedy for weeds is constant cultivation.

Some naturalized plant citizens, with attractive flowers, one might like to have in the garden, if they were not so aggressive. But, if admitted, they would selfishly shoulder out the weaker and possibly more desirable inmates. The place for such vagrants is, therefore, the roadside where they will thrive on a hard bed and a crust of earth. Bouncing

Bet [*Saponaria officinalis*] and butter 'n' eggs [*Linaria vulgaris*] may be cited as examples. A blue ribbon should be awarded them for certain sterling qualities. During protracted droughts, when other vegetation has succumbed and even the grass blades have shriveled, they alone put out their blossoms and brighten what would otherwise be a bare and desert waste. The name Bouncing Bet probably refers to the luxuriant growth; but the other name, old maids' pinks, seems especially applicable. For to do their duty cheerfully under adverse circumstances is the metier of spinsters. The pale and the deep yellow colors of the flowers of *Linaria vulgaris*, so well set off by the slender, sage green leaves, are aptly characterized by the rustic name, butter 'n'

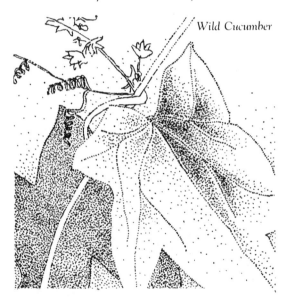

Wild Cucumber

eggs. The nectar held in the sharp pointed spur lures the humble bee to the lips of the blossom, stubbornly closed, as in the related snap-dragon, to other insect rovers.

Three sister composites—eupatoriums—grow together in the meadows. The homeliest, *E. perfoliatum*, has rather a coarse aspect, and its dull gray flowers scarcely command a glance from the passerby. Yet, under closer observation, they will not fail to please and will not be ignored when properly arranged in a vase. Every natural growth has a beauty of form, if not of color, that needs only to be seen to be appreciated. As Emerson said, "We are immersed in beauty, but our eyes have no clear vision." Folks brought up in the old-fashioned way have a bitter memory

of this eupatorium under the name of thoroughwort or boneset, which in the spring was dealt out copiously to every member of the household, as a thorough remedy to prevent or to remove influenzal bone aches and, in general, "to purify the blood."

The tall Joe-Pye weed, *Eupatorium purpureum*, succeeds the rosy-hued swamp milkweed in furnishing red tones to the meadows, a red, however, of a subdued, crushed raspberry hue. It is named for a New England Indian who concocted medicine from it for fevers, that once had a ready sale.

The most beautiful of the eupatoriums is the white snakeroot, *E. urticaefolium* [*E. rugosum*], also of medicinal repute. It is of value not only on account of its profuse, soft, starry inflorescence of harmonious white, but because it is easily cultivated and can be depended upon to bloom after frosts have set in. In one garden at least in Minneapolis, besides the wild one, where it stars the ground in late summer, it is the most prized ornament. The flowers yield not a whit in beauty to those of the ageratum, which they resemble so much in form that they once bore the name ageratoides [i.e., *Eupatorium ageratoides*]—meaning like ageratum.

Woods without vines are comparatively bare, formal and unduly trim. Best of all, vines form tangles in which birds nest and sing. Of the annual vines, none has a more graceful and riotous growth than the common wild cucumber (*Echinocystis lobata*). Lacking an upstanding object to embrace, it will run along the ground and form borders of bewitching spires of bloom. The fibrous, netted inside of the seed vessel, sometimes called balsam apple, resembles on a smaller scale that of a vine of the South known as the towel gourd [*Luffa aegyptiaca*, sponge gourd], which is sold in the market as a bath sponge.

The gourd family can produce huge fruits, as the mammoth squashes and pumpkins, the prize winners of county fairs. Prominent among the tropical gourds—for the family is most largely represented in the tropics—is the calabash [*Lagenaria siceraria*], whose hard-rinded fruit, when cleared of its contents, is indispensable to the natives as receptacles for food. The big pumpkins on a calabash tree [*Crescentia cujete*] might brain, in falling, the luckless wayfarer.

Common Plantain Is Compared with the Alisma Plantago, Otherwise Known as the Water Variety, by Miss Butler   August 13, 1911

THE COSMOPOLITE WEED, the common plantain or ribwort (*Plantago major*) is presented in this paper for comparison with the somewhat more decorative water plantain, *Alisma plantago* [*A. triviale*]. But it is hoped that the former will win some favor, although universally considered a homely weed. The contrast of the wandlike, fruiting spikes with the deeply ribbed rosette of leaves is surely not without charm. The leaves illustrate one of the methods of preventing over-shading, a difficulty met with in the rosette habit. In the plantain each leaf gets its modicum of light and air, by the upper and inner leaves being smaller and shorter stalked than the lower ones. Birds are fond of the seeds enclosed in the little rounded pods, which are lidded like snuff boxes. Farmers put the leaves in their hats to protect from sunstroke in haying time. Again, when macerated, the leaves are deemed a sovereign remedy to use as a poultice for inflammatory bruises.

The water plantain, fringing pools and lakes, is no relation to the roadside weed. It has received its name from the similarity of the leaves in shape, arrangement and venation. The small flowers are entirely different, being white and arranged in a large, loose, many branched cluster.

Veritable fields of cloth of gold are now gleaming with sunflowers, coneflowers and golden rods, not for kings alone, but for all the people. In this display of gold the tall coneflower, *Rudbeckia laciniata* [wild golden glow], takes the lead—a brother of black-eyed Susan, with eyes of golden brown, fringed with longer, drooping lashes of paler yellow. The palmi-parted leaf readily shows that it is the original of the popular favorite, the cultivated golden glow. Many prefer the single wilding, for it is less insistent to be observed and does not pall upon the taste. It fulfills, moreover, its purpose in nature, that of producing seed.

Lepachys pinnata [*Ratibida pinnata*, gray-headed coneflower] has a longer cone and more drooping rays. It is abundant on the prairies. *L. columnaris* [*Ratibida columnifera*, long-headed coneflower] is distinguished by a still longer and slenderer cone, but with shorter rays. A variety has lovely velvety petals of dahlia red, with a dash of yellow at the base. This long coneflower, with its variety, is the pride of a beautiful garden in the city, whose owner delights in native plants.

A much admired annual is now in bloom in the wild garden—the partridge pea, *Cassia chamaechrista* [*Chamaecrista fasciculata*]. The beauty of the large flower of clear, bright yellow is enhanced by a purplish brown eye formed by the stamens and the blotching of some of the petals. The delicate, fresh, green leaflets of the compound leaf close together when touched and also for protection from cold at night. Sensitiveness is an endowment of all forms of life. As plants have no nerve fibers, stimuli are conveyed from cell to cell. . .

Common Plantain

The tendrils of the common pea and the tendrils or stems of all climbers must have this quality in order to find the required support. The foliage of the mimosas, plants common in warm regions, make instant response to disturbing influences. "At the tramp of the horse's hoof on the turf of the prairies far in advance are closed the leaves of the shrinking mimosa." The natives call the mimosa "shame"; for, presto! a filmy mass of green turns at a touch into a bunch of seemingly dry twigs, which slowly erect themselves and resume their leafy appearance when the danger is past.

A large crop of mushrooms—edible and inedible, of all sizes, shapes and colors—promoted by the frequent warm showers, are daily harvested. The mental, if not the physical, appetite is keenly whetted [in] those inoculated with a passion for those interesting forms of vegetable life. . . . Although the mushroom is taken as a type of rapid growth, the "spawn"—the slender, many-branched, subterranean fibers—are of slow formation and may be of great age. Small round "buttons" appear on these fibers and expand quickly into the aerial, spore-producing bodies. In one species of *Lepiota* [*L. procera*], the cap at the top of the stalk at first resembles a small cone. It finally spreads out like a Japanese parasol, breaking away the veil—a membrane covering the gills—a vestige of which remains in the form of a movable ring, that may be pushed, umbrella-wise, up and down the stem. In the ring on the stem and the scaly top of the cap, this fungus is like a deadly *Amanita*, but it is without the volva or cap at the base, a character of the poisonous genus.

The question is often asked, how can edible fungi be distinguished from the poisonous form? No infallible rule can be given. One must learn to distinguish carefully one species from another, and never taste of an unknown or doubtful specimen.

Wild Balsam Occupies Low Places in Wild Gardens; Leaves Shine Like Silver When Put in the Water   August 20, 1911

EVERY INCH OF SPACE on low, moist soil not held firmly by tufted meadow grasses and sedges is occupied by the wild balsam [*Impatiens*, touch-me-not or jewelweed]. The smooth, glossy stem has a translucent appearance, and its joints are swollen, affording another proof, of course, that rheumatism is induced by dampness! The leaves are thin and delicate. When dipped in water, their under-surfaces appear to gleam like quicksilver, an appearance due to tiny hairs that catch the water and enmesh air bubbles. The hairs keep the pores that are abundant on the under side of the leaves from being clogged with water. Some water beetles show the same phenomenon when they dive; but, in their case, the air bubbles supply them with the requisite oxygen during the period of immersion.

Little girls are familiar with the plant as jewelweed. By means of the curved nectar spur, they hook the flowers in their ears and are fine ladies, for the nonce, with gold ear-drops. The most common species of balsam has flowers usually spotted with brown, of varying shades of orange and yellow, and sometimes pink or white. This is called *Impatiens biflora* [*I. capensis*, spotted touch-me-not]. *I. pallida* [pale touch-me-not] has larger, pale yellow, often unspotted flowers, with stouter spurs.

The term *Impatiens* refers to the nature of the seed-vessel, the origin of another common name, touch-me-not. If you gently press the plump, ripe seed-pod between your thumb and forefinger you will be startled by its breaking

Jewelweed

up into writhing, wormlike pieces, and by the seeds snapping out several feet into space. Many other plants are seed-catapults, among them the violets. If you do not pick your pansies before they go to seed you may lose your eyes some day when leaning over the pansy bed.

Fur-bearing animals are involuntary agents of seed-dispersal. Cows have been seen patiently chewing their cuds with their faces plastered over with "beggars' lice" and their tails festooned with burdock burrs. People are brought into service. You will be busy for some time after a walk in the woods in getting rid of the various stick-tights that have taken a free ride attached to your clothing, some even burrowing into the flesh. The tick trefoils

[*Desmodium* species] will be in the crowd. You will know them by the scalloped pea-pods, covered with small barbed grapplers. When you pull them off, the scallops separate, each one having a single seed. The tick trefoils have, as the name implies, compound leaves made up of three leaflets. The blossoms are bright purplish pink, clustered in long racemes.

We stop long to admire the delicate, pure white flowers and splendid leaves of the arrowhead or sagittaria, which densely fringes the margins of brooks and ponds. Disappointment will follow if we are tempted to pick them for a bouquet, for the flowers and leaves wither quickly, when detached from their natural element, the water. . . . Their beauty might be preserved in decorative designs for leather, metal or wood. The leaves of sagittarias vary greatly in width. Some are very slender and others are without the arrow lobes.

Further east, thickets of tall, leafy buttonbush, *Cephalanthus occidentalis*, abound in the neighborhood swamps. The "buttons" are creamy balls over an inch in diameter, composed of closely packed, small, tubular flowers. A specimen of this interesting plant, with many other species, was shipped from Massachusetts for planting in the wild garden in July of the first year of its founding. The location of the plant was not recorded, and it was supposed to have died out. The next year another plant was obtained, which produced one blossom the following season, and the next summer a dozen or more blooms. While admiring these, a random glance perceived a bush some distance within the swamp luminous with starry globes. It was the first buttonbush, all covered with buttons à la mode, which had grown to maturity, undetected in the rank vegetation.

The buttonbush must not be confused with the buttonwood [*Platanus occidentalis*], a tree which is also strung with buttons hanging from long, fibrous stems. This tree is [not] a native of Minnesota. It is called also plane tree, because of its smooth bark, which scales off in patches, leaving light-colored spots, as if it were affected with leprosy. It reaches a magnificent growth on the river bottoms of the Middle West, where it is known by another name, the sycamore. You remember the sobriquet of Senator Vorhees of Indiana—the "Tall Sycamore of the Wabash."

The present season seems favorable to the

wild onion, *Allium cernuum* [*A. stellatum* is the common species], for pink balls of fairy grace lifted on slender, leafless stalks give a magical brilliancy to the billowing grasses of large expanses of the prairie. Do not be disconcerted by the name. The onion is, after all, a sort of lily, considered by every one a flower queen, and the odor is not perceptible, except when the plant is bruised. The leaves of this *Allium* are very narrow, unlike those of the early leek, so abundant in the woods in early spring.

If you should peer under the boughs of a dense plantation of prickly ash in the wild garden, you would see stars—not from being cruelly pricked by the thorns, nor do you see them as a reflection from the sky, but actual stars—geasters, literally, earth-stars—not revolving in space, but grubby, toad-colored bodies attached to the ground. In fact, a species of puffball, with a thick envelope that breaks up when mature into starlike rays reflexed to the ground. Before the rays are formed the geaster looks like a big, dull acorn. . . . The collar earth-star [is] *Geaster triplex* [*Geastrum indicum*]. Other species are collarless and in some the spore-bearing part is unstalked. A tiny species has been found at Minnehaha, about the size of a pea. The edibility of the earth-star has not been tested.

Prickly Armor Furnishes Protection for the Thistle; Caterpillars Crawl By and Browsing Horses Shun Plant   August 27, 1911

THE SCOTCH MADE NO MISTAKE in selecting the thistle for their national flower. Bristling with needle-like prickles, a type of stern independence, it does not admit of close intimacy. But we are captivated by its reddish purple blooms, fragrant as roses and brimmed with sweetness. Economical and thrifty, the thistle can wrest a living from the scantiest means; but "ower canny" as it is, it sends out myriads of plumy seeds, by which it will establish itself in richer soil wherever the opportunity offers. The voracious caterpillar crawls by it to plants with unarmed herbage; the thistle is browsed only by underfed donkeys. It is often decked with winged visitants of black and gold, the thistle birds or goldfinches, surrounded by drifting clouds of silvery plumes, as they lightly swing on the matured flower heads and eagerly break them apart to obtain their favorite food. The buds, the beautiful flower clusters, the feathery balls of fruit, and the deeply lobed leaves with ruffled margins of the thistle, all readily lend themselves to designs for ornament.

The field thistle, *Cirsium discolor*, is particularly lovely by reason of its pale pink, or sometimes white flowers, and long, drooping leaves. The bull thistle [*C. vulgare*, from Europe] has larger heads and still more formidable prickles; while the tall swamp thistle [*C. muticum*] is less stout and spiny. These species are not undesirable for a garden, if one has space enough to keep them at arm's length. But no good word can be said for the

Tall Swamp Thistle

Canada thistle [*Cirsium arvense*], an emigrant from Europe that multiplies apace, although allowed no rights of citizenship. It seems useless to legislate against it; for it has a running root stock that spreads while we sleep, and the seeds fly over the country to sow discomfort elsewhere. It is a pest because it is so difficult to keep within bounds. If you wish to know just how Theophilus Thistlewaite thrust three thousand thistles through the thick of his thumb (too low an estimate by far!), clear by hand a plot of land that has been overrun by Canada thistles.

A vegetable pariah, also of foreign origin, humbly occupying waste places, is especially abundant about drains and pig sties, and is stigmatized by the rude Saxon term,

"stinkweed" [*Anthemis cotula*]. It is also known as dogfennel and as May weed, although it blooms throughout the summer until nipped by frost. It is as pretty as its much admired cousin, Marguerite [*Chrysanthemum leucanthemum*]—cultivated here, but an injury to the hay fields in the East—for it has the daisy beauties of pearly white ray flowers encompassing golden tubular flowers of the disk. The leaf [of the May weed], too, may be favorably compared with that of the fern. But the weed is without regard on account of its associations and fetid odor. It bears the scientific name *Maruta cotula* [*Anthemis cotula*], and its nearest kin are the garden and medicinal chamomiles.

One might be justified in asking the mower to stay his scythe in the meadow until the fleeting beauty of the grass of Parnassus [*Parnassia palustris* and *P. glauca* in Minnesota] is past. It is not a grass, but it is always found among the grasses. The glossy leaves are clustered in a rosette close to the ground. The cream white flowers grow singly on the stalk, and the deeply veined petals are marvels of perfectness in detail. Poets drew inspiration from similar species on Mount Parnassus, in the legendary days of Greece.

Happy is he who finds in brooks winding through meadows the tiny blossoms that vie with the violet and the rose in popular favor— the forget-me-not. It is not easy to forget these pale blue flowers with yellow eyes—an unequalled harmony of color. The brook forget-me-not [is *Myosotis scorpiodes*. Butler planted both the Minnesota native *M. laxa* and the European *M. scorpiodes* in the garden. *M. scorpiodes* survived.] After three unsuccessful attempts, [it] has been firmly established in the wild garden, where it blooms the summer long. The parent stock in Needham, Massachusetts, grew waist high in prodigal profusion. "Oh!" said one admirer, "these flowers are just like those we see on hats!"

In pastures, giant puffballs [*Calvatia gigantea*] may be seen breaking through the grass. . . . Several over four pounds in weight have been noted this season. Some of the small puffballs have a smooth surface, some are covered with tiny tubercles of spines, and some are stalked. In the puffballs, the spores are enclosed instead of being exposed to the air on the surface of gills or tubes as in the umbrella or bracket forms of fungi. As far as is known, the true puffballs are edible. They are to be used for food when the inside is firm and white-like cottage cheese. When mature, the puffball splits regularly or irregularly, according to the species, discharging a mass of dark, powdery spores. Those fond of this delicacy are much grieved when they see a specimen that has been used as a football and kicked to pieces. If one realized that a puffball when fresh is good, palatable food, he would resist the impulse that impels him to destroy it.

Virgin Minnesota Prairie in Full Bloom Surpasses Flora of Tropics; Earth's Tapestry Shows a Riot of Color before Autumnal Frosts   September 3, 1911

VIRGIN MINNESOTA PRAIRIE AT THE height of its bloom surpasses the far-famed flora of the tropics in brilliancy of coloring. Here all shades of red, blue and gold are intricately interwoven in earth's tapestry before it is destroyed by autumnal frosts and replaced by winter's carpet of snow. Prominent in the riot of color and beauty of design are the liatras [Liatris] or blazing stars, with their flower heads loosely arranged in slender wands, or in splendid, compact spikes, sometimes over a foot in length. The flowers might be mistaken for thistles, but they have no stabbing prickles. Other popular names, as gay feather and button snakeroot, show the esteem in which the plants are held.

Minnesota has [five] species of liatras, and three of them—L. pycnostachya, L. cyldrinacea, and L. scariosa [L. ligulistylis in Minnesota] have been introduced into the wild garden. L. pycnostachya has gone by, but the other two species are still in full bloom. They are easy to cultivate on account of their thick, bulbous rootstalks.

Not many years ago the gum plant, Grindelia squarrosa, was not to be found within the limits of Minneapolis. It is common on the great plains, and it has spread from the western part of the state until it is now a common weed by sandy roadsides and in vacant lots, and one against which our gardeners and farmers wage battle. Nevertheless, it is an attractive plant with its profuse, pure yellow flower heads resembling sunflowers and its lettuce-green

leaves. We are glad, moreover, to learn that [it] is of some use, as a specific for ivy poisoning. But why is it named gum plant? Not that it furnishes a delectable wad for the ruminating folk, but because under the flower clusters a mass of sticky, resinous matter is exuded to keep out from the blossoms the crawling insect tribes that are unable to do the work of pollination. It is unnecessary to glue the flower heads to the herbarium sheets, for they provide their own mucilage.

Helenium autumnale [sneezeweed] is a glorious, late composite in rich, low land. From now on it will unfold its golden disks as long as any flower endures. It blossoms freely and often attains a height of six feet. The soft yellow ray petals are divided like those of

Liatra

coreopsis and surround a convex disk. The leaves are pale green, just the right shade to harmonize with the flowers. They run down on the angles of the stem, making narrow, winglike projections. If the leaves are dried and pulverized they make a titillating powder as efficacious as snuff for those who enjoy sneezing, hence its common name, sneezeweed. Florists cultivate the plant and have produced from it varieties [Helen's flower]. It is excellent for formal gardens on account of its height, refined color and its late, profuse blooms. It never fails to respond under transplanting. . . . A colony of sneezeweed in the wild garden of two successive seasons which was lifted when in full bloom . . . has repaid the labor by continuing to bloom at its appointed time.

143

High above the lovely grass of Parnassus rise the spikes of the tall lobelia [great blue lobelia, *Lobelia siphilitica*] in such opulence that the meadows appear to be gemmed with lapis lazuli rimmed with goldenrod. The tubular portion of lobelia flowers is split down to the base for the convenience of the nectar-seeking insects, and the stamens, five in number, are united in a close ring around the pistil so that, to the novice, stamens and pistil seem to be a single body. The lobelias may be recognized, whatever their size or color, by these peculiarities.

A certain botanist arriving at a house where he was expected as a guest found the whole family assembled in the front yard in a state of excitement and the host, with coat off, tearing up the flooring of the piazza.

"What is the matter, good people?" he asked.

"Oh, a rat or some other animal has died under the piazza and we shall have typhoid if the body is not removed."

"Poor souls!" the botanist exclaimed, "that is no dead rat. It is only a stinkhorn [probably *Phallus impudicus*], a small fungus that will soon disappear. It is not necessary to unfloor your piazza on its account. Why, here it is outside in the grass, and you have had all this work for nothing!"

The reason for alluding to this vile smelling form of vegetable life is to prevent a similar occurrence. The odor, to be sure, is as bad as that of carrion; but, once perceived, it will never afterward be mistaken for anything else. Therefore, it would be a good idea to get one whiff of it at least from the mushroom table at the state fair, where it will be kept tightly corked so as not to befoul the air.

Examining the structure through the glass in which it will be encased you will note a cylindrical stem set in a cup of jelly. The stem is capped when mature by a cone perforated at the top and smeared with dark green slime, which holds the spores. It is from this slime that the bad smell chiefly comes, which is attractive to flies, the active agents in distributing the spores. The stem is covered with an exquisitely fashioned network. When in the bulbous state, before the stem emerges from the cup and the strong odor is developed, the plant is eaten by the peasantry of Europe, with whom wild mushrooms are a staple article of food.

Fringed Gentian, Termed Loveliest of Blue Flowers, Now in Bloom; Asters and Goldenrod Indicate Autumn Has Reached Minnesota September 10, 1911

SEPTEMBER BRINGS US what is pronounced the loveliest blue flower of the world—the fringed gentian [*Gentianopsis crinita*]. The indescribable color of rich, deep blue, the exquisite finish of the petals, the large number of flowers borne on a single individual, together with the late time of blooming, make this species of extraordinary value. The poet Bryant has given it immortal fame. Every one knows his beautiful poem, "To the Fringed Gentian." It is somewhat captious to criticize this venerated master of literature and keen observer and lover of nature. Perhaps the case was different in Bryant's Berkshire home but, with us, this "blossom bright with autumn dew, and colored with the heaven's own blue," does not "come alone, when woods are bare and birds are flown." Late August finds it here with a large company of other flowers, and the trees are still in full leafage. The color of the flower, also, is not "sky blue." But who can say what sort of blue may not be found in the sky? Among the many tints gentian-blue will sometimes be seen there.

> Then doth thy sweet and quiet eye
> Look through its fringes to the sky,
> Blue - blue - as if that sky let fall
> A flower from its cerulean wall

A smaller fringed gentian [*G. procera*], with slight stem, linear leaves and fewer and paler colored blossoms, grows with the showier species. These flowers are annuals. Florists desirous to cultivate them were long baffled in their attempts. It was at length discovered that the seeds were biennial, that is, that they do not germinate until two years old. We must always leave some of the flowers to go to seed, however much their beauty tempts us, in order that the plant may not be exterminated.

Less local in the meadows is the closed blue gentian, or "chimney flower," (*Gentiana andrewsii*). The tubular flower never expands. It displays all shades of blue. It is sometimes tinted with pink, and sometimes white, or white striped with blue. There are other small-flowered gentians, with white or blue flowers. The prairie gentian [downy gentian], *Gentiana puberula* [*G. puberulenta*], has a large, handsome, arm-shaped blossom of the deepest, darkest blue imaginable for petals. It looks almost black when seen across the prairie.

Sure signs of approaching autumn are the asters and goldenrods, the lambent flames of dying summer, that leap up and blaze with unwonted vividness before they are banked with snow. Gray enumerates fifty-six species of goldenrod and fifty-nine of aster, a large proportion of which are native to Minnesota. Both are difficult for beginners in botany to determine, but a few of them have such well marked characters that he who runs may read their names. For example, the sweet, flat-topped prairie goldenrod, *Solidago rigida* [stiff goldenrod]. Another flat-topped species is the

Fringed Gentian

narrow-leaved, early-blooming *S. graminifolia* [*Euthamia graminifolia*, grass-leaved goldenrod] found in damp soil. Among the more usual types with many-branched, elongated flower clusters are *S. latifolia* [*S. flexicaulis*, zig-zag goldenrod], a wood species, with broad, ovate leaves pointed at both ends, zigzag stems and with flower heads in bunches among the leaves; and in bogs *S. uliginosa* [bog goldenrod], that exemplifies the name in the inflorescence forming a straight, slender reed.

The aster flower head is constructed like that of the daisy. It may be tiny or have a diameter of two inches or more. The ray petals are dark or pale blue, lilac, or white, according to the species. The New England aster [*Aster novae-angliae*] is tall and many-flowered, with

long, bright purple rays; *Aster puniceus* is a swamp species with flowers of paler blue and hairy, red stems; *A. umbellatus* [flat-top aster] is a tall, flat-topped, white swamp aster; and on the prairies are the small leaved and small flowered *A. multiflorus* [*A. ericoides*], as lovely as the spiraea, known as bridal wreath; and, loveliest of all, *A. sericeus* [silky aster], a silver gray, silky-leaved aster with large, bright, red-purple flowers.

No mention has yet been made of the grasses and sedges. Nature has not granted them bright colors, fragrance or nectar, because they are pollinated by the wind instead of by insects, but in place of these attractions, [they have] grace and beauty of form, qualities not to be ignored. They are social plants and live together in large companies. Many sedges have three cornered, solid stems, while all the grasses have round stems which are hollow except at the leaf joints. Colonies of *Zizania aquatica* [*Z. palustris*], wild or Indian rice, may be noted in the shallow waters of lakes and ponds. The leaves are long and slender and the tall, attenuated flower spikes pierce the air like needles. The wild rice was carefully harvested by the Indians for breadstuff, and the grain-eating birds eagerly cull its seeds.

No one fond of mushrooms fears to gather and eat freely the shaggy mane, *Coprinus comatus*, for it is easily recognized. There is a lively contest for it on the parade ground, where it abounds, and the first comers in the morning often carry off basketfuls in the season. . . . The cylindrical cap covered with large scales like turkey feathers finally expands into a disk and deliquesces, dripping with a black fluid containing the spores. The mushroom is eaten, of course, before this change takes place and when the flesh is firm and white. The black liquid treated with a preservative may be used as ink. It has been suggested that the government should use this fluid for printing bank notes to insure against counterfeiting. The microscope would at once expose a fraud, for the spores in the ink have a definite size and shape.

Two other copriri are common and also edible—the ink cap, *Coprinus atramentaries* [*C. atramentarius*], whose cap is usually smooth, gray and cup-shaped; and the little ink cap, *C. micaceus*, a small yellowish brown mushroom, common on lawns, especially above decaying roots of trees, throughout the season. The cap of this species is sometimes covered with gleaming, mica-like scales. The gills turn black when mature, but the plant generally dries without deliquescing.

Acrid Taste Gives Name to the Smart Weed; Miss Butler Describes Wild Grasses in the Park   September 17, 1911

SMART WEEDS [ARE NAMED] not for their enterprise in taking possession of the wet lowlands wherever they can get roothold, or for their smartness in attire—many species being decked with gaily colored, graceful, drooping flower spikes of rich shades of rose graded down to pale pink, flesh color and white, which brighten large expanses of moorland—but because, if tasted, the acrid, peppery sap will make one's mouth burn or smart.

A very humble relative—small-leaved, prostrate and a spreading pest, unnoticed except when you investigate the cause of the disappearance of the velvety turf on your lawn—is the knot weed, or dooryard grass. Do not be misled by the latter name, for it is not a grass. The term knot weed refers to a character of the family—the enlargements or "knots" of the stem just below the sheathing stipules. These are close together on this plant and the most noticeable feature, for the greenish flowers in the axils of the leaves are exceedingly small. The weed well illustrates the meaning of the generic name, *Polygonum* (many knees or joints).

The water pepper, an aquatic polygonum [*Polygonum amphibium*] with oblong, floating leaves, has a heavy, rose-colored spike that beautifies the borders of ponds. The tear-thumb, a malignant polygonum [*P. sagittatum*] with sparse white flowers, forces acquaintance, when we are botanizing in meadows, by making jagged wounds with its sharp, reflexed teeth that bristle on the edges of the angled, prostrate stem.

The familiar climbing false buckwheat [*P. scandens*], a slender vine with pendant racemes of small, greenish white flowers, is another species of this large genus. This will remind you that the cultivated buckwheat, *Fagopyrum* [*F. esculentum*], is a cousin of the polygonums.

A wild morning glory, *Convolvulus sepium* [hedge bindweed], is everywhere present,

running over waste places and doing good service by concealing unsightly objects with its lovely large flowers of pale pink or white, and making dense tangles in the woods, which, in the struggle to break through, forcibly impress one to rename it bindweed. Being common and a weed, it is not properly appreciated. It might be improved and varied by cultivation, and it would outrank its relative, the tame morning glory, *Ipomaea*, as a porch vine, for it is a perennial and can always be depended upon to furnish shade. A certain piazza in Nova Scotia, decorated with a long established specimen of bindweed, is admired by all who see it.

A turtle takes a daily sunning on a rock in the little pond in the wild garden. His tail

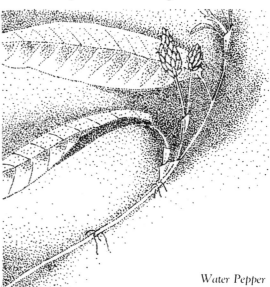

Water Pepper

held stiffly erect suggested to someone a marlingspike, the tool that is associated with a boatswain. Accordingly the turtle was dubbed Bos'n, and a little one that has lately appeared, Bos'nette. Very appropriately, a plant with white-flowered spikes, named *Chelone* (turtle) [*C. glabra*, turtlehead], graces the sides of the same pond. It is easy to understand how the name turtlehead was applied to this plant growing in the damp places that turtles frequent, when one has an opportunity to compare the lips of the animal with those of the flower.

Who has not seen a tall, stout weed with a long dense spike of sweet-scented flowers with rather large, deflexed, yellow petals? But how many take the trouble to know its name,

Oenothera biennis, or common evening primrose? The flowers are succeeded by stiff, four-valved pods splitting at the top, from which the seeds are threshed out by the wind. The seeds that sprout will form a rosette lying flat on the ground and made up of row upon row of oblong leaves narrowed at the base and becoming shorter and shorter above and towards the center—a fine example of one of the methods of preventing overshading. The rosette has varied autumnal tints and survives the winter to form, from a central bud, an erect flowering stalk that often branches like a candelabra, and completes its course when the seed is ripened. Such plants are biennials like many garden vegetables, cabbage, beet, etc. In flower, this weed decorates the roadside. Some native oenotheras are prized ornamental plants, particularly *O. fruticosa* (sundrops) [an eastern species], a low perennial of easy cultivation and with bright yellow, profuse blooms.

The season must not go by without some attention to the ferns. The dearly loved shade or vernal plants flower and disappear when the trees are fully leaved. Then we find but few plants in bloom in the woods, and most of our pleasure in woodland walks, aside from the trees, comes from observing the fungi and the ferns. These do not usually need strong sunlight for their development. The attractiveness of ferns is wholly due to their foilage. The leaves or fronds of restful green, and usually finely dissected, are types of delicacy and grace. Justly popular is our one species of maidenhair fern, that favorably compares with the exotic forms cultivated in greenhouses. Maidenhair ferns [*Adiantum pedatum*] are characterized by dark, polished leafstalks, and branched leaves of many pinnules with marginal spore cases protected by little inturned teeth. Groups of these ferns in the wild garden have fronds that are fully three feet high and that measure eighteen inches across.

The shelf-like mushrooms found on stumps and trees may be called bracket fungi. Some of the woody forms are used for brackets in summer cottages and are often etched with fanciful designs. Many of these fungi belong to the genus *Polyporus* (many pored) [*Grifola*]. The under surface of the bracket is studded with minute pores—the terminations of tubes which are lined with spores. Such fungi are hurtful to trees.

Through a fissure in the bark the spores gain entrance, germinate, and form a network of fibers that prey upon the wood. The bracket grows out from these threads and is the fruit of the plant. Some of the softer brackets are edible when young, among them the sulphur polyporus [*Laetiporus sulphureus*]. This fungus, as one would infer from the name, is bright yellow in color. *Polyporus betulinus* [*Piptoporus betulina*] particularly affects birches. It is dull gray, while other species are a rich, red brown. Sometimes the bracket fungi assume strange shapes. Some have been found that resemble the head of Napoleon. Some species are phosphorescent and light up the dusky woodland with a ghostly glow that makes the bones of the timorous quake.

Late Blooming Flowers Dot Meadows with White, Blue and Gold; Asters, Gentians, Lobelias, and Sunflowers Greet Field Lovers September 24, 1911

FOR THE LATE-BLOOMING FLOWERS we must turn to the floodplains and meadows still glorious in the white, blue and gold of the moisture-loving asters, gentians, lobelia and sunflowers, tricked out here and there with the deep red of the cardinal flower—the purest red found in nature. The brilliant salvia now blooming in the cultivated gardens has a tinge of yellow in its redness, but that cannot be said of the red lobelia known as the cardinal flower [*Lobelia cardinalis*]. Conspicuous in this notable company is the large-flowered, pale pink *Hibiscus militaris,* locally abundant on the river bank. The hibiscus from the wild garden . . . is *H. moscheutos* with a larger and brighter colored flower. This species is not indigenous to Minnesota but is the glory of the swamps ranging from Massachusetts to Ontario and Missouri.

The swamp betony, *Pedicularis lanceolata* [swamp lousewort], would be of interest to the close observer, with its dense, leafy spikes of pale yellow [and] laterally compressed, two-lipped flowers, but who can spare a glance for it when awed by the miraculous blue of the fringed gentians that surround it? Reference was made last May to *P. canadensis* [common lousewort], similar to this betony, that was abundant on the prairie and adjacent woodland slopes, early in the season.

The sweet fragrance, however, of the tiny *Spiranthes cernua* [nodding ladies' tresses], an orchid slender as a grass blade, makes one conscious of its presence, and its pearly whiteness intensifies the celestial blue of Bryant's flower. Most of the orchids are early bloomers. The blossoms of this delicate late-comer are arranged in a curiously twisted raceme, so that it has been given the name ladies' tresses.

The naturalized plants have enforced their citizenship on cultivated land and contest their rights by defensive and offensive methods. For instance, the Russian thistle [*Salsola iberica*] appears to be in its youth harmless and innocent; but later it grows prodigious,

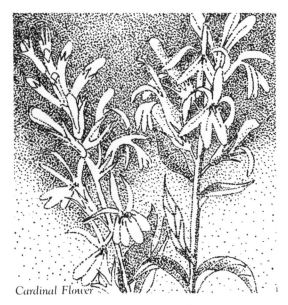

Cardinal Flower

develops numerous short spines and overspreads the ground, destroying other vegetation. When the seeds are ripe, the plants are uprooted by the wind and, like a huge cartwheel, roll over the ground, sewing evil broadcast for another season until they come to a fence, where their advance is checked until piled to the top, when the procession is formed again.

This plant, introduced from Russia several years ago, is not a true thistle, although so called on account of its prickles. It belongs to the goosefoot family, which numbers other tumble weeds. The smooth pigweed or lamb's quarters [*Chenopodium album*], whose young, tender leaves are superior to spinach for the table, is of close kin.

A part of the wild garden recently acquired by the park board was once used for a pasture. Consequently, several naturalized weeds, as Canada thistles [*Cirsium arvense*] and creeping Charley or ground ivy [*Glechoma hederacea*], are firmly established in excess. The thistle is discouraged by being pulled up wherever it shows its head, but it continually breaks out from the newly budding, creeping rootstalks. Another method is taken with creeping Charley, who, with pretty, scalloped, round leaves and bright blue flowers, is not uncomely, if only he could be taught to keep his proper place. Various other rampant, naturalized plants, with pleasing foilage or flowers—butter 'n' eggs [*Linaria vulgaris*], cypress spurge [*Euphorbia cyparissias*], Aaron's rod [*Thermopsis caroliniana*], bouncing Bet [*Saponaria officinalis*]—have been planted around him, which, together with the native goldenrods, will tussle with one another for possession of the field. We shall watch the scrimmage with somewhat, we fear, of the Irish delight in a shindy. Last November tansy [*Tanacetum vulgare*] also was planted among the contestants. Every root has grown and blossomed, and it bids fair to spread and hold its own with odds in its favor. Tansy is found on the sites of burned down or abandoned houses in the country and is associated with days long past. The finely cut leaves have a pungent odor, and the flower disks, bright and golden as sunlight, are fine for large bouquets.

Your attention is called to another edible bracket mushroom *Polyporus frondosus* [*Grifola frondosa*], pale gray and velvety, and made up of many overlapping brackets. The pores on the under surface are barely perceptible to the naked eye. This fungus particularly affects the roots of oaks, and was found in the wild garden at the foot of "Monarch," an aged white oak. It often attains great size. One was discovered a year ago by an oak stump on the top of the highest bluff in Lake City, too big for removal. The specimen in the wild garden weighed 20 pounds. The one who took it up thought it might weigh fifty as he tugged it to the waiting automobile. It was displayed for a few days on Nicollet Avenue in Mr. Hoffman's (the optician's) window, until it began to shoot its spores all over the store, covering everything with a white, dustlike powder.

Cultivation of Native Ornamental Plants

In this article published in 1912 in the Minnesota Horticulturalist, Eloise Butler advocated "wild landscape gardening," or landscaping with native trees, shrubs and perennials, leaving dead trees and vines as cover for birds, and allowing grasses to remain unmown about homes.

IN PLANNING A HOME, comfort, utility and the essentials for healthful living—light, air, drainage—must first be provided for; but all these can be obtained without the sacrifice of beauty, about "the best thing God invented." To observe the principles of good taste does not entail greater expense but merely forethought. The laws of artistry are well known to lovers of the beautiful. Why cannot they be followed by everyone, and why should anything ugly be tolerated? Every home should be a joy to the eye, every block a harmonious picture, every street a visa of enchantment, the horizon framing a scene of splendor. To make this ideal possible, a duly qualified art commission should be appointed to supervise the buildings of the city, and all owners of adjacent grounds should consult one another and submit their plans to this commission for approval. As it is, everything is done at hap-hazard, and harmonious results are achieved, if at all, by happy accident.

A house should be adapted to the site and the environment, harmonizing in color and mode of architecture with the neighboring buildings. The living rooms should be so arranged as to command the most beautiful prospects, including, if possible, sunrise and sunset. But what has all this to do with the cultivation of plants? Everything, for the decorative features of one's grounds should not be meaningless tags, but a part of an integral whole.

Strive to retain the natural features of the site, for you can seldom improve upon nature. In the clearing of land for building, notable plants are often destroyed that cannot be restored for a price. The best intentioned efforts in grading and planting have the taint of artificiality and are stiff and commonplace compared with the inimitable graces that nature, the greatest landscape architect, has for so many years perfected. Instead of staling the infinite variety of nature by reducing the land to a monotonous level, we should cherish the native plants, boulders and outcropping ledges—the harbors of ferns, mosses and lichens—and irregularities of surface that afford differences in light, exposure and moisture, and thus make possible a greater variety of vegetation.

Unfortunately, most people cannot begin anew but can improve only or make the best of what they have. It is not necessary to call to your attention certain principles of planting,

149

too often disregarded: that trees and shrubbery should harmonize with the lines of architecture and connect the buildings with the ground, and be confined in the main, especially in restricted areas, to the vicinity of the walls of the buildings and to the borders of lawns and paths. Shrubs and flower beds otherwise placed have a patchy effect and dwarf the space. If privacy were no object, spaciousness would be best attained by treating adjacent lawns as one. Plants should also be selected with reference to color, form, size, beauty of foliage, flower or fruit, for succession of bloom and all-the-year-around effects—for winter is not cheerless and devoid of color. A landscape with the delicate tracery of deciduous trees against the sky, gleaming with the red, green and gold stems of shrubs hung with fruit ranging from white to blue, red and purplish black, set off by snow and the dark green foliage of evergreens, I, for one, would not exchange for perpetually blooming roses.

Avoid, above all, imported plants of unusual color, like the copper beech and weeping trees, or plants trimmed into formal or fantastic shapes. In general, native species should be used, for plants torn from their natural setting may strike a false note in the landscape. There are many plants just as effective as the cultivated canna, castor bean, crimson rambler, fall hydrangea, golden glow, admirable in themselves, that now pall upon the taste by reason of monotonous reiteration.

Outside of the city there is no excuse for ugliness. If you own a tract of land in the country that you can afford to keep for a pleasure ground, you have a source of perennial pleasure. The most attractive adjuncts of a place are always the native ones. You will never go astray if you endeavor to maintain the indigenous flora of brook, pond and lakeside, bog, meadow, rocky slope, wood and prairie, since each is beautiful and peculiar to itself, and exemplifies unity in variety, an essential of good art. Your favorite plants can be introduced and will flourish if properly placed. You will learn what to transplant and where by observing the conditions under which the species grow most luxuriantly. Many plants, however, can adapt themselves, within certain limits, to different life-relations. You can often better the conditions, for seeds scattered by accident may have germinated where the wind, or other agent of dispersal, listeth. Besides giving your transplants the

environment they prefer, you can enrich the soil, discourage competition by thinning out and improve the breed, or produce new varieties, by grafting or cross-pollination. . . .

In regard to trees, much depends upon the space available. They should be selected with an eye to scenic effects and for durability. Keeping these two points in mind, since each species has individual merit, one will make no mistake if he indulges his preferences in habit of growth, foliage, flower, fruit or autumnal coloring. Evergreens are admirable in winter but must be placed discreetly to avoid somberness. Oaks, elms, hackberry, basswood, [and] hard maple are all splendid trees. The red maple (*Acer rubrum*), although a soft wood species, well repays cultivation. It glows like a torch in the spring with its vivid flowers and fruits, and turns a gorgeous red even before frosts set in. Another small tree, black alder, or holly (*Ilex verticillata*), is extremely pleasing by reason of its wealth of red berries.

As for small trees or notable shrubs, their name is legion: the wild crab, plum, cherry and Juneberry, decorative in flower and in fruit and of culinary value as well; the waahoo, a veritable burning bush; the wild roses and dogwoods, whose bright stems warm the snow and display together the national colors in their fruit; and the viburnums, among them the high bush cranberry with its large flower clusters made up of blossoms that produce the scarlet, acid drupes, rimmed by a row of larger, neutral blooms. Man has transformed these clusters entirely into neutral flowers, making the snowball, uninteresting and pompous with its big heads, that are of no use to him or bird, and of much less beauty than those of the wilding.

In plant decoration, vines are especially important. Picturesque and graceful, they disguise faults of architecture, cover bare, unsightly places, relieve stiff formality, and furnish shelter—and often food—for birds. Room can always be found for vines on wall, fence or screen, and, if one is not over-precise or neat, he will leave here and there an upstanding trunk of a dead tree to support them and for homes for wren or bluebird— delightful songsters with endearing ways. As one recalls the luxuriant growth of the wild grape, the resplendent autumnal coloring of the Virginia creeper, the persistent, brilliant berries of the bittersweet, the profuse white flowers and grayish, fluffy plumes of the clematis, he will want them all.

For the most part, perennial herbs are to be preferred to annuals, for, when once established, they will require but little care. Some annuals, however, will seed themselves. Of especial value is the sensitive, or partridge, pea (*Cassia chamaecrista*) [*Chamaecrista fasciculata*]. The foliage is refined, the flowers large, of bright, clear yellow with brown centers. *Cleome serrulata* [spider flower], another annual—although the odor of the foliage is somewhat rank—is sure to please, because it attains a large growth and produces for more than a fortnight a profusion of pink, feathery blooms.

Your choice of herbaceous plants should be regulated by the light exposures, for you can change the soil and provide the needed moisture if you care to take the trouble. On the north side of buildings, or wherever there is shade, ferns can be planted. They will take the place of the early flowers, which are chiefly shade plants. All are delightful, from the tall, lush osmundas to the tiny crevice, or rock, ferns, with their exquisitely cut foliage and their cool, restful tones of green. With herbs on small grounds, a succession of bloom must also be planned for. On a large estate, where conditions are varied, this point does not need to be considered. Nature will attend to it.

By all means leave some grasses and sedges unmown. They soften hard edges, and nothing is lovelier in winter than their waving plumes, transfigured at times with hoar frost, ice crystals or snow.

The early flowers are usually delicately tinted—far otherwise are those of mid and late summer. Then, nature uses blues and white to tone down the garish reds and yellows and to harmonize discordant colors. White flowers in succession, of all heights and adapted to different situations, can easily be obtained. Among them—to mention only a few—are the Canadian anemone, the filmy northern bedstraw, starry campions, larkspur with ethereal wands, the stately late meadow rue, the late-blooming eupatorium, and the huge cow parsnip (*Heracleum lanatum*).

. . . I would mention particularly our native phloxes, blue and pink—social plants, excellent for massing; the pale-leaved, bright-flowered *Aster sericeus*, and the better known New England aster, of especial value on account of its height and large, richly-colored flowers; the cardinal flower, of incomparable hue; the wondrous orchids; our glorious lilies; the unique closed gentians; the wild sunflowers; the tall, profusely flowered sneezeweed; and the great St. John's-wort, whose large blossoms are as lovely as yellow roses by reason of their innumerable stamens.

To procure these plants I should deplore a reckless despoliation of the wilderness. Many of them can be found in neglected places, or where it is the intention to till the soil, or to lay out roads in the march of improvements. They are also cultivated by a number of nurserymen and florists, who offer them for sale.

Appended to Butler's article was a list of more than 200 native ornamental plants. Lists of native plants suitable for home landscaping and gardening may be obtained from the National Wildflower Research Center in Austin, Texas, and at the Minnesota Landscape Arboretum in Chanhassen.

The front gate of the Eloise Butler Wild Flower Garden and Bird Sanctuary in 1991. *Martha E. Hellander.*

Annals of a Wild Garden

Eloise Butler planned to write a book, Annals of a Wild Garden, chronicling the natural history of the preserve. She intended to use as material her contributions to the monthly round-robin bulletins of her botanical correspondence club, the Gray Memorial Chapter of the Agassiz Association. After her death, Butler's friends assembled a two-volume selection of her writings, entitled Early History of Eloise Butler Plant Reserve and Annals of the Wild Life Reserve. The volumes were placed in the Minneapolis Public Library, Minneapolis Collection. These writings have been rearranged and are largely reprinted here, including additional pieces not in the two bound volumes. Modern botanical names are as supplied by Gerald B. Ownbey, Thomas Morley, and David McLaughlin of the Department of Plant Biology, University of Minnesota, from authoritative sources.

HAVING A RETICENT NATURE, I must confess to shivering on the brink before taking the plunge into self-revelations. I was born not long after the middle of the nineteenth century in the little village of Appleton, on the St. George River, about twelve miles from the seashore, Knox County, Maine. Here I lived until I was about fifteen, attending district and private schools, my chief amusement being then what it still is—roaming the woods. An aunt who lived with us taught my sister and me to know the plants of the neighborhood. My mother said I was abnormally good when I was a baby, but got bravely over it when I grew up. Indeed, some of the neighbors thought I must be idiotic because I lay quietly in the cradle, making no demands for attention. They said, too, that I hadn't any nose—only two little holes in my face where my nose ought to be. Accordingly, everyone was pinching my face in order to make the organ grow. Who can tell how much my lack of good looks is due to that practice?

My father was a farmer. Before marriage my father and mother had both been teachers, and at that time and place no other career than teaching was thought of for a studious girl. So, after completing the courses at high school, Lynn, Massachusetts, and normal school, Castine, Maine, I began the work that I am still engaged in. (In my next incarnation I shall not be a teacher.) My father sold his farm and moved to a small town in northern Indiana, on Lake Michigan, just as I left the normal school. I taught a few months in Indiana. I have a keen recollection of a ludicrous experience. We New Englanders slur the sound of r. In northern Indiana, settled largely by Germans, the r is exaggerated and the speech bristles with bur-r-s. My pupils could not understand what I said, and a child where I boarded, who had learned my language, had to act as interpreter. The report went abroad that the new teacher was tongue-tied. With what circumlocutions I tried to avoid words with r's! The result of my efforts to acquire the new tongue had the following sequel: I remained West seven years before visiting East. Then my relatives threw up their hands in astonishment, exclaiming, "Good heavens! *Where* did you get that brogue?"

Not finding a situation to my liking in Indiana, I secured a place in the Minneapolis schools and here I have lived since 1874. The monotony of my life has been broken during the long summer vacations. I have taken courses of study at Harvard, at Woods Hole and our State University and have enjoyed particularly the instruction of Dr. J.C. Arthur and Dr. Charles Bessey, the latter the greatest and most enthusiastic teacher I have ever met. The summer of 1896 I spent abroad, revelling with the old masters in art—my greatest hobby after plants. And I have collected chiefly algae and ferns for three seasons in Jamaica, West Indies. Those were memorable occasions, to which I must add a most enjoyable sojourn at the seaside station of the University of Minnesota, on Vancouver Island, a camp sixty miles from civilization.

As you well know, I chiefly live and move and have my being in and for the Wild Botanic Garden.

I haven't had a photograph taken for twenty years. [On page 97] is a "snapshot" fired this summer as I was crossing a stream surrounding a quaking tamarack bog.

Early History of
Eloise Butler Plant Reserve, 1911

The Wild Botanic Garden

IN THE EARLY '80s Minneapolis was a place of enchantment—a veritable fairyland. Along the river banks grew in profusion trillium, bloodroot, wild phlox, anemones, Dutchman's breeches, and hepatica; the meadows were glorious with Indian paint brush, both red and yellow, with gentians, purple fringed orchids, and royal clumps of blue violets. In the tamarack swamps of the suburbs might be seen long vistas of our state flower, the showy lady's-slipper, together with the wild calla, and pitcher plants without number. And who could describe the outlying prairies, rioting in colors far exceeding the brilliancy of tropical flora. A long procession beginning with the pasque flower, "the crocus in chinchilla fur," the rosy three-flowered avens, and the equally profuse bird's-foot violet, that gave way in turn to the more gorgeous blooms of midsummer and early autumn, as the purple blazing stars, giant sunflowers, goldenrods and asters of many species and hues. Various lily-rimmed pools and lakes were teeming with algae, among them microscopic desmids and diatoms

of extraordinary beauty, many of which were new to the world.

What changes have been wrought by the rapid growth of the city and the onward march of "improvements"! The shy woodland plants are fast dying out on our river banks; the tamarack swamps have been drained, and with the drying up of the water have disappeared the wondrous orchids and the strange insectivorous plants. The pools with the desmids and diatoms have been filled in and houses built over them; and the prairies have been plotted into building lots. The land has been ruthlessly stripped of the exquisite features that Nature, the greatest landscape gardener, has wrought through the ages, and "all the king's horses and all the king's men" can never make the place the same again. The foreign plants used to replace our native species, and introduced with so much labor and expense, removed from their natural setting, look formal and stiff, and impress one much as impaled butterflies do in a museum case. Again, it is cleared land that is invaded by unwelcome foreigners like burdock, sand-bur, and Russian thistle; for most of our vegetable tramps, like the human ones, are from the Old World. Inured to keener competition, they multiply rapidly and crowd out our native wildings. Cottagers on the suburban lake shores have fettered ideas of planting that are more appropriate for city grounds, and condemn their neighbors who strive to preserve the wildness, for a lack of neatness in not using a lawnmower and in not pulling down the vine tangles in which birds nest and sing—apparently dissatisfied until the wilderness is reduced to a dead level of monotnous, songless tameness. What does one go into the wilderness for to see? A reed shaken by the wind, if you please; but surely not geometric flower beds, nor mounds of the ubiquitous canna and castor bean.

Hence, to preserve intact and within easy reach some of our vanishing wild land, to maintain a supply of native plants for educational purposes, to study at firsthand the problems of ecology and forestry, to preserve the indigenous flora and to introduce, if feasible, the flora of all the other regions of Minnesota for the benefit of students of botany and lovers of wild life—the teachers of botany in Minneapolis petitioned the city park commissioners to set aside a tract of land for a wild botanic garden. The site selected by the teachers and generously granted by the commissioners lies in Glenwood Park, the largest and perhaps the most beautiful of all our parks, containing three ponds of fair extent, a diversity of soil and slopes, and wooded heights commanding extensive views. In autumn, the scene is of surpassing loveliness with the beautiful groups of trees on the hills, in the valleys, and about the ponds, the vivid reds of the maples and the oaks, and the gold of the poplars set off by the white boles of birch and the dark green foliage of tamaracks.

A particular reason for selecting this place was the undrained tamarack swamp, such a swamp being the abode of most of our orchids and insectivorous plants so interesting in habit and structure. Indeed, most lovers of wild plants are bog-trotters and find in the depths of a swamp an earthly paradise. The indigenous flora was found to be captivating. Among the notables were sundew, pitcher plant, Linnaea, Turk's-cap lily, the two species of fringed gentian, [and] showy and yellow lady's-slippers.

In the spring of 1907, the experiment began on a tract about three acres in extent, comprising the small tamarack bog with meadows on the south and west merging into wooded slopes. Longing eyes were cast upon a marsh overgrown with willows on the eastern side of the bog. This was private property, but before a year had passed it was purchased by the park commission and added to the garden together with the adjacent hillside. Later, meadows on the north and west were also annexed so that the garden now contains about twenty-five acres.

A tiny stream threaded the bog and emerged into a depressed area of slimy ooze flanked by low banks. A dam was constructed that converted the depression into a lovely pool that has become a favorite sketching point for artists. It has proved too shady for aquatics and it is proposed to make a small pond by excavation in the open north meadow where the stream from the bog unites with one that flows from a spring on the eastern boundary. The delicious water of this spring is not one of the least important adjuncts of the garden.

It was planned from the beginning to make the garden a living museum of the flora of Minnesota and to preserve strictly the wild appearance of the place. There were to be no formal beds. Plants were to be allowed to grow according to their own sweet will and not as humans might wish them to grow, and without any restraint except what would be essential for health and mutual well-being. Each plant introduced to the garden is provided with an environment similar to its original one and then left to take care of itself as in the wild open, with only the natural fertilizers such as decaying wood and leaves. No watering is done after the plants are firmly established. Plants growing in excess and pestilent weeds are removed to make room for more desirable newcomers.

Minnesota has a flora of wide range, with representatives from the forest region of the east, the prairies of the west, the Alpine region of the north, and even a few species from the arid Great Plains.

Plants are obtained for the Reserve by collection, by exchange, and by purchase from nurserymen who deal in native species. As a rule they thrive best from regions of similar climatic conditions. The largest plantings are made in the spring and fall, the early flowering plants being set in the fall and the late flowering in the spring, although specimens have been successfully transplanted in full flower in midsummer—anything desirable being taken whenever procurable. This is a risky procedure, but bog plants can be lifted at any time if not allowed to become dry in transit. Whether fall or spring planting is preferable depends for the most part upon succeeding conditions of weather. With reliable forecasting, all doubts would be settled. Do not plant heavily in the fall when the winter will be open or in the spring when early droughts are expected. The greater rush of work in the spring is an argument in favor of fall planting.

At the very beginning a garden "log" was installed in which a record of the plantings, period of blossoming, and other data have been faithfully transcribed. A brief history and the location of each species are also preserved in a card catalogue. A species is not indexed until it has wintered, and the necrology is noted by merely withdrawing the name from the catalogue. Only a small percentage refuse to flourish. Sand and lime are imported for species requiring an excess of that diet; tannic acid and ammonium sulphate for greater acidity. Trailing arbutus, *Viola lanceolata* [lance-leaved violet], and *V. rotundifolia* [round-leaved violet] are found to be the least persuasive. It is probable that these could be established if they could be raised *situ* from the seed. Some annuals, like *Campanula americana* [American bellflower], have been raised from self-sowing by being planted when in flower.

It was soon found that the term "Wild Botanic Garden" was misleading to the popular fancy, so the name has been changed to "Native Plant Reserve."

"Is this the wild garden?" was a common query accompanied by widely roving eyes.

"Yes."

"Well, where are the flowers?"

"All about you. But many do not grow in masses. They are planted naturally and not in beds, and must be looked for as in any wilderness. Some have been picked by vandals; others are out of blossom, and many of the leafy flowerless stalks which must have room to grow, will not blossom for weeks to come."

*Early History of
Eloise Butler Plant Reserve, 1926*

Notable Features of My Wild Garden

AMONG THE NOTABLE FEATURES of the garden, first of all should be noted the lie of the land and the admirable situation, consisting as it does of morainic hills commanding wide-spread views with intervening valleys, ponds and bogs. My twenty acres of garden within a park of about 600 acres, includes one small tamarack bog, but none of the ponds. One pond, however, full of lilies, lies not a stone's throw off, and the other can be seen from my highest hilltop; while a third is distant but a few minutes' walk. I have a pool in the garden that was formed by building a dam across my brook, and it is proposed to make by excavation a sizable pool in one of my meadows for more aquatic plants. As it is, I have varied conditions of soil, moisture and light exposure that satisfy the needs of all the imported plants from other parts of the state.

The beauty of the landscape is enhanced by the character of the trees and shrubs and their natural grouping. There are many white birches and white oaks, also red maples. These in the fall—the white stems of the birches, the peculiar mulberry red of the white oaks, and the many shades of color afforded by other

plants, all set off by the dark green of the tamaracks—make one understand why the term *poignant* should be applied to remarkable beauty. Someone voiced this feeling on seeing the garden in autumnal dress by saying, "It makes me *ache* to look at this!" One of my white birches on a hillside has eight bolls, while opposite in the meadow a yellow birch rejoices with seven. Between them "Monarch," the largest white oak in Minneapolis, lifts his aged head and rules the landscape.

The season is unusually late this year and we have no flowers as yet, save those of the white maple and the yellow aments of hazel, but the swamp is gay with a cordon of red-osier dogwood, interspersed with yellow stems of willows and saffron-colored *Cornus circinata*. Since early March, innumerable pussies on the willows have been purring, "Spring is here!" although more warmth is needed to bring out the yellow stamens and pistils.

*Annals of the Wild Life Reserve,
March 1915*

* * *

I am often asked when one can derive the most benefit or pleasure from a visit to the wild garden. Every week, from April through October, presents new attractions. First are the early spring flowers, appearing a little later than in some other places, on account of the deeper shade in the cup-like depression occupied by the bog. There is an unparalleled display of marsh marigolds, making golden vistas through the tamaracks and surrounding marshes, accompanied by the fragrant white violet and all the other notable flowers then due, indigenous or introduced, from other parts of Minnesota. Within a space of twenty acres may be seen in an hour what would be impossible to find in traversing the state for several days. From May on, the ferns, some forty species in all, compel attention, from the time that the wooly crosiers of the interrupted fern unroll, densely clothing with its long fronds the wooded slopes, even until winter, when the evergreen species are conspicuous against the snow. In the latter part of May, the hawthorns transcend description, freighted with white flowers, from which, in the fall, will mature bright red fruits. About Decoration Day, the much admired yellow and pink lady's-slippers are in bloom. June brings the roses, the strange flowers of the pitcher plant, and the marvelously beautiful showy lady's-slipper. In July, the garden is resplendent with lilies, while in August, the meadow flowers are in full force, forming brilliant mosaics of white, blue, yellow and red. Again, not one of the city parks surpasses Glenwood in scenic beauty during autumn, offering, with its morainic hills and ponds, wide-spreading views and a great variety of landscape. In addition to the common autumnal foilage, swamp maples yield vivid scarlet, and numerous white oaks, rich tints of mulberry red, [are] set off by the white stems of birches and the dark green foliage of tamaracks, while the meadows are blue with gentians and the hills carpeted with asters unaffected by frosts.

Letter to Theodore Wirth, 1 January 1914

* * *

In specifying the herbs, mention must be made of the large specimen of *Aralia racemosa*, or spikenard, growing on the borders of the swamp. Near by the wild calla flourishes in its adopted home and its relative *Symplocarpus*, the skunk cabbage, one of our earliest bog plants to bloom, for it literally thaws its way through the ice. Deep in the recesses of the swamp are the orchids—coral root, habenarias [rein orchids, now *Platanthera*], and our state flower, the showy cypripedium [lady's-slipper].

Of the orchid family, either indigenous or introduced, are now in the garden six species of cypripedium, eight of habenaria [*Platanthera*, rein orchid], *Orchis spectabilis* [*Galearis spectabilis*, showy orchis], *Pogonia* [*P. ophioglossoides*, rose pogonia or snake mouth], *Calopogon* [*C. tuberosus*, grass pink], *Arethusa* [*A. bulbosa*, dragon's mouth], two species of twayblade (*Liparis*), *Aplectrum* [putty-root], coral-root, and three species of rattlesnake plantain (*Epipactis*) [*Goodyera*].

Imbedded in the sphagnum, close by the lady's-slippers, is the pitcher plant, the only species of this latitude. . . . In the treeless swamp is an abundance of the tiny, round-leaved sundew (*Drosera rotundifolia*), another insectivorous plant. . . .

Cat-tails abound in the neighborhood of the brook. Near them have been established colonies of sweet flag (*Acorus*) and fragrant vanilla grass, used by the Indians in basketry. In their season the rosy swamp milkweed (*Asclepias incarnata*), asters and

goldenrods glorify the meadow. One of the most precious possessions of the garden is the twin-flower named for the great Linnaeus and said to be one of his favorite flowers. The day is memorable on which it is first enjoyed in its perfection. The wild garden is its only station in Minneapolis.

With the *Linnaea* is found the dwarf cornel, also local in Minneapolis, the herbaceous relative of the dogwood shrubs, valued for hedges on account of their ornamental fruits and stems. The fruit of this cornel is red and edible and is commonly called bunchberry. Other indigenous rarities of the meadow are three-leaved smilacina, *Menyanthes* [buckbean], *Tofieldia* [*T. glutinosa*, false asphodel], *Chelone* [turtlehead], marsh rosemary and the small cranberry (*Vaccinium oxycoccus*). Especially prized are the gentians—the larger and the smaller fringed and closed, all abundant and of magnificant growth. The former, pronounced the most beautiful blue flower of the world, florists have but recently learned how to cultivate. The tall blue lobelia and three eupatoriums—the pale purple Jo-Pye weed, the less striking boneset, with its grayish flowers, and the pure white-flowered snakeroot—are other adornments of the meadow.

. . . In the rich soil under the trees, adjusted to their requisite degrees of moisture, are our most conspicuous shade plants, among them *Sanguinaria* [bloodroot], three species of *Erythronium* [trout lily], five of *Trillium*, and two dicentras—Dutchman's breeches and squirrel corn.

For the instruction of the unwary harborage is given to poisonous plants like the water parsnip and hemlock, poison ivy and sumach, and to the pernicious parasite, the *Cuscuta* or dodder, the enemy of the cereals.

On the treeless slopes, the prairie plants are well established—euphorbias [spurges], liatras [blazing stars], asters, golden-rods, petalostemums [prairie clover], *Vernonia* [ironweed], *Heliopsis* [ox-eye] being the leading genera. . . .

A wild garden is beautiful at all seasons. After the heavy frosts and before the kindly snow covers up in the cultivated gardens the unsightly, bare earth—suggestive of newly-made graves—and the dead bodies of herbs, and the tender exotics, stiffly swathed in winding sheets of burlap or straw, awaiting the spring resurrection, I turn with pride and relief to the wild garden, whose frozen ruins are graciously hidden by the shrubs, which then enliven the landscape with their glowing stems and fruits. And how lovely are the waving plumes of the grasses, how endless the varieties of seed-pods, how marvellous the modes of seed-dispersion! The eye, no longer distracted by the brilliant flower-mosaics, sees the less flaunting beauty and rediscovers "the commonplace of miracle."

Bulletin of the Minnesota
Academy of Science, September 1911

* * *

One of my banks in early spring is thronged with the pretty *Anemonella thalictroides* [rue anemone]. This gives way to an equally profuse growth of wild geranium or cranesbill, followed for the rest of the season by sunflowers, chiefly *strumosus* and *tuberosus* [Jerusalem artichoke]. It is a wonder that the soil can support such a rank succession. I have several other sunflowers in other places, and splendid masses particularly of *H. grosseserratus, giganteus, maximiliani* and *scaberrimus.* Just now large patches of the little wood anemone, *Anemone quinquefolia,* vie with the *Anemonella.* Visitors are interested in comparing these two species with the false rue anemone, *Isopyrum biternatum,* usually confused by novices. Marsh marigold is now a golden glory. It is so abundant that cartloads could be removed without apparent loss. This is also true of the interrupted fern. The marsh fern is equally abundant in the meadows. The bog is stocked with splendid growths of cinnamon fern and sensitive fern is much in evidence on the borders. Lady ferns and maidenhair rank next in abundance. We now have forty-one species of ferns, ten of which are indigenous.

The bog is now fragrant with *Viola blanda* [*V. incognita*]; among it is one lovely large mass of *V. conspersa* [dog violet]. A little later, the adjacent meadow will be perfumed with my favorite *Smilacina,* the *trifolia* [three-leaved false solomon's seal]. We have quantities, too, of the other smilacinas and the closely related *Maianthemum* [false lily-of-the valley].

. . . The most notable spring event is the blossoming of the hawthorns. We have many trees that may be seen near at hand and in the far distance loaded with a snowy fleece of bloom. They blossom like apple trees, more profusely every other year. This is the good year.

Annals of the Wild Life Reserve, 1915

* * *

My wild garden is run on the political principle of *laissez-faire.* Fallen leaves are not raked up unless they lie in too deep windrows and are likely to smother some precious specimen but are retained to form humus. But the tall dead canes of herbs like Jo-Pye weed and wild golden glow, which are allowed to stand during the winter to protect the dormant vegetation underneath, are removed from the meadows in the spring for a clear view of the clumps of marsh marigolds, trilliums, etc. I also gather and burn all fallen branches, and in the fall while the late flowers are still blooming, all unsightly evidences of decay. Of course, I do not allow at any time any outside litter to be brought in—not the tiniest scrap of paper, or string, or peanut shell. The great mass of herbaceous plants, as asters, goldenrods, and most composites, I admire in their fluffy state, after they have gone to seed. Some species, however, are to me the reverse of ornamental in old age. These are snipped to the ground or torn up by the roots and reduced to ash. Red clover is one of the offenders. It becomes unkempt and scraggly; and the stalks of the common milkweed that are without fruit, after shedding their leaves, turn black and look like long rat tails. Touch-me-not, *Impatiens biflora* [*I. capensis*] and *I. pallida,* collapse with the first frost and cumber the ground with a brown slime; and wood nettle, *Laportea canadensis,* is smitten as with a pestilence. A few type specimens of stingers and stick-tights are permitted on the grounds. *Laportea* is a persistent spreader and sometimes gets the upper hand, busy as I am with many other things. In the fall, I grub it out and plant something else in its place. Then I learn its encroaching ways: The roots are not very deep, but they are woven and knotted together into a dense mat that seems as hard as rock.

Annals of the Wild Life Reserve,
February 1920

The Plateau

THE "PLATEAU," HERETOFORE mentioned, is a natural terrace of about half an acre in extent that cuts in twain the south hillside. Here, in [1915], was erected the Curator's office, a small building subdivided by a partition, serving as a tool house and a reception room for visitors. On the north and east side of the office is a pergola-trellis that supports wild grape, *Vitis vulpina;* Virginia creeper, *Psedera quinquefolia;* and bittersweet, *Celastrus scandens.* At the right of the entrance on the south wall clambers the common clematis, *C. virginiana,* and on the left an uncommon clematis, *C. verticillaris* [*C. occidentalis*]. It was procured from northern Wisconsin and was tended assiduously for eight years before it responded by displaying lilac blooms fully four inches in diameter that endured the whole latter half of May. The common bindweed, *Convolvulus sepium,* is confined with some difficulty to trellises on the east side of the building, where also are growing wild yam, *Dioscorea villosa;* moonseed, *Menispermum canadense;* wild smilax, *S. hispida;* and climbing nightshade, *Solanum dulcamara;* also occasionally the lovely climbing fumitory, *Adlumia fungosa.* The last named I have some difficulty in establishing. On the north side flourishes a stalwart Dutchman's pipe that loves the shade and is festooned with its curious "pipes" before the leaves attain their splendid maximum size.

At the southern rim of the Plateau and on the winding path leading to the south gate, a large granite boulder has been set that has been chiseled out for a bird bath in a series of steps on a half-inch gradient to a depth of five inches. The birds like to step from shallow water into deeper, and the steps are left rough so that their feet will not slip. The bath is partially surrounded by a covert of thickly planted evergreens—white pine, spruce, and arbor vitae. Clusters of evergreen exclamation points, *Juniperus virginiana,* stand on each side of the south gate and accentuate the entrance to the "deep, tangled wildwood" to which the primal soul responds.

A few other evergreens have also been set near the southeast boundary. No evergreens are endemic in the Reserve. Representatives of all of the Minnesota conifers form a small pinetum on the western bank, and many hemlocks [*Tsuga canadensis*], which have but one stand in the [northeastern] part of the state, have reached a sturdy growth in the vicinity of the garden pool where they are protected from hurtful dry winds of winter.

This evergreen with its low-spreading delicately sprayed branches and the blue-berried mats of junipers, *Juniperus communis* and *J. horizontalis,* are not only highly decorative but form ideal shelters for birds.

Early History of
Eloise Butler Plant Reserve, 1926

Trees in the Wild Garden

A CENSUS WAS TAKEN at once of the most obvious inmates of the Reserve, which has been increased from time to time by many delightful surprises. To begin with the trees, the most conspicuous is a majestic white oak, 700 years young, the largest and oldest in the vicinity of Minneapolis. "Monarch," as we call him, was slowly dying atop. So, in obedience to the scriptural injunction, his dead limbs were cut off and cast away, and decayed portions of his "heart"—not essential as with humans for circulation—were taken out and replaced with concrete. Thus, lopped and reinforced, he bade fair for many more years to hold sway. Alack and alas! In the tornado of last June [1925], large chunks of concrete were belched out and all the limbs torn off. How long will he yet stand without his crown?

The leading tree in the swamp was the tamarack. They were piled up like jackstraws by the tornado, and but few left standing. But most of the white birches, which were nearly equally abundant, were spared by reason of their deeper root system, as was also another prime ornament of the garden—a much be-photographed eight-boled white birch that dominates the eastern hillside. A few clumps of yellow birch reside in the swamp, the rarer small tree, *Betula sandbergii,* and many dwarf birch, *B. pumila* [*B. glandulifera*]. One river birch, *B. nigra,* has been planted at the base of the south hillside. A few ash trees, both black and white, border the swamp, and the green and the red ash have been introduced. A single tall hackberry, with its beautiful corrugated bark, adorns the west side of the pool. Younger trees will be developed in time to take its place. Next in size to "Monarch" are the white and the red elms, more or less defaced by the storm. Two cork elms have been planted on the west bank. A goodly sized basswood stands in the east meadow and young basswoods are springing up on every side. A fine specimen of large-toothed poplar,

Populus grandidentata, is on the "Plateau" near the south entrance to the garden, and innumerable youngsters are springing up that must be held in check. The smaller quaking [aspen] is much in evidence, and two cottonwoods are beginning to tower above the landscape.

In the garden's second spring, a small balm of gilead was planted at the base of the west hillside. It has grown into a lusty tree, and, after a shower, the fragrance of the young leaves is wafted over the whole enclosure. In September 1919, the curator, on a trip to the North Shore of Lake Superior, dug up a balsam poplar, as fragrant as its variety, the balm of gilead, and added it to the treasures of the garden. It is planted near the gate on the south side of the tarvia road that divides the precincts.

Besides "Monarch," there are many other white oaks whose leaves in rich shades of maroon lend a special glory to the autumnal coloring. And red oaks vie with them when dressed in reds and browns, not to speak of the tender blush of the young leaves just escaping from the bud. Several bur oaks express their gnarly individuality—the Carlyles among the oaks. A few swamp white oaks, *Quercus bicolor,* have been introduced; also *Q. prinoides,* the chinquapin oak, the latter from Boulder, Colorado.

The most popular tree in the Reserve is commonly called the "fire tree," the red swamp maple, *Acer rubrum.* It really is aglow twice a year. The young leaves and keys warm the landscape and often in August, before frosts, the trees are aflame throughout the swamps. Our other native maples have been introduced to the Reserve, even the common white or silver maple and the hard or sugar maple which form large "orchards" in many sections of Minnesota. Very interesting additions are two northern species, *Acer spicatum,* the mountain maple, thickly hung with yellowish flower plumes which develop into highly decorative small rose-red keys, and the striped maple, or moosewood, whose showy striped bark is a tidbit for moose. It bears drooping green racemes and the largest leaves of any of our maples.

The ten most abundant trees in the Native Plant Reserve, Minneapolis, are: tamarack (*Larix laricina*), white birch (*Betula alba var. papyrifera*), ironwood (*Ostrya virginiana*), northern pin oak (*Quercus ellipsoidalis*), white oak (*Quercus alba*), red oak (*Quercus rubra*), white ash (*Fraxinus americana*), red maple (*Acer rubrum*), basswood (*Tilia americana*), [and] large-toothed aspen (*Populus grandidentata*).

The least frequent trees in the Reserve are: scarlet oak (*Quercus coccinea*), one tree only; white maple (*Acer saccharinum*), one tree endemic; [and] hackberry (*Celtis occidentalis*), one tree endemic and a few young ones.

The other trees in the Reserve are not rare in the immediate vicinity. Two other rare trees in Minneapolis are [the] Kentucky coffee tree (*Gymnocladus dioica*) [and the] swamp white oak (*Quercus bicolor*).

*Early History of
Eloise Butler Plant Reserve, 1926*

* * *

In winter, a more intimate acquaintance can be made with deciduous trees. For it is only after the leaves have fallen that the architecture of trees can be clearly discerned. Every species has a different form. No individual, ever, is exactly like another. A tree with its delicate tracery of leafless branches is a thing of beauty to eyes that are adjusted to see it. Note, then, the different kinds of bark; the direction of the cleavage; whether it is deep or shallow, smooth or shaggy; laid in smocking, as in white ash, or broken into coral-form bosses, as in hackberry; or in plates with curled edges, as in black cherry. Sober colors merge and blend in trunk and branches to break in the outmost twigs into livelier tints of olive, ash-pink, red, or yellow, according to the species. To one versed in tree-craft, a single twig is sufficient to identify the species. Is the twig stout or slender, rigid or flexible? How are the buds arranged, and what [is] their shape, size, surface, and color? The leaf and flower buds, if separate, can be distinguished by their size and shape, the flower buds being usually the larger. Particularly decorative is the alder, displaying three sorts of buds—purple oblong leaf buds, tiny buds of pistillate flowers, and staminate in three-finger aments—together with brown cones, the receptacles of last year's fruit. The buds of basswood are coated with red shellac, of box elder with mouse-colored fur, while those of sycamore are hidden within the hollow leafstalk. Buds of swamp hickory are sulphur yellow; buds of white elm resemble apple seeds; those of red elm are covered with rust colored wool. The leaf scars below the buds vary, also the arrangement on them of the little dots—the ends of wood bundles that divide to form the venation of the leaf. The rings of bud-scale scars, marking off the annual growths of the branch, also instance the saying that "Nature repeats herself with a difference." In the maples, for example, these rings are wider and shallower than in the poplars, where they are deeply indented.

A small pinetum has been established on the hillside northwest of the tamarack swamp. As the deciduous tamarack is the only conifer growing naturally in the garden, all the evergreen trees therein are juveniles. They have been placed in accordance with their predilections for dryness or moisture—red cedar, jack, white, and red pines [and] prostrate junipers highest on the slope, followed to the level below by white spruce and black, balsam fir and arbor vitae, with yew (*Taxus canadensis*) and hemlock along the brook. Hemlock has not been listed among Minnesotan plants; but it has been sneaked in, contrary to rule, with the idea that it may sometime break across the Wisconsin border. In order that the face of nature may be changed as little as possible in our trained wilderness, only a few specimens each of the state flora not indigenous to the garden are admitted.

Annals of a Wild Garden, c.1914

Shrubs in the Wild Garden

THE BRIGHTLY HUED BERRIES of the shrubs are but a "fleeting show" in the garden, being scarcely allowed to ripen by the fruit-loving birds. The sweet fruit of the shadbush or Juneberry vanishes like dew before the sun, shortly after the eye is gladdened by the gracefully drooping sprays of *Amelanchier canadense* in flower and the more upright plumes of the low gray-leaved *A. oblongifolia*.

The dogwoods richly furnish forth the bird tables. The gray dogwood, *Cornus paniculata*, is the most abundant of all. The inflorescence does not unfavorably compare with white lilac, and the profuse white berries, borne on red stalks, are very pleasing. Red-osier dogwood, *C. stolonifera*, forms a cordon around the swamp, warms the snow, and enlivens the winter landscape with its red stems. The stems turn brown as the leaves develop, but then it is soon adorned with flowers and white or bluish fruits, and has the further recommendation of blossoming twice during the season. This shrub is selected by a certain sawfly for an egg depository, and hundreds of her larvae banded with olive green and pale yellow may be found coiled like little serpents on the underside of the leaves. *C. alternifolia* [pagoda dogwood] is certainly our handsomest dogwood, its glossy leaves forming tufts at the ends of the branches, and flower clusters so large that it is often mistaken for an arrow-wood; but the four-parted corolla shows that it is not a kin. *C. circinata* is another fine species that may be distinguished by its larger round leaves and greenish, warty stems. The silky dogwood, *Cornus amomum*, with its waxy blooms and dull purplish stems, is distinguished by being the favorite *kinnikinnik* of the Indians. The bark of the red-osier dogwood was also used by the Indians for tobacco, but the former was preferred. *Cornus baileyi* [a variant of red-osier dogwood], also a native of Minnesota, naturalized, but not endemic in the Reserve, bears a general resemblence to *C. stolonifera*, although it does not form a thicket by the stolon habit. All these dogwoods are bog-trotters, except that *C. circinata* will also thrive on woody hillsides. Also a dweller in bogland is the lovely herbaceous member of this genus, the dwarf cornel or bunchberry, *Cornus canadensis*. The flower cluster with four showy white bracts surrounding a bunch of small inconspicuous flowers that develop into red berries, resembles on a smaller scale that of its beautiful congener, the flowering *Cornus florida*, which, alas, is too tender for the rigorous climate of Minnesota. The dwarf cornel spreads by slender creeping rootstocks and makes an excellent ground cover for low shady places. The "bunch" of sweet berries is considered delectable by children, despite a doubtful suspicion of being poisonous. I, myself, have devoured them by handfuls without any ill effect. *Cornus asperifolia* [*C. drummondii*], the rough-leaved dogwood . . . is not found in the neighborhood of Minneapolis and has not yet been planted in the wild garden.

Our arrow-woods or viburnums are even superior to the dogwoods for bird food. Some of the fruit is, indeed, appreciated by humans. The flower clusters are larger and more striking, and the foliage is vividly conspicuous in autumn. Nannybush, or sheepberry, *Viburnum lentago*, takes the lead in height, the trunks often clustered. The leafstalks have wing-like margins, [and] the buds are shaped like candle extinguishers; the drupes are bluish black, as are also the fruits of the lower and almost equally attractive downy arrow-wood, *V. pubescens* [*V. rafinesquianum*]. The fruit of *V. dentatum* is an exquisite shade of blue. The last named species is not endemic in the Reserve. Other introduced species are hobblebush or moosewood, *V. alnifolium*, a resident of northern woods; witherod, *V. cassinoides*, very decorative in fruit, its wand-like stems wreathed with globes in varying shades of green, reddish brown and blue-black; dockmackie, the maple-leaved arrow-wood, *V. acerifolium*, common in New England; and the few flowered high-bush cranberry, *V. pauciflorum* [*V. edule*], endemic in northern Minnesota. The widely distributed highbush cranberry, *V. Opulus var. americanum*, is fortunately one of the native adornments of the Reserve. With showy inflorescence and bright red fruit, it vies in beauty with the famous flowering dogwood. The fruit, as acid as genuine cranberries, is esteemed for jelly. It hangs on the bushes late in the season, and the Bohemian waxwing may be seen culling from them his dessert for Thanksgiving. As you all know, the useless stupid garden snowball was produced from the European *V. Opulus*, which is almost identical with the American variety, by converting the small fruit-bearing flowers into showy neutrals like those bordering the clusters, at the expense of beauty and food for man, bird and bee. Thereby was overturned the House that Jack Built, for Dame Nature, who practices economy when she can, had intended the neutrals for guide boards to insects that, in getting the food prepared for them in the numerous small perfect flowers, would do service, in turn, by insuring fruit for birds and humans.

The ten shrubs most common in the Reserve are: willows, of which the most abundant are *Salix discolor, S. petiolaris*, [and] *S. rostrata*; common hazel (*Corylus americana*); prickly ash (*Xanthoxylum americanum*); beaked hazel (*Corylus rostrata*); smooth sumach (*Rhus glabra*); gray dogwood (*Cornus paniculata* [*C. foemina subsp. racemosa*]); red-osier dogwood (*Cornus stolonifera*); dwarf birch (*Betula pumila* [*B. glandulifera*]); wild buckthorn (*Rhamnus alnifolia*); [and] round-leaved thorn (*Crataegus rotundifolia* [*C. chrysocarpa*]).

Of the many other species of endemic shrubs, none are infrequent except *Ilex verticillata* [holly or black alder].

Of the undershrubs, even more abundant are: blackberry (*Rubus allegheniensis*), raspberry (*Rubus idaeus var. aculeatissimus* [*R. strigosus*]), wolfberry (*Symphoricarpos occidentalis*), [and] poison ivy (*Rhus toxicodendron* [*R. radicans*]).

The above undershrubs may be denominated "weeds" and are grubbed out continually. Others [that are] abundant, but not allowed to be rampant, are: *Rosa blanda* [smooth wild rose], bush honeysuckle (*Diervilla lonicera*), [and] New Jersey tea (*Ceanothus americanus*); and the vines: bittersweet (*Celastrus scandens*), wild grape (*Vitis vulpina*), [and] Virginia creeper (*Psedera quinquefolia* [*Parthenocissus quinquefolia*]).

Early History of
Eloise Butler Plant Reserve, 1926

Asters in the Wild Garden

FROM YEAR TO YEAR I become more and more attached to wild asters. They are so varied in color, habit and form. They bloom from August well into October, defying frosts. The one I look at last, I like best of all, for each species has a charm peculiar to itself.

Asters indigenous to the wild garden:
Aster azureus [*A. oolentangiensis*] still burgeons on the hillsides (October 5). It is a *sine qua non* [absolutely necessary] not only on account of its late blossoms, but because of their profusion and bright, pure color.

Aster junceus [*A. borealis*] is a pleasing adjunct of the meadows. It appears early and has a long period of bloom. The flowers, white or palely tinted, the slender stalks, and linear leaves, make it a fitting companion for its associate, the marsh bellflower, *Campanula aparinoides*.

Aster laevis with richly colored flowers, smooth, thick leaves, and sturdy habit, is also still in evidence on dry, sandy soil.

"O, you cunning little thing!" we exclaim at the wee blossoms peeping out through the leaves densely clothing the diffusely branched stems of *Aster lateriflorus*—the so-called calico aster—the purple disks and pale rays forming a pattern on the background of the small green leaves. . . .

Aster multiflorus has been largely planted in the garden, but last season I found a specimen of it well established in my swampy meadow, where I never should have thought of planting it—the inhabitant of dry prairies. This aster with its small rigid leaves and multiplicity of flowers might well be called *ericoides* if the name had not been preempted, for it looks like a heath. Robust specimens are fully as fine as the overworked *Spiraea van houttei*.

Aster novae-angliae [New England aster] is truly a splendid plant—tall, late-blooming, with prodigal large flowers of many shades of rich blue and pink purple. It often has the striking tone of the ironweed.

Aster paniculatus [*A. lanceolatus*] is often mistaken for *Boltonia* in the distance. The inflorescence, however, is not flat-topped like that of *Boltonia*, and the disk-flowers are of a deeper color. This aster is highly decorative, growing as it does in large masses.

Aster salicifolius [*A. hesperius*] has a similar habit and, when the flowers are white, is scarcely distinguishable from it.

Aster puniceus, the red-stemmed swamp aster, is nearly as showy as *A. novae-angliae*. The typical plants, tall and bushy, their flowers with narrow rays, deep blue or pale, or even white, with orange disks, look as if studded with stars.

Aster puniceus var. lucidulus [*var. firmus*] is a late bloomer and the most abundant aster in the garden, growing in large masses in the meadow bordering the west side of the tamarack bog. The stem is yellowish brown, more simple and far less hairy than that of the type. The flower is of the palest blue and somewhat smaller. The leaves are glossy and shining.

Aster sagittifolius [*A. urophyllus*] is of refined beauty. It has a wand-like habit and is crowded with blossoms of medium size, generally white or pale blue, with purplish disks.

Aster drummondii is said to be hardly distinct from it; but, with me, *A. drummondii* has larger, thicker leaves, larger and darker blue flowers, a less brittle stem, and a more gregarious habit.

Aster umbellatus is highly esteemed because of its tallness, its ample flat-topped flower clusters of mingled gray and yellow that set off and harmonize with the luxuriant masses of Joe-Pye weed.

Introduced asters:

Aster commutatus [*A. falcatus var. commutatus*] is a sort of glorified *Aster multiflorus* [*A. ericoides*]. The flowers are quite a bit larger. I have but two roots in the garden and they have not yet blossomed.

Aster divaricatus, sparsely introduced, has entirely died out.

This is also the case with *Aster ericoides*. Both species were obtained from Massachusetts and probably could not withstand the rigours of our severer climate.

The large, rough, basal leaves of *Aster macrophyllus* give the plant a marked individuality. The flowers, though pale in color, attract attention by their size and abundance. This aster is local in the vicinity of St. Paul and takes kindly to cultivation.

Aster novi-belgii is not yet well established in the garden. I am not very familiar with its characteristics.

Aster oblongifolius is local on our prairies. It is pleasing by reason of the size, color and aromatic odor of the blossoms.

Aster patens did not put in an appearance this season. A particularly fine aster, its stems thickly clothed with sessile, cordate leaves, the flowers [are] large and of rich purple hue.

Aster ptarmicoides [*Solidago ptarmicoides*, actually a goldenrod] behaves like a biennial. I think every other year that it has petered out, but it comes up serenely the next season. The small flowers have the pure whiteness and texture of camellias.

If I have any special favorite, it is *Aster sericeus*. The flowers are lilac tinted, a shade peculiar to themselves, and the contrast with the silky, pale gray foliage is altogether charming. It is abundant on the hillsides just outside of the garden, and I have introduced it in large quantities.

Aster cordifolius is abundant in the woods along our river banks. I have specimens of remarkable beauty where I have planted it in burnt-over tracts, branching diffusely and crowded with pale blue flowers whose disks take on a richer tone in maturity.

Aster undulatus, also introduced from Massachusetts, perhaps on account of its thick epidermis thrives well in the garden. Its flowers are pleasing and about of the same tone as those of *A. cordifolius*. . . .

I find that I have omitted from my list of introduced species, A. linariifolius. They have not yet reached the blossoming stage.

Annals of the Wild Life Reserve,
June 1915

Ferns in the Wild Garden

TEN FERNS ARE INDIGENOUS to the wild garden. Indeed, the most spectacular feature of the garden is a hillside densely clothed with the interrupted fern, Osmunda clintoniana [O. claytoniana], and the tamarack swamp abounds with cinnamon fern, O. cinnamomea, and the lovely evergreens, Aspidium spinulosum [Dryopteris carthusiana] and A. cristatum [Dryopteris cristata], with the second in point of numbers—the marsh fern, A. thelypteris [Thelypteris palustris], which is also massed in the marsh on the eastern side of the swamp. We also have an abundance of lady fern, Asplenium filix-femina [Athyrium angustum]; sensitive fern, Onoclea sensibilis; and maidenhair, Adiantum pedatum, which forms mats of unusual size and height. The rattlesnake fern, Botrychium virginianum, is frequent, and the brake, Pteris aquilina [P. aquilinum], is rapidly spreading, although, when the garden was started in 1907, it was not in evidence, and I recall that three of the teachers of botany tried and failed to dig up a root of it to transplant in the garden. This may repeat the history of the royal fern, Osmunda regalis, which has been introduced on the border of the swamp. Much to my surprise I found a single specimen, not large, but beyond the period of childhood, in the center of the swamp where it had not been consciously planted. The query is, how did it get there? Possibly in the sod from some other plantation, for it is too soon for it to develop from the spores of the introduced specimens. The fern is abundant in a thicket about two and one-half miles from the garden.

The other ferns that grow about Minneapolis and have been introduced in numbers in the garden are the ostrich fern, Onoclea struthiopteris [Matteuccia struthiopteris var. pensylvanica], which is locally abundant in moist ravines, [and] in one place, I have been told, fronds grow six feet high; Cystopteris bulbifera [bulblet-fern] with very long fronds on moist, rocky banks; the less frequent fragile bladder fern, C. fragilis; [and the] common polypody, Polypodium vulgare [P. virginianum] on the bluffs of the Mississippi. I know of one limestone bluff that is carpeted with it and close by another that has an equally rank growth of Woodsia obtusa [woodsia]. On our river bluffs is also found perhaps the most interesting fern of all, Cryptogramma stelleri, the filmy rock brake, differentiated, small as it is, into two sorts of fronds, the sterile and fertile.

I have had to go several miles farther afield, a journey by rail farther south along the river, for the purple cliff brake, Pellaea atropurpurea, where I find it abundant in crevices of bold, outcropping rock; and my nearest point for the walking fern, Camptosorus rhizophyllus, is over the border in Osceola, Wisconsin. Here, too, I have obtained the pretty oak fern, Phegopteris dryopteris [Gymnocarpium dryopteris] and Woodsia ilvensis. For the other beech ferns, P. polypodioides [Thelypteris phegopteris] and P. hexagonoptera [Thelypteris hexagonoptera], I have had to depend upon florists. I find that P. hexagonoptera [Thelypteris hexagonoptera] prefers a shady hillside, while the two other beech ferns do well in the swamp. I have obtained besides from Eastern florists Asplenium trichomanes [maidenhair spleenwort]; A. angustifolium [Athyrium pynocarpon], the narrow spleen-wort; A. acrostichoides [Athyrium thelypteroides], the silvery spleenwort; Polystichum braunii, one of the most beautiful evergreen ferns; Aspidium noveboracense [Thelypteris noveborcensis], the New York fern; A. filix-mas [Dryopteris filix-mas], the male fern; A. Goldianum [Dryopteris goldiana] (a fine species); A. bootii [a hybrid Dryopteris] (another favorite); and the varieties of A. cristatum [Dryopteris species and hybrids] and A. spinulosum [Dryopteris species]; also the hay-scented fern, Dicksonia punctilobula [Dennstaedtla punctilobula] (which I like best of all; so did also Thoreau!); adder's tongue, Ophioglossum vulgatum [O. pusillum]; [and] the grape fern, Botrychium obliquum.

Colorado has furnished me with the little Woodsia scopulina, and I have myself successfully transported from Malden and Franklin, Massachusetts, the Christmas fern, Polystichum acrostichoides; the marginal shield fern, Aspidium marginale [Dryopteris marginalis]; and the precious ebony spleenwort, Asplenium platyneuron—the last three evergreens especially to be commended. The thick, blue-green fronds of *Aspidium marginale* [*Dryopteris marginale*] persist each season until after the new leaves are formed, doing duty the whole year round.

All my ferns are prospering except *Pellaea atropurpurea* and *Asplenium trichomanes*, which require renewing. . . .

Of the fern allies, three species of horsetails are indigenous—*Equisetum arvense, sylvaticum,* [and] *hyemale,* and I have imported *E. scirpoides.*

I have not succeeded in naturalizing lycopodiums [clubmosses]. Conditions do not seem favorable. They live a season or two and then peter out. One specimen of *Lycopodium lucidulum* was found growing naturally in the swamp, but it has disappeared. However, a large mat of transplanted *Selaginella rupestris* is completing its third year in the garden. Neither have I one snippet of *Isoetes* [quillwort] (of which there are three species in Minnesota), nor *Salvinia natans* [*S. rotundifolia,* salvinia], nor *Azolla caroliniana* [water fern], both of which are listed in our flora.

Annals of the Wild Life Reserve,
June 1915

* * *

. . . In my recently planted Fern Gulch, maidenhair, lady fern, and *Aspidium spinulosum* [*Dryopteris carthusiana*] are self-established. It was my aim to make a plantation in this gully of all the ferns native to Minnesota that were not indigenous in the garden and that could be induced to grow under the prevailing conditions of light and moisture. . . . The ferns were set out with reference to size and conditions of light and moisture, as well as drainage.

I have also outside of the Gulch well established *Osmunda regalis* [royal fern] and large colonies of *Onoclea struthiopteris* [ostrich fern, *Matteuccia struthiopteris var. pensylvanica*]. These I did not place in the Gulch because of their need of space and more moisture. I have, besides, a few highly cherished specimens of the dainty little cliff brake, *Cryptogramma stelleri,* and *Ophioglossum vulgatum* [*O. pusillum*]; and, when I left the garden last November, a quantity of *Azolla caroliniana* [water fern] and *Salvinia natans* [*S. rotundifolia*], planted during the summer, were bravely green on the surface of my little pond.

Annals of the Wild Life Reserve,
September 1919

Liverworts, Lichens, Mosses, and Evergreen Ferns in the Wild Garden

NATURE-STUDY IS AN all-the-year-round pursuit. Several birds, among them the snow bunting and the evening grosbeak, sporting a yellow vest, are with us only in the winter. Lichens, also, are then potent to charm, when the attention is not diverted by the more spectacular features of other seasons. Some tree trunks are gardens in miniature, when encrusted by these symbionts of fungus and imprisoned alga, forming yellow patches, or ashy gray, or grayish green rosettes, pitted here and there with dark brown fruit-disks. The tamarack boughs are bearded with gray *Usnea*; and, when the snow melts away, ground species of *Cladonia,* allied to "reindeer moss," can be seen, with tiny branches tipped with vivid red or studded with pale green goblets. Rock lichens, however, must be sought for elsewhere, as the wild garden does not provide for them either ledges or boulders.

As the snow disappears, and before Mother Nature's spinning wheels whir rapidly and her looms turn out a new carpet for the earth, a glance can be given to the mosses. A love for these tiny plants will surely awaken, if your "eyes were made for seeing," and a keener zest will be given to your out-of-door life. They are gregarious for the most part and everywhere present—by the roadside, on damp roofs and stones, as well as in the forest. Although it is especially true of mosses that "By their fruits ye shall known them," several genera can be readily determined by their leaves. The fruit, or spore case, is usually a little urn-shaped body borne on a slender stalk. Some species fruit early. I have seen before March was half over, *Bartramia,* the "apple moss," a mass of little globes—Rhode Island greenings, one might pronounce them—which turn a rich brown when mature.

Sphagnum, or bog moss [peat moss], may be recognized by its pale green color and the compact bunches of minute leaves terminating the stems. Its paleness is due to large water cells which make this plant of great value to florists for packing plants for distant transportation. We are also indebted to sphagnum for peat, which in the course of ages has been formed from it by reason of antiseptic properties that render it [almost] immune from decay.

Among other abundant mosses of the

165

swamp are *Thuidium*, the fern-moss, with branches so finely divided that it resembles filmy lace; *Leucobyrum*, nearly white in color, in dense mounds around the stumps; *Bryum proliferum* [*Rhodobryum roseum*], with its leaves arranged in rosettes that have been likened to green roses; *Mnium*, attracting attention by its trailing stems and leaves of lucid green, small indeed, but larger than the leaves of most mosses; *Timmaea* [*Timmia*], a rarer moss, resembling *Mnium*, but with a persistent little bristle projecting from the base of the fruit; *Climacium*, or tree moss, that might pass for an evergreen tree in a dwarf-garden.

On the "Plateau" may be seen clumps of *Polytrichum*, a comparatively tall moss, with brownish, somewhat rigid leaves. Large masses of this moss bear rosettes which shelter sperm that will fertilize the ova enclosed in apparent buds tipping other masses of the same species. The "buds" will finally develop into conspicuous fruits with shaggy caps of pale tan, aptly named "pigeon wheat."

In evolutionary order, liverworts should be mentioned before mosses. A few of them somewhat resemble in form their allies, the mosses; but the most common species in the garden are like branching green leaves coating the ground. The fruit of *Conocephalum*, the giant liverwort, is borne on small toadstool-like growths, and the sperm on other individuals, in sessile disks. Liverworts "invented" the so-called breathing pores, or stomates [that may be seen] with the naked eye, looking like pin pricks in the center of the diamond-shaped divisions into which the surface of the plant is divided. The stomates of mosses, by the way, are found only on the fruit capsules.

Marchantia polymorpha—liverwort of many forms, as the name implies—seems to the novice to be three distinct species. The vegetative form displays exquisitely fashioned green nests lined with tiny green eggs—not eggs, really, but what answers to bulblets in higher plants. On another individual, little stalked disks with scalloped margins carry the sperm, while a third form develops the fruit on the under surface of little, deeply fringed umbrellas. As these points are observed, one more character of liverworts will probably be noted—the cloying sweet odor.

Evergreen ferns make the woods attractive when other vegetation is brown and shriveled. They refresh eyes half blinded by reflection from the snow and serve to "keep in memory green" the delights of the growing season. Two species frequent tamarack bogs: the spinulose shield fern, whose dissected fronds have all the grace and delicacy of the well known lady fern's, and the crested shield fern that shows marked individuality in its deeply etched venation. The Christmas fern, so common farther east, but here [in the garden] an introduced species, takes kindly to the bog as well as to the rich black soil of the wooded slopes. It is sometimes mistaken for a short leaved variety of the cultivated Boston fern, but a comparison of the fruit dots on the backs of the fronds will show the difference. Also, on the same hillslope, have been naturalized the prostate, glossy holly fern, *Polystichum braunii*, and the marginal shield fern, *Aspidium marginale* [*Dryoptis marginalis*], which can be especially recommended as one never wearying in well-doing. For its cheerful, blue-green fronds persist each year until the new annual growth is well developed. The rock fern, common *Polypody*, that elsewhere mats the sides of overhanging bluffs, has been bribed to take root in the garden by a diet of ground rock and a bed of sunken stones.

Annals of a Wild Garden, c.1914

Children's Forage Plants in the Wild Garden

I HAVE BEEN THINKING LATELY about the plants I used to browse upon when I was a child and am trying to persuade my sister to write a paper on the subject. I wonder if any of you can add to the list from your own experience.

I ate but little at the table when beech leaves were young and tender. I do not know how delectable their acid would seem now, for I have but one small beech in the garden and no leaves to spare for experiments. The beech barely reaches the eastern border of Minnesota. The white starchy bud of the interrupted fern was a delicious morsel well worth long and hard digging to procure. It has a taste peculiar to itself, and I think it would make an excellent salad. We used to dig industriously also for the tubers of dwarf ginseng (*Panax trifolium*); "ground nuts" we called them. Do they have the same properties as the commercial ginseng? I have naturalized them in the garden from tubers sent me from Maine. It bloomed for me May 22. After fruiting, it dies down to the ground. We nibbled quantities of the nutlets of sweet fern, *Myrica asplenifolia* [*Comptonia peregrina*]. Boys made cigarettes of the leaves. It wasn't fashionable in our set for girls to smoke. I have failed to induce this plant to grow, although I try every season. I have succeeded with *Myrica gale*, another fragrant plant of the genus. I have never tested the edibility of its fruits. It loves water, while sweet fern affects a gravelly soil. Young shoots of raspberry and blackberry, peeled of their prickles, and the tips of wild grape tendrils were good fodder, too. The common red raspberry is in excess in the garden. It is uprooted when I want room for something else. I discovered only last summer a few roots of the thimbleberry, *Rubus occidentalis*. The stems are covered with thick white bloom. In Maine, everyone is fond of the young leaves of ivory plums, *Gaultheria procumbens*. We called them "youngsters," and the spicy fruit, "boxberries." Another name for the leaves was "ivries," the meaning of which is not apparent to me. The inner bark of slippery elm and of sweet birch, *Betula lenta*, were especially esteemed—the latter not a native of Minnesota.

The spore capsules of the moss called "pigeon wheat," *Polytrichum*, were culled for their slightly acid taste; but for extreme tartness, leaves of sheep sorrel were resorted to, which caused a peculiar sensation in the hinges of the jaw most often employed with the product of the spruces. Spearmint and pennyroyal supplied aromatic flavors, also bits of sarsaparilla, *Aralia nudicaulis*, and sweet flag root, *Acorus calamus*. In Minneapolis, children also eat the berries of common sumach, *Rhus typhina*, and the roots of sweet cicely, *Osmorhiza*. Of course, all sorts of berries were eaten—sweet or otherwise, puckery, juicy or stony. Besides those mentioned above, bunchberries, *Cornus canadensis*, snake berries (rare in Minneapolis)—a local name for partridge berries—*Mitchella repens*, [and] creeping snowberry, concealed on the under surface of the delicate vine, were especial favorites, notwithstanding the "horrid smart-bug" that was often popped into the mouth along with the sweet bunchberries. Thorn apples and bird cherries, nearly all stone, were made to yield their pulp. Chokecherries were devoured to the right degree of puckerment

for [saying] "papa, prunes, and prisms."

Other edible fruits in the wild garden are chokeberry, blackberry, dewberry, two species of Juneberry, two species of strawberry, flowering raspberry (rather tasteless), salmon berry, wild crab, the two cranberries, sheep berry, high-bush cranberry, May apple, blueberry, huckleberry, high-bush blueberry, two species of gooseberry, three of currant, purple-berried elder, black cherry, Bessey's cherry, [and] sand cherry, *Prunus pumila*.

Of nuts, there are only hazel—two species. Other nut bearers are introduced, but not old enough to fruit.

To . . . [the] list of substitutes for tea I can add *Amorpha canescens* [leadplant]. It is used for the sake of economy by some western farmers.

A German lady comes to the garden for *Galium circaezans* [wild licorice], which she uses as a flavoring for Rhine wine and lemonade.

Annals of the Wild Life Reserve,
January 1915

The Fragrance of the Wild Garden

BARRING THE MALODOROUS skunk cabbage which had to be introduced into my bog, the equally offensive carrion flower which is forgiven on account of the picturesque vine and big bells of dark purple berries, and the unspeakable fungus, the stinkhorn, tolerated as a curious freak of the vegetable kingdom, at all times the garden dispenses sweet fragrance.

First, there is the nice woodsy smell so delightful in the spring when the wilderness is free from snow. The tamaracks yield a slight aromatic blend to this, leafless as they are. My juvenile evergreens—all introduced—will increase this quality in the future.

The liverworts coating the ground in the bog, with their flat, leaf-like growths, have a cloying sweet odor, so individual that they could be recognized by that alone.

We know from afar when the willow catkins merge from furry pussies into yellow flower clusters, as well as the bees which are attracted by the honey-like smell that comes from the little nectar scale situated at the base of each staminate or pistillate flower above each downy bract.

The odor of plum and cherry blossoms is reminiscent of their fruits, while one is almost overpowered by the fragrance of the hawthorns—spectacular features of the garden when covered with their fleece of bloom.

Most agreeable and sweetest of all is the small white violet which carpets the swamp. The Canadian violet, introduced in large numbers, is also delicately fragrant.

But for delicacy and sweetness I think every flower must yield the palm to Linnaea.

I have not yet succeeded in naturalizing trailing arbutus, which is perhaps a more universal favorite. Our showy orchid might compete with this in beauty and richness of perfume.

It is impossible to describe an odor. Comparison with other odors fails in indicating the individual quality, which is always *sui generis* [one of a kind]. For instance, the odor of cypripediums reminds me of that of strawberries, but this conveys no true idea of it.

For spicy odors we resort to the rootstalks of sarsaparilla, *Aralia nudiflorum* [*A. nudicaulis*], wild ginger, and sweet flag with its peculiar tang. Their leaves hold them in less degree. Unfortunately, sassafras is not a native of Minnesota.

Who does not love the fragrance of wild grape blossoms? And again that of the ripe fruit? It would be interesting to determine how much of our enjoyment in tasting fruits comes from their pleasing fragrance. . . .

Now and then I find a fragrant specimen of marsh fern, *Aspidium thelypteris* [*Thelypteris palustris*], and at times the interrupted fern is slightly fragrant. Very delightful is the odor of the beautiful *Dicksonia*—introduced—my favorite fern and also Thoreau's!

After a rain, we sniff the air with delight, saying, "Oh yes, there's balm in Gilead!" as we pass a young balsam poplar that has been planted near one of the foot paths.

Favored visitors are allowed to bruise a leaf to extract the perfumes of sweet gale, benzoin (introduced), wild bergamot, wild anise, *Galium circaezans* [wild licorice], *Dalea alopecuroides* [*D. leporina*, foxtail dalea] (elusively sweet), mountain mint (*Pycnanthemum* [*P. virginianum*]) which must nearly equal the European sweet basil in fragrance, and aromatic sumach (introduced). Some also like to revive the memories of childhood by inhaling the stronger odors of tansy, catnip and ground ivy [creeping Charlie] (all naturalized species). The common wild

mint, *Mentha* [*Mentha arvensis var. glabrata*], makes its presence known as we walk over it in the meadows.

Pungent and less agreeable odors we obtain from bruising the fruit of mountain ash and the leaves of the pasque flower, *Anemone patens* [*Pulsatilla nuttalliana*]; prairie clover, *Petalostemum* [*P. candidum*]; and wormwood, *Artemisia* [*A. serrata*].

June, of course, is redolent with wild roses and the blossoms of locust. In September, the meadows abound in the lovely, sweet-scented ladies' tresses, *Spiranthes* [*S. cernua*]. Lastly, in the fall, we are greeted by a compound of agreeable odors as we walk scuffling the leaves under our feet.

Early History of
Eloise Butler Plant Reserve, February 1915

Effective Coloring in the Wild Garden That Is Not Due to Flowers

I HAD DECIDED TO WRITE a little on this subject before reading in the November [1915] *Garden Magazine*, Mr. E.H. Wilson's delightful paper on "The Glory of the Autumn." He says, "No scene in nature is more delightful than the woods of eastern North America in the fullness of their autumn splendour." The forest region of Minnesota may be included in this eulogy. . . .

The first note of the brilliant color of the waning year is struck by the red maple, *Acer rubrum*, which is abundant in all stages of growth in the wild garden. Its poignant beauty persists until after the first heavy frosts. In the spring, this tree glows brilliant in fruit as well as in flower. When the maple leaves fall, the oaks begin to put on their gorgeous crowns in many shades of red, bronze, and russet brown, set off by the yellow leaves of the birch and poplars, the gleaming white stems of the birches and the dark green foliage of the tamarack. The white oaks lend a distinctive tint of a peculiarly rich mulberry red. Nature makes a lavish use of pigments on many of the shrubs and low bushes. The sumachs cover the landscape here and there with floods incarnadine; and the woodbines, or Virginia creepers, are trailing clouds of glory; the viburnums show deep red; the dark pink leaves of the waahoo are succeeded by fruit-tassels of coral pink and red; the foliage of the black currant, *Ribes floridum*, is rimmed and streaked with red; and the blackberry's vicious prickles are forgiven when its leaves are like the petals of damask roses.

The ground blazes where the blueberry appears, or the malignant poison ivy, and flecks of crimson or scarlet mark the position of flowering spurge, *Euphorbia corollata* and of *Epilobium coloratum* [willow herb]; and the miniature poinsettia, *Euphorbia heterophylla* [*E. ayathophora*], decks its green bracts with a scarlet blotch at the base.

All this brilliancy is enhanced in the garden by the young evergreen trees, the evergreen ferns and trailers in the swamp, and by the persistent green of some of the deciduous trees and shrubs, like locust and *Ceanothus* [*C. americanus*, New Jersey tea]; and variety is added by the mottled leaves of *Geum macrophyllum* [large-leaved avens], *Heuchera americana* [alum root], and the rosettes of evening primrose, while the patches of *Epipactis* [helleborine], of three species, in their white tracery are a never-ending delight.

Fruits often excel flowers in richness of color. I have already mentioned the fruits of red maple and waahoo. To classify by color, various shades of red are represented by the following: *Sambucus racemosa* [red-berried elder] appears early in summer, a veritable Queen of Sheba against a background of green; the birds scarcely allow us a glimpse of the sweet Juneberry, and the children cull the fragrant strawberries on the hillsides; the brilliant pomes of the hawthorns and the rosehips endure for a longer period, also the fruits of mountain ash. The red raspberry disappears quickly, but not in the same way; the strawberry-blite, *Chenopedium capitatum*, or the red baneberry; the fruits of trillium, smilacina [false Solomon's seal], Jack-in-the-pulpit, wild calla, green dragon, twisted stalk, bearberry, coral berry, *Ilex verticillata* [holly], Canadian holly, *Lonicera* [honeysuckle], and of the vines, bittersweet, matrimony vine and *Solanum dulcamara* [bittersweet]. The bright berries of *Panax quinquefolium* [*P. quinquefolius*, wild ginseng] may not escape the ginseng hunter, but he passes by the smaller *P. trifolium* [dwarf ginseng or ground-nut]. Birds and children quickly despoil the various cherries and the yellowish red wild plum and the buffalo berry of their fruits, but the swamp affords some protection from children to bunchberry (*Cornus canadensis*), cranberries,

May apple, *Mitchella repens* [partridgeberry], dewberry, [and] red currant. The introduced boxberry, *Gaultheria procumbens*, and mountain cranberry, *Vaccinium vitis-idaea*, are too sparse to attract attention. The large, showy thyrsi of the stag-horn sumac must not be omitted from this list; neither many vermilion-hued fungi—the red cup of early spring, *Sarcoscypha coccinea*; the swamp *Boletus pictus* [*Suillus spraguei*]; the little *Hygrophorus conicus* [*Hygrocybe conica*], rosy russulas; and the deadly *Amanita muscaria*. Very pleasing, too, are the red tipped lichens, species of *Cladonia*. I had nearly forgotten the berry-like fruit of "ground hemlock," *Taxus canadensis*, and the beautiful high-bush cranberry, delicious preserves for the Bohemian waxwing and jelly for humans.

Among blue or purple fruits we have the wonderful blues of cohosh, clintonia, of *Cornus amomum* [red willow], *C. circinata* [*C. rugosa*, round-leaved dogwood], [and] *C. alternifolia* [pagoda dogwood]. Other blues, lighter or darker, are blueberries, grapes, moonseed (*Menispermum*), fruits of woodbine, juniper, *Lonicera caerulea* [*L. villosa*, mountain-fly-honeysuckle], [and] *Viburnum pubescens* [*V. rafinesquianum*, downy arrow-wood].

Dark purple or black fruits: buckthorn, *Rhamnus alnifolia*; blackberry; thimbleberry, *Rubus occidentalis*; sheepberry; smilax of several species; black currant, *Ribes floridum* [*R. americanum*]; *Aralia nudicaulis* [sarsasparilla]; *Aralia racemosa* [spikenard]; Solomon's seal; gooseberry; chokeberry, *Sambucus canadensis* [common elder]; [and] hackberry, purplish brown in color.

Yellow fruits: *Crataegus punctata* [hawthorn]; horse gentian, *Triosteum perfoliatum*; deerberry; [and] chokecherry [*Prunus virginiana*] var. *leucocarpa*.

Greenish white or white fruits snowberry; creeping snowberry, *Chiogenes hispidula* [*Gaultheria hispidula*]; wolfberry; white baneberry; poison ivy; poison sumach, *Cornus asperifolia* [*Rhus vernix*]; *C.* Baileyi [*C. stolonifera var. balieyi*]; *C. stolonifera* [red-osier dogwood]; *C. paniculata* [*C. racemosa*, dogwood]. The fruits of white baneberry and *Cornus paniculata* [*C. racemosa*] are given additional beauty by their red stalks. Under this head may be placed the fluffy appendages of dry fruits or seeds which add in their season a conspicuous note to the landscape: clematis; cotton grass, *Eriophorum angustifolium*; the pappus of many composites, as dandelion, thistle, *Senecio* [ragwort] . . . and [the] appendages of seeds, as willow and milkweed.

Quaker grey and silver are furnished by many of the artemisias, by the foliage and fruit of the silver berry, *Elaeagnus argentea*; by poverty grass, *Hudsonia tomentosa*; cudweed; and *Salix candida* [hoary willow].

The tones of grasses are potent to charm and almost defy classification. I will mention a few of my favorites without attempting to define the color: Indian grass, *Sorghastrum nutans*; *Andropogon scoparius* [little bluestem, *schizachyrium scoparium*]; *A. furcatus* [*A. gerardi*]; *Eragrostis pectinacea*; *Phragmites communis* [*P. australis*]; *Bromus ciliatus* [Brome-grass]; *Glyceria canadensis* [rattlesnake-grass]; and of the sedges, *Scirpus validus*, *S. sylvaticus* [*S. microcarpus*], [and] *S. atrovirens*.

Our oaks, except *Quercus macrocarpa* [bur oak], retain their leaves in winter, and though turned to dusky brown, still give variety to the landscape. When the birds have eaten the fruit and the deciduous trees and shrubs are bare, the stems of dogwoods and roses make a cordon of red and purple about the garden swamp, and the willows light up gray days with sunshine-yellow. The sense of color can also be gratified in noting the gradations of tints in trunk, branches and outmost twigs. It is interesting to distinguish trees by the color of their bark as well as by their leaf forms and general architecture. The twigs of trees show soft, bright tints, and there is much individuality in the color of buds. To note but a few: the mouse-colored buds of box elder; the bitter nut, sulphur-tinted; the American elm, appleseed brown; those of basswood like red shellac. Of course, the color of tree trunks varies with age. Everyone admires the conspicuous bolls of the white birch, but [those] of the yellow birch [are] like old brass; the mountain ash like copper; the red maple is ash-pink; the aspen, pale greenish gray.

I particularly love the color tones of spring when the buds are beginning to unfold. They are more difficult to characterize, and I wish to renew my impressions before I make the attempt.

Early History of
Eloise Butler Plant Reserve,
December 1915

Experiences in Collecting

THE WILLOW HERB, or fireweed, is . . . [a] plant with a history. I thought that this showy flower would have a fine effect massed in the meadow against the background of tamaracks. The fireweed is scarce in the immediate vicinity of Minneapolis, but I knew where a full acre of it grew in Massachusetts. Whence a large quantity of what was supposedly fireweed was dug up, transported, and planted in the garden [in 1907], only to learn at blossoming time that it was not fireweed at all but another insignificant species of the genus already established in the garden and, if anything, too abundant in the place.

The next season, at the close of the summer's vacation, after having enjoyed for a week or more huge bouquets of fireweed, I went confidently to the place again for specimens to take to Minneapolis, when not a blade of the plant was to be seen. The ground had been burned over, ploughed and harrowed, and seeded down with another crop. I looked for it at another station, a mile distant, but there a cow had been tethered, and had left not a wrack behind in her foraging.

For some other plants I had scoured in vain wild land in Massachusetts, although I was assured that they were common and might be found anywhere. My friends said consolingly, "Perhaps you can get them on the way back to Minneapolis." But I said, "Impossible. Everything at a railway station is cleared away, and there is nothing but a desolate sandy waste, or else a spick-and-span garden of geraniums, castor bean and canna, with unclimbable barbed wire fencing off the wilderness."

The prophecy, however, was fulfilled. My train was wrecked (fortunately without loss of life) in the wilds of Ontario; and there, on either side of the track, were growing the elusive fireweed, [and] the other long-looked for plants, with rarities besides—and nothing to dig them up with but a broken penknife! In the enforced delay, lasting from morning till night, this small difficulty was overcome. Going farther afield in every direction, although false alarms and the fear of missing the train were the cause of briar-rent gown and headlong tumbles in the frantic rushes back to the track, I found, it seemed instinctively, just what I most desired; and my suitcase, regardless of the rights of clothing, was crammed with the spoils of accident.

But, shortly after my return, such is the contrariety of Fate, I came across a quantity of fireweed in several happy hunting grounds beyond White Bear Lake, so we are no longer dependent on a foreign land for a supply of it.

Who of the participants in the adventure can ever forget about the acquisition of squirrel corn [*Dicentra canadensis*]? Much to their delight, the teachers of botany learned of a station for squirrel corn on one of the large islands [Big Island] of Lake Minnetonka. This plant is local and is found abundantly in a few favored places, unlike its relative, the Dutchman's breeches, which grows all about us in rich woodlands. The squirrel corn has a similar foliage, but the flowers are white and larger, and heart-shaped, like another of the same genus—the cultivated bleeding heart— and are delightfully fragrant. The name comes from the small, subterranean tubers—round and yellow, like kernels of Indian corn.

After a long journey by water and pathless woodlands, the teachers came to the designated place, where they stood aghast before a recently constructed fence, some nine feet high, of strong, large meshed chicken wire, attached to stout iron poles, with a row of barbed wire close to the ground, three more rows of barbed wire at the top, surmounted by three horizontal rows of the same sort.

Experienced as they were in getting over barriers of all sorts, they thought this, at first, unsurmountable. Nevertheless, one of the party seized a trowel and began to dig in desperation a passage-way under the fence. How long a task this would have been is an undetermined question. Another collected long poles, which she wove in and out over the top wires. These were draped by a thick waterproof recklessly sacrificed to the cause, and then the fence was scaled, and the plants gathered in deathly silence, from fear of arrest for trespass.

[The teachers] were then informed by a loyal neighbor of the owner of the property, who had deemed the fence beyond their powers, of a hole on the other side of the enclosure, where a sewer was being dug, through which, by dint of flattening themselves to the ground, they wriggled and crawled like rats—dusty and triumphant!

A Wild Botanic Garden, 1911

I had but one clump of white cypripedium [lady's-slipper] in my wild garden and that had been given to me. What I bought from eastern florists refused to grow. This clump has blossomed for three years in succession, but this spring I had but one blossom because some vandal had picked the flowers the year before. I find that when the flowers of cypripediums and trilliums are picked that they do not flower the following year. If any blossoms appear they are due to leafy stems that were infertile or without flowers. For, as you know, if the leaves—the food manufacturers—are picked off, no more food is stored up in the roots below for the next year's growth.

The white cypripedium is local. I had been told of various places where it grew profusely but failed to find them. A friend phoned me a few days ago that she had spotted them several miles out of town. So we planned to "go for" them. We had to get up at five o'clock in order to make the train. When we left the train we expected to be met by another friend who was to drive us to the place to be explored several miles farther away. But no one was there. It had rained heavily the night before and was not yet clear so that no one dreamed that we would make the venture.

Should we take the next train home? No, never! We kilted our skirts and, weighted with impediments, trudged through the wet grass some three miles across the country until we found a farmer who was willing to take us where we were bound to go. We had a pair of stout farm horses and a long heavy truck, big enough and to spare. The *Tradescantia* [spiderwort] was out in full force, set off by great clumps of orange puccoon, *Lithospermum gmelini* [*L. carolinense var. croceum*]. Now and then we passed patches of the strikingly beautiful large-flowered Pentstemon. We drove as far as we could. Then we had to walk a long distance through meadows to reach our plants. It did not rain, and the overcast sky was the ideal condition for such a tramp. The meadows were full of yellow cypripediums, both the large and small varieties, and scores of the showy cypripedium in bud. We came upon large expanses of *Castilleia coccinea* [Indian paintbrush] with heavy heads of luxuriant scarlet bloom, with a few yellow ones by way of contrast. Never had we seen them in such magnificent profusion.

The haunt of the white cypripediums was an open meadow full of hummocks of tufted grasses and sedges surrounded by deep pools of water. The flowers grew on the hummocks and were hard to spade on account of the intertwined and matted roots of the sedges. In drier meadows we found *Polygala senega* [seneca-snakeroot], *Valeriana edulis* [*var. ciliata*, valerian] just going out of blossom, and zygadene [white camas] and Turk's-cap and wood lilies in bud. On an unwooded hill was a spring surrounded by pitcher plants in full flower and all the different cypripediums again. I had never seen pitcher plants in such a situation before. The soil was peculiar—a fine gray-colored clay, seemingly intermixed with sand.

We were enthusiastic over our "finds." My friend said, "California can't offer anything equal to this!"

We packed our treasures in gunny sacks and had no difficulty in getting them home, as we were met by autos at the other end of the line.

Annals of the Wild Life Reserve,
May 1914

* * *

The photographer of the garden [Mary Meeker] and the curator, the latter part of August, were so fortunate as to be the guests for a few days of Mr. Hazzard, the Superintendent of the Minnesota Division of the Interstate Park of Minnesota and Wisconsin, at Taylors Falls. We were given possession of Mr. Hazzard's summer cottage at the park, which is luxuriously fitted for the accommodation of several guests. Although the park is of primary interest to the geologist on account of its wonderful rock formations, it is a first-class hunting ground for the botanist.

I will not attempt to describe the geologic features of the place, for I was familiar with them and gave them only a cursory glance, and I was determined to discover the rare, fragrant fern, *Aspidium fragrans* [*Dryopteris fragrans*], listed some thirty years ago in Upham's *Catalogue of the Flora of Minnesota* [1884], at Taylors Falls. I have never seen a greater display and denser massing of *Polypodium vulgare* [*P. virginianum*, polypody], *Woodsia ilvensis* [woodsia], *Camptosorus rhizophyllus* [walking fern], *Cystopteris bulbifera* [bulblet fern], and *C. fragilis* [fragile bladder fern]. All that I had to help me in my search

was a mental picture of the illustration of *Aspidium fragrans* [*Dryopteris fragrans*] in [Willard] Clute's *Ferns and Their Allies* [probably *Our Ferns in their Haunts: A Guide to all the Native Species* (1901)]. The young and mature fronds of *Woodsia ilvensis* differ considerably, and many a time I was falsely lured to climb precipitous ledges. My chief reliance in identification was the sense of smell. So I climbed sniff-sniffing at every frond that had a suspicious appearance. I found several fragrant fronds, but I was not positive that I had secured the prize. On the third and last day of our visit, when I was making a farewell round of the place and had given up all hope of finding the fern, I espied a specimen that sent a thrill along my spinal cord. "There's my fern!" I exclaimed.

"No, it isn't," scoffed the photographer. "It's only another rusty woodsia, just like hundreds all around here."

"O, I am sure this time," said I.

"Don't you try to get it. You'll break your neck if you do!"

"You keep still!" I commanded. "I can and will get it!"

By holding onto a not-overly-strong root of sumach, I managed to secure the plant. One sniff at it made assurance doubly sure—such an indescribable compound of sweet odors!—and the plant was tossed to the photographer with a "There, didn't I tell you so?"

I have no doubt but that more of this aspidium could be found at Taylors Falls under more favorable conditions. The season was so dry that many fronds were reduced to powder and could not be distinguished. This one specimen grew in a cool, sheltered place.

I was also able to obtain specimens of the floating white water crowfoot. I had never found specimens of it before in Minnesota. In a deep ravine skirting an ancient Indian trail that had on its course an as-yet-unexplored mound, I found an unusually rich growth of *Epipactis pubescens* [*Goodyera pubescens*, downy rattlesnake-plantain]. I also added to my collection a species of cactus which I have not identified. It grew in moss in the crevices of a ledge.

Annals of the Wild Life Reserve,
October 1916

The Quest of the Walking Fern

CAMPTOSORUS RHIZOPHYLLUS is popularly known as the walking fern, on account of the runners that develop from the tips of the mature leaves and take root to form new plants, which thus "walk" on from year to year.

The fern is local and is said to flourish best in soil of limestone origin. Two founders of the Wild Garden went to Osceola, Wisconsin [in May 1908] to obtain some of the fern. Osceola is a picturesque little village, with high, limestone bluffs overlooking the St. Croix River. It is about two hours by rail from Minneapolis and has two daily trains, one leaving Minneapolis in the morning and the other returning in the early afternoon. Considerable time and labor were spent the day before in transporting and forming a bed of calcareous earth for the reception of the plants in the garden. On arriving at Osceola, as the day proved hot, the collectors obtained permission to hang their wraps in the office of the station, to be free of unnecessary impediments in the toilsome climb before them. The present fashion of pocketless gowns also necessitated that the one having a convenient handbag should carry the valuables of the other.

Although the collectors were familiar with the grounds and knew from former visits just where to look for the specimens, a long and patient search failed to reveal them. The place had evidently been despoiled. Keen, indeed, was their disappointment. They finally became separated in their search, and one of them did not appear at the station in time for the journey home. The other [Eloise Butler], fancying that her companion might, at the last moment, reach the train from the opposite side, snatched the wraps of both in desperate haste and boarded the train, only to discover her error and hence to get off at the first stop to investigate the cause of the apparent accident. She found herself at the farther end of a very long and high railroad bridge, which must be crossed to get back to Osceola. It was then broiling hot, and she was weighed down with the heavy wraps and all that she could lift of earth and plants. She essayed the bridge with fear and trembling, lest she should be hurled into the depths below by a passing train. The sleepers were far apart, and, looking down to keep her footing, she became dizzy

and had to summon all her grit to . . . get across the bridge. "How long is the bridge?" she asked. "Half a mile," was the reply. It seemed to her more than twice that distance. And even then she was nearly five miles from the village, and with no conveyance except a hand-car, which could not leave until the close of the working-day. During the long wait, she pictured her friend lying dead, or with broken bones, in some dark ravine. Under other circumstances, the ride on the hand-car would have been enjoyed as a novel experience. The car was piled high with pickaxes and spades, among which were perilously perched some fifteen Italian laborers. A seat was arranged at the back of the car for the distracted woman, who sat bent forward to avoid the revolving machinery, and with dangling feet, which were drawn up quickly, every now and then, as they struck the sleepers. The rare plants of the railway cutting, so close at hand and easily seen by reason of the slow movement of the car, were passed unheeded.

Reaching Osceola, she could find no trace of the missing one. She hoped against hope that her companion was safe somewhere in the village and would appear in time for the next morning's train, but her heart failed when she thought that she must finally telephone the circumstances to the relatives in Minneapolis, perhaps needlessly alarming them and causing them a sleepless night. It was now nearly dusk. The town marshal was summoned to aid in the search. As she hurriedly climbed the cliff again, shouting at intervals the name of her friend, what did she see in the failing light but a large mass of the walking fern! Up it was torn, or rather, *clawed*, root and all—the ruling passion strong in death, so to speak—she, blunting the pricks of conscience by the resolve to throw the plants away if any harm had come to her friend. At length it was learned from inquiries at the station, which had been closed through the period of searching, that the lost one was slowly but safely pursuing her homeward way by freight train, carrying with her the purse and return ticket of the other, who was, in consequence, obliged to beg from strangers food and lodging and money for the fare to Minneapolis.

The walking fern was planted in the wild garden, where it has survived one winter's cold, and where we trust it will continue to commemorate its story.

The Quest of the Walking Fern, 1909

Garden Experiences

"Mistress Mary, so contrary,
How does your garden grow?"

LIKE MISTRESS, LIKE GARDEN is the reply. In quirks, in whimsies, and in sheer contrariness a wild garden surpasses Mistress Mary. This is true especially of the introduced species. Last summer a robust specimen of *Aster multiflorus* [*A. ericoides*] appeared in the marsh, although it had been placed where it ought to be contented when transplanted from the dry prairie. *Gentiana andrewsii* [closed gentian] has been naturalized by the brook, and now it comes spontaneously on the dry hillsides. *Viola conspersa* [American dog-violet] was found in large masses putting to shame carefully nurtured specimens planted at the opposite end of the swamp. The showy *Liatris pycnostachya* [blazing-star] has chosen to appear of itself in the meadow, and the little twayblade, *Liparis loeselii*, has established itself at a distance from the planted colony. The royal fern, *Osmunda regalis*, not indigenous to the garden, as was supposed, but laboriously dug and transported from miles away to the borders of the swamp, has mysteriously sprung up in the center. The most superb growth of *Orchis spectabilis* [*Galearis spectabilis*, showy orchis] is also unaccounted for, in somewhat dry and infertile soil, where no thoughtful gardener would ever think of placing it. *Castilliea coccinea* [Indian paintbrush], suspected of root parasitism, and accordingly lifted in large blocks of sod, rewarded repeated efforts last season with a single stalk; but at the same time another specimen was found in a seemingly unsuitable place. I have failed in cultivating *Epilobium angustifolium* [fireweed], although I have planted it both in the spring and in the fall—in season and out of season, from various places and in different situations. Two years ago it broke out in two widely separated spots where it had not been consciously introduced. I have had a similar experience with Indian pipe, *Monotropa uniflora*, but difficulty with a saprophyte was to be expected. Last summer there was no sign of Indian pipe, although to my surprise and joy it was abundant for the two previous seasons.

I have thought that I knew every foot of my garden and the position of every sizeable plant in it, but I have had so many surprises that I am no longer confident. *Lythrum alatum* [winged loosestrife] is a case in point. I wanted to obtain some for the wild garden and looked for it in vain through four seasons. Then I came across a large patch of it in full bloom in the garden! It is not uncommon, and I have since found it in abundance elsewhere.

The hazelnut, *Corylus americana*, is a superfluity in my garden, but I have been watching with interest the development of some introduced specimens of *C. rostrata* [*C. cornuta*]. I felt rather foolish last summer when I discovered a lot of the latter in my bog loaded with the long beaked fruit. It is listed for the northern part of the state, and I never dreamed of finding it in Minneapolis. With the exception of the fruit, it differs but little from *americana*. At about the same time I discovered also the thimbleberry, *Rubus occidentalis*. This, too, was in fruit and thereby easily distinguished from the more common red raspberry. But how blind I was not to notice before the thick white bloom on the stems!

Teucrium canadense [American germander] is another newcomer. This has followed in the wake of the extermination of Canada thistle.

Shaking my digger at *Zygadene chloranthus* [*Zigadenus glaucus*, white camass] and *Veratrum viride* [false hellebore] and threatening to replace them with something more tractable, brought them to luxuriant blossoming, although they had not shown even a smitch of a flower bud during five years of zealous care. The *zygadene* bears an elongated raceme of attractive greenish-white shallow bells. The *Veratrum* . . . is a stout, tall plant with large plaited leaves and a many-branched panicle of innumerable small green flowers. Its hugeness makes it noticeable.

A specimen of *Rubus odoratus*, the beautiful flowering raspberry—its large rose-colored flowers and maple-like leaves familiar to many under cultivation—was procured from cold Ontario, but it died down to the ground every winter and was as effortless as the first Mrs. Dombey [a character in Charles Dickens' novel *Dombey and Son* (1846)]. Last season it was piqued by jealousy to sprouting into a big bush which blossomed and blossomed, outdoing every plant of that kind that I have ever seen. I merely planted around it a quantity of *Rubus parviflorus*, the salmon berry, saying, "I am sure I shall like these as well. They have beautiful white flowers, leaves as fine as yours, *Odoratus*, and better tasting fruit of an unusual color."

... I have planted a good deal of *Erythronium albidum* [white trout lily], but have had but two blossoms, although I have been careful to select two-leaved specimens after the fruit has matured. The leaves come up all right. It seems to require a long time to recover from transplanting. I have seen the flowers in abundance in open meadows and again on limestone bluffs. *E. americana* [*E. americanum*, yellow trout lily], on the other hand, blossoms freely in my bog near where I have set the *albidum*.

A florist in New York raises *Gentiana crinita* [fringed gentian]. He says that the first season's growth from the seed is very tiny. His methods may be learned from consulting *Garden Magazine* some four years back.

Annals of the Wild Life Reserve, c.1916

* * *

While I am about it, although destroying the literary unity of my paper—but where may one not ramble, if not in a wild garden?—I will give ... a more complete idea of how we have fought, bled and nearly died for the cause by recounting another adventure that might really be called a *hair-breadth* escape: I took two boys to the Wild Garden to help clear up the fallen brushwood and to put the place in order for the spring awakening. I was working some distance from them. Going near them to direct *their* work, I was astounded by their running to me, shouting at the top of their voices and beating me excitedly over the head. Do not form a hasty conclusion: They were young gentlemen and what they did was perfectly right and proper. I had been attending to the burning of the brush. In some way a spark had kindled on the top of my hat, and I had been moving serenely about, emitting flames and smoke, like a small volcano, while a crater was forming in the crown of my hat. I had been wondering all the while at the peculiar odor of the burning brush and supposing, when blinded and choked by the smoke, that the wind had veered since the starting of the fire. If the boys had not been at hand, the accident might have been serious. As it was, my hat was a charred ruin and my hair, which I could ill afford to lose, was about one-quarter burned away. Some visitors came into the garden during the afternoon, but I sent every one home and waited alone until it was dusk, skewering my hat together with safety pins and filling up the hole in the crown with a big rose that had survived the fire. I hoped that in the crowd [on the streetcar] and darkness, my peculiar head-gear would pass unnoticed.

A Wild Botanic Garden, 1911

* * *

The enforced rest due to three years of drought and a goodly amount of snow last winter resulted in an unusual abundance of fruit on trees and shrubs. I cannot recall a like harvest. Dogwood, mountain ash, prickly ash, viburnum, shadbush, cherry, and hawthorn, vied with the glorious autumnal foliage in making a brilliant landscape.

At Miss Leavitt's request, I will add an account of one of the many vagaries in wild gardening: Are you all familiar with prairie dock, *Silphium terebinthinaceum*, belonging to the same genus as the famous compass plant, *S. laciniatum*? It is a native of Minnesota but is not found near Minneapolis. A single specimen was given me nine years ago, and I planted it near my office. Every season it sent up its large green banners, but nary a flower. I hesitated to change the plant to another situation because of its large root and lest I might lose it altogether. So this last spring I gave it a "good talking-to" and bought half a dozen more prairie dock and planted them elsewhere. To my astonishment, the obstinate specimen sent up at once two tall stalks that burgeoned out into a number of sizable yellow flowers! I have had somewhat similar experiences. Does it mean that plants are sentient beings?

Annals of the Wild Life Reserve, December 1932

Occult Experiences of a Wild Gardener

"WHAT'S THIS, MISS BUTLER?" asked a pupil, holding up a wilted flower, as she took her seat in the classroom.

"I don't know. It is a cultivated flower, is it not?"

"No, it grows wild on the prairie."

"That doesn't seem possible. I never saw it before. What do *you* call it?"

"An anemone."

"I have never seen an anemone like that.

Bring me the whole plant, and I will analyze it."

As I was familiar with the prairie flora of the neighborhood, I continued to think that the plant was an escape from the garden. About a week afterward, the plant was brought in just as recitation was beginning. At one glance, without taking it in my hand, I said, "You are right. It *is* an anemone. It is the Carolina anemone." Then I was immediately stricken with astonishment at my own words, for I had never seen the Carolina anemone and could not have described it to save my life. But at the first free moment, I found that the botanies confirmed my rash statement.

Not many days later a group of teachers were talking about violets. One asked another, "How many violets are native to Minnesota."

"I do not know," was the reply. "Can you tell us, Miss Butler?"

"Seventeen," I flashed, as one would answer to "What is twice three," but immediately exclaimed, "*Why* did I say that? I haven't the slightest idea of the number." However, consulting two authorities, we found that the answer was confirmed.

Associates in botany have remarked to me, "You always find the plant you look for." I wished to get some leatherwood for the wild garden. It had died out from the place where I had found it years ago. One day a University student inadvertently asked me, "Do you know leatherwood?"

"Indeed I do. That is just what I wish most to see. Tell me where I can find some, and I will get it this very day."

Her ideas of its whereabouts were vague. She had seen it two years before near St. Thomas' School, but on what side of the buildings, or the road, she could not tell. With this direction, I scoured all the region about St. Thomas, without success. As it was then past the dinner hour and high time for me to go home, I left the place reluctantly and started for the streetcar. Suddenly, without conscious volition, but obeying a blind, unreasoning impulse, I turned and plunged on a bee-line into the woods. "Eloise Butler," I said to myself, "what are you doing? You are due at home." But on I went and walked directly into a pocket lined with leatherwood in full blossom—a place that I had never visited before. The whole affair seemed uncanny to me.

The following summer, merely out of curiosity, as I have no belief in spiritistic phenomena, I had a "sitting" with an alleged "medium," who was visiting the family. Among other queer remarks she said, "When you want a plant, you always find it. This is the cause of it: You have two friends, botanists, who are deeply interested in your work. It is as if they put their hands on your shoulders and pushed you toward the right place."

Then I laughed, saying, "That explains my experience with leatherwood." The medium, by the way, knew nothing about my work.

Two or three times since, I have put the matter to a test. When delayed by a railway wreck in Ontario, I wanted to find sweet gale. I walked aimlessly for some distance and came right upon it. Then I tried the other side of the railway in the same way, and successfully, for the yellow round-leaved violet.

At another time I wanted *Gentiana puberula* [*G. puberulenta*, downy gentian]. I had never gathered the plant. I only knew that it grew on the prairie. So I betook myself to the prairie and hunted until I was tired. Then I bethought myself of my *ghostly* friends and murmured, "Now, I will let 'them' push me!" Thereupon, I wandered about, without giving thought to my steps, and was just thinking, "The spell won't work this time," when my foot caught in a gopher hole, and I stumbled and fell headlong into a patch of the gentian.

September 20, 1913, I was planting more *Gentiana puberula* in the wild garden. I had just unwrapped the plants to set them in the holes prepared for them, when I was seized with another uncontrollable impulse, and I dropped my hoe, leaving the roots of the gentians exposed to the hot sun, and went quickly to the pond. [*Here the account ended, without further explanation. Butler's Garden Log entry dated 20 September 1913 reads: "Saw two crested wood ducks swimming in the little pond!"*]

Annals of the Wild Life Reserve,
c.1917

* * *

Old Andrew's Mount [is] the highest point in the garden. . . . The western slope of the mount and the meadows to the west and north are the most recent acquisitions of the garden. . . . A gravelly pit on this western slope marks a mystery. It was hollowed out and roofed over by a solitary called Old Andrew. Here, mailed in silence, he lived for several years, and no one knew his history. One day he disappeared. Weeks afterward, the body of a man past recognition was found in the vicinity. It may have been Old Andrew's, but there was no definite proof. At any rate, he was never seen again. His cave and trenches furrowing the meadow below, which he attempted to farm, are the only traces of his life among us.

Shortly after Old Andrew's cave was included in the garden, the curator's work was interrupted by the sound of an axe coming from that direction. Rushing up the incline to ward off the trespasser, she found no one, and heard nothing; but, when her work was resumed, the experience was repeated. This happened again and again, for two or three days in succession.

> A sense of mystery the spirit daunted,
> And said, as plain as whisper in the ear,
> The place is Haunted!
>
> [source unknown]

Old Andrew used to cut wood for the neighbors. Could he be the ghostly woodchopper? Means were at once taken to exorcise him. The cave was cleared of fallen tree trunks and branches. Basketfuls of violets, hepatica, wild columbine, and trailing fern, with a generous amount of rich loam, were dibbled in. And thereupon the "perturbed spirit" was induced to rest.

Annals of a Wild Garden, c.1914

Animal, Bird, and Insect Life in the Wild Garden

A LARGE NUMBER OF BIRDS nest in the garden, and during the season most of the migrants reported from the state have been noted in the garden. The tangled vine coverts, abundance of food and water, and protection from sportsmen have made the place a favorite resort of the birds. Song, vesper and swamp sparrows, catbird, bluebird, rose-breasted grosbeak, Baltimore oriole, brown thrasher, bobolink, marsh wren, scarlet tanager, [and] indigo bunting hold matins and vespers in the leafy aisles along the brook, while those of brilliant plumage, together with goldfinch, Maryland yellow-throat, yellow warbler, and the ruby-throated hummingbird gleam like jewels in the foliage or as they dart through the air. I have stroked baby crows too young to be timid, followed the whip-poor-will in his short flights through the swamp, seen bluebirds chase out the long-eared owl, the great bittern stiffen like a stick when he heard my footstep, and a pair of the rare created wood ducks swimming in my little pond. The red-shouldered hawks have nested and reared their young in the garden, and just the other day a covey of nine bobwhites were found in their retreat in the meadow.

All sorts of sappers and miners have homes in the garden. On the sides of the brook, round holes bordered with a ring of mud show where the cray-fishes abide. Many heaps of pulverized earth, sometimes, alas, in the midst of a plantation of choice flowers, are the roofs of gophers' dwellings. Big tunnels, probably enlarged by dogs in chase, mark the refuge of woodchucks. Squirrels find winter quarters in basements of decayed tree trunks, their roomy summer residences of interlaced twigs being high in the branches above. Immense mounds, which must have been built up from time immemorial, testify [to] the industry of the ant.

Trees and shrubs are hung with wasps' nests of various sizes. One season I counted fifteen of them and hardly a day passed when I was not warned by a painful prod that I was intruding on their premises. One kind of wasp has made a labyrinth in the ground, with the grass cut from the tunnelled entrance as if by a scythe. Another wasp built on the ground a flat paper nest as large as a dinner plate.

There are various despoilers of the garden. Last winter, mice—on account of some unusual condition, I suppose, as it never happened before—girdled, a foot or more up from the base, all the many young red maples in my swamp. (I applied melted paraffin, but its efficacy remains to be proved.)

A red aphid is a persistent pest on the wild golden glow, and sometimes it attacks goldenrod. Another species of aphid, noted too late for routing, curled up nearly every leaf on one of my beloved hawthorns.

The eggs of a vile smooth caterpillar are laid in the leaf buds of the common sumach. They hatch and eat the branches bare. Our two heavy frosts, which mowed down my ferns for the first time in the history of the garden, served one good turn by killing the sumach buds and with them the caterpillars. The second crop of leaves are free from the "varmints."

Another flying insect selects the buds of the sunflowers for an egg depository. Scarcely a bud escapes this infliction and my hillslopes are covered with thousands of sunflowers of several species. At this time, pulling apart the leaves of the buds discloses little wrigglers. These develop into slimy, sluglike creatures with prodigious appetites. My remedy is to "scrunch 'em,"—an endless and unpleasing task.

Among the doings of the animal folk in the garden, I was interested in noting the habit of the striped ground squirrel or gopher, *Citellus tridecemlineatus*. This pretty creature, with stripes mottled like the toad, although said to be the most carnivorous of squirrels, I saw eagerly eating panic grass, and again, the ripe heads of white clover.

Annals of the Wild Life Reserve,
June 1914

* * *

As I went into the garden early this morning, I had another surprise: a half-grown pig lay asleep on the hillside below my office! A neighboring farmer caught him by turning a big box over him, and he is now housed in the dog kennel on the place where I live. I thought of naming him Roley-Poley because he is so fat, or Endymion because we found him sleeping; but the boy in the house said, "Miss Butler, you must call him Rip, because his ear has been ripped on a barbed wire fence, and he sleeps like Rip Van Winkle."

Discovered a shapeless mass of damp earth and moss on the top of a wren bird-house set under the eaves of my office. It looked as if some sportive youth had flung it there. A few hours after it had taken a more definite shape, and I saw that it was the work of Mistress Phoebe. Will war be declared if the wrens take possession below?

Letter to Gray Memorial Botanical Chapter,
May 1916

* * *

The latest acquisition in my wild garden is a big boulder hauled in on a stone drag by four pairs of horses and chiseled out by a stone mason into a bird bath with four shelves, each about seven inches wide on a half-inch grade. It is much appreciated by the birds, who bathe in it early in the morning

and late in the afternoon and stop to take a drink in passing.

My phoebe, who raised two broods last year in a nest that she built over a wren box under the eaves of my office, returned this season and is now feeding her second brood.

The first of June, as I was clearing away the dead stalks of perennials near the edge of my swamp, I flushed a bird that I had only seen in pictures or as stuffed specimens in museums. It made a short, low flight and fluttered feebly to the ground as if it were wounded unto death. As I followed it, the bird repeated the feint several times, sometimes running for a little distance and peeking out at me from behind a bush with one bright eye. Of course, I understood that the bird was trying to lure me away from her nest, and I recognized from the long bill and bobbed tail that it was a woodcock. The next day I found her in the swamp with three little ones.

Annals of the Wild Life Reserve,
June 1917

The Wild Garden in 1925

A MOST UNUSUAL SEASON—spotted, indeed, if due to sun spots. In April, very hot weather that unduly stimulated vegetation. Then late frosts—ice forming May 26—that nipped aspiring flower buds. Some things were frozen four times. Therefore, no wild grapes, no May apples, nor several flowers. During May, heavy rains and cold weather, so that we said, "We'll not complain when the sun roasts us." June 2 a tornado swooped upon us from the northwest, uprooting trees and laying everything flat with wreckage. Fortunately, only a few lives were lost. The damages cannot be repaired in years. Through August and not yet fairly broken, the most protracted drought ever recorded in Minnesota. The hillsides in the Reserve have suffered severely, but the asters are holding their own fairly well. The usual crop of mushrooms [is] a complete failure.

Have had some pleasant outings to break the general dismalness. Went out on the prairies early in July when the wood lily mingled with the tall cream-colored spikes of zygadene [*Zygadenus elegans*, white camass] at its height, and on the low lands, large masses of showy moccasin flowers disported themselves. In August, spent two days at Lake Kabecona, about twenty-seven miles east of Itasca Park. There I saw for the first time in their native haunts the spurred gentian (*Halenia deflexa*), and the northern grass of Parnassus (*Parnassia palustris*). On a creek floated the pretty white water crowfoot in full bloom, and all the land was blue with harebells.

Strange to say, a little earlier, a single specimen of halenia was brought to me from the north to identify. From the venation, I thought it must be an endogen and tried to place it in the lily or orchid families. Over the telephone I got a hint from one who knew, that it must belong to the gentian family, although the name could not be recalled. The small flowers were cream colored and spurred. Then, "spurred gentian" flashed through my mind, and also the scientific name, *Halenia deflexa*, although I had no consciousness of previous knowledge. The botanies confirmed the wireless telegram. This is another instance of several experiences that I have had of unconscious registration. We all really know much more than we are aware of. . . .

Letter to Gray Memorial Botanical Chapter, October 1925

Spring Exhibits in the Native Plant Reserve

I ARRIVED HERE as usual April 1 [1928]. There had been abundant snow during the winter, but at this time the weather was dry and warm. On account of the drought there was nothing in evidence except white [silver] maple, hazel, willow and alder. But on the afternoon of April 2, one or two buds of hepatica showed color and the venturesome flowers of *Trillium nivale* [snow trillum] began to open. The hepaticas were truly wonderful the greater part of the month. They withstood two heavy snowfalls on the 5th and the 13th, and several succeeding frosts with undiminished loveliness, and now the beautiful clumps of new leaves are fully grown and will be a joy throughout the year.

Before *Trillium nivale* had finished shedding, the showy red-purple *T. erectum* [purple trillium] appeared, followed before the 10th of May by all the glorious rout—*T. declinatum* [*T. flexipes*, declining trillium], *grandiflorum* [large-flowered trillium], *recurvatum* [recurved trillium], *sessile* [sessile trillium], and last of all the endemic *T.*

cernuum [nodding trillium]. The petals of *grandiflorum* have turned pink and are now beginning to shrivel, but the purple *recurvatum* with its pretty blotched leaf and the western specimens of *declinatum* are still holding their own, while *T. cernuum* is at the height of bloom. [*Trillium nivale, T. declinatum, T. grandiflorum,* and *T. cernuum* are Minnesota natives.]

Shortly afterward, the next great pageant was staged—literally acres of lowland bespread with [a] "cloth of gold"—marsh marigold. I sincerely pity those who are not privileged to see this flower in bloom. With marsh marigold came lovely *Mertensia virginica* (virginia bluebell), delighting the eye with its pink buds and lead-blue bells. At this writing the northern *M. paniculata* [bluebell, or tall lungwort] is beginning to blossom.

At the same time dense mats of spring beauty, *Claytonia virginica*, vivified the swamp. This pretty bell(e) is a welcome spreader. Its seeds are widely scattered, and the flower crops up in unexpected places, while *C. caroliniana* [broad-leaved spring beauty], with similar flower but shorter and broader leaf, remains stationary.

May is the time of flowering shrubs. Shadbush came early and soon disappeared, so also did the wild thorn, *Crataegus rotundifolia* [*C. chrysocarpa*]. I have yet to know if anything can surpass *Malus coronoria* [*Pyrus coronaria*, an eastern wild crab] in wealth of bloom. *Cornus stolonifera* [red-ozier dogwood] is now in full blossom and the other dogwoods and all the viburnums are preparing to follow speedily.

In April, the pretty yellow *Viola rotundifolia* [round-leaved violet] came and went, but the others were at their height the middle of May. The mats grow larger and denser every year. The prettiest one of all is . . . *V. septentrionalis* (early). It is clear white with a pale blue center and favors damp soil.

I had a clump of twisted stalk, *Streptopus roseus*, as big over as a bushel basket. It is a charming plant with the habit of *Uvularia* [bellwort] and hung with many tiny pink bells. The "twist" is in the pedicels.

The west path in the Reserve is called "Geranium Path," thickly beset, as it is, on either side with *Geranium maculatum* [wild geranium]. One would think that nothing else could find room there. But no, there is a succession before and after their advent. *Phlox divaricata* [wild blue phlox] is now in the ascendant. It came in late this season. I have known it to blossom with violets. I never tire of this phlox in many shades of pink and blue lavender merging into white. . . .

Masses of May apple, *Podophyllum peltatum*, and the cypripediums [lady's-slippers]—*C. parviflorum* [*C. calceolus* var. *parviflorum*, yellow], *pubescens* [*C. calceolus* var. *pubescens*, large yellow] and *acaule* [stemless]— now lend a tropical air to the Reserve. One clump of *C. candidum* [white lady's-slipper] has over forty blossoms. June 15 is expected to usher in the crowning event of the year—our wonderful state flower, *Cypripedium hirsutum* [*C. reginae*, showy lady's-slipper].

Letter to Gray Memorial Botanical Chapter,
June 1928

The Wild Garden in 1930

IT SEEMS AMAZING THAT Mother Nature—by blending two factors, temperature and moisture, in different proportions—can form an endless variety, no two seasons alike, [with] consequent variations in vegetation.

Spring was late and cold with continual downpours. The early blooms were much belated, but the last heavy frost was later than usual, so that the new foilage had had time to develop a resistant epidermis and did not suffer as in the year before, when May apple and twisted stalk were blighted and fern fronds seared. The flower buds of dogwoods and viburnums were, however, badly affected, and the food for birds was materially diminished. The unfolding buds of walnuts and hickories were, as usual, frozen. I despair of ever having any nuts develop.

The display of spring and summer flowers was fine—hepaticas, bloodroot, spring beauty, anemonella [rue anemone], anemones, marsh marigold, mertensia [bluebell], trilliums, violets, dentaria [toothwort], wild geranium, buttercups, showy orchis, habenarias [rein and fringed orchids], cypripediums [lady's-slippers], lilies, etc. Lupine (*Lupinus perennis*) was a great joy. As I have but little sandy soil, I have found it difficult to establish. I think that it is now a permanent possession. So also is horsemint (*Monarda punctata*) which thrives on a coal cinder diet. This plant is particularly effective in masses, growing, as it does, in large clumps, with its flower spikes made up of

whorl upon whorl of the pale yellow spotted corollas subtended by the more showy pink, velvety bracts.

Then followed the unprecedented midsummer drought. The wild garden suffers less than other places on account of the lie of the land—drainage flowing into it from three sides. But this season foliage of shrubs on the hillsides shriveled and dropped off. I did not mind the prickly ash dying, of which I have a superfluity. On this shrub during the early wet season there developed a disgusting scale insect enwrapping nearly every twig. The heroic remedy applied was pruning and burning, lest the pest might spread to other plants. I cannot tell until next season how many plants were killed outright by the drought. The most apparent effect was the smaller crop of autumn blooms and the scarcity of mushrooms. In one respect I was surprised. A year ago a drought prevented the annual appearance of the huge edible fan tuft (*Polyporus frondosus* [*Grifola frondosa*]) at the base of our venerable white oak. Sometimes it has attained a weight of over eighty pounds. This year it sprang up again and grew to a goodly size. It was taken up while still growing for the delectation of the Mushroom Club [the Minnesota Mycological Society].

Since I left Minneapolis this fall, an interesting discovery was made. A wild duck was given to a pair of ardent nature lovers [William and Martha Crone]. In dressing the bird, some undigested seeds of American lotus (*Nelumbo lutea*) were found in the gizzard. This was enough to start an investigation, for the lotus has been nearly exterminated in the vicinity of Minneapolis. The duck was shot near the neighboring town of Stillwater [actually Shakopee]. My friends thought that they knew every square rod of the territory. But a vigorous search revealed much to their delight a large tract of lotus that had been concealed in blossoming time by a rank growth of tall grasses. A quantity of seeds were collected and encased in balls of clay to serve as sinkers. The ponds around my garden were bombarded with these balls, and a quantity of seeds were sent me to distribute in Massachusetts. I have sent some to the director of Harvard's botanic garden, and some will be planted in the cemetery where my sister, Mrs. Cora E. Pease, lies buried. The lotus is said to be the largest flower of this latitude. The appearance is striking when the flower is in

full bloom. And the large top-shaped
receptacle is very singular. It breaks off [and]
rolls over and over in the water, shedding the
seeds through the perforated disk like a patent
seed dropper.

*Letter to Gray Memorial Botanical Chapter,
February 1931*

The Attractiveness of Vegetables and Common Weeds

I SOMETIMES THINK, if I have any mission
in this world, it is to teach the decorative value
of common weeds. A weed is simply a plant
out of place; or, as Emerson says, "A plant
whose virtues are not yet understood." I amuse
myself in summer by decorating the home
with what are generally considered ugly weeds,
often to be greeted with the exclamations—
"What a beautiful thing! Where did you get it,
and what do you call it?"

"Mullein," I may answer, or "sheep
sorrel," as the case may be, "which you well
know."

"Of course I do, but I never really saw it
before."

A sympathetic interest in nature is a
never failing source of delight. . . .

When in Massachusetts I never miss an
opportunity to see Mr. C.W. Parker's place at
Marblehead Neck. Mr. Parker is a wealthy
Bostonian, a prominent member of the
Massachusetts Horticultural Society, and an
enthusiast in regard to our native plants. He
has left his grounds facing the sea in their
natural ruggedness—a refreshing contrast to
some of the neighboring estates, whose owners
have failed to improve upon nature with their
artificial walls of masonry. The rare plants
from abroad do not stand out obtrusively but
blend with the landscape, every plant
appearing to belong in the place it occupies.
The haunting graces of wild life are retained;
no pruning is done except on fruit trees, and
the meadow is left unmown, that one may
enjoy the seldom appreciated flowers and fruits
of the grasses and sedges. Despised weeds are
raised to the dignity of cultivated plants and
rise uncropped from the well-kept turf, in
thriving luxuriance, as the mullein, the evening
primrose, and the Indian poke, to demonstrate
the truth that nature makes nothing
unbeautiful. . . .

On the borders of copses a graceful

composite, *Prenanthes alba*, may still be seen.
One notices the broad, halberd-shaped leaves
long before the flowering time and wonders
what sort of plant it is. And later one is sure
to mark the pendant bells of the flower heads
with their delicate, mauve-colored bracts
enclosing whitish petals. A closely allied species
has local repute in South Carolina and
elsewhere as a remedy for snakebites, so the
genus is known as rattlesnake root. This
"gall-of-the-earth" has subterranean tubers that
are bitter enough to counteract any virulence,
if, as was once believed, the more ill tasting the
medicine, the more potent it is to cure. The
flowers go to seed like the dandelion, but the
parachute of fine hairs that wafts the seed
abroad is tawny brown instead of white.

Dock is synonymous with backache to the
gardener, who unearths the long tap root again
and again; for it is difficult to remove in
entirety, and the usual result of his efforts are
more vigorous growth and a multiplication of
progeny. To use the leaves for greens is his
only compensation. The flowers of the docks
are a dull greenish yellow; but many achieve
beauty in the myriad [of] small, flattish,
triangular and slightly winged fruits in all
shades of red, yellow, and brown. You would
sing "Rule Brittania!" to see an arrangement of
tall swamp dock (*Rumex britannica* [*R.
orbiculatus*]) in an appropriate vase. Every
weed has decorative possibilities, and can be
used when hot-house or garden flowers are
lacking.

Life will be richer by the discovery of
beauty that we have hitherto passed
unheeding. Attractive bouquets can be made
even from the common sheep sorrel (*Rumex
acetosella*) that earlier in the season clothed
sandy hillsides with its low, spiry inflorescence
of red and yellow. The plant is a naturalized
weed, originally from Europe. Children know
the acid leaves as "sauer kraut." They can be
used for salad. A form similar to sheep sorrel
is cultivated in France for this purpose.

The large, coarse, basal leaves of the weed
burdock, novices are apt to mistake for
"pie-plant." A taste of the leaf would convince
them that this disagreeable composite is no
relation to the acid rhubarb which is allied to
the burless docks, just mentioned. The
burdock is a naturalized biennial from the old
world. The seeds that sprout this season form
the big leaves. Next year a large, bush-like
plant will develop, crowned with pink heads

surrounded with row upon row of barbed grappling hooks.

We can admire the symmetry of the rank growth and rejoice with the little girls who furnish their doll houses with elegant sofas, chairs, and bureaus made of the burs; but, before the seeds mature, the plant should be uprooted and burned to protect dogs and cattle from the discomforts of stinging prickles and matted fur, not to speak of the mortification of people who find themselves the "observed of all observers" on returning from an autumn walk, festooned and kilted by these "sticktights."

. . . A pink flowered variety of yarrow is a favorite in cultivated gardens. A botanist [Eloise Butler] from this country (exploring Jamaica, where what are to us rare and costly exotics grow wild by the roadside, free to any one who cares to gather them), was entertained by a wealthy planter. His hostess took much pride in her garden. What she cared for most of all and pointed out as curiosities were a few common northern plants, among them a lone, lorn, scraggly specimen of potted yarrow. In his surprise he exclaimed, "Oh, you cultivate our weeds and we cultivate yours!" Thus the unusual and foreign, even if inferior, is, by the majority, preferred.

We may esteem the yarrow for its steadfastness. In the middle of last November, when the surrounding vegetation was limp and blackened by frost, it was in full blossom. Any flower appeals to us when it blooms on the verge of ice-bound winter.

A Wild Botanic Garden, 1911

* * *

My household [has] been enjoying the last two weeks a peculiarly attractive plant: A cabbage was discovered by the cook that had developed a stalk over six inches long, bearing at the top a flat bunch of tiny flower buds. The outer leaves of the head were thin, papery and pale gray. The leaves along the stalk varied from silvery white to shades of delicate pale green. The cabbage was placed in a Japanese porcelain bowl that just fitted it and had the same shades of gray and green. No water was added. The stalk is now nearly two feet tall and the flat topped bud-cluster has burgeoned into a spreading panicle of pale yellow drooping flower bells. The cabbage in every stage has been a dream of beauty and the joy of all beholders. It might even get a

blue ribbon in the great horticultural exhibit now displayed in Boston.

My pupils were always delighted with a living hanging basket that I used to prepare for them. I selected a large carrot, cut off a due amount of the narrowed tip and hollowed out a portion of the center for a cavity to hold water, and made holes just before the rim for the insertion of suspension wires. The carrot was hung in a window, and, in a short time the incised, feathery leaves grew up reversely, revealing through them the rich orange yellow of the carrot.

I cannot help admiring the pariahs of my garden, although competition is so fierce I must needs destroy them. If rare and difficult to cultivate, one would travel miles to see the golden heads of dandelion or the gossamer balls of down when in seed. If it were not for its pernicious pollen, I would spare some ragweed on account of the beauty of its finely dissected foliage; and I like the massed effect of burdock, but cannot endure the matted, clinging burs. One of my most pleasing photos is that of the common horseweed, or Canada fleabane, *Erigeron canadense* [*Conyza canadensis*]—tall, graceful and fluffy in tropical luxuriance, which must be ruthlessly destroyed on account of its aggressive habit. Three stalwarts often attract the eye—dock, the bane of gardeners, with its curled leaves (the swamp *Rumex britannica* [*R. orbiticulatus*] has full sway with me); hemp, with its palm-like leaves; and mullein clothed in gray plush with large basel rosettes and heavy spikes of pale yellow. Nor can I resist the charm of sheep sorrel, *Rumex acetosella*, when it carpets the ground with rich colors, bearing dainty spikes of red and green. I often take up a mat to decorate the table. . . . The curly, prickly leaves and the softly bright flower heads [of the thistles] are to me altogether lovely. I make room for them, all except the Canada thistle which is a greater pest than quack grass when it once gains a foothold. I suppose it is unlawful to harbor the thieving dodder with its yellow stems looping, twisting and coiling about its victims and drinking their life-sap. Have you ever seen the species *glomerata* [*Cuscuta glomerata*] in blossom, enwreathing its host with a dense mass of tiny white blossoms? But I call "Halt" when it attacks my orchids.

I must add, however, that I haven't any sentiment to waste on sand burs, agrimony, or beggar's ticks with their beguiling flowers like

small forget-me-nots; or pitch forks, *Bidens*,
though they flaunt in their season a glorious
yellow. Life is too short to spend it a-picking
off stick-tights from one's clothing.

*Annals of the Wild Life Reserve,
April 1931*

Mallard Pool

EVER SINCE THE Native Plant Preserve
was started, I have wished to have a pool
constructed where two small streams converge
in an open meadow, the only pool in the
Preserve being too shady for aquatics. The
hard times gave this joy to me, for a jobless
expert did the work for a sum that could be
afforded by the Park Commissioners. The pool
is about thirty-five feet long, several feet
narrower, and of irregular outline. Indeed, the
contour is beautiful. The excavation was made
in a dense growth of cat-tails. While digging,
the workman saw a mallard duck wending its
way through the meadow with a train of four
little ones. Hence, the name of the pool, as this
duck had never been listed before in the
garden.

The voracious muskrat was also observed,
and I began to fear that the roots of my water
lilies would be gobbled up. It was thought that
stout wire netting at the top and bottom of the
pool would prevent the muskrats from
entering, but my adviser knew little of their
predatory habits. Some white water lilies were
planted in the pool. In two days, only a
fragment of the leaves could be found. Then it
was decided to encircle the pool with the
netting, sinking it two feet in the ground.
Before this work was completed, a muskrat
preempted the pool with two little ones. We
thought we could trap them inside and throw
them over the fence, but before the circuit was
complete, they left of their own accord,
probably in search of more food, and the gap
was closed against them. It is possible that they
will burrow under the fence. Traps must be set
next spring.

A neat rustic [bridge] of unpeeled
tamarack poles has been built across the
narrow lower end of the pool. Here one can
see at advantage the pool and the border.
Opposite, at the upper end, is "The Gurgler,"
the water entering gently by a short series of
low rapids. Here my ingenious bridge-builder
will insert a waterwheel made of galvanized tin
and about five inches in diameter, designed to
throw a mist-like spray over plants like
Pinguicula [butterwort] that flourish on
dripping rock. We call the place "Atlantic
City" because, at each end of the bridge a
plank walk was laid over the cat-tail slough.

Many desirable plants were already
established near or on the border of the pool:
Sagittaria latifolia [duck potato], *Eupatorium
maculatum* [Joe-Pye weed], *E. perfoliatum*
[boneset], *Verbena hastata* [blue vervain],
Epilobium coloratum [willow-herb], *Lythrum
salicaria* [purple loosestrife], *Mentha
canadensis* [M. arvensis var. glabrata, mint],
Rumex brittanica [R. orbiculatus, water-dock],
Solidago canadensis [Canadian goldenrod], *S.
uliginosa, Aster puniceus* [red-stalked aster], *A.
junceus* [A. borealis], *A. umbellatus, A.
paniculatus* [A. lanceolatus], *Asclepias incarnata*
[swamp milkweed], *Helianthus tuberosus*
[Jerusalem artichoke], *H. grosseserratus*
[sunflower], *Rudbeckia laciniata* [wild golden
glow], *Chelone glabra* [turtlehead], *Galium
asprellum* [rough bedstraw], *Caltha palustris*
[marsh marigold], *Impatiens biflora*
[jewelweed], *Aspidium thelypteris* [Thelypteris
palustris, marsh fern], *Onoclea sensibilias*
[sensitive fern], and an overplus like water
cress and cat-tail, and others that must be
grubbed out with ruthless hand—like *Cuscuta
gronovii* [dodder] and *Bidens cernua* [stick-
tight]. In the near vicinity are the grandest
species of our flora: *Cypripedium hirsutum* [C.
reginae, showy lady's-slipper], *C. parviflorum*
[C. calceolus var. parviflorum, small yellow
lady's-slipper], *C. pubescens* [C. calceolus var.
pubescens, large yellow lady's-slipper], *C.
candidum* [white lady's-slipper], and far
enough distant not to shade the pool, *Cornus
stolonifera* [red-ozier dogwood], *C. paniculata*
[gray dogwood], *Viburnum lentago*
[nannyberry], *V. opulus* [highbush cranberry],
and a few tamaracks.

The soil is a rich peaty loam. Here and
there on the border this was mixed with a due
proportion of sand to accommodate the plants
that will not grow except in wet sand. Large
sods of sand-lovers have been contributed by
friends of the garden, packed full of *Polygala
sanguinea* [milkwort], *P. cruciata* [cross
milkwort], *Viola lanceolata* [lance-leaved
violet], *V. sagittata* [arrow-leaved violet], *V.
arenaria* [V. adunca, hooked violet], *Eriocaulon
articulatum* [E. septangulare, pipewort], *Gratiola
aurea* [hedge-hyssop], *Steironema quadrifolium*

[loosestrife], *Xyris flexuosa* [*X. torta*, yellow-eyed grass], [and] *Hypericum canadense* [Canadian St. John's wort]. . . . This may seem too large a number of plants for a border, but the border is of indefinite width. It comprises nearly an acre and extends across the sunlit area of the marsh. I shall probably think of more desirable plants!

I intend the fence barring out the muskrats to be concealed by the tall herbaceous perennials.

Annals of the Wild Life Reserve,
October 1932

* * *

The little water wheel (to be removed during the winter lest the paddles be bent by ice) has been inserted in "The Gurgler," but the name has been changed to "The Jolly Spindrift." It chugs around so merrily, the spray splashing in the sunlight, that everyone smiles audibly when he sees it. I gave it the name at first sight, to find afterward that it is a new coinage, the compound not being in the dictionary. Below the rustic bridge another excavation has been made, continuous with the first, but more like a little pond, while the first is like a winding river emptying into it, increasing the length of the water area to fifty feet. I needed the "pond" for the display of the aquatic buttercup—white and yellow—which I hope the muskrats will find too bitter to eat. Otherwise, the pond must also be fenced. Some yews, "ground hemlock," have just been contributed to the border, whose bright green foliage will greatly add to the *toute ensemble*. Gratiola continued to blossom for some time after planting and marsh marigold began to bloom for the second time on the border. Even now, at the beginning of the work, the place with its setting is truly enchanting and I have to tear myself away from it. I shall dream of it all winter and conjure up the futurity of the plantings.

Annals of the Wild Life Reserve,
December 1932

Selected Bibliography

Published writings of Eloise Butler:

"An Active Desmid." *American Naturalist,* Vol. 16 (July 1882): p. 584.

"Desmids (*Desmidieae*)." *Botanical Gazette,* Vol. 11 (June 1886): pp. 148-149.

"Botanizing in Jamaica." *Postelsia, The Year Book of the Minnesota Seaside Station, 1901* (St. Paul: The Pioneer Press, 1902): pp. 87-131.

"Back to Nature: A Little Patch of God's Creations in Connection with School Studies." *The Labor Digest,* Vol. 1 (May 1908): pp. 24-25.

"The Minneapolis Wild Botanic Garden." *School Science and Mathematics,* Vol. 10 (March 1910): pp. 229-234.

"The Wild Botanic Garden in Glenwood Park, Minneapolis." *Bulletin of the Minnesota Academy of Science,* Vol. 5 (September 1911): pp. 19-24.

"Cultivation of Native Ornamental Plants." *The Minnesota Horticulturalist,* Vol. 40 (October 1912): pp. 365-373.

"The Native Plant Reserve." *Bulletin of the Garden Club of America* (January 1924), No. 15 (new series): pp. 61-62.

"A Native Plant Reserve." *Wild Flower* 1 (1 October 1924): 27.

Eloise Butler's annual letters to Theodore Wirth were published in the Minneapolis Board of Park Commissioners' *Annual Report* for the years 1911-1914 and 1930-1932.

Eloise Butler's weekly articles on Minnesota wildflowers were published in the Sunday Minneapolis *Tribune,* 16 April through 24 September 1911.

Eloise Butler's scrapbooks I and II (in archives of the Minneapolis Park and Recreation Board), and III (in archives of The Friends of the Wild Flower Garden, Inc.), contain clippings of numerous newspaper articles (often undated) by and about Eloise Butler.

Unpublished writings of Eloise Butler:

The unpublished papers of Eloise Butler are located at the Minnesota Historical Society (*Garden Log, Diary,* correspondence, photographs, unpublished writings); the archives of the Minneapolis Park and Recreation Board, Eloise Butler file (unpublished writings including "Annals of a Wild Garden" [c. 1914], "A Wild Botanic Garden" [1911] and "The Quest of the Walking Fern" [1908]); and the Eloise Butler biography file at the Minneapolis Public Library, Minneapolis Collection. The latter's holdings include numerous photographs, as well as *Early History of Eloise Butler Plant Reserve* (with forty black and white plates), a

36-page typescript of selected letters from Eloise Butler to the Gray Memorial Botanical Chapter, Agassiz Association (1911-1915) and *Annals of the Wild Life Reserve, Theodore Wirth Park*, a 40-page typescript of selected letters from Eloise Butler to the Gray Memorial Botanical Chapter, Agassiz Association (1914-1932).

Index

Leadplant, 167
Leatherwood, 121, 176
Leavitt, Clara, 20, 25n.23, 51, 67, 93
Leopold, Aldo, 60
Liagora decussata, 118
Licorice, wild, 167
Lilies, water, 133
Lillie, Miss, 57-58, 63n.1
Linnaea. See Twinflower
Linton, Laura, 27n.46
"List of Freshwater Algae Collected in Minnesota
    During 1893" (Tilden), 50
"Liverworts, Lichens, Mosses and Evergreen Ferns in
    the Wild Garden," 165-166
Lobelia, Great blue 143-144
Longfellow, Henry Wadsworth, 130-131
Loosestrife: purple, 84, 183; winged, 174
Lotus lily, American, 95
Lousewort, 126
Lupine, 128, 180
Lynn, Massachusetts, 8-9
MacMillan, Conway, 30, 50, 52, 53
"Mallard Pool," 183-184. *See also* Wild Botanic
    Garden
Man and Nature (Marsh), 60
Manning, Sara, 36n.34
Maple: red swamp, 121, 160, 168; sugar, 122
"Marine Algae of Vancouver Island" (Collins), 51
Marine Biological Laboratory, 43-44
Marsh arrow-grass, 78
Marsh marigold, 69, 104, 121, 156, 158, 179, 183
Mathias, Lillian, 20
Mayapple, 105, 180
McLains Mills, 4
Meeker, Mary, 91, 92, 172
Mermaid's shaving brush, 40
Middlesex Fells, Massachusetts, 22
Milkweed, 69, 132, *132*, 157, 183
Millay, Edna St. Vincent, 4, 6n.16
Minerva, 92
Minneapolis Audobon Society, 93
Minneapolis Board of Park Commissioners, 63, 67, 77
Minneapolis: in 1874, 17-18, 20-21; in 1880s, 154
Minneapolis *Journal*, 91
Minneapolis *Tribune*, 91
Minneapolis Woman's Club, 77, 78
Minnehaha Falls, 58, 69, 81, 136
Minnesota Academy of Science, 20, 26n.23, 91
Minnesota Algae (Tilden), 53
Minnesota Department of Natural Resources, 79
Minnesota Endangered Species Act, 101n.12
Minnesota, Geological and Natural History Survey of,
    xi, 34
Minnesota Horticultural Society, 92
Minnesota Landscape Arboretum, 106, 107
Minnesota Native Plant Society, 107
Minnesota Mycological Society, 94
Minnesota River, 79, 81
Minnesota Seaside Station, 49-53, 54n.17
Minnesota State Fair, 92, 100n.5
Mint, 83, 137, 183
Mississippi River, 69
Mitchell, Maria, 8, 14n.7

Monarch. *See* Wild Botanic Garden
Montagne, Jean Francois Camille, 41
Moravians, 31, 35n.14
Morning glory, wild, 146
Mound, Minnesota, 69
Mountain laurel, 88n.31
Moyer, Lycurgus R., 88n.26
Mushrooms, 59, 129, 139-140, 145-146, 147, 148
Muir, John, 60
Nachtrieb, Henry, 68
Naftalin, Mrs. E., 85
National Science Club for Women, 43
National Wildflower Research Center, 107
"A Native Plant Reserve," 93
Native plants: decline in Minneapolis, 67; decline in
    nineteenth century, 60; preservation movement,
    61-62; use in home landscaping, 149-151. *See also*
    Wild Botanic Garden
Nature Conservancy, 107
Nature Magazine, 94, 98
New England Botanical Club, 34n.4
New England Wildflower Society, 107
New England Women's Club, 43
New Jersey tea, 134
"New Missionary Work" (Clarke), 62
New York Botanical Garden, 51, 61, 62, 93
Nordstedt, Otto, 32
Northern bedstraw, 131
Northrup, Cyrus, 68
"Notable Features of My Wild Garden," 156-158
Oaks, 160
"Observations on Rhodymenia" (Butters), 53
"Occult Experiences of a Wild Gardener," 175-177
Oconee bells, 106
Odell, Clinton, 104, 106
Oestlund, O. W., 68
Old and New Club, 37
Old Andrew, 78-79, 176-177
Onion, wild, 141
Orchids, 71, 78, 82, 83, 93, 97, 130, 148, 171. *See also*
    Wild Botanic Garden
Osceola, Wisconsin, 173
Our Ferns in Their Haunts (Clute), 172
Owen, Maria, 34n.4
Ownbey, Gerald B., 79
Ox-eye, 133, 157
Ox-eye daisy, 83
Paige, Emma, 19
Paige, Mabeth Hurd, 25n.14
Park Board. *See* Minneapolis Board of Park
    Commissioners
Parker, C.W., 181
Partridge pea, 139
Pasque flower, 69, 80, 119, *119*
Pease, Curtis, 11, 45n.5, 95
Pease, Cora E.: and Frank S. Collins, 37-38, 42;
    early life of, 12, 22; in Jamaica, 111-118; later years
    and death of, 95; at Marine Biological Laboratory,
    43-44; seaweed collecting, 38-42, 45; and Wild
    Botanic Garden, 70-71; wild garden of, 60;
    writings, 3, 4, 22, 39, 40, 42-43, 46n.34, 47n.39, 61,
    71. *See also* Butler, Cora
Pease, Ethelwyn, 95